# Japanese Sports

# Japanese Sports

## *A History*

ALLEN GUTTMANN
LEE THOMPSON

University of Hawai'i Press
Honolulu

**Library of Congress Cataloging-in-Publication Data**

Guttmann, Allen.
    Japanese sports : a history / Allen Guttmann, Lee Thompson.
        p.   cm.
    Includes bibliographical references (p.  ).
        ISBN 0–8248–2414–8 (cloth : alk. paper) — ISBN 0–8248–2464–4 (pbk. : alk. paper)
        1. Sports—Japan—History.   I. Thompson, Lee (Lee Austin)   II. Title.

GV655 .G88 2001
796'.0952—dc21                                                           00-066665

Designed by Bookcomp, Inc.
Printed by The Maple-Vail Book Manufacturing Group

*To Hideo and Fusako Higuchi (A.G.)*
*To Marjorie and George B. Thompson, Sr (L.T.)*

# Contents

*Plates follow page 150*

# Acknowledgments

References to "internationalism" have become a refrain in twenty-first-century Japan. We can join the chorus with expressions of gratitude to a thoroughly international set of friends and colleagues. We have received invaluable assistance and encouragement from Harold Bolitho, Michel Brousse, Gordon Daniels, Higuchi Hideo, John Horne, Cameron Hurst, Ikeda Keiko, Inagaki Masahiro, Inoue Shun, Kiku Kōichi, Kodama Sanehide, William W. Kelly, Wolfram Manzenreiter, William May, Matsumoto Yoshiaki, Oinuma Yoshiro, Sōgawa Tsuneo, William Tyler, Uda Yoshitada, Yamamoto Norihito, and from many unnamed members of the International Society for the History of Physical Education and Sports, the Japan Society of Sport History, the Japan Society of Sport Sociology, and the North American Society for Sport History. Not all those acknowledged may agree with everything we have written, but we hope that they will appreciate our attempt to bring the history of Japanese sports to an English-speaking readership.

Several institutions have aided and supported our efforts. Dōshisha University and Dōshisha Women's College opened their libraries and computer centers to us. Dean of the Faculty, Lisa Raskin, waved her magic wand, and Amherst College opened the coffers of its research funds. Assistance was also provided by a 1999 grant from Osaka Gakuin University and by the staff of OGU's library, which tracked down innumerable hard-to-find resources.

Kate Wittenberg encouraged our project when we began it; Patricia Crosby patiently guided it to its conclusion. Finally, heartfelt thanks go also to those closest to home and heart: Doris G. Bargen and Masako, Hitomi, and Kei Thompson.

# Introduction

Every June, when the hydrangea are at their best, the Fujinomori shrine on the outskirts of Kyoto hosts an exhibition of *kemari,* a traditional Japanese sport. A team of men dressed in the colorful robes of eleventh-century courtiers kick a ball back and forth, skillfully keeping it aloft. Next to the ground on which they play their game stands a large rack from which are suspended hundreds of *ema,* the small wooden votive tablets on which supplicants can write their prayers. Most of the prayers at the Fujinomori shrine are for good luck at the races. Pictures of horses and jockeys are captioned with explicit appeals to the gods (e.g., "Let Hikaru win the Japan Derby!"). This juxtaposition is by no means unique. From Nagasaki in the south to Sapporo in the north, sports spectators are enthusiastic about *sumō* wrestling, generally believed to have its origins in prehistoric times, and about baseball, which many Japanese consider the epitome of modernity. And sumō is certainly not the only traditional sport to survive and flourish side by side with the modern sports that have elsewhere driven all rivals from the field and forced them into the precincts of folklore societies and museums.

Foreign visitors to Japan are often fascinated by this nearly unique[1] peaceful coexistence of traditional and modern sports, but the Japanese seem—with very few exceptions—to take it for granted. They are no more jarred by it than they are by weddings in which the bride makes her first appearance in a splendid red kimono and her second in an equally splendid Western-style white bridal dress.[2] In short, hardly anyone in Japan seems to mind the eclecticism that characterizes contemporary Japanese culture. The Japanese have assimilated aspects of European and American culture just as, centuries earlier, they assimilated aspects of Chinese culture. Japanese traditionalists, a minority in their own country, are more often than not resolute defenders of what their ancestors borrowed from China. Criticizing the widespread use of English words as "un-Japanese," they pen their polemics in *kanji,* that is, Chinese characters.

1

We must quickly acknowledge that the foreigner who marvels at Japanese eclecticism almost certainly comes from a culture that is similarly eclectic. "'Happy Birthday,' sung always in English, and 'Auld Lang Syne,' sung always in Japanese," comments Edwin Reischauer, "are . . . solid and natural parts of Japanese folk culture today."[3] And what is an American Christmas without the glee club's rendition of "Adeste Fideles" and a few verses of "O Tannenbaum"?

Implicit in the striking contrast we have drawn between traditional and modern sports is the concept of modernization. From Robert Bellah's *Tokugawa Religion* (1957) to S. N. Eisenstadt's *Japanese Civilization* (1996), an array of sociological studies have discussed and debated the modernization of Japanese society.[4] Masao Miyoshi has sought to obviate the necessity of serious discussion of Japan's modernization by announcing that modernity is "a regional term peculiar to the West,"[5] but he is definitely not representative of the scholarly consensus. Most scholars continue to believe that "modern" is an appropriate word to describe the present state of Japanese society and that one must, therefore, consider Japanese history from 1868 to the present as an instance of modernization. It must be emphasized, however, that specialists in Japanese history no longer assume, if they ever did, that the modernization of the West is a standard and that "failure" to follow the same path or to follow it at the same pace is a deviation.[6] Like Otto von Bismarck's Germany, which many nineteenth-century Japanese took as their model, Japan found its own *Sonderweg*—its own "special path"—to modernity.

There also seems to be a consensus that the preconditions for modernity had to have been present in the Edo period, under the Tokugawa sho-gunate, for Japan to have modernized as quickly as it did, but there is, not surprisingly, disagreement about what those preconditions might have been. We assume that, whatever they were, they also account for the undeniable fact that the Japanese were more receptive to modern sports than other Asians were. To document that remarkable receptivity is one of our main concerns.

Our purpose is more descriptive than explanatory. Although it should be clear from our text and our notes that we are deeply indebted to the many foreign and Japanese scholars who have discussed and debated Japan's modernization, we have not attempted to provide answers to the very large questions that these scholars have raised. Both of us have ventured into the realm of theory,[7] but we are more concerned in this study with practice. That may irritate readers who are, as John Keats (almost) said, half in love with easeful theory, but it is a risk to which we are reconciled.

That said, we do want to locate briefly our position on the theoretical map and to summarize what we think are the distinguishing features of modern sports. When the formal-structural properties of modern sports are contrasted with those of premodern sports, one discovers certain key characteristics that can be presented in paradigmatic form.[8]

*Secularism:* despite their tendency to become ritualized and to arouse the deepest passions, modern sports are not related to some transcendent realm of the sacred; sports in premodern societies often occurred as part of religious observances. *Shinji-zumō* (ritual sumō), for instance, was performed at temple and shrine festivals.

*Equality:* modern sports require, at least in theory, that everyone be admitted to the game on the basis of his or her athletic ability and that the rules be the same for all contestants. Premodern sports like *yabusame* (mounted archery) are usually restricted by social class and gender.

*Bureaucratization:* local, regional, national, and international bureaucracies now administer every level of modern sports, from Little League to the Olympic Games. Sports in premodern societies usually lacked this kind of administrative structure.

*Specialization:* many modern sports (rugby, soccer, American football, Australian Rules football) have evolved from earlier, less differentiated games, and many modern sports (baseball, cricket) have a gamut of specialized roles and playing positions. Premodern sports such as the early forms of archery and swordsmanship tended to evolve directly from the world of work or warfare and they rarely demonstrated role specialization.

*Rationalization:* the rules of modern sports are constantly scrutinized and frequently revised from a means-ends point of view; athletes train scientifically, employ technologically sophisticated equipment, and strive for the most efficient use of their skills. The rules for premodern sports tended to change much more slowly and the level of instrumental rationality (Max Weber's *Zweckrationalität*) was much lower.

*Quantification:* in modern sports, as in almost every aspect of our daily lives, we live in a world of numbers. The typical samurai scorned the use of mathematics, which he associated with the mercantile class.

*The Obsession with Records:* the unsurpassed quantified achievement, which is what we mean by a sports record, is a constant challenge to all who hope to surpass it; without the prerequisite of quantified results, participants in premodern societies were unable to set—and perhaps unable even to imagine—sports records.

Before the modern era, some of Japan's sports—like kemari and *ōyakazu* (a form of archery)—demonstrated *some* of these seven characteristics, but none of them demonstrated all seven. In considering the contrast between premodern and modern sports, one must bear in mind that these seven characteristics are not a random collection of attributes. They interact systematically. One might even invent a (false) teleology and maintain that, in order to achieve records, the first six characteristics are necessary preconditions. The modern quest for records is certainly unthinkable without quantification. The 3:30 mile may well be a will o' the wisp, but the unclocked 3:30 mile is an impossibility. It is also impossible, after a certain point reached by the untrained body, to set records without specialization and rationalization, but specialization and rationalization usually imply bureaucratic organization, without which world championships cannot be staged or rules established or equipment standardized or records duly certified. The quest for records also assumes certain kinds of equality. There must be equality within the rules of the game. When the Maharajah of Kashmir came to bat in Indian cricket matches, special rules went into effect and his opponents made no effort to put him out, which rendered his "records" meaningless. There must also be—in the theory if not in the practice of modern sports—equal opportunity to enter into competition. If the fastest runners or swimmers are barred from the contest because of race, religion, nationality, occupation—all of which *have* been criteria for exclusion—then the alleged record is devalued, if not rendered farcical. Finally, the very notion of a record is probably more compatible with the standards of secular society than with one closely oriented to the transcendent realm of the sacred. "When qualitative distinctions fade and lose their force, we turn to quantitative ones. When we can no longer distinguish the sacred from the profane or even the good from the bad, we content ourselves with minute discriminations between the batting averages of the .308 hitter and the .307 hitter."[9] It may be—although the hypothesis is probably untestable—that there is an inverse relationship between conventional religious faith and the quest for that special kind of immortality conferred by the sports record.

If there is, indeed, this stark contrast between the "ideal types" (Max Weber's term)[10] of premodern and modern sports, the transition from one to another can reasonably be considered an instance of modernization. Unfortunately, modernization theories have fallen into disfavor. Writing specifically about "the writing of sport history in the postmodern age," Colin D. Howell asserts that modernization theories are "widely discredited."[11] Although few of those who dismiss modernization theory feel an obligation to indicate the grounds of their dismissal, their critique can be summarized and debated.[12]

Rejection is usually based on modernization theory's allegedly simplistic assumptions about the inevitability, ubiquity, and desirability of modernization. Michel Foucault has been especially critical of such assumptions in his many influential studies of historical discontinuity. Since we remain committed to modernization as a useful heuristic concept, we feel obliged to offer clarifications and caveats. The history of nineteenth-century and early-twentieth-century sociology is, to a remarkable degree, the history of successive attempts to describe and explain sociocultural differences across time and space. The contrast between medieval rule by divine right and modern legitimation by appeals to popular sovereignty is, like the contrast between the work habits of preliterate tribes and the bureaucratic organization of the modern corporation, too immense to be ignored or dismissed with pieties about the unity of "the family of man." Various terms have been used to analyze these contrasts. Karl Marx wrote of feudalism and capitalism, Ferdinand Toennies of community and society, Emile Durkheim of mechanical and organic solidarity, Max Weber of traditional and modern societies, Talcott Parsons of particularistic and universalistic forms of social organization, Norbert Elias of the transition from "uncivilized" to "civilized" behavior. Their efforts were, of course, only the most famous conceptualizations (and they were, obviously, far more subtle and complex than the reduction to single phrases can possibly imply). We take none of these efforts as gospel truth, but neither are we persuaded by "postmodernism" that "grand theory" is tantamount to delusion.

Although we cannot imagine a more useful approach to the fundamental transformation that every historian recognizes, the paradigm of modernization has undeniable drawbacks. It is too abstract to account for every detail in history's vast panorama. It can easily be misinterpreted to mean that the observed changes occurred as part of some uniform and inevitable process that must of necessity and by some preordained schedule transform each and every aspect of each and every society in precisely the same way. Most important, modernization theory can be misused as a facile instrument of ethical judgment—as if modern ways were somehow a *moral* as well as a technological advance beyond traditional customs. Richard D. Brown has wisely cautioned against this arrogant assumption:

> As an organizing theme "modernization" bears some resemblance to the old idea of progress as the major process in Western society. It also resembles the dialectical materialism of Marx, and from a historiographical perspective it may indeed be descended from both interpetations. But unlike its predecessors, the idea of modernization does not imply inevitability or even necessarily improvement. Technical development, complexity, specialization, and rationality do not necessarily generate a better, more just, more humane, or more satisfactory society.[13]

While nineteenth-century observers may have felt optimism about the future, those of us who have experienced the twentieth century have reason to ponder the adverse effects as well as the benefits of modernization. Toxic wastes and nuclear catastrophes are as much a part of modernity as are laser surgery and telecommunications.

Finally, if such qualifications and caveats seem an inadequate response to the criticisms of modernization theory as a framework, one may reasonably ask: Is there a better way to conceptualize the differences between New York and New Guinea (or between eleventh-century Heian-kyō and twentieth-century Tokyo)? Is there a better way, in the domain of sports, to understand the contrast between the medieval free-for-all known as folk-football and the globally televised spectacle of the World Cup (or between an eleventh-century kemari ceremony and a twentieth-century baseball game)? As Peter N. Stearns long ago remarked in a perceptive discussion of the historiographical advantages and disadvantages of the concept of modernization, "There is more sense of dissatisfaction with the approach than coherent comment or presentation of alternatives."[14]

Despite the manifest possibility that the concept of modernization can be misunderstood and misrepresented, we continue to find it more useful than the "postmodernism" that is currently fashionable in what once were called the social sciences. An imperfect account of the historical facts seems preferable to the startled discovery that there is no such thing as Absolute Truth.

If one looks at the history of Japanese sports through the lens of a modernization paradigm, one is surprised to discover that much of what is marked as "traditional" about Japanese sports turns out to have been invented in the modern era.[15] This seems, at first, contrary to common sense, but a little reflection reveals why it is so. The way we live our daily lives—what Pierre Bourdieu refers to as "habitus"[16]—is usually unremarkable and is ordinarily taken for granted. Where tradition is alive, where it survives in the form of habitus, it tends to be invisible: it is just the way things are done. It is only when a practice loses its original, unquestioned, taken-for-granted meaning and function that it either disappears, unnoticed and unmissed, or becomes a candidate for willed preservation as "tradition."

In the latter half of the nineteenth century the Japanese began to experience uneven, sometimes imperceptible, sometimes jarringly obtrusive changes in their habitus, in the ways that they lived, worked, and played. Collectively, these changes, which historians of Japan have commonly referred to as "modernization," were often perceived by the Japanese as "Westernization." In other words, they tended to see the transformation of their world as the result of foreign influences rather than as the outcome of developments within their own culture. This attribution, which overstated the importance of the borrowed and underestimated the importance of the indigenous, created a problem for Japan's political, economic, social, and cultural leaders who were (and still are) trying to reimagine their rapidly changing nation. Small wonder that they, and the ordinary men and women who looked to them for leadership and guidance, experienced a crisis of cultural identity.

One response to this crisis was the reaffirmation—or the invention—of tradition, a concept that is properly understood as the antithesis of modernity. Tradition is what modernity is not; the two concepts define each other. If the modern is scientific, rational, and concerned with ends, then the traditional is spiritual, not accessible to logic, and concerned with means. Since modernity was (and still is) identified with the West, it seemed to follow that Japan's indigenous culture—its traditions—must stand in opposition to European and North American culture. To adopt Western ways was, therefore, to turn one's back on the Japanese past. This, at least, was the dilemma faced by many Japanese who reflected upon their habitus.

Modern sports were introduced from the West. How were they to be made compatible with Japanese traditions? One response to this problem was to claim that modern sports are pursued somewhat differently in Japan. In Japan the "spirit" is emphasized. "Samurai baseball" is very different from the game played in Yankee Stadium and Fenway Park. Another response to the arrival of European and North American sports was to preserve, revive, or revise Japan's traditional sports. Some attempts at preservation, revival, and revision were more successful than others, but they all involved modernization as well as what we term—somewhat awkwardly—"retraditionalization." In other words, "traditional" Japanese sports as they exist today were consciously formed or reformed in the context of the modern-traditional dichotomy. In a modern society, there can be no such thing as "innocent" tradition.

From this perspective, then, we have attempted to present the history of sports in Japan. We first describe several sports that were prominent before the modern era. Then we narrate two related stories, one about the arrival and diffusion of modern sports from the West, the other about the development of sumō, the martial arts, and kemari in reaction to the wave of Westernization and modernization.

We have also sought to contextualize our narrative within the larger narrative of Japanese history. In one of the earliest approaches to a social history of sports, Joseph Strutt wrote,

> In order to form a just estimation of the character of any particular people, it is absolutely necessary to investigate the Sports and Pastimes most generally prevalent among them. War, policy [politics], and other contingent circumstances may effectually place men, at different times, in different points of view, but, when we follow them into their retirements, where no disguise is necessary, we are most likely to see them in their true state, and may best judge of their natural dispositions.[17]

We are properly wary of simple correlations of sports with "the character of any particular people," but Strutt's main point remains as valid as when he offered it some two hundred years ago. "Sports and Pastimes" are especially good indicators of values because they occur in a domain of relative freedom. People normally have more choice in their play, in their "true state," than in their work.

We must also remember that the nation of Japan was not a continuous and coherent entity throughout the fourteen hundred years covered by our text. The concept of a nation called Japan, the land areas that it was thought to cover, the relationships of power between those areas, the degrees of cultural similarity and difference within those areas, the loyalties and identification of the people residing in those areas—all these important components of nationhood have constantly changed throughout history, and are changing even today. We remind our readers and ourselves that this history necessarily projects something we now know as "Japan" back into eras where current assumptions of cohesion and uniformity did not yet apply.

For most Europeans and Americans (and for quite a number of Japanese), the two related stories that we have narrated about traditional and modern sports will be largely unfamiliar. On the assumption that most of those who begin to read this book will in fact know very little about Japanese sports, we have endeavored to strike a balance between too much detail and too little: enough to inform a reader and hold his or her interest, but not so much as to produce the bewilderment that comes when one confronts a plethora of unfamiliar names and dates. We have, for instance, felt it necessary to explain at some length the rules of kemari but not those of baseball. A number of individual athletes and famous sports events appear in our text, but we have most emphatically not aimed for encyclopedic coverage.

Finally, a word about language. Since Japanese words are often an important clue to the significance of the object or the phenomenon to which they refer, we have not hesitated to use them. We have, however, been careful to explain them upon first use and to include them in the index so that a reader can quickly return to our initial explanation. To avoid the overuse of italics, we have used them for only the first appearance of Japanese terms. Japanese names appear in the Japanese order—family name first—except when our notes cite the authors of books and articles published in Western languages.

# Part I

## Sporting Practices
## Before the Black Ships

# 1

# Sumō, Ball Games, and Feats of Strength

A ll sports," wrote the German scholar Carl Diem, "began as cult."[1] This generalization is as much an exaggeration as the Marxist assertion that "all sports were originally one with the means of production,"[2] but Diem was right to call attention to the easily forgotten fact that, in the centuries before our more secular age, adults who participated in sports were often—perhaps usually—engaged in religious ritual. Examples abound: the athletic contests at ancient Olympia, which were staged quadrennially in honor of Zeus; the ball games of the Mayans and Aztecs, which culminated in human sacrifice; the wrestling matches of the Nuba, the Diola, and other African peoples, which were often fertility or prenuptial rites. In this respect, the Japanese may have been no different from other peoples, but the evidence is often unclear. By the time that the Empress Gemmei established her capital at Nara, in 710, the imperial court's ceremonial calendar was marked by a number of ritual sports events whose origins and possible religious significance are obscure even to Japanese scholars.[3] By the eighth century, if not earlier, politics may have been more important than religion.

## SUMŌ

Despite their extensive digging into the past, archeologists have been able to tell us very little about the sports of the prehistoric inhabitants of Japan. We can safely assume, however, that they, like all peoples, wrestled. Whether or not their wrestling matches should be identified as sumō, the peculiarly Japanese form of the sport, is a matter of some debate. Among the terra-cotta figures from the Tumulus period (250–552) are a few that are assumed to depict wrestlers. This assumption is based mainly on their state of (un)dress: they stand naked except for a loin cloth, the appearance associated with sumō wrestling throughout most of recorded history. Citing the evidence of these terra-cotta figures (known as *haniwa*), P. L. Cuyler asserts that "sumo was performed as part of Shinto ritual at least from the Tumulus period."[4] Jörg Möller agrees that the haniwa figures are wrestlers and he claims "a purely religious function" for prehistoric sumō.[5] Cuyler and Möller echo the opinion of most Japanese scholars, but one has to wonder about a case made from the testimony of silent clay figures. In fact, this interpretation of sumō's origins is an anachronism reflecting views formed in later centuries (especially our own).[6]

The same can be said about the early written historical record. Although modern scholars consider material from before the sixth century A.D. to be more legend than reliable history, stories from the ancient chronicles of Japan collected in the *Kojiki* (712) and the *Nihongi* (720) are customarily cited to explain the origins of sumō. For example, the potter Nomi no Sukune is said to have engaged in the first sumō match between two mortals. This match, which is alleged to have taken place in 23 B.C., occurred when Nomi no Sukune was asked by Emperor Suinin to deal with Taima no Keyaha, a notorious braggart who boasted that he was the strongest man "under the heavens." Nomi no Sukune engaged the braggart in fierce hand-to-hand combat, broke his ribs with one kick and his back with another, and became "the father of sumō."[7] This famous encounter is obviously a far cry from sumō as we know it today.

Nomi no Sukune may, nonetheless, seem like an appropriate predecessor of the modern *sumōtori* (sumō wrestler), whom Japanese admirers see as an epitome of masculinity, but close attention to language discloses an irony. The earliest use of the term "sumō" actually refers to matches among women. Emperor Yūryaku, who is said to have reigned in the fifth century A.D., was annoyed to hear a palace carpenter boast that he never made a mistake. Yūryaku arranged for some of his female attendants to strip to their waistcloths and grapple in plain view. After watching the women, the agitated carpenter resumed his work, only to slip and ruin the edge of his plane, whereupon the emperor ordered him to be executed.[8]

It should be noted, however, in this earliest written use of the term "sumō," that the activity itself was not described. Whatever it was, the sight of women naked except for their waistcloths—like the terra-cotta haniwa figures—was obviously a sexually provocative spectacle. As such, it has been an embarrassment to modern historians who want to make a case for sumō's religious origins. The story of the women's matches is often ignored or retold with the salacious bits deleted. Wakamori Tarō, for instance, mentions that Yūryaku had his female attendants perform sumō, but he is silent on the women's near-nakedness and he omits the bragging carpenter altogether. Having removed the incident from its actual context, Wakamori provides it with a new interpretation. Ignoring the obvious implications of the text, he comments that the emperor's female attendants also performed as dancers and concludes that the incident supports his thesis that sumō originated as a religious dance.[9]

There is some evidence to support Wakamori's thesis about sumō's religious origins. It is true, for instance, that sumō is held as a part of festival celebrations at Buddhist temples and Shinto shrines all over Japan. The most famous example is probably *karasu-zumō* (crow wrestling), which takes place at the Kamo shrine in Kyoto. Boys representing the god Takemikazuchi wrestle against other boys representing the worldly sphere.[10] At the Ōyamazumi shrine on the island of Ōmishima *hitori-zumō* (one-man sumō) was performed. Twice a year, before the spring planting and before the fall harvest, a lone wrestler enacted a struggle against the spirit of the rice plant. The spirit always won and was expected to express its pleasure in the form of an abundant crop.[11] The lack of concern for equal competition, like the variation from place to place, is typical for traditional sports.

Most scholars join Wakamori in interpreting the existence of these rituals as proof that sumō had its origin as a religious ceremony, and many scholars specify that the ceremony was an agricultural ritual.[12] We cannot assume, however, that the rituals performed represent practices common some two thousand years ago. As Nitta Ichirō points out, the historical roots of these rituals and the degree to which they retain their original forms are unknown. In fact, sumō rituals at village shrines and temples are unlikely to predate the thirteenth century because the villages themselves were not established until the development of the feudal state at the end of Japan's medieval period. Although a few shrines and temples have older antecedents, most were created as a focal point for these villages. The practice of sumō at the largest shrines and temples may date from the Heian period (794–1185), but sumō at provincial shrines probably dates from no sooner than the late middle ages. In fact, the earliest reliable record of one-man sumō at the Ōyamazumi shrine dates from sometime between 1716 and 1736.[13] Kaneda Eiko argues in a recent article that women's sumō frequently served as a rain-making ceremony, but her evidence comes from the eighteenth and nineteenth centuries and cannot be used to argue that sumō began as a religious ritual.[14]

Questions can also be raised about the meaning of sumō performed in conjunction with harvest and other festivals. In most cases sumō seems to have been a secular entertainment rather than a religious ritual. Nitta makes a useful distinction between *sumō shinji* (divine sumo), in which the act of sumō itself has an unambiguously ritual meaning, and *hōnō zumō* (offerings of sumō), in which sumō is a separate performance presented to the deity on the occasion of a ritual. Most of the performances of sumō at shrine and temple festivals have little to do with the content of the central ritual. Like most of the festivity surrounding a medieval European archery contest or a modern American football game, sumō was an ancillary event. Along with music, dance, and theatrical performances, it was an added attraction. In Nitta's terms, most sumō performed at temples and shrines around the country, today as in the past, should be categorized as "offered" rather than "divine sumō," an entertainment rather than an act of worship.[15]

If we set aside compilations of myth and speculations based on the assumption of unbroken continuity from the distant past, the earliest form of sumō about which we have reasonably reliable evidence dates from the eighth century. It was intimately related to the new system of government instituted with the Taihō Code, which came into effect in 702. The sovereign, who until that time had been merely the primus inter pares, became, or attempted to become, a Chinese-style emperor, a ruler whose absolute authority was exercised through a centralized bureaucracy. The annual sumō ceremony at court symbolized this ideal version of the new state.

After Japan's imperial court was established at Nara in A.D. 710, sumō matches took place on the seventh day of the seventh month of the lunar calendar. The first of these annual events occurred in 734. When the court moved to Heian-kyō (today's Kyoto), sumō continued to be performed. In 826 it was moved to the sixteenth day of the month and no longer conflicted with the Tanabata Festival.[16]

If it is true that life at court was a matter of "intolerable tedium,"[17] the wrestlers must have been welcomed with heartfelt enthusiasm. The earliest detailed descriptions are from the early ninth century. Although the ceremony changed over time, Möller describes its basic structure.

The annual tournament was held on the grounds of the imperial palace. There was no raised earthen ring (as there is in modern sumō). A flat area adjacent to the Shishinden (Hall for State Ceremonies) was strewn with white sand for the ceremonial occasion. As thirty-four wrestlers entered the garden they were announced by drums and gongs. They were followed by officials, musicians, and dancers. The "left" team wore paper hollyhocks in their hair; the "right" wore calabash blossoms. Although sumō matches are now won (a) when one's opponent touches the ground with any part of his body other than the soles of his feet or (b) when he is forced from the ring, court sumō matches, lacking a ring, were decided only in the former manner. After each match, the musicians beat their drums, struck their gongs, and performed a ritual dance. The results were recorded by arrows thrust into the sand.[18] There was no independent referee. According to the eleventh-century historical tale *Eiga monogatari*, the emperor determined the winners of close matches.[19]

What exactly was the significance of this annual event? It was certainly more than an occasion for a group of high-spirited men to flex their muscles and display their physical prowess. Although there was nothing in the ceremony itself to support the conventional view that court sumō began as an agricultural ritual, one cannot rule out the possibility. It seems much more likely, however, that the sport was a political statement rather than a prayer for fecundity. Obinata Katsumi, an authoritative guide, has analyzed the structure and administration of the ceremony and has convincingly demonstrated that sumō served to display and reconfirm relationships of power. The wrestlers were recruited from all parts of the territory over which the Heian court claimed authority. Despite the promulgation of the centralizing Taihō Code, some local jurisdictions retained a large degree of autonomy. Requiring such jurisdictions to send representatives to Heian-kyō to wrestle in an annual ceremony performed before the emperor was tantamount to having them acknowledge imperial authority. This much is constant throughout the history of the ceremony, but the roles that the emperor and his officials played in the ceremony underwent changes reflecting shifts in the balance of power at court.[20]

The venue for the ceremony, which had political implications, was not fixed before the end of the eighth century. From 811, sumō was held annually at the Shinsen'en, a park adjacent to the imperial palace grounds. From 837, it was held at the Shishinden, the main ceremonial hall in the inner palace, where the emperor conducted affairs of state. (The archery ceremony *jarai*, discussed in the next chapter, also had a change of venue around this time, from the Shinsen'en to the inner palace.) The ceremony was attended by all government officials.

To coordinate events, a temporary sumō office, the *sumai no tsukasa,* was set up every year about one month before the ceremony. It was staffed by twelve court officials and supervised by a royal prince. Every year, wrestlers were sent from the provinces to participate, as a form of tribute, in the court sumō ceremony. They were appointed as palace guards.

The *Dairishiki,* a text compiled early in the ninth century, describes the ceremony as it was then conducted. Seating at a sumō ceremony was as socially significant as the seating in an ancient Roman arena or at a medieval tournament. Special seats for the emperor, royal princes, and the highest court ranks were prepared at the main building in the Shinsen'en. Seats for the lower-ranking government officials were prepared in the open yard south of the building, and places were prepared on the east and west sides of the court for the sumō officials. Entering first, the emperor ordered the ceremony to begin. The other spectators followed and took their seats. Then the sumō officials entered, accompanied by the wrestlers. A dance was performed, after which the wrestling began.

A distinguishing characteristic of early Heian court sumō is that royal princes and court nobles were included as sumō officials. The highest levels of court society were not present merely to enjoy the spectacle of sumō. Like the wrestlers, albeit rather less strenuously, they were in attendance as a sign of political loyalty and subservience to the emperor.

In time, however, political authority shifted from the emperor, who lost much of his personal power to a small group of noble clans. From the mid-tenth century, the most powerful men at court were members of the Fujiwara clan. (It was Fujiwara policy to have their daughters marry into the imperial family. After the birth of a son, the reigning emperor abdicated and his Fujiwara father-in-law acted as regent for the child-emperor.) This change in the power structure was reflected in court sumō.

One manifestation of this change was that the annual ceremony was no longer administered by a sumō office (sumai no tsukasa) staffed by royal princes and high court officials. Instead, a "sumō station" (*sumaidokoro*) was established in the headquarters of the inner palace guards. Wrestlers arriving in Kyoto practiced there under the supervision of officers of the guards (who were also in charge of preparations for the ceremony). At the ceremony itself, royal princes no longer made opening addresses to the emperor. This role was assumed by officers of the guards. The members of the royal family and other high court nobles were promoted to the role of spectators. They no longer served the emperor, but took their place alongside him.

In response to their loss of political power, the imperial family, in 1086, created the Office of the Retired Emperor "from which successive ex-emperors were able to conduct family and administrative affairs in competition with the Fujiwara."[21] That same year, 1086, saw the inauguration of sumō performed for the retired as well as for the reigning emperor. The retired emperor Shirakawa (1053–1129) encroached on another prerogative of his successor: setting the date to issue the formal summons calling the wrestlers from the provinces to the capital. The fact that the retired emperor Goshirakawa (1127–1192) joined the reigning emperor Takakura (1161–1181) at the last recorded instance of court sumō, in 1174, can be read as an attempt to shift the balance of symbolic power from the reigning emperor to his retired predecessor.[22]

While the imperial family and the major clans were struggling for control of the court, Heian-kyō gradually lost its control over the country as a whole. Sumō tournaments became sporadic and only two were held after the early decades of the twelfth century, one in 1158 and one in 1174.[23] Then, for a period of some three hundred years, records of sumō of any kind became very sparse.

In the Kamakura period (1185–1333), warriors replaced courtiers as Japan's rulers. Needless to say, prowess in armed combat was prized above rhetorical skill and mastery of etiquette. In battle, the bow and arrow were most effective at a distance. When closing with the enemy, the sword and spear were the weapons of choice. When all else failed, one relied on one's skills at barehanded combat. Accordingly, sumō was valued for its usefulness as preparation for battle, and Minamoto no Yoritomo (1147–1199), the founder of the Kamakura shogunate, encouraged its practice. He established special commissioners (*bugyō*) to supervise the warriors' training in sumō. He also had sumō performed regularly, along with equestrian archery, horse races, and dances, at the shrine he built in Kamakura for Hachiman, the god of warriors.[24]

Oda Nobunaga (1534–1582), one of the three unifiers of feudal Japan, was passionate about sumō and sponsored a series of tournaments between 1570 and 1580. For a tournament held in February 1578 he assembled over 1,500 wrestlers at his stronghold, Azuchi Castle.[25] The second unifier, Toyotomi Hideyoshi (1537–1598), shared his enthusiasm for the sport.

Nitta Ichirō speculates that after the discontinuation of court sumō in 1174, wrestlers may have continued to perform at festivals sponsored by shrines and temples in and around Kyoto. The evidence is sketchy, but from at least the fourteenth century, perhaps earlier, temples and shrines did begin to hold performances of sumō for which they charged admission to raise money for construction, repairs, and other projects. These performances were known as *kanjin zumō* (benefit sumō). Performances of kanjin zumō were recorded in the Kyoto area in 1605, 1644, and 1645. In Edo, benefit sumō was performed around 1640.[26]

The sumō patronized by Nobunaga and Hideyoshi and performed at shrines and temples had already begun to exhibit one of the most important characteristics of modern sports: the specialization of roles. Specialization of space was soon to follow. It is characteristic of modern sports that athletes are segregated from spectators and that fields of play are spatially differentiated from one another as well as from workspace. In the development of sumō as in the evolution of modern soccer and rugby from the medieval European sport of folk-football, roles became as specialized as the space in which the sport occurred.[27]

In the early years of court sumō, wrestlers were recruited from the peasantry and selected more for their physical strength than for their technical skill. In all likelihood, there was no specifically developed technique for sumō as a combat sport and there was little or no sense of the wrestlers as professionals for whom the sport was a way of life rather than an occasional event. Around the twelfth century, however, the status of the wrestlers who appeared at the court tournaments seems to have become fixed, and certain provincial families regularly sent their sons to the court tournaments. (This gave them a connection to the central government through which they obtained posts such as provincial governor.) In this development we can see the beginning of the role specialization that is characteristic of modern sports.[28]

Benefit sumō also seems to have contributed importantly to the specialization of the sport. The temples and shrines employed the services of professional or semi-professional groups of wrestlers which, if they had not existed already, were formed in conjunction with this new demand.

Eventually, some of these professional wrestlers began to hold performances of sumō for their own profit. In other words, they continued down the path that led to sumō as a more or less modern spectator sport. As in most modern spectator sports, economics rather than religion or politics was the driving force. It is also important to note that the origins of modern sumō were urban. The sport took shape in the three major cities of Edo (the former name of Tokyo), Osaka, and Kyoto. The promoters of sumō were not the wrestlers themselves, or even former wrestlers, but townsmen—the Japanese mercantile equivalent of the European bourgeoisie whose role in the modernization of Western sports can hardly be overstated. Thus began a differentiation of functions that, as often happens in the history of sport, eventually gave rise to what are now two distinct sports. As sumō became primarily a spectator sport, it began to lose its value as a practical, combat-oriented skill. The martial function of barehanded combat was emphasized by other activities. The Takeuchi school of unarmed combat, for example, emerged in the middle of the sixteenth century. The martial arts techniques taught in this and other schools were called *totte, koshimawari*—or in the Edo period (1600–1868)—*jūhō* or *jūjutsu*. The last term is, of course, more familiar today.[29]

Another direct outcome of the development of sumō as a spectator sport was the specialization of space as evidenced by the creation of the *dohyō*, the raised earthen ring characteristic of modern sumō. Before the seventeenth century, there was no clear boundary designating sumō's competitive space. There is some disagreement over exactly when a boundary was established, but Ikeda Masao's analysis of seventeenth-century drawings and paintings demonstrates that it must have been in the latter part of that century. No marked boundaries are depicted before 1660. In a picture dating from the 1660s, wrestlers are shown grappling in a space marked off by a rope wound around four pillars. In other pictures from the period, sumō takes place within an area marked off by rice bales placed on the ground. Since the first appearance of a marked boundary coincides with the government's first attempts to ban sumō, Ikeda conjectures that the boundary was drawn to separate participants from spectators and thus to reduce the likelihood of fights and other disturbances of "public order." Whatever the motives behind its invention, the dohyō was an innovation that completely transformed the sport in that matches came to be decided when a wrestler was forced from the ring as well as when a wrestler was thrown to ground.[30]

The existence of the ring was also a prerequisite to some of the rituals accompanying sumō matches. Strewing the ring with salt before the bouts is thought, for instance, to have been begun around this same time, that is, about 1690.[31] This particular custom, which was probably copied from Shinto rituals of purification, served as a technique of legitimization.

Legitimization of Edo-period sumō was a long and slow process. Tokugawa Iemitsu (1604–1651), the third Tokugawa shogun, banned sumō from Edo in 1648. The reason for the ban was the shogunate's characteristic concern for public order, which was often disrupted by *tsuji-zumō* (street-corner sumō).[32] "Unemployed warriors and rough townsmen came into violent contact in these street-corner contests fought for small amounts of money tossed down by the onlookers who gathered around the impromptu wrestlers. Clashes between hot-tempered masterless samurai and commoners were incessant; drawn swords and the untimely death of a combatant or spectator were not unheard of."[33] Bans on sumō were issued periodically throughout the Edo period—at least fifteen by the mid-nineteenth century[34]—which testifies to the helplessness of the authorities in the face of the populace's determination not to be deprived of one of its principal pleasures. Eventually the outright bans were directed only at street-corner sumō. The authorities were content to regulate rather than to forbid benefit matches held at shrines and temples. These efforts to diminish the sport's level of random expressive violence exemplify what Norbert Elias has called "the civilizing process."[35]

Promoters promised to control the incipient sport better and to donate a share of the profits to public works. Accordingly, benefit sumō was permitted in Edo in 1684, in Osaka in 1691, and in Kyoto in 1699. The authorities granted permits to hold benefit sumō almost every year after that.[36]

From around 1750, the yearly calendar of meets settled into a pattern: spring and fall in Edo, summer in Kyoto, fall in Osaka. This did not mean, however, that stable sumō organizations existed in each of the three cities. The cities were merely centers where sumō groups gathered for major performances. Many of the wrestlers, especially those retained by a *daimyō* (lord of a domain), resided in their own regions. For these seasonal tournaments, wooden stands holding several thousand spectators were erected on temple grounds. Then, as now, wrestlers were ranked for each new event, but the ranks were not determined as they are now by performance in a previous meet. Rankings had to be rough and ready because the participants varied from meet to meet as promoters negotiated with various groups of wrestlers for each meet. With the passage of time, however, there was a degree of rationalization. Promoters identified the more capable wrestlers, invited them back for each performance, and ranked them less arbitrarily.[37]

In some ways, however, Tokugawa sumō as a spectator sport still resembled the simulated mayhem of modern "professional" wrestling. At meets held in Osaka, for example, wrestlers who lived and practiced in the city and its surrounding region played the role of the good guys while wrestlers from elsewhere were the "heavies." It was the same in Edo and Kyoto. It was good business to let the hometown heroes win. Like the enthusiasts studied by Roland Barthès in *Mythologies* (1957), the fans were enthralled by the allegorical drama enacted in the ring and seemed not to mind the fact that fixed matches were hardly unknown. The prestige of a retained wrestler's lord sometimes influenced the outcome of a match. Comparing records from the Edo period (1600–1868) is like taking at face value the results of modern "professional" wrestling.[38]

Another uncanny resemblance to modern "professional" wrestling can be seen in *onna-zumō* (women's wrestling), performed mostly, it seems, for men's titillation. The names assumed by the women (or given to them by promoters) suggest the debased nature of the attraction: "Big Boobs," "Deep Crevice," "Holder of the Balls."[39]

Another characteristic of modern sports is a tendency toward national and international bureaucratic organization. The predecessor of today's Japan Sumō Association can be traced back to an organization established early in the eighteenth century when the men who ran the centers where sumō wrestlers lived and trained formed a loose organization called the *sumō kaisho.* This organization achieved a stable form in 1751—the year that the English established their first national sports organization, the Jockey Club.[40]

In 1772 a suit against village "amateurs" was resolved in favor of the Edo organization. The judgment ruled that amateurs not belonging to "proper groups" had to apply for permission before they were allowed to charge admission fees for sumō performances. The kaisho thus achieved a virtual monopoly on sumō performances. The basis of their authority was their supposed preservation of "ancient practices" (*kojitsu*).[41]

Toward the end of the eighteenth century, most of the best wrestlers appeared regularly in the four-season circuit of the three main sumō centers. Gradually, however, Edo established itself as the place to be, the equivalent in the sumō world of Broadway in the American theater. This was mainly because the shogunate that ruled Japan during the Edo period demanded that the daimyō reside in Edo rather than on their provincial domains. Residence in Edo precluded the daimyō's development of regional rivalry.

The sumō kaisho's strategy was to gain the recognition of the ruling shogun and to forge a closer association with him and his lords. To accomplish this, the sumō organization petitioned successfully to hold a special performance before the shogun. (The parallel with the court sumō of the Heian period was presumably in mind.) The organization sought the help of Yoshida Zenzaemon, a vassal of the Hosokawa domain in present-day Kumamoto. The Yoshida were a prominent family of referees who claimed to have had centuries of association with sumō that gave them special knowledge of "ancient practices." Ironically, the Yoshida who claimed to have access to tradition were actually innovators. In an effort to produce sumō suitable for performance before the shogun, Yoshida Zenzaemon introduced the *dohyō matsuri* (ring ceremony) that is now performed before the beginning of each tournament. In this colorful ceremony, the head referee, playing the role of a Shinto priest, purifies the ring. Yoshida also introduced a special ceremony performed immediately before the bouts. Two of the top wrestlers of the day entered the ring, separately, with thick white ropes, the spectacular *yokozuna*, tied around their ample waists. Another ritual, the *yumitorishiki* (bow dance), is said to have first occurred when the shogun expressed his pleasure after a bout by handing a bow to Tanikaze Kajinosuke. Tanikaze's presumably spontaneous dance was an expression of his gratitude for the gift. Taken together, these innovations changed the nature of the sport. "Shogunal sumo lifted the sport out of the vulgar world of entertainment," writes Cuyler, "and imparted to it a sense of ritual that later became its major characteristic."[42]

The Yoshida family maintained a strong influence on sumō for two hundred years. On the basis of their family records, the Yoshida claimed a number of rights. They licensed referees and decided who was and who was not entitled to wear the yokozuna. They preserved what were (wrongly) supposed to be the ancient traditions of the sport. The sumō kaisho, for its part, obtained legitimacy through its connection to the Yoshida family. The alliance was eventually able to dominate sumō in most of the country.[43]

Despite the efforts of the Yoshida and members of the kaisho to organize, control, and legitimize the sport, nineteenth-century sumō remained a distinctly vulgar phenomenon. Francis Hall, an American who resided in Yokohama from 1859 to 1866, admired sumō wrestlers as "the perfection of animal nature," but he was bothered by their near-nakedness and appalled at the "immodest" behavior of the female spectators. When a young woman climbed over a gallery rail and descended a ladder, the rail "caught her garments and exposed her unprotected limbs in all their proportions." Hall was similarly shocked at a subsequent match when a female admirer denuded herself "to the last skirt" in order to present her clothes to her hero. Hall was not alone in his distaste for "the corrupt taste" of the Japanese.[44] After a visit to Edo's Ekō-in temple, the city's most popular sumō venue, two Englishmen expressed their acerbic view in John Murray's *Handbook for Travellers in Japan:*

> Ekō-in might well be taken as a text by those who denounce "heathen" temples. Dirty, gaudy, full of semi-defaced images, the walls plastered with advertisements, the altar guarded by two hideous red Ni-ō [divine temple guardians], children scampering in and out, wrestlers stamping, crowds shouting—the place lacks even the semblance of sanctity.[45]

The English were horrified. How did the Japanese react?

Harold Bolitho notes that Ekō-in temple, which stood on the banks of the Sumida River, was situated in an area famous for its freak shows. He goes on to suggest "that, just as the world of the sideshow booth and the sumō stadium intersected at the Ekō-in, so did the world of the wrestler and the freak, the two shading imperceptibly into each other." The spectators stared at the wrestlers as they gawked at the freaks— with a "blend of fear and amazement." The wrestlers embodied "mythic terror." Bolitho's argument is based largely on the evidence of popular woodblock prints. "What the . . . prints display, quite unambiguously, is bulk, and what they suggest, with equal force, is phenomenal strength accompanied in many instances by an indefinable air of menace."[46]

The bulk is obvious and the strength is implied, but the menace is questionable. Some of the wrestlers whom the artists depicted were indeed freaks whose distorted bodies were the result of endocrinal abnormality. Utagawa Kunisda, for instance, portrayed the deformed giant Mitateyama Kisaku, who never actually wrestled. While those who did wrestle resembled the hugely muscled Ni-ō dismissed as hideous by ethnocentric Englishmen, it should be remembered that these temple figures were guardians. They were presumably looked upon with gratitude because their fearsome strength was reassuringly protective. Sumō wrestlers were likewise held in awe. Successful wrestlers like Raiden Tameimon, Tanikaze Kajinosuke, and Inazuma Raigorō were idolized rather than feared. Hall, who observed many sumō performances during his seven-year sojourn in Japan, noted the enthusiasm of the spectators and their adulation of the wrestlers.[47] Like the actors of the kabuki theater, who were also pictured—sometimes grotesquely—in innumerable woodblock prints, sumō wrestlers were seen by the Japanese, then as now, as an embodiment of their culture.[48]

A summary comment is in order. Although there is some truth to the claim that sumō is an ancient rite, the form of sumō that emerged in the middle ages, established itself during the Edo period, and survived—with modifications—into the twentieth century was not the same as the sumō alleged to have been performed by the gods and by the inhabitants of prehistoric Japan nor was it the same as the politically inflected court sumō of the Heian period. Edo-period professional sumō was looked down upon by most of the warrior class as useless in battle and akin to begging. In response to samurai scorn, the men involved with sumō performances in Edo and elsewhere sought to raise the status of their sport by stressing its allegedly ancient origins. They sought to enhance their own status and authority by claiming to have arcane knowledge of the "ancient practices" surrounding sumō. Like their contemporaries who were forging the myths of the emerging modern state, the creators of modern sumō were "inventing tradition."[49]

## KEMARI

### *How It Was Played*

There are many accounts of sumō in English and other Western languages, but the game of kemari (kick-ball) remains almost completely unknown in Europe and the Americas. The game's cultural importance requires extended treatment.

No one knows exactly when the Japanese began to play kemari. The earliest writings on kemari are from the twelfth century. They allege that the game, like so much of Japanese culture, came from China. That allegation has been accepted by most works on kemari to this day, but the style of play of Chinese kemari is different from the Japanese version of the game and a different ball is used. Emphasizing the Japanese contribution, Kuwayama Kōnen, asserts that there are no cases where Chinese sources can be shown to have influenced the rules, techniques, or customs of Japanese kemari. None of the old Japanese treatises on kemari refers to the Chinese texts.[50]

The earliest reference to kemari—in the *Nihongi*—seems to date the game from the year A.D. 644.[51] From the twelfth century, reigning and retired emperors as well as the highest levels of the nobility attended and participated in what Watanabe Tōru calls *hare no marikai* (formal ball games). As kemari took root, its field of play, equipment, techniques, customs, and costume were standardized. From the late thirteenth century, the rules of the game were systematized and codified in various treatises.[52]

It was not only the nobility that contributed to the development of the game. Treatises on kemari and other records of the time show that the more skillful players tended to be of lower social status, and they were the ones who initially exerted the greatest influence on the game's development. In time, however, the nobility adapted the game to their own beliefs and institutions. Their courtly version of the game, what Watanabe calls *kuge mari* (courtiers' ball), became the standard and subsequently spread throughout the country.[53]

Kemari deserves detailed consideration because it was the first Japanese game to achieve a high level of development, because it provides an interesting contrast to the development of other sports in Japan, both indigenous and imported, and because it is very little known outside Japan.

The game seems to have been a secular rather than a religious activity. A text dated 1593 referred to kemari performed as a supplication for rain during a drought in 1215[54] and kemari also seems occasionally to have functioned as a ceremony of appeasement designed to dispel the accumulation of misfortune,[55] but these are rare instances of kemari as *shinji* (religious ritual). For the most part, kemari seems to have been played solely for the enjoyment of the players and the spectators.

Watanabe has described kemari as it was played in the thirteenth century. The game was played outdoors on a square earthen court with sides about 6 or 7 meters in length, depending on the space available. At each of the four corners of the court there was a tree. These trees were so central to the game that playing kemari was often referred to as "standing under the trees." The ball, made of deerskin, was hollow. Existing balls are about 20 centimeters in diameter, and weigh around 100 to 120 grams. These light balls were so delicate that they were liable to collapse if kicked too hard. The balls were coated with albumen (egg white). Some were then given an additional coat of white face powder mixed with glue; still others were dyed yellow by smoking them over a pine-needle fire. The "smoked" and white balls were sometimes said to symbolize not only the sun and the moon but also the opposing principles of yin and yang.[56]

Other items of equipment needed for kemari included poles (for retrieving balls caught in the trees), nets (for keeping the ball off roofs and from under the verandas of nearby buildings), and blinds (to block the rays of the setting sun).

We do not know when trees first appeared as constituent elements of kemari or when the specific kinds of trees were first stipulated. The first mention of *kakari no ki* (the trees on the court) is from around 980. It was apparently still the custom in the tenth century to locate the kemari court among trees that had grown naturally. In the eleventh century, however, trees were purposely planted for use in kemari. Four different kinds of trees were considered appropriate: cherry, willow, maple, and pine. "Especially high status was accorded to courts marked by four pine trees, but these were allowed only within the palace grounds . . . and at the courts of the Asukai and Namba houses."[57] In ordinary games, the plum tree was sometimes substituted for one of the other four. Each tree was assigned a corner of the court: northeast, southeast, southwest, and northwest. Which tree belonged in which corner was an important component of kemari's "ancient practices" (kojitsu). Like many aspects of traditional sports, the placement of the trees was a contentious issue for the competing "houses of kemari." Trees were either *motoki* (rooted to the spot) or *kiritate* (stuck in the ground like a post and destined to wither).[58]

Whether a tree was permanent or temporary, it was important to prune it with an eye to the possible paths taken by the ball as it tumbled down through the branches. A good pruning job left a pattern of branches that created a variety of interesting courses for the ball to take during its descent.[59] Although a modern observer is likely to compare this descent to that of the metal balls in a pinball machine, the irregularity of the branches also resembled the irregularities—architectural rather than arboreal—that were a fascinating part of medieval European court tennis.[60]

In the ninth century, players seem to have worn *kariginu* (hunting dress), which was certainly more suitable for vigorous activity than courtly garb, but the players' costumes underwent a process of refinement and elaboration. By the thirteenth century, ceremonial attire, including the Heian courtier's distinctive tall black hat, was worn. "In their choice of kimono and in the combination of colors, players had to conform to strict rules."[61] Tucked into the players' belts were the decorated paper fans that normally indicated a courtier's rank—the more ribs the fan had, the higher the rank. Needless to say, the clogs worn for everyday use were inappropriate for a kicking game and special shoes, made of leather and bound to the calf by cords, were also required.[62]

Eight players normally participated, one on each side of the four trees.[63] The player enjoying the highest court rank stood closest to the pine tree. He was the first to kick the ball, which he was required to pass to the player with the next highest rank.[64] Once play began in earnest, the eight players moved freely to follow the ball, but they returned to their original positions whenever play was interrupted. The ball was kicked with the right foot, often several times in succession, before it was passed to another player. The object was to keep the ball in the air for as many kicks as possible.

When a formal count was kept, the game was called *kazumari* (number ball) and an official was designated to keep score. He counted silently until 50 and then announced every tenth kick. Sometimes, when a player executed a particularly skillful kick, the official awarded a bonus. Counting silently, "51, 52, 53," he saw an especially impressive kick and shouted "60!"

At most *marikai* (ball meets), there was an upper limit—usually set before the game—at which a volley was to be discontinued. One treatise mentions limits of 120, 300, 360, 700, and 1,000. These numbers, which might at first glance be thought to anticipate the modern craze for quantifying sports, actually came from astrology.[65]

Played in this way, kemari had no winners and no losers, but contests could be and were arranged. Two teams of eight players each performed a preset number of trials, and the team with the most kicks in a single trial was the winner. This contest was called *shōbu mari* (competitive ball).

The number of times a player kicked the ball before passing it on was not fixed, but three was considered most appropriate. One kick to receive the ball and bring it under control, one kick to send the ball straight up (often high above the player's head), and one kick to pass the ball on to another player. Gender distinctions appeared in the terms used for these three kicks. The first and third kicks—slow, low, and easily handled—were *meashi* (a woman's kicks). The second kick—quick, high, and gracefully performed—was *woashi* (a man's kick).

These terms raise an intriguing question. Did women play kemari? If ladies of the court did play, it was a rare event. This can be inferred from *The Confessions of Lady Nijō* (1307). In this memoir, Lady Nijō reported a game of kemari suggested by the priest Sukesue: "Let's select eight court ladies . . . and dress them in the attire of . . . kickball players.

Then we can set out the traditional trees in the garden and have the ladies act out a kickball game. That certainly would be a rare sight." Although the women whom Sukesue selected were allowed to catch the ball in the sleeves of their kimonos rather than to keep it in the air, they found the whole affair "acutely embarrassing."[66]

To keep the ball in the air, team play was very important. The players coordinated their movements with a variety of calls. There were three calls, one for each of the three kinds of kicks. Receiving the ball from another player, one called out "*Ooh!*" when the ball was at the peak of its arc. If more than one player called out, the one who called the longest received the ball. For his second kick, which propelled the ball straight up, the player cried "*Ari!*" On his third kick, passing it to another player, he called "*Ya!*" Some treatises describe various patterns of movement the players should take in following the ball.[67]

A player was evaluated on the basis of what were called the "three virtues of the ball" (*mari no santoku*): proper posture; swiftness and skill; and mastery of the strategy, "ancient traditions" (kojitsu), and etiquette of the sport. Excellence in any one of these three virtues was an attribute of expertise. There were also three techniques, any one of which was considered the sign of a skillful player. Reaching for a ball coming down at a difficult distance was called *nobiashi*. Since it was considered bad form to kick with one's back to the center of the court, a player would catch an errant ball on his shoulder, then turn quickly as it rolled down his body to face the center, a move called *kaeriashi*. The third acclaimed technique was *mi ni sou mari*, absorbing the force of a hard-kicked ball with one's upper body and controlling it as it rolled down to the foot.[68]

Records of the number of kicks (presumably including bonuses) date from the beginning of the tenth century. In 905, eight courtiers reached a count of 206. At a game played in 953, the count rose to 520.[69] Watanabe, commenting on the way that each score surpassed the previous one, suggests that the author he consulted understood the concept of the sports record and provided only the numbers that surpassed the previous quantified achievement. If this was indeed the case, the author anticipated what is widely thought to be the uniquely modern concept of the quantified sports record.[70]

Although kemari was played throughout the year, spring was considered to be the most appropriate season. Play started in the early afternoon and lasted until dusk. At games attended by a reigning or a retired emperor, there were certain prescribed procedures to inaugurate and end play, beginning with *tsuyuharai*, in which real or metaphorical dew was shaken from the trees. The proper form for these procedures was an important component of the "ancient practices" transmitted by each of the "houses of kemari." They were the subject of much dispute.[71]

There were three stages in a day's marikai. These divisions apparently came from *bugaku*, a form of music and dance that was performed at court. The first stage (*jo no dan*) is the warm-up. The players practice the basic moves and kick the ball into the trees to see how it falls. Once they are warmed up and have a feel for the trees, they move into the second stage (*ha no dan*), in which they demonstrate their skills to the admiring spectators. When the sun begins to set and shadows start to lengthen, the players enter the third and final stage (*kyū no dan*). They move into the center of the playing area, away from the trees, and begin to play kazumari, aiming for a high number of volleys. Here the point is to show teamwork rather than individual skill. The players try to keep the ball out of the trees, and to make good passes. When darkness approaches, it is time for *torimari*. The best player calls for the ball, kicks it once, and then gracefully catches it in his kimono sleeve, ending the day's meet with aristocratic flair.[72]

Commenting in her famous *Makura no sōshi* (*Pillow Book*) on what scholars have taken to be a game of kemari, the tenth-century writer Sei Shōnagon was unimpressed by the players' attempts to comport themselves elegantly. She wrote that their movements were "interesting" (*okashi*) but an "unpleasant spectacle" (*sama ashi*).[73] In her even more famous *Genji monogatari* (*Tale of Genji*), Sei Shōnagon's slightly younger contemporary, Murasaki Shikibu, renders a similar assessment. In Chapter 34, Genji's son Yūgiri and his rival Kashiwagi indulge in this "less than genteel sport." "Spring mists enfolded trees in various stages of bud and bloom and new leaf. The least subtle of games does have its skills and techniques, and each of the players was determined to show what he could do. Though Kashiwagi played only briefly, he was clearly the best of them all."[74] As ladies of the court, Sei Shōnagon and Murasaki Shikibu seem to have had standards of elegance that were even more lofty than those of their male counterparts.

### *History*

The retired emperor Shirakawa (1053–1129) was apparently quite fond of kemari (although it is not known whether or not he stood under the trees himself). From the end of the eleventh to the beginning of the twelfth centuries, emperors and regents—the most prestigious members of court society—held many kemari meets.[75]

Kamo Narihira (1081–1136) may have been the first recognized master of kemari. Trained from a young age by his father, he, in turn, taught Fujiwara Narimichi (1097–1162), known to posterity as the "saint of kemari."[76] Narimichi, whose passion for the game is described in *Kōden nikki* (1197), boasts of having dedicated seven thousand days to the practice of kemari, two thousand of them without a break in the sequence.[77] "During this time, when I was unwell, I kicked the ball while lying down. When there was a pouring rain, I went to the Taikyoku Hall and played indoors. Was there ever anyone who loved the game as much as I do?"[78] Narimichi is said to have mounted the rail of the high balcony of Kiyomizu temple, built on the slopes of the mountains on the eastern edge of Kyoto, and to have walked the rail—like some daredevil tightrope artist—while kicking a kemari ball, first from west to east, then east to west.

Narimichi taught Fujiwara Yorisuke (1112–1186), the founder of two of the main houses of kemari, Namba and Asukai, and wrote the oldest known treatise on kemari, *Sanjū kajo shiki*. Although this work no longer exists in complete form, it can be pieced together from references and quotations in later works. Compared to these later works, Narimichi's offers a rather lighthearted approach to kemari. Narimichi does not stand on ceremony. For him, kemari is a game that should be enjoyed without excessive attention to proper etiquette. When asked about the origins of the yellow (smoked) ball, he ignored the opportunity for esoteric analysis and replied that it came about by accident.[79]

Later commentators criticized Narimichi for his informality. He wrote mainly about technique, they complain, and little about appropriate manners. Watanabe interprets this complaint to mean that kemari had not yet become, in Narimichi's time, a solemn ceremonial occasion.[80] Since *Sanjū kajo shiki* contained no instructions for different forms of dress for players of differing status, Kuwayama concludes that the early-twelfth-century version of the sport had not yet developed into the status-marker that it subsequently became.[81]

The first emperor or retired emperor identified by Watanabe as a kemari player rather than merely a spectator was the retired emperor Goshirakawa (1127–1192). Goshirakawa was quite fond of the game, held meets during his reign, and even stood under the trees himself, which was a significant factor in establishing the popularity and status of kemari at the court. Fujiwara (Namba) Yorisuke, Goshirakawa's kemari instructor, provided a detailed description of Goshirakawa's involvement with the game in his *Kemari Kōdenshū*. Whether or not his praise for the ex-emperor's skills was exaggerated is impossible to decide.[82] Yorisuke's accolades, like those that flattered Henry VIII as a tennis player, may have been merely politic.

Apart from the account of Goshirakawa's prowess, the *Kōdenshū* is a treatise on the techniques and traditions of kemari. Yorisuke related and assessed the achievements of Narihira, Narimichi, and other illustrious players. While accomplished players of relatively low status were included in Yorisuke's book, Watanabe notes that the frequent appearance of emperors, retired emperors, regents, and other representatives of the courtly elite served to legitimize the traditions and customs Yorisuke propounds and to raise the social status of kemari. There were at the time other established houses of kemari and other accomplished players, but they are given only a minor role in the *Kōdenshū*, as Yorisuke emphasized the importance of his own circle.

The retired emperor Gotoba (1180–1239) was an even greater fan of kemari than his grandfather Goshirakawa and he, too, was an accomplished player. According to his diary, during the fourth month of 1214 he played kemari sixteen out of thirty days. In 1208, while at the Minase Imperial Villa, he participated in a kemari meet that had important repercussions for the later development of the game. In the first round, the count reached 980 and in the second round the group kept the ball in the air for over 2,000 kicks. Gotoba was so pleased that he bestowed an official court rank on the ball, one that conferred the right of access to the palace. Shortly afterwards the three individuals most prominent in court kemari of the day—Narimichi's heir Yasumichi, Namba Munenaga and Asukai Masatsune (the latter two, the grandsons of Yorisuke)— awarded Gotoba the honorary title of "Patriarch of kemari" (*kono michi no chōja*). Watanabe believes that the three men bestowed this title in order to elevate the game's status at the court.

Three years after becoming "Patriarch" of the sport, Gotoba contributed to kemari's traditions and customs by issuing the "Regulations Governing Stockings" (*Tabi no teihin*). These regulations stated that the color and pattern of the stockings worn inside the players' shoes, which were also quite special, should indicate the status and skill level of the player. The color and pattern that denoted the highest rank were reserved to players honored by the "Patriarch" himself.

What the original colors and patterns were cannot be said for certain, but, predictably, they soon became the subject of conflict among the different houses. The Mikohidari house, which dominated kemari in the capital from the mid-thirteenth to the late fourteenth centuries, based its claim to precedence on the fact that Mikohidari Tame'ie had received Gotoba's permission to wear the highest rank of stockings in 1214. The Kamo line, on the other hand, whose superb players had done much to promote kemari in the past, were denied permission to wear the most coveted stockings. The reason was apparently the family's relatively low social status. Watanabe considers the "Regulations" and their selective use—providing legitimacy for some houses while denying it to others—to have been important in the development of the courtly version of the game.

At the same time that the retired emperor Gotoba acted to enhance the status of kemari in Kyoto, the Kamakura shogunate had its own enthusiast in the form of Minamoto no Yoriie (1182–1204), the eldest son of the first Kamakura shogun, Minamoto no Yoritomo (1147–1199). Between Yoriie's accession in 1199 and his death in 1204, the *Azuma kagami*, which chronicled the events of the Kamakura shogunate, recorded sixty-three instances of his engaging in sport. Kemari was mentioned thirty-five times compared to eleven mentions of mounted archery, eight of hunting, and five of standing archery. In 1201, Yoriie's kemari team achieved counts of 700 and 950. In 1202 he played kemari three times in one day, in the morning, afternoon, and evening. After only two years as shogun, Yoriie was forced to surrender his position. Implying that a man obsessed by a mere ball game was obviously unsuited for the onerous obligations of political leadership, the *Azuma kagami* may have emphasized Yoriie's involvement with kemari in order to justify his removal from office. His successor as shogun, his younger brother Minamoto no Sanetomo (1192–1219), almost never played kemari.[83]

The popularity of kemari in Kyoto and Kamakura intensified the endemic quarrels among the three great thirteenth-century houses of kemari, the Mikohidari, the Namba, and the Asukai, each of which claimed sole legitimacy for its traditions. The Mikohidari house was preeminent in kemari in Kyoto from the mid-thirteenth century. The Namba house also had some influence in the capital. In Kamakura, on the other hand, the Namba and Asukai houses competed for influence. Namba may have had an advantage because it was the older house. (Asukai was a branch of Namba.)[84]

By the time of the establishment of the Tokugawa shogunate in 1600, however, the Asukai all but monopolized the right to transmit kemari's "ancient traditions." The Namba and Kamo families were allowed by the Tokugawa shoguns to acquire disciples and to teach kemari, but the Asukai effectively controlled the authoritative "texts of transmission" and they dominated kemari until the end of the Edo period in 1868.[85]

Differences concerned such matters as the arrangement of the trees, the colors and patterns of the stockings, and the proper way to tie (or not to tie) the *hakama* (the divided skirt worn by men). From the perspective of someone who takes modern sports as the norm, the space given to such matters in the records of the time seems totally disproportionate—especially in light of the sparseness of detail about the way the game was actually played. For both the Heian courtier and the Kamakura warrior, form took precedence over content.[86]

Sometime around 1291 Asukai Masaari compiled the *Naige sanjisho*. The motive for his labor was probably the desire to preserve certain house secrets for oral transmission by the hereditary head of the house. Whatever Masaari's motive, Watanabe notes that his compilation represents a systemization of kemari not found in earlier treatises. It is organized into regular categories to a degree that earlier treatises were not.[87]

During the fourteenth and fifteenth centuries, both nobles, who had lost their political power but clung to their superior social status, and samurai, who ran the country but never overcame their sense of social inferiority, looked to the Asukai as kemari's ultimate authority. The Asukai house began to issue "texts of transmission" (*densho*) to those who enrolled as formal pupils of the game. After the Ōnin War (1467–1477), which destroyed much of Kyoto, the culture that had developed in the capital in the five hundred years since its foundation was carried to the provinces by the city's fleeing residents. As a result of this diffusion, the Asukai house issued its "texts of transmission" to followers scattered far and wide, from the Tōhoku region in the northeast to present-day Kagoshima on the western tip of the main islands. A kind of social diffusion paralleled kemari's geographical diffusion. Urban merchants were among the recipients of the "texts of transmission" and records from the Edo period show that urban merchants, rural landlords, priests, and others all indulged in regular games of kemari.[88]

Although the Kamo family was allowed to teach a form of kemari to the common people, various restrictions were placed on the sport as played by the lower classes. Some who violated the restrictions were sent into internal exile, but this did not hinder kemari's diffusion among city dwellers and even among the peasantry.[89]

We can catch a glimpse of the commoners' game in the diary of Sejimo

Yoshitada, who lived in Shinano, in the mountains of central Honshu, far from the ancient capital of Kyoto and far from Edo, seat of the shogunate. Yoshitada was a devotee of kemari, which he mentions often in his diary. The first reference came in 1715 and the last in 1782, the next-to-last year of the diary and a few years before Yoshitada's death.

In the spring of 1751, a kemari court was set up on the grounds of a temple in the village of Nozawa, where kemari was performed "almost daily from summer to fall." Samurai and townspeople also gathered to play the game at a local official's house. Yoshitada specifically mentions the construction of no fewer than five kemari courts in the village. Every year, on the seventh day of the seventh month, a special meet was held in Nozawa, at which individual rankings were determined.[90]

Yoshitada writes that the heir of the domain lord played kemari at a local temple. Just as the second round started, rain began to dowse the players. The young heir was disappointed but resourceful. He ordered that the tatami mats in the main hall of the temple be removed. The game then resumed on the temple's wooden floor.

In 1754 Yoshitada visited the regional capital, Matsumoto, where he received instruction in kemari from a local representative of the Asukai family. On a trip to Edo in 1759 he played more than twenty games of kemari with prominent players. This devotion to kemari in one small corner of Shinano Province suggests that the game was popular in a myriad of local variations throughout Edo-period Japan.[91]

## DAKYŪ

*Dakyū* is a team game in which the players, either on foot or on horseback, swing sticks in order to propel a ball into a goal. The word, made from the Chinese characters for "strike" and "ball," is often translated as "Japanese polo," but the translation is a misnomer because the game resembled modern lacrosse as well as modern polo.[92]

Like polo, dakyū originated in Persia, came to China by way of the Silk Road, and was then introduced to Japan, probably sometime in the seventh century. From the *Man'yōshū*, an eighth-century collection of poetry, we know that dakyū was played by court aristocrats in Nara in 727. For the next five hundred years, the game was popular among the court nobility.[93] During the Heian period, samurai guards at the imperial court included the game among the annual events of the fifth lunar month. With the rise to power of provincial samurai, however, the power and influence of the court samurai diminished and dakyū died out. The last recorded performance occurred in 986.

The game reappeared in the eighteenth century. In an attempt to revive the martial arts and reinvigorate the male population, Yoshimune, the eighth Tokugawa shogun (1684–1751), brought back dakyū and a number of other nearly forgotten sports. For reasons unknown, however, dakyū was revived in an altered form. As the name implies, in the original form of dakyū (also called *mariuchi* [ball hitting]), the ball was struck with a stick. When the game was revived, however, the end of the stick was provided with a net in which the ball was scooped and thrown. The field was asymmetrical in that both teams threw their balls into a goal or goals located on the same end. Two teams, one red and one white, each threw a predetermined number of balls into the goal. The officials who oversaw the game also came in pairs—one red and one white. Unlike the situation in modern sports, there was apparently no single neutral authority.

Later in the Edo period, as different schools advocated different versions of the game, dakyū underwent constant modification. The goal, for example, was changed from an arch on the ground to a round hole in a facade. Most of the Edo-period changes distanced the game from any possible martial application and emphasized the purely ludic nature of the sport.

In the Meiji period (1868–1912), dakyū lost favor once again. It survives today as a traditional cultural asset in two different forms. *Kagamiryū dakyū* is preserved in Hachinohe in Aomori Prefecture; a second style is preserved in Yamagata Prefecture and also by the Imperial Household Agency.

There are three main differences between the two surviving forms. The sticks used in the Hachinohe style are longer than those used in the Yamagata–Imperial Household style. The goal is round in the latter style. The Yamagata–Imperial Household style is complicated by the *agemari* rule (which involves a specially marked ball for the final goal).

In the Hachinohe style, which dates from the middle of the Edo period, two teams of four players each compete, one wearing red and one white. The stick used is approximately 2.27 meters long. The balls, which are about 30 centimeters in circumference, are made by wrapping a small rock in straw, then in hemp or cotton cloth, and finally in paper or leather. Each side uses four balls, red for the red side, white for the white side.

The two teams ride into the playing area, scoop up their balls, and throw them toward their goal from behind a line marked at a distance of 18 to 27 meters from the goal. (The distance is set beforehand according to the skill of the players.) There are two goals, one for the red team, one for the white team. When the white team scores a goal, drums are beaten; when the red team scores, gongs are sounded. The first team to place all its balls in its goal wins the round. Three or four rounds are played to determine the winner.

The Yamagata–Imperial Household style of dakyū dates from late in the Edo period. The sticks are of the same shape and material as in the Hachinohe style, but they are much shorter, only about one meter long. The playing area has a single, round goal. The ball is made in the same way, but it is only about 4.5 centimeters in diameter. In the Yamagata version, five balls are used, while the Imperial Household version is played with eleven.

Play is similar to that of Hachinohe dakyū, but the balls are hurled at the raised goal from a distance of 3.6 to 5.4 meters, depending on the skill of the players. The drums and gongs indicate the score as in the Hachinohe game. When one side has scored all its balls, a final ball is put into play, the agemari, which is marked by a black cross. The team that sends the agemari into the goal wins the game. In both versions of the game, the winning team exits mounted, while the losing players remove their headgear and exit on foot, leading their horses.[94]

## GITCHŌ

The game of gitchō may be an offshoot of the original form of dakyū. A round disk, shaped like a hockey puck, is struck with an implement more closely resembling a golf putter than a hockey stick. These instruments can be seen in a Heian-period drawing depicting seven boys playing gitchō in the streets of Kyoto at the New Year. A written description of the game exists from the middle of the nineteenth century.

Several versions of the game were played in the latter half of the nineteenth century. Sōgawa Tsuneo divides them into two main types. There are several versions in which the game is territorial. In one of these versions, two teams line up in the center of town facing each other across a short distance. The first team throws the puck along the ground toward the second team, which receives and returns it, advancing to the point where the puck had been stopped while the first team retreats and prepares to receive and return the puck. The puck flies back and forth until one team is pushed out of town. In other versions of the game points are scored, but the basic concept is the same: not allowing the puck to penetrate your defense. The two teams hit the puck back and forth between them. If the puck is not returned, the opposing side gains a point.

Like medieval European folk-football, which was customarily played at Christmas and at Whitsuntide, dakyū and gitchō were both seasonal games.[95] Mounted and unmounted versions of dakyū were traditionally played at *tango,* the boys' festival that falls on the fifth day of the fifth month. Gitchō was intimately associated with celebrations of the New Year. From the Heian period on, the game was a common iconographical representation of that holiday. Implements used in the game were sold as New Year's presents for Edo-period boys.[96]

## CHIKARAISHI

*Chikaraishi* (written with the characters for "strength" and for "stone") is the practice of lifting heavy stones. The term also refers to the stones themselves, which are found on the grounds of temples and shrines throughout Japan. We know a good deal about sports like sumō, kemari, and dakyū because the participants and the spectators were for the most part literate people who left written or visual records from which we can now reconstruct their activities. The strong men who competed at chikaraishi left few records and most of these are fairly recent. The inscriptions found on some of these stones constitute our best source of written information. The oldest known inscription, found on a rock at Tokyo's Shinobu shrine, is from 1664. The second oldest inscription, dated 1705, is on a rock in a shrine in adjacent Saitama Prefecture. Rocks in other parts of the country have much later inscriptions. Over five hundred chikaraishi have been confirmed on Awaji Island in Hyōgo Prefecture, but only one is dated—and that date is 1928.

It may not have been accidental that many of these chikaraishi stones have been found at Shinto shrines. One wonders if the gods were thought to have had a hand in the contests (as they did in the funeral games described by Homer in Book XXIII of the *Iliad*).

There are various theories about the origins of chikaraishi, but the paucity of hard evidence forces historians to rely on speculation. Like workers everywhere, the stalwart Japanese who lifted heavy sacks of rice to their shoulders or carried cargo from a ship's hold to the dock challenged one another in feats of strength. In the *shitamachi* area of Edo, impromptu contests became, no later than the seventeenth century, the sport of chikaraishi, in which large stones took the place of sacks of rice. The sport seems to have reached the peak of its popularity in the early nineteenth century as the Tokugawa shogunate approached its end.[97]

The stones used in these contests were often sculpted into a smooth, flat, oval shape, but natural rocks were also used. Most chikaraishi are blank, but some have inscriptions, especially those found on the grounds of temples and shrines. The inscriptions give the weight of the rock, its name, a date, a place name, and the names of the person(s) who lifted it and of others who supervised the event.

The form of competition varied with region and with time. Among the common forms of competition were *ishizashi, ishikatsugi, ishihakobi, ashiuke,* and *ishiokoshi.*

In ishizashi, both hands were used to hoist rocks weighing around 70 kilograms from the ground to the stomach, then to the chest, where the lifter adjusted his grip, then overhead. Ishikatsugi was more complicated. Employing a circle of rope under the rock to make their task easier, contestants lifted rocks weighing approximately 70 to 210 kilograms, first to the waist and then to the chest, at which point the rope was dropped and the rock shifted to a shoulder. From there the rock could be rolled behind the neck to the other shoulder in a move called *ishimawashi.*

Ishihakobi was a competition in carrying a heavy rock. Who was able to carry the rock the greatest distance? In ashiuke, another variant of the sport, a rock weighing as much as 245 kilograms was used. The brave contestant lay on his back with his legs in the air while assistants placed the rock on the soles of his feet. Rocks too heavy to be lifted from the ground were suitable for ishiokoshi. The object was to raise one end from the ground so that the stone stood on edge.

The weight of many of the uninscribed stones was probably known, since some blank rocks are still called by their weight in sacks of rice, for example, as the "one-sack-of-rice-rock." Early inscriptions are simple and shallow, as if they were just meant to be simple reminders of the weight of the rock. Later, the weights were inscribed deeply in the center of the face of the stone. The weight is given in *kan,* a fairly standardized unit roughly equivalent to 3.75 kilograms. Although the inscribed weight is usually heavier than the actual weight, some inscriptions testify that their numbers are "true weight."

This concern for measurement indicates a small step in the direction of the ubiquitous quantification that characterizes modern sports.

On the basis of this simple form of quantification, some historians see chikaraishi as a prototype of modern sports,[98] but their argument is unpersuasive. Although a list compiled in 1836, "Men of Strength in Edo," does indeed prove that there was some effort to rank the strong men on the basis of their achievements, fewer than a quarter of the stones had their weight inscribed upon them and even these stones varied in size and shape—in stark contrast to the standardized iron plates hoisted by the modern weightlifter. It was possible, as it always has been, for local bards to sing the praises of strong men, but it was not yet possible to identify a national champion or to imagine a sports record in the modern sense of the term.[99]

# 2

# Martial Techniques

## ARCHERY

According to the most authoritative Western scholar of Japan's martial arts, "Archery was the first of the traditional Japanese combat techniques to become modified into a sport form."[1] In part, this is probably because it was easier for archery to make that transition. The bow and arrow was used for hunting as well as combat, and the substitution of inanimate targets for live ones was not a complicated procedure.

Millennia before the dawn of history, inhabitants of the Japanese islands hunted with bows and arrows and used these implements as weapons. Like the hunters and warriors of other cultures past and present, they must have challenged one another in tests of skill. Archeologists have found obsidian arrowheads from the Stone Age,[2] but the earliest documents relating to archery as a sport date from late in the seventh century A.D. Both the *Kojiki* and the *Nihongi* "firmly link archery and its accessories . . . with the deities and their descendants, the rulers of Japan." The mythical Jimmu, the first of these rulers, was said to possess "heavenly-feathered arrows" as one token of his right to rule. In 682, Emperor Temmu (d. 686) had his courtiers perform a ceremony at the Nagatsuka shrine in which they shot at targets from horseback.[3]

Although the Japanese gripped the bow in the Mongolian fashion, with the thumb wrapped over the bowstring, they used the long bow derived from Southeast Asia rather than the much shorter Mongol bow. The long bow, which measures over 2 meters, is still used to this day and is still gripped as it was in Heian times, with two-thirds of the bow's length above the archer's hand.[4]

Archery, like sumō, became incorporated into the annual calendar of ceremonies performed at the imperial court "designed to preserve harmony between Heaven and Earth and secure the political order."[5] In the *Dairishiki* (833) and other chronicles of the court for the years 646 to 930, archery matches far outnumbered all other ceremonies.[6] Archery was divided into two main types, standing and equestrian, both of which were subdivided into several kinds.

Standing archery first appeared as a court ritual in the form of jarai (the shooting ceremony), which was performed in the middle of the first lunar month of the year. Twenty noblemen, including imperial princes, were selected to participate. Another group of archers was selected from the palace guards. On the fifteenth of the month, the two groups practiced separately. Two days later, the archers presented themselves to the emperor at the Burakuin (Court of Abundant Pleasures). Standing on mats made of calfskin, aiming at deerskin targets, the nobles shot first, followed by the guards. A gong rang once to indicate that an arrow had hit the target's outer ring. The gong rang twice if the arrow lodged in the middle ring, thrice if the innermost ring was struck. Whether or not the concentric rings were the basis for quantified results is uncertain, but equality in the conditions of competition, another characteristic of modern sports, was not present. Members of the imperial family aimed their arrows at a target some 20 percent larger than the one provided for the nobility.[7]

After an archer had released his arrow, a herald announced the result along with the contestant's name, rank, and office. Prizes, consisting of bolts of cloth, were given for degrees of accuracy, but the event was not a direct competition producing winners and losers. The archer's rank influenced the prize he received: the higher his rank, the more lavish his reward, a form of inequality characteristic of many premodern sports.[8]

Although archery contests of some sort occurred at the palace as early as A.D. 483, the first reference to jarai is from 647. Jarai became an annual ceremony late in the seventh century at approximately the same time that Japan's first unified state took shape. At jarai, all the top government officials gathered before the emperor and displayed their skill in archery. In the early tenth century, punishments were set for nobles who failed to show up for the ceremony. Participation in the ceremony served a political purpose similar to that of court sumō. Shooting with the long bow symbolized the archers' inclusion in the state and allegiance to the emperor. In the early years of the ceremony, *bankyaku* (visitors from areas outside the emerging state) also took part, but they shot with their own bows, thereby demonstrating that they were subservient to the emperor even if they were not among his subjects.[9]

The jarai ceremony underwent a change after the middle of the ninth century. The emperor no longer attended the ceremony and, in his absence, the royal princes and the highly ranked nobles withdrew from the contest, becoming passive spectators rather than active participants. The venue shifted from the Burakuin to an open space in front of the Kenreimon, the south gate of the outer wall of the inner palace. As a result of these changes, the ceremony ceased to fulfill its function as a physically enacted statement of fealty to the emperor.[10]

In the course of the Heian period, as the emperor lost much of his power to the Fujiwara regents, two new forms of standing ritual archery ousted jarai from ceremonial centrality. *Noriyumi* and *yuba hajime* were in closer accord with late-Heian political reality.[11]

Noriyumi (prize archery) was held on the eighteenth day of the first lunar month, the day following jarai. Initially, it was merely an auxiliary to the jarai ceremony. Archers from the inner palace guards and the military guards competed before the emperor at the archery range of the inner palace. Ten pairs of archers from the inner palace guards competed first. Two archers, one from the Left and one from the Right, came forward and shot three arrows each. A round was concluded when each of the ten pairs had had its turn. After each round, the winning side received a bolt of cloth and the losers drank sake from "the cup of defeat," which presumably increased the likelihood of defeat in the next round as tipsy archers took uncertain aim. When the inner palace guards were done, they stepped aside while seven pairs from the military guards took their turns. (The competition was internal, between the Left and Right sides of the two guard divisions; there was no direct competition between the inner palace guards and the military guards.) This procedure, in which direct head-to-head competition was clearly more important than it was in jarai, was repeated for a maximum of ten rounds. At the conclusion of the contest, the head of the inner palace guards invited all the contestants to his residence for a banquet. Like all aristocratic entertainments, this one was enlivened by the consumption of alcohol.[12]

The earliest record of noriyumi is from 824. From 848 on, the emperor attended noriyumi almost annually. Jarai, in which the emperor no longer played a role, lingered on throughout the Kamakura period (1185–1333) and seems to have disappeared by the end of the fourteenth century. (By that time, noriyumi had also ceased to exist as a court ceremony.)[13]

The other form of ritual archery that developed in the middle of the ninth century, yuba hajime (opening the archery gallery), occurred on the fifteenth day of the tenth month. The archery range in the inner palace was set up annually by the gate guards on the third day of the tenth month and dismantled on the second day of the fourth month. This was the season in which the facility was available for use by the emperor. Yuba hajime probably had its origins in a ceremony in which the emperor shot the first arrow to inaugurate a new season of archery.

In the ninth-century form of yuba hajime, a place was set aside for the emperor to shoot and a bow and arrows were placed next to him for his use. These objects, like the swords worn on state occasions by twentieth-century monarchs, were clearly symbolic. Demonstrating the emperor's familiarity with the warrior's weaponry, they testified to his unity with his subjects. At the emperor's command, the royal princes and high court nobles entered. (Officials of lower rank who participated in jarai and noriyumi were excluded from the yuba hajime ceremony.) Once the contestants were assembled, the emperor's "shooting seat" was removed and the competition began. The first appearance of the term "yuba hajime" occurred in 898, but there are earlier records of the emperor's attendance at archery matches that took place in the inner palace in the tenth and eleventh months. The yuba hajime ceremony must have taken shape in the middle of the ninth century at approximately the same time that jarai was declining in importance and noriyumi was becoming more prominent.[14]

The second main type of archery performed as an annual court ritual was *kisha*, mounted archery, performed at the Butokuden (Hall of Military Virtues) on the palace grounds. This ceremony was also intimately related to military technique. Like the mounted knights who dominated medieval European battlefields, armored warriors astride their steeds were the terror of early Japanese warfare. All government officials were required by law to own horses, to master the techniques of equestrian military discipline, and to provide military service to the emperor. This policy, an intrinsic part of the military system of the new state, was so thorough that fashions in dress were modified in accordance with the requirements of mounted warfare. Late in the seventh century, clothes worn at court underwent a mandated change and men switched from skirt-like lower garments to trousers, suitable for straddling a horse.[15]

It is hardly a surprise, therefore, that mounted archery became an important court ceremony from early in the eighth century.[16] This ceremony occurred annually, with occasional interruptions, on the fifth and sixth days of the fifth lunar month. The participants—forty-two inner palace guards and twelve military guards—were selected at practice sessions held about one month earlier.

On the twenty-eighth day of the fourth month, a preliminary event was held at which horses raised in the provinces surrounding the capital were presented to the emperor. Provincial governors, leading their gift horses, paraded before their sovereign. In an age when the mounted warrior was the ultimate in weaponry, the offering of horses demonstrated the political loyalty of the provinces as well as a readiness to bear arms in defense of the emperor and his realm.[17] In the presence of the presumably grateful emperor, the inner palace guards rode some of the horses and performed mounted archery. The versatile guards also provided music for the occasion.

On the fifth day of the fifth month, mounted on the horses that had been presented as tribute, the guards raced and competed in target archery. (It was the guards who raced because most Heian courtiers were poor horsemen.)[18] The targets used were 1 *shaku* 5 *sun* (ca. 42 centimeters) in diameter. (The ability to hit a 1-shaku 5-sun target with every shot was, in fact, a requirement for the inner palace and military guards.) On the following day, the sixth, another round of races and mounted archery was held, but participation was much more limited and the targets were about one-third the size. Archers of exceptional skill were selected to display their superior talents. Dakyū was also held, which provided an additional opportunity to display equestrian skills.

All government officials were represented at the main event of mounted archery held on the fifth, while the ceremony on the sixth was restricted to the upper ranks. Here too, spatial arrangements had symbolic importance. On the sixth, the emperor sat nearer his subjects than he had the previous day, a visible expression of his closer relationship to the upper ranks of the nobility.[19]

There is some evidence that the horse races run on the sixth were fixed. On or about the twentieth day of the tenth month, it was the custom for the emperor to go to the Shishinden to receive offerings and be entertained by the side of the guards that had lost the horse races on the sixth day of the fifth month. The losing side, however, was almost always the Right. Obinata Katsumi speculates that it was probably a dictate of ritual custom that the Left win.[20]

The custom of mounted archery on the fifth day of the fifth month began to decline early in the tenth century. Kisha was discontinued in 986 and there are no unambiguous records to show that it was ever revived.[21] When the mounted warrior returned to prominence, after the relatively peaceful years of the Heian period, other forms of equestrian archery were devised.

In addition to jarai, noriyumi, yuba hajime, and kisha, private archery competitions in which prizes were given were also common at the mansions of Heian nobles.[22] The Heian historical tale, *Ōkagami* (*The Great Mirror*), depicts the powerful statesman Fujiwara Michinaga (966–1027) as a skillful archer. In one contest, his rival is his nephew Korechika, who at that time outranked him. The contest takes place at the southern palace in the presence of Korechika's father Michitaka, then the regent. When Michinaga outperforms Korechika, Michitaka suggests another round of two shots each.

> "All right, extend it," Michinaga said, somewhat annoyed. As he prepared to shoot again, he said, "If Emperors and Empresses are to issue from my house, let this arrow hit the mark." And didn't his arrow strike the heart of the target?
>
> Next Korechika prepared to shoot. He was extremely nervous, and it may be that his hands trembled. At any rate, his arrow flew off into the sky without coming near the target. Michitaka turned pale.
>
> Michinaga got ready again. "If I am to serve as Regent, let this arrow find the mark," he said. The arrow hit the very center, striking with such force that the target almost broke. The Regent's cordiality vanished, and he showed his displeasure by ending the match.[23]

Poor losers, it seems, are not a recent phenomenon. And Michinaga did, after his brother's death, become regent.

Feats of archery also appear frequently in classical Japanese literature's most famous historical narrative, the *Heike monogatari*. Since this fourteenth-century text tells of the war between the Taira (also known as the Heike) and the Minamoto (or Genji) clans, archers appear principally in their deadly role as warriors for one side or the other, but there is also a famous demonstration of toxophilic skill that is applauded by both armies. At the Battle of Yashima (1185), Nasu no Yoichi, a renowned archer, is asked by Minamoto Yoshitsune (1159–1189) to shoot at a red fan that was conspicuously attached to a pole propped on the gunwale of one of the Heike's ships. Nasu no Yoichi mounts his horse, rides some distance into the sea, prays to the gods, swears that he will kill himself if his arrow misses the target, and shoots. "The whirring sound of the arrow reverberated as it flew straight to its mark." The Minamoto rattled their quivers to signal their delight, and the Heike beat the gunwales of their boats to acknowledge their admiration of an enemy's skill.[24]

The Minamoto vanquished the Taira, and Yoshitsune's half-brother Yoritomo (1147–1199) became the first Kamakura shogun in 1192. Yoritomo was so fond of archery that he incorporated exhibitions of another form of mounted archery, *yabusame,* into the festivals of the Hachiman shrine, dedicated to the god of war, near his capital of Kamakura. He was, however, troubled by the tendency of poorly performing archers to commit ritual suicide. His clever response to their unfortunate over-reaction was to order that the targets be enlarged.[25] Yoritomo was also a renowned hunter and quite concerned that his eldest son Yoriie (1182–1204) become skillful with bow and arrow. During a famous hunt, in 1194, the twelve-year-old boy shot his first deer, an event celebrated by a coming-of-age ceremony.[26] (As indicated in the previous chapter, however, the boy's favorite sport was to be kemari.)

The geographical move from the imperial court in Kyoto to the shogun's palace in Kamakura signaled a shift in political power from courtiers to warriors. The imperial court continued to hold the annual ceremony of jarai, but it had lost its relevance. Since archery was a vital combat skill for the warriors of the Kamakura shogunate, they quite naturally included it among their ceremonies, which they tended to fashion in imitation of court traditions. The three forms of archery most popular among Kamakura-period warriors were *kasagake,* yabusame, and *inuoumono.*

Kasagake might be translated as "the hanging hat." It occurred during the Heian period—the oldest record is from 1057—but became more popular in the Kamakura period, when the course, target and costume became standardized. The first instance of kasagake recorded in the *Azuma kagami,* the chronicles of the Kamakura shogunate, is from 1184.

The sport probably evolved from an amusement warriors engaged in during lulls in battle or pauses in a hunt. While remaining on horseback, they took practice shots at a round hat (*kasa*) hanging from a bush or tree or set on the ground. There was no special site for early kasagake. Almost any flat, open ground, such as a field or a sandy beach, served the purpose. The contestants needed only to run their horses in a straight line to make a track.

In the developed version of the sport, the target was a wooden plank covered with cowhide, stuffed with cotton, and suspended from a frame about 18 centimeters above the ground. Contestants galloped at full speed down a straight track more than 100 meters in length. A single arrow was shot at the target erected 8 bow-lengths (about 20 meters) from the left side of the track. In later years, as the skills of the archers apparently declined, the distance to the target was shortened to 7 or 6 or even fewer bow-lengths. A special kind of arrow was used, the *hikimeya*, which had an attachment to its head that whistled as it flew through the air. It was said that hikimeya were used because Minamoto Yoritomo liked the sound they made.

To begin the event, the archers gathered and galloped down the course one at a time to familiarize themselves with it. After that, the contest began in earnest. There was no set number of participants. Ten rounds were usual. As in most Japanese sports that were codified in premodern times, there was a prescribed costume. Several officials assisted in the event, the number depending upon the formality of the occasion. Referees, called *kenmi*, were sometimes assigned for the competition, but it was more common to do without them. The *kaizoe* helped prepare the archers' costumes and implements, the *yatori* sat by the target to retrieve the arrows, and the *nikkizuke* recorded the results. When performed as a ritual, kasagake was conducted in an appropriately grave fashion, but as a rule it was not accompanied by strict ceremonies. Kasagake was popular in and around Kamakura and Kyoto until the middle of the thirteenth century, after which it declined. It made a small comeback in the fifteenth century, but there are almost no records of it after the beginning of the sixteenth century.[27]

A form of mounted archery that might be considered a forerunner of yabusame was practiced at Kyoto's Kamo shrine. The annual event was so popular that disorderly crowds of spectators gathered and Emperor Mommu (683–707) found it necessary to ban the ritual in 698. Three reigns later, in 738, Emperor Shōmu (701–756) relented and the ritual resumed.[28] Although there are records of a yabusame contest performed expressly for the retired Emperor Shirakawa in 1096, the sport's golden age was during the Kamakura period, when it was popular among the samurai. It was first mentioned in the *Azuma kagami* in 1187.[29]

As with most of Japan's traditional sports, there were, from school to school, subtle variations in yabusame. In general, this form of archery was similar to kasagake in that contestants drew their bows and loosed their arrows while riding down a straight track some 220 to 270 meters long. A major difference, which greatly increased the difficulty of the task, was that they were required to shoot in quick succession at three targets. Contestants "had to nock, draw, and shoot twice more after releasing the first arrow, all at a full gallop."[30] The targets, which were about 55 centimeters square, were placed on meter-high poles 7 to 11 meters from the track and spaced at intervals of 72 to 90 meters. Special arrows—*kaburaya* (howling arrows)—were used, which, like hikimeya, made a whistling sound in flight. In their second pass, the mounted archers shot at tiny clay targets a mere 8.2 centimeters in diameter. Any number of riders participated.[31]

At the first recorded yabusame contest held at the Tsurugaoka Hachiman shrine in Kamakura, in the eighth month of 1187, Minamoto Yoritomo ordered Suwa Morizumi, a captured warrior from the Taira clan, to demonstrate his skill. "Despite having to ride an ill-tempered horse, Morizumi managed to hit all three targets on his first ride. On his second ride, he shattered the three clay targets." Yoritomo then ordered Morizumi to aim at the tiny pegs that held the targets in place. Morizumi prayed, rode, shot, and "to the amazement of the crowd he hit all three pegs."[32] Yoritomo was so impressed by this feat that he freed Morizumi and took him into his service.

Yabusame, like kasagake, was thought by the mounted warriors of the Kamakura period to be enjoyable sport as well as good practice for the battlefield. In addition, yabusame was sometimes performed as a religious ceremony, one purpose of which seems to have been to cure illness.[33]

The last recorded instance of regularly performed yabusame occurred in 1484, and then there are no records for two and a half centuries until the sport was revived by Tokugawa Yoshimune (1684–1751).[34]

Inuoumono (chase the dog), the largest and most elaborate of the mounted archery contests, was immensely popular during the Kamakura and the following Muromachi (1333–1573) periods. In this ritual, mounted archers pursued and shot blunted arrows at unfortunate dogs. The oldest written reference to this noisy (and to modern sensibilities noisome) event dates it from 1207. The *Azuma kagami* records several occasions, the first of which dates from 1222.

The playing field was approximately 200 square meters. Within this area two concentric circles were marked off with straw rope. The outer circle was approximately 12 meters in diameter, and the inner circle, called the *inutsuka* (dog's mound), was 2 meters in diameter. Thirty-six riders participated, divided into three teams of twelve riders each. The first group of twelve rode around the outer circle, where a handler held a single dog. When the dog was let loose, the riders aimed at it with blunted arrows. The first team shot at ten dogs, one after the other, and then it was the next team's turn. Five turns for each team required a total of one hundred fifty dogs. Winners were judged by their riding and shooting technique as well as by the number of hits, which is quite typical in premodern sports, and victory in the contest depended in part on where exactly the dogs were struck.[35]

Whistling arrows were used in inuoumono as they were in other mounted archery contests, but they were larger than the ones used in kasagake and were lacquered black instead of red. There was a prescribed costume for the riders, of course, and a number of attendants and officials were present to assist in the ceremony. Each rider was aided by two attendants. The list of officials included two mounted referees (each with two attendants). Like the heralds and scribes of a medieval European tournament, two officials announced the referees' decisions and a third official recorded them.

The hundred-year period from 1467 to around 1570 is known as the *Sengoku jidai* (Era of Warring States). The central government was weak, and regional warlords waged incessant battles to expand their influence at their neighbors' expense. By the early seventeenth century, however, the country had been reunified, and for the next two hundred and fifty years Japan was at peace under the rule of the Tokugawa shogunate. Centuries of peace had a negative effect on the various forms of archery, especially mounted archery. By the early seventeenth century, yabusame was rarely performed. When the Dutch observer Hendrick Hagenaer witnessed the ceremony in 1636, he found it "strange and incomprehensible."[36]

Yabusame was, however, unexpectedly, revived by the eighth shogun, Tokugawa Yoshimune (1684–1751). Yoshimune required the daimyō and the different schools of archery to submit their secret documents relative to the different forms of archery. Relying on this research, he revived a number of obsolete rituals. In 1724, Yoshimune ordered Ogasawara Tsuneharu to teach the art of mounted archery. A year later, ten mounted archers were summoned to the capital from the Province of Ki, where Yoshimune had been a daimyō before a series of unanticipated deaths brought him to the shogunate. A trial performance of yabusame took place on November 30. (It was witnessed by Hans Jürgen Keyserling, who was in Japan to care for a herd of Dutch horses that Yoshimune had imported from Europe.) Three years later, forty-six archers participated in a full-scale revival of the ceremony.[37]

The men, who had been sexually abstinent for as long as seventeen days, galloped between two low earthen mounds, one identified as male, the other as female. The targets were on the male side. The display of masculine prowess was successful and the archers were rewarded with suitable gifts. More important, Yoshimune's eldest son Ieshige (1711–1761), who had been afflicted with a mysterious skin disease, was cured. There was another performance of yabusame in 1738 to celebrate the birth of another son, Ieharu, and to protect him from harm. Yoshimune's comment on his own motives did not, however, emphasize the religious element nor did he comment on the participants' sexual abstinence, which was similar to that required before American Indian stickball games.[38] He explained that he had revived yabusame because "I regretted that the ancient ceremony of mounted archery had died out and also because I wanted to test my retainers."[39]

Inuoumono, which had died out during the warfare that preceded the Tokugawa period, was also occasionally revived. In 1842, the shogun Tokugawa Ieyoshi (1793–1853) viewed inuoumono, but his successor banned the activity in 1862, probably as a concession to Westerners who found the event distasteful. It was, however, performed for ex-president Ulysses Grant during his 1879 visit to Japan. His Japanese hosts may have thought that Grant's experiences during the Civil War rendered him immune from the sight of cruelty to canines, but he, like other Westerners privileged to witness inuoumono, expressed strong displeasure. The last known performance, for the Meiji emperor (1852–1912), was in 1881 at a residence of the Shimazu clan.[40]

As archery developed, standardized, and specialized, it was increasingly organized on the master-disciple principle characteristic of Japanese arts and crafts. In the Heian period, there were subtle differences in the archery practiced and taught by Ki no Okimichi, Tomo no Waketamaro, and Sakanoue no Tamuramarō, but these differences seem not to have been institutionalized in the form of schools that persisted through centuries. In the Muromachi period, several families of archers vied for preeminence and the favor of the shogunate. Ogasawara Sadamune (1294–1350) compiled the rules for mounted archery in the *Inuoumono mokuanbumi* (1341). His great-grandson Ogasawara Mochinaga (1396–1462), the teacher of the eighth Muromachi shogun, Ashikaga Yoshimasa (1436–1490), added five more volumes to the book, but Mochinaga's best-known work was the *Jarai shiki* (Personal Record on Ceremonial Shooting), which covered every aspect of the sport.[41]

The Ogasawara family's authority was "unrelated to any achievements this house had shown in archery and horsemanship on the battlefield. Its position as the highest authority on martial arts stemmed from its codification of what had become the rules of a sport."[42] The Ogasawara school taught a ceremonial form of archery that did not emphasize practical skill. Repudiating Ogasawara authority, many contemporary schools of archery trace their origins back to the legendary Heki Danjō Masatsugu, who died in 1502. Unlike the archers of the Ogasawara family, Masatsugu distinguished himself on the battlefield and in archery contests rather than as a writer. G. Cameron Hurst describes Masatsugu's distinctive stance as it was portrayed in a drawing:

> Barefoot and with the left sleeve of his jacket off, baring the shoulder for freedom of movement, Masatsugu stands with his feet about shoulder width apart, splayed outward in ducklike fashion. The bow is pulled back as he takes aim, and the pull extends only to the right breast, a mid-pull, as opposed to the full pull employed today in [Japanese archery].

Masatsugu transmitted his style of archery to Yoshida Shigekata (1463–1543), with whom the proliferation of various schools and branches of schools began in earnest.[43]

During the pacific Tokugawa era, the importance of archery as a battlefield skill declined. The samurai continued to practice with bow and arrow, but the motivation for their practice was not what it had been when the accuracy of one's aim made a life-or-death difference. Archery was simultaneously a recreation, a sport, and a form of spiritual training. This last aspect of Japanese archery—spiritual training—has received much attention, especially in the West. As Hurst comments, the intense "concern with form and decorum has been important to Japanese archery since it was first introduced as one of the six accomplishments of the Chinese noble. Archery was part of the training of the gentleman, with spiritual and civilizing qualities, as well as practical skill, emphasized."[44]

This emphasis on spiritual training is often attributed to the influence of Zen Buddhism,[45] but archery as a form of spiritual training predates the arrival of Zen Buddhism in Japan. When the spokesmen of the various schools of archery began to proliferate, and to systematize and codify the rules and techniques of their particular styles, they tended to express their thoughts in the religious terminology—Shinto, Buddhist, Confucianist, and Daoist—that was the common currency of the learned men of their day. "Samurai authors," wrote E. J. Harrison, "who had been taught composition by the Zen priests, quite naturally copied their teacher's style when they sought to express themselves in literary form."[46] Zen Buddhism contributed to the idea of archery as a spiritual activity, but it was only one of several influences. Hurst notes that a member of the famous Ogasawara family of archers does not mention Zen or any other Buddhist sect in an article on Japanese archery written for a major Japanese encyclopedia.[47]

The Portuguese introduction of firearms in the middle of the sixteenth century did not immediately render the bow obsolete as a weapon, but the emphasis in archery did shift even farther along the spectrum from warfare to sports competition. "If mental and physical discipline were essential elements in archery from antiquity, what distinguished archery in the Tokugawa period from archery before then was the rapid rise of competitive sport archery."[48]

This can be seen most clearly in a unique archery contest, known as *tōshiya* (clearing arrows). First recorded in 1606, it continued in existence until 1861. Although the contest seems to have been entirely secular, it was held at Kyoto's Rengeō-in temple. (The temple is popularly known by the name of its main hall, the Sanjūsangendō, where the contest was held.) Sitting at one end of the long veranda on the west side of the Sanjūsangendō, a single archer shot a series of arrows that were supposed to traverse the 120-meter length of the veranda without touching the structure's roof, pillars, or wall (which explains the term "clearing arrows").

In the 255 years during which the event was held, a total of 823 archers (counting repeaters) tested their skills at tōshiya at the Sanjūsangendō. The first was Asaoka Heibei, who was apparently satisfied with clearing fifty-one arrows. His record, set in 1606, was quickly surpassed. By 1623, Yoshida Ōkura had raised the record to 1,333 arrows. Starting with Ōkura, the total number of arrows shot was also recorded (2,087 arrows), which allows us to calculate his percentage of successful shots (63.4%).

In time, the contest became more complicated and evolved into four main categories: the *ōyakazu*, which lasted for twenty-four hours; the *hiyakazu,* which lasted twelve hours; the thousand-arrow contest; and the hundred-arrow contest. The proliferation of different distances and separate categories for minors eventually produced an array of eleven different events. Several officials oversaw the contest. There were three judges—one from the archer's own school, and two from rival schools. They held flags with which they signaled the success or failure of each effort.

Since ordinary arrows shot from ordinary bows flew in too high an arc for the low corridor of the Sanjūsangendō, shorter bows and lighter arrows were developed specifically for use in tōshiya. These bows and arrows were unsuitable for warfare because the arrows struck with much less impact than those propelled by the long bow. For this reason, traditionalists who wanted to maintain archery as a martial skill criticized the competition as impractical and militarily useless. The Ogasawara family, which played such an important role in the development of ritual archery, also refused to compete in tōshiya.

From 1606 to 1861, ōyakazu was held 598 times, but over half of those contests—54 percent to be exact—took place in the first 30 years, which suggests that the sport's popularity leveled off as records reached new and intimidating heights. In 255 years, the record for ōyakazu was set 41 times. A memorial tablet from 1669 marks the achievement of Hoshino Kanzaemon, who scored an amazing 8,000 successes with 10,542 arrows. A second tablet commemorates the feat of Wasa Daihachirō, who surpassed Kanzaemon's record in 1686 when he achieved 8,133 successes with 13,053 arrows. In order to do this, he had to shoot nearly 6 arrows a minute for 24 hours, from sunset to sunset, a nearly unimaginable athletic achievement. Although the contest continued for another 156 years after Daihachirō's extraordinary record, the 24-hour ōyakazu was held only 8 times after 1750, while the less demanding 1,000-arrow competition was held 51 times during the same period. "Tōshiya, which began as a simple test to see if an archer could shoot an arrow or two down the long veranda at Sanjūsangendō, was thus developed into a well-organized competitive sport."[49]

The competition became known to archers throughout the country, not all of whom were able to journey to Kyoto in order to compete. To accommodate the skilled archers in Edo, a Sanjūsangendō was constructed in that city in 1642. There, between 1645 and 1852, 544 archers (counting repeaters) tested their skills at tōshiya in twenty-one different events over varying times, distances, arrow limits, and age limits. The most spectacular achievements were those of the legendary Kokura Gishichi. In his first appearance, at the age of eleven, in 1827, he missed only five of his thousand shots at the "half-hall" distance.

Edo was not the only place where a replica of the Sanjūsangendō was constructed. The Sendai and the Shōnai clans, for example, built their own more or less authentic Sanjūsangendō on their domain lands and held their own tōshiya contests. Other domains held similar contests in existing facilities. The Aizu clan, for instance, used a warehouse with a long veranda located on their castle grounds in present-day Fukushima Prefecture.

Unlike other traditional sports, tōshiya emphasized quantification, one of the main characteristics of modern sports. This emphasis appeared in Japan during the seventeenth century, at precisely the same time that European sports began to manifest a similar mania. If this impulse to quantify athletic achievement was widely present in Japan two centuries before the British and Americans introduced modern sports to the Japanese, then the quick acceptance of these sports is somewhat easier to understand.

Some Japanese historians are ready to take an additional step. Like Arnd Krüger and Itō Akira, who argued from the evidence of chikaraishi that Edo-period sports exhibited typically modern characteristics, Sasajima Kōsuke maintains that the tablets placed at the temple to commemorate the achievements of Hoshino Kanzaemon and Wasa Daihachirō are proof that the seventeenth-century Japanese understood the concept of the quantified record, which is another of the distinguishing characteristics of modern sports.[50] Indeed, according to Sasajima, ōyakazu "went out of vogue" because "people found it difficult to break the record."[51]

While it is intriguing to think of tōshiya as an example of what might be called incipient or anticipatory modernity, one should also take note of what distinguishes tōshiya from modern sports. The most obvious difference falls under the category of rationalization. When archers in other parts of the country wanted to take part in a similar contest, they did not simply construct a "tōshiya gallery," a specialized structure of standard length, height, and width—they built a copy of the entire structure (minus its one thousand and one gilded statues).

## SWORDSMANSHIP

The bow may have been a more effective weapon than the sword, but from the Tokugawa period it was the latter that conquered the heart of the Japanese warrior. Nitobe Inazō wrote in 1905 that the sword was "the soul of the samurai" and subsequent historians of the martial arts have agreed.[52] When the bow and the sword had both become militarily obsolete, it was the latter that survived as an aesthetic object and as one of the most potent symbols of Japanese culture.

Arrowheads of obsidian prove that archery began in paleolithic or, at the latest, neolithic times. Swords came later. Awkward stone swords were made as early as the Jōmon period (ca. 10,000 B.C.–ca. 300 B.C.), but it was not until the Yayoi period (ca. 300 B.C.–A.D. 300) that bronze swords came into use. They were quickly rendered obsolete by iron swords introduced from Korea.[53]

In Japanese mythology, the gods wielded swords rather than the bolts of lightning, spears, and arrows favored by Greek, Roman, and Nordic deities. According to the mythology of the imperial house, when the sun goddess Amaterasu sent her grandson Ninigi no Mikoto to rule the Japanese archipelago, she presented him with a mirror, a jewel, and a sacred sword. The sword, later known as *kusanagi no tsurugi* (the grass-mowing sword), had been found by Amaterasu's brother in the tail of a dragon he had slain. These "three treasures" later became symbols of imperial authority, and their transfer became a part of the emperor's enthronement ritual.[54]

While the bow was probably used by hunters before it was adopted as a weapon, the sword's original use was presumably in warfare. In time, of course, soldiers turned "work" into "play" and engaged in mock combats similar to those of medieval European tournaments. This was especially true during the Kamakura period, which followed the decades of deadly warfare between the Taira and Minamoto clans. With the final victory of the latter in the Battle of Dannoura in 1185, swordsmanship became less immediately necessary for survival, but it was cultivated all the more as a sign of status. The shogunate that ruled from the town of Kamakura (south of modern Tokyo) prized rough martial prowess above the refined aestheticism that had characterized the court of Heian-kyō, but the aesthetic instinct was not to be wholly denied. Weaponry became art. As early as the Heian period, the double-edged sword (*ken*) was replaced by the single-edged curved sword (*tō*) that was a thing of beauty as well as a lethal weapon. From the Kamakura period the names of more than eleven hundred swordsmiths have come down to us (as compared to the 450 names from the Heian period).[55] The swords they produced were far superior, as weapons and as works of art, to anything produced by their European contemporaries.[56]

Since these deadly weapons were unsuitable for the sport of fencing, bamboo swords were devised. These implements can be traced back to the sixteenth century. "Kendō tradition holds that Kamiizumi [Hidetsuna] . . . first fashioned the fukuro shinai, the bamboo sword contained within a silk swordcase."[57] The first documented use of the device was in 1563.[58] Hidetsuna explained that he used the bamboo sword so that he could practice without holding back and without injuring his opponent.[59] The famed swordsman Miyamoto Musashi (1584–1645) ridiculed the bamboo sword as fit only for cowards, but, by the middle of the Tokugawa era, its use was widespread.

While some scholars count over seven hundred schools of swordsmanship, most of them are derived from three major styles.[60] There is considerable uncertainty about the history of these schools, and much scholarly disagreement, but it seems that the oldest of these was founded by Iizasa Chōisai in the middle of the fifteenth century.[61]

Born in the village from which he took his name, Iizasa lived for a period at the Katori shrine in what is now Chiba Prefecture. He moved to Kyoto in the service of the shogun Ashikaga Yoshimasa (1436–1490), who was a devotee of the martial arts. After one of Iizasa's students offended the god of the Katori shrine, Iizasa dedicated himself to a thousand days of austerity and purification, during which the deity of the shrine appeared to him in a dream and transmitted to him the secret techniques of swordsmanship. Iizasa's style, which he called the *Tenshinshō-den Katori shintō-ryū* (Heavenly True, Correctly Transmitted Style of the Katori shrine), is commonly known as *Shintō-ryū*.[62]

The claim of divine revelation to the founder of a school was typical.[63] It is, in fact, still assumed by many of the more fervent members of each school that *their* school was created "by the grace of divine guidance" and that they are protected by a divine power that works through the medium of an oracle at a Shinto shrine.[64]

The greatest master of the Shintō-ryū school, Tsukahara Bokuden, was born in Kashima in 1489 or 1490. He was adopted by Tsukahara Yasumoto, lord of the local castle, who taught him Iizasa's techniques. For Tsukahara Bokuden, the sword was clearly a weapon as well as an item of "sporting equipment." He was famed for having fought in nineteen duels and thirty-seven battles in which he killed 212 people. Despite the bloodshed, he was renowned for "the ability to detect danger and avoid it." A hundred students were said to have followed him about in order to learn the secrets of his skill. He died in 1571.[65] A related school, the *Kashima-shinryū,* was established by the legendary Matsumoto Masanobu. The school, several branches of which still survive, took its name from the god's shrine at Kashima in what is now Ibaraki Prefecture. It was said that the god Takemikazuchi-no-Mikoto, patron of swordplay and tutelary deity of the Fujiwara clan, came to Masanobu in a dream and inspired him to found a school.[66]

The sixteenth-century innovator, Kamiizumi Hidetsuna—one of the greatest swordsmen of the late Muromachi period—is credited not only with introducing the bamboo sword but also with establishing the

*Shinkage-ryū* (New Shadow school). Hidetsuna's style was based on the one already developed by Aisu Ikō, who was said to have learned *his* style from a simian deity who appeared at the Udo shrine in Kyushu. Since Aisu called his style the *Kage-ryū* (Shadow school), Hidetsuna merely added the word *shin* (new) when he founded *Shinkage-ryū.* The Shinkage school produced many skilled swordsmen.[67]

Another important school—*Ittō-ryū* (One Sword school)—was founded late in the sixteenth century by Itō Ittōsai. Itō was famed for having been victorious in thirty-three duels. The "one sword" in the name of the school does not refer to the number of swords employed; although most schools taught the use of just one sword, Itō instructed his disciples in the use of two swords, one in each hand.

> The term and the school's concept of one sword were derived from analogy to the Daoist idea that all things spring from the One and return to the One. Thus One Sword changes into all swords, and all swords return to the One Sword. Ittō-ryū was one of the first ryū to add a philosophical dimension to the developing martial art of swordsmanship.[68]

In the first half of the seventeenth century there were still battles to be fought as the Tokugawa government overcame the last resistance to its dominance. Swordsmanship continued to have some practical value. Warriors were expected to be capable in the "six arts" (bow, horse, spear, sword, gun, and unarmed combat); they were expected to be proficient in several of them. Specialization by weapon had not yet taken place. Iizasa Chōisai's Shintō-ryū, for example, was a comprehensive system that included instruction in military tactics and in the use of the sword, spear, halberd, and cudgel. One of the last truly versatile martial artists was Marume Nagayoshi Kurando (1540–1629), who was allegedly master of twenty-one different weapons. "Versatility decreased with peace and the martial arts specialization that evolved in Tokugawa times."[69]

The most famous swordsman of the century, perhaps the most famous of all time, was Miyamoto Musashi, mentioned earlier for his scorn of bamboo swords. Thanks to the kabuki stage, to Yoshikawa Eiji's novel *Musashi,* (1935–1939), and to the modern mass media, Musashi is "the king of Japanese popular culture."[70] He fought in the Battle of Sekigahara (1600), in the sieges of Osaka Castle that solidified Tokugawa Ieyasu's rule, and in the Shimabara Rebellion (1637). His most famous duel, which may have been apocryphal, occurred in 1611, when he allegedly met and defeated Sasaki Kojirō on the island of Ganryō-jima. Musashi's book, *Gorin no sho* (*Book of Five Rings*), which he completed just a few weeks before his death, remains a classic.[71]

Musashi was utilitarian rather than philosophical. "To master the virtue of the long sword," he wrote, "is to govern the world and oneself." He did, however, allow himself this enigmatic epigram: "By knowing things that exist, you can know that which does not exist. That is the void."[72] His disciples founded several schools of swordsmanship.

Another important figure in the history of swordsmanship is Yagyū Munenori (1571–1647), head of the shogun's office of swordsmanship. (He served three Tokugawa shoguns: Ieyasu, Hidetada, and Iemitsu.) Working with his father's catalogue of military techniques, written in 1601, Munenori systematized the practice and explored the religious and philosophical aspects of swordsmanship in a 1632 volume entitled *Heihō kadensho* (Transmissions of the House Regarding Military Techniques). This classic work was widely regarded "as a bible by practitioners of martial arts during the Tokugawa period."[73] The first part of the book—a strictly utilitarian catalogue of military techniques—is followed by sections entitled *Setsunintō* (The Killing Sword) and *Katsuninken* (The Life-Giving Sword). These sections were written under the influence of the Zen Buddhist monk Takuan (1573–1645), whose book, *Fudōchi shinmyō roku* (Divine Record of Immovable Wisdom), was written for and addressed to Munenori. Takuan quotes the Chinese sages Mencius and Shao K'ang Chieh on the need to release the mind. The mind must not tarry. "If you put an empty gourd on the water and touch it, it will slip to one side. No matter how you try, it won't stay in one spot. The mind of someone who has reached the ultimate state does not stay with anything, even for a second. It is like an empty gourd on the water that is pushed around."[74] Munenori expands upon Takuan's wisdom. Among his many adages is this: "When nothing remains in your mind, everything becomes easy to do."[75]

The *Heihō kadensho* is a work "whose logical structure and sophisticated discussion of technique and mental preparedness go far beyond earlier swordsmanship texts, riddled as they are with obscure magical elements."[76] Munenori's book surpasses the other classics of seventeenth-century swordsmanship, Takuan's *Fudōchi shinmyo roku* and Musashi's *Gorin no sho*, because Munenori combined in one person both practical experience and philosophical sophistication.

During the warfare of the sixteenth century, there were only a few schools of swordsmanship and instruction was for the most part oral. As the years of peace continued in the seventeenth century, as there was less and less opportunity to demonstrate skill on the battlefield, the number of instructors paradoxically increased. And all of them, it seems, wanted to form their own school. They developed new techniques and certified their students' proficiency in them. "It was during the Tokugawa period (1600–1867) that battlefield techniques became true martial arts and, in the case of some popular schools of swordsmanship, were transformed into combat sports as well."[77]

As the peace continued, the role of the samurai class underwent a gradual transformation from warrior to bureaucrat. The leaders of the Tokugawa government began to stress a Confucian education for the samurai. As an important component in the education of a "complete" samurai, the martial arts were taught in the domain schools. Since these schools required a steady supply of instructors, various professional schools (*ryū-ha*) were created to grant certificates of proficiency to trainees and instructors. Training in the martial arts also developed as a hobby: for recreation, for health, and as a sport.[78]

The evolution of the martial arts was, inevitably, accompanied by a transformation of the language used to denote them. Until the early seventeenth century, swordsmanship was just one category of a comprehensive fighting system known as *heihō* (military methods). Specialization in the sense of concentration on a single weapon to the neglect of others brought a shift in terminology. Midway through the Tokugawa period, schools that concentrated on swordsmanship began to call their activity by various names—*kenjutsu, kenpō,* or *kengei,* terms roughly equivalent to "techniques of the sword" or "the art of the sword." With the passage of time, however, heihō, used in a narrower sense to denote swordsmanship, became the most common term. Today's word for Japanese swordsmanship, *kendō* (the way of the sword), is a modern coinage. The same is true for the modern term for Japanese archery, *kyūdō* (the way of the bow). In fact, the general term *budō* (the martial arts) was rarely used before the Meiji era (1868–1912).

As literacy spread among the samurai, many of them felt the desire to transmit their experience and their wisdom in written form. In their writings they gave a theoretical basis for their practice that naturally enough reflected their educational background. Like their contemporaries who codified archery, they were proponents of Confucian, Buddhist, Daoist, nativist, and other perspectives. The appearance of texts "discussing not only military techniques but also the requisite mental training and philosophical principles underlying those techniques . . . contributed to the development of the martial arts as a means for 'self-perfection.'"[79]

Some swordsmen saw the sword as a means of pursuing the study of Zen Buddhism; hence the adage *kenzen ichinyo,* "the sword and Zen are one." This association of Zen with the martial arts has received particular attention in the West, where Zen-based kendō has been championed by Minoru Kiyota and other seekers after *mushin* (the "nonmind"), but an exclusive concern for the influence of Zen can, as G. Cameron Hurst has shown, produce a distorted view of the martial arts.[80] Examining kendō and the other martial arts solely through the lens of Zen Buddhism is like explaining modern European and American sports entirely on the basis of the nineteenth-century vogue of "muscular Christianity."[81]

There were economic as well as religious and philosophical reasons for the publication of texts and treatises. These publications, called *densho,* were provided to qualified pupils for a fee. Schools also received income for certifying various grades of accomplishment and for issuing licenses (which the domains began to require for certain positions and prerogatives). In order to obtain as many students as possible and to gain the patronage of powerful families, it became common practice to award ranks and certificates "for considerations of money or personal obligation."[82] The skill of the buyer was not always the most important consideration.

In a peaceful era, professional teachers of swordsmanship faced a difficult problem. How were they to train their students and judge their ability without subjecting them to dangerous combat? Adoption of the bamboo sword was clearly a step in the direction of "safe sport," but even bamboo swords were liable to cause severe injury when wielded by a skilled and determined fencer. Two different approaches developed to solve this problem: the use of *kata* (patterns or forms of movement that the student practices in preparation for real combat) and the development of protective gear and conventions that allowed the simulation of combat without the risk of injury. The latter, especially, were the preconditions for the development of fencing as a sport.

Late in the seventeenth century a number of schools of swordsmanship began to emphasize kata. Typically, the founder of a school developed a series of repetitive exercises simulating the movements of a warrior engaged in actual combat. The "fastest and most accurate method of mastering swordsmanship techniques was deemed to be the constant repetition of these kata under the supervision of an unchallenged teacher."[83] Kata were arranged by skill level and it was essential for beginners to master the elementary kata before they were allowed by their teacher to advance to the next level. It was not unusual for a student to practice for years before he was certified as proficient in the highest level of kata. This system was an important aspect of the professionalization and what might be called the "sportification" of swordsmanship.

The repetition of basic moves is part of the acquisition of any physical skill, even today, but, in the absence of actual combat, the polished performance of kata was often transformed into an end in itself. Constant repetition led all too frequently to "an extreme formalism that emphasized the outward elegance of the kata."[84] This tendency was probably exacerbated by the fact that there was little contact among the schools, each of which was free to disparage its rivals and claim superiority for its own untested techniques.[85] In fact, the shogunate banned challenges between experts proficient in different styles, and the individual domains followed suit. Then the schools themselves issued similar prohibitions. The lack of opportunity to test one's abilities against other swordsmen inhibited innovation and encouraged sterile formalism and idle boasts.

The emphasis on formalism led to the theatrical display of complicated kata. Early in the eighteenth century, Matsushita Kunitaka complained about effeminate samurai who plucked their eyebrows and powdered their faces. He "noted wryly that the hand techniques of a swordsman looked like those of a Noh dancer who had simply exchanged a sword for his fan, and their foot movements resembled those of court nobles and priests kicking a *kemari* ball."[86]

The second solution to the fencing master's problem—how to train and compete without incurring injury—is well illustrated by *shinai uchikomi keikō*. In this style of swordsmanship, which was developed in the eighteenth century, the use of bamboo swords and protective gear allowed a realistic but nonetheless safe simulation of combat. While "the practice of kata kenjutsu—rote, formal swordplay—never died out, it was superseded by *shinai uchikomi keikō*, the forerunner of modern kendō."[87]

The practitioners of shinai uchikomi keikō developed a variety of protective gear to make their sport safer: *kote* (gloves for the hands and lower arm); the *men* (a cotton helmet with a metal protector for the face); the *dō* (a chest protector); and the *tare* (armor for the waist and groin). This equipment was not devised all at once, but gradually over time. Members of the *Jikishin kage* school were probably the most avid developers of protective gear, and one of its instructors, Naganuma Shirozaemon Kunisato, is credited with important contributions. By the beginning of the eighteenth century, the mask, gloves, and trunk padding had achieved something like their present form, and the Jikishin kage school had begun to use them for simulated combat. "Protective gear represented a dramatic step forward in the transformation of military techniques into the sport forms that we know today."[88]

Like most innovations, this new form of practice with bamboo swords and protective equipment was controversial. When Nakanishi Tadazō introduced the equipment in his school, his best pupil left in disgust.[89] The predictable objection from traditionalists was that the innovations distanced the sport too far from the conditions of actual combat. They refused even to admit that shinai uchikomi keikō was more realistic than the practice of formalized kata then in vogue.

Since higher-ranked samurai tended to be attracted to what were considered more refined cultural pursuits, like calligraphy or the composition of haiku, the most prominent swordsmen came from the lower ranks of the samurai class. In the domain academies, competition was often stifled by hypersensitivity about rank and status (how awkward to be defeated by a man of lower social rank!), but serious competition flourished at urban training centers. Although the right to bear swords was technically limited to the samurai, commoners too flocked to the urban training centers, especially after simulated combat with bamboo swords became popular. In the nineteenth century, a number of townsmen became accomplished fencers.[90]

Unlike most traditional sports, which tend to exclude people on the basis of their race, ethnicity, gender, or social class, modern sports are— at least ideally—egalitarian. Achievement matters more than ascribed status and there are no artificial barriers to equal access to competition. As training to kill underwent what Norbert Elias called "the civilizing process," swordmanship became a sport accessible to men (and eventually to women) who were not members of the samurai class. Shinai uchikomi keikō was hardly an example of pure egalitarianism, but it was at least an approach. "Late Tokugawa fencing . . . became an activity in which samurai and commoner were brought together, helping to further blur the class distinctions between lower-ranking samurai and upper peasants or merchants."[91] It was a small but important step on the path to modernity.

# Part II

## Modern Times

# 3

# The Arrival and Diffusion of Western Sports

### CLOSURE

Franciscan and Jesuit missionaries from Portugal and Spain arrived in Japan in the sixteenth century, decades before Tokugawa Ieyasu (1543–1606) defeated his rivals and consolidated his control over a more or less unified nation. These European missionaries actively propagated their religion among the "heathen," many of whom were eager to embrace Roman Catholicism. The missionaries proved to be too successful for their own good. The large number of converts to Christianity, especially in the area around Nagasaki, led to a viciously xenophobic reaction. The shogunate banned Christianity in 1614, murdered thousands of Japanese who refused to renounce their new religion, ordered the expulsion of the European priests, executed those who defied the order to leave, and sought to seal the country off from foreign influence.

The closure was never total. Some intercourse was permitted through a small Dutch settlement on the island of Dejima in Nagasaki harbor. (Protestants were thought to be less dangerous than Catholics.) The *Tokugawa jikki* records that the eighth shogun, Tokugawa Yoshimune (1684–1751), watched what may have been the first Western sport introduced to Japan: an exhibition of fencing by the Dutch.[1] Of course, European and American sports had not yet developed into the forms familiar to us today.

The rare Japanese whom the ever-suspicious government permitted to visit this small replica of a Dutch town was able to observe the long-nosed barbarians at their amusements, which included a precursor of badminton. The game was described in 1787 by Morishima Chūryō in his *Kōmōzetsuwa* (Tales of the Red Hairs), a book provided with illustrations of the racket and the shuttlecock.[2] A woodblock print of the Tokugawa period shows the Dutch at a game of billiards. Such interest was unusual. While a number of eighteenth-century Japanese were eager students of Western medical science and military technology, which they studied in Dutch texts, few of them left evidence of curiosity about Western sports.[3]

## OPENING

On July 8, 1853, Commodore Matthew Perry arrived at the port of Uraga with a letter to the Tokugawa shogun from President Franklin Pierce in which the Japanese were informed that the United States expected the Japanese to open their islands to trade and to provide humane treatment for shipwrecked American seamen. Perry returned the following February, with a larger naval force, and a treaty was signed on March 31, 1854.[4] Eight months later, Sir John Stirling successfully negotiated a similar treaty between Japan and the United Kingdom.

Mercantile motives brought Perry to Japanese shores, but sports played a small part in his initial interactions with his reluctant hosts. In addition to a minstrel show, Perry's sailors put on a display of manly fisticuffs. The Japanese responded with an exhibition by a score of beefy sumō wrestlers. Neither party seemed properly impressed by the other. The Americans were disgusted by the massive wrestlers, "over-fed monsters" who glared "with brutal ferocity at each other, ready to exhibit the cruel instincts of a savage nature."[5] The Japanese, on the other hand, produced a woodblock print that shows "bulky sumo wrestlers delivering the shogun's gift of bales of rice to the scrawny American sailors."[6] During Stirling's negotiations, the British were allowed to land and indulge in "athletic sports."[7]

Townsend Harris, the first American consul, arrived in August 1856 and was met with "consternation."[8] Additional treaties with France and other European powers brought more diplomats, more merchants, and more dismay. For a dozen years, the shogunate was riven by internal disagreement and undecided about what to do with these foreigners who seemed to arrive in increasingly large numbers with increasingly inconvenient demands. Inconclusive debates within the government led to ambiguous policies and general confusion. The resolution came in 1868 in the form of the "Meiji Restoration."

The term "restoration" suggests that the revolution of 1868 that ended centuries of Tokugawa rule returned Japan to imperial rule, but the emperor enthroned in Tokyo was more or less the same figurehead he had been in Kyoto. In fact, real power was in the hands of clan activists for whom "restoration" was actually part of a bold venture in what might be termed instrumental modernization. The new rulers were plagued by power struggles among the leading clans, but there was a consensus about foreign policy. Japan should acquire from the West the modern science and technology necessary to defend the islands against the very real threat of foreign domination. (China's helplessness in the face of European military might was an ominous indication of the danger to Japan.) In addition to the Western experts who were invited to Japan, over eleven thousand Japanese went abroad for study between 1868 and 1902. Among them was Itō Hirobumi, the nation's first prime minister.[9]

The modernizers' emulation of the West's scientific and technological achievements was often constrained by the desire to preserve what began to be identified as Japanese culture. The five-volume published report of the Iwakura Tomomi mission's two-year sojourn in Europe and the United States advocated modernization ("Human knowledge rushes toward enlightenment"), but the authors cautioned against the hasty abandonment of "old institutions and practices."[10] There were, however, some intellectuals whose admiration of the West (and denigration of their own culture) was uncritical and extreme. Mori Arinori suggested in 1872 that the country adopt English as the national language and Takahashi Yoshio, writing in 1884, urged that Japanese husbands divorce their wives and marry Western women of robust physique and superior intellect.[11]

Inevitably, uncritical enthusiasm for Europe and the United States aroused nationalistic opposition. Motoda Nagazane (Eifu), for instance, condemned what he saw as the effort "to convert Japanese into facsimiles of Europeans and Americans."[12] Criticism of the modernizers often took the form of verbal or pictorial satire. The nineteenth-century novelist Kanagaki Robun ridiculed his countrymen for aping the "barbarians" by wearing top hats, carrying umbrellas, eating beef, and ostentatiously consulting their pocket watches.[13] Cartoons in conservative journals lampooned sandal-shod students with thick-lensed spectacles and arm-loads of foreign books. Hostility was also expressed through the murder of foreigners resident in Japan. Townsend Harris's secretary, Hendrik Heusken, was killed in January 1861 and British diplomats were attacked that July. A number of foreign nationals were ambushed and hacked to death by samurai wielding their razor-sharp swords.[14] Xenophobia also accounted for the 1889 assassination of Minister of Education Mori Arinori, who was accused of having betrayed Japan's traditional culture.[15]

The "Imperial Rescript on Education" of 1890, promulgated after two decades of modernization, was a more positive assertion of Japanese culture. Calling upon all Japanese to venerate the emperor, the rescript was a powerful statement of "invented tradition."[16] Its goal was to transform the deified emperor into the focal point of patriotic sentiment.[17] To "revere the emperor" was not, however, necessarily to "expel the barbarians." The men behind the "Imperial Rescript"—men like Motoda Nagazane (Eifu) and Nishimura Shigeki—wanted to slow but not to reverse the drive to bring Japan into the modern world.[18] S. N. Eisenstadt's shrewd comment about the recent past applies as well to the crosscurrents of change in the Meiji period: "Tradition or traditionalism . . . tended to become a crucial . . . symbol of legitimation for new patterns of behavior, organization, cultural creativity, and discourse."[19]

Steamships, telegraph lines, and modern weaponry were very much on the modernizers' minds, not cricket bats and rowing shells. On their extended missions to Europe and America, Japanese officials investigated mines and factories, not baseball diamonds and tennis courts. Children's songs, which were certainly composed for and not by children, listed lightning rods and gas lamps, not sports equipment, among "worthy objects."[20] The enthusiasm for modern sports, like the vogue among the Meiji elite of Western dress and cuisine, was an unintended consequence of the desire for locomotives and coastal artillery. To put it in the language of the businessmen who arrived in Japan along with the foreign diplomats, advisors, and teachers, the modernizers got more than they bargained for.

In the course of the Meiji period (1868–1912), a gamut of modern sports popular in the West were introduced to Japan.[21] Government attempts to modernize the military led to the introduction of gymnastics, fencing, rifle-shooting, riding, and skiing. European and American residents in the trading communities of Yokohama or Kobe introduced football, rowing, athletics, tennis, baseball, cricket, and golf. The Meiji government invited many scholars from Europe and America to teach in the newly established school system, and they introduced their students to baseball, soccer, rugby, rowing, athletics, tennis, and ice skating.[22]

Foreign missionaries, especially those associated with the YMCA, propagated basketball, volleyball, field hockey, and badminton. Students and other Japanese who had lived abroad brought back with them table tennis, handball, basketball, and volleyball. Voluntary sports clubs took up activities such as yachting and climbing.[23] After 1912, participation in the Olympics and other international sports events introduced Western-style wrestling, weightlifting, and canoeing.

Although some scholars have seen the global diffusion of these sports as proof of "cultural imperialism,"[24] coercion played a very small part in their adoption by the Japanese. On the contrary, the modernizing elite seemed as eager to emulate Westerners at play as they were to learn from Westerners at work.[25] It should be emphasized, however, that enthusiasm for British and American sports was for the most part limited to just this modernizing elite. This was especially true in the early years of the Meiji period. Farmers, who were still the vast majority of the population, remained for the most part content with the physical contests traditionally associated with their seasonal festivals.

In most non-Western societies en route to modernity, the military have played an important role, and Japan was certainly no exception. The Meiji leaders imported the weaponry of modern warfare and passed legislation to reconstitute the nation's ineffective military. A conscript army replaced the samurai who had been Japan's traditional warriors.[26] (The samurai, deprived of their principal function, also lost their right to wear the swords that had distinguished them from lesser mortals.) Between 1867 and 1880, French officers supervised the new army's training. Reorganization included the adoption of Western notions of physical fitness and the proper way to attain it. At the newly established Toyama Military School (1874), the French instructed their Japanese counterparts in the gymnastic principles that they had learned from Francisco Amoros at their military academy in Joinville. They also taught the Japanese officers how to ride and to fence in the European manner.[27] In the dissemination of modern sports, however, French officers were soon supplanted by British businessmen and diplomatic officials and by American educators and advisors to the Japanese government.

Despite the fact that Japanese terrain was seldom suitable for cricket, a sport that requires an extensive and well-tended field of play, the British bowlers and batsmen refused to deny themselves the pastoral pleasures of their favorite game. On October 16, 1869, eleven Britons resident in the port city of Kobe met a team from H.M.S. *Ocean*. A cricket club was promptly organized three days later, thanks largely to the initiative of Arthur Hesketh Groom (who was also an active mountain-climber).[28] Shortly thereafter, the Yokohama Cricket and Athletic Club was founded by the British in that harbor town (where occasional matches between the garrison and visiting naval personnel had taken place as early as 1864).[29] Although a few Japanese tried their hand at cricket, the sport never became popular. "Today cricket is almost the only major foreign sport that does not interest Japanese at all."[30] Readers consulting the *Kodansha Encyclopedia of Japan* will find an entry under "cricket"; it provides information on insects of the order Orthoptera.

As early as 1862, the British organized horse races in Yokohama, gala spectacles attended by the entire foreign community. In 1868, the British residents of Kobe followed suit and celebrated Christmas Day with a horse race. It was not an unqualified success. The Japanese mounts bolted when the race went by their stables. Three of the jockeys were thrown.[31] This mishap was not enough to extinguish the ardor of the Victorian toff. The Kobe Jockey Club was organized in 1870. Within a few years, the turf became a popular theme for woodblock artists. Prints from the 1880s show the emperor and his entourage in the grandstand at Ueno.[32]

Both forms of another British passion, football, were played at Japan's private universities during the Meiji period. Soccer was brought to the School of Engineering around 1873 by "an Englishman named Jones."[33] That same year, the game was introduced to Japanese naval personnel by Major Archfield Douglas.[34] Soccer failed to gain much of a foothold. According to Kinoshita Hideaki, it was not until 1907 that two Japanese teams met on the soccer pitch.[35] The sport was not organized nationally until 1921 and the national federation was not admitted into FIFA, the international soccer federation, until 1929. Rugby, then the more popular of the two football "codes," was played at private universities like Keiō and Waseda. In 1890, only a year after Cambridge graduate E. B. Clarke introduced the game to Keiō, the students played against the British members of the Yokohama Athletic Club.[36] In the Kansai area, which includes Kobe, Osaka, and Kyoto, Dōshisha University emerged as a hotbed of rugby enthusiasm. In 1927, these private schools joined with the nation's most prestigious public universities (Tokyo and Kyoto) to form a national federation for rugby.[37] In Japan as in Great Britain, rugby was perceived as a quintessentially masculine sport.[38] Some sanguine British observers believed that "the day is not far distant when [rugby] will eclipse baseball in popular esteem,"[39] but that has not yet happened— despite the excitement that accompanied Kobe Steel's unprecedented string of seven consecutive national titles from 1989 to 1995.[40]

Athletic (track-and-field) events were introduced as part of the *undōkai* (sports days) at various schools. The earliest of these may have been the "Student Competitive Games" held in 1874 at the Naval Academy in the Tsukiji section of Tokyo. The initiative apparently came from the thirty-four British naval officers who had assumed posts at the academy the previous year.[41] Prizes were awarded to the top placers.

Four years later, an American educator, William S. Clark, introduced track-and-field to the students of Sapporo Agricultural College. Educated Japanese learned to quote Dr. Clark, in English, "Boys, be ambitious," but interest in "athletics" remained minimal until the initiatives taken in 1883 by Frederick W. Strange, an Englishman who arrived in Japan in 1875 to teach at what became Ichikō, the nation's most prestigious preparatory academy.[42]

Imbued with the Victorian conviction that sports are the proper antidote for an excess of intellectual endeavor, Strange summoned the students "to come out and play games." He staged a historic track-and-field meet on June 16, 1883. The participants were the students at Ichikō and at the college that eventually became Tokyo University. A 300-yard bamboo-fenced track was laid out on the college grounds. All the customary running, jumping, vaulting, and throwing events were included, along with running a three-legged race and hurling a cricket ball. For the shot-put and the hammer-throw, Strange made do with whatever equipment was available. "Instead of a pistol shot, the start was signaled by swinging down a folded Western-style umbrella."[43] There was also "a story that he brought out the school benches for use as hurdles."[44] Thanks to the prestige of Tokyo University, this particular undōkai greatly influenced the development of athletics on other campuses (where students were also keenly interested in foreign sports).[45]

To spread the gospel of manly sports, Strange wrote a short book entitled *Outdoor Games* (1883), which Shimomura Yasuhiro translated in 1885. In 1900 Shiki Shuji published *Rikujō kyōgi* (Track-and-Field Contests), the first book on the subject written by a Japanese. The term *rikujō kyōgi* is still employed for track-and-field events.[46]

At the turn of the century, distance races became popular. When Yamaguchi Higher School staged an 11-mile race in 1899, other schools were spurred to hold their own distance races, each one longer than the one before. In November 1901 the newspaper *Jiji shimpō* sponsored a 12-hour race around the perimeter (1,478 meters) of Tokyo's Lake Shinobazu. A 25-year old rickshaw-puller, Andō Shotarō, won the event, circling the lake 71 times. In March 1909, a newspaper, the *Osaka mainichi*

*Shimbun,* sponsored what was publicized as the "Kobe to Osaka Marathon Race." (The distance was actually 19.56 miles.) A military reservist from Okayama Prefecture, Kenko Chōnosuke, won in 2 hours, 10 minutes, and 54 seconds.[47]

In the fall of 1902, Tokyo University's Law Department sponsored an undōkai at which one of the students, Fujii Minoru, was clocked in the 100 meters at 10.24 seconds, an astonishing time. The president of the university, Hamao Arita, proudly announced the time as a world record and it was listed as such by *Spalding's Athletic Almanac.*[48]

According to Fujii Minoru's memoirs, reproduced in the 1997 bulletin of the Tokyo University Track and Field Club, his time was measured by an electric device developed by Tanakadate Aikitsu, a professor of physics who was also apparently the head judge at the meet. The start and finish of the race activated an electric current in a machine that wound a tape at a speed of 3 centimeters per second. The current was cut when Fujita crossed the finish line, and the length of the tape was then measured to determine the elapsed time to 1/100 of a second.[49] Noting that Fujii never again approached his sensational time of 10.24, sports historians have been skeptical about the alleged world record. In 1906 Fujii was said to have pole-vaulted 3.9 meters, which was 12 centimeters better than the world record, but this remarkable achievement was not recognized outside Japan.[50]

Japanese men have never done very well in track-and-field competition with European and American sprinters. In 1912, for instance, when the world record for 100 meters was 10.6 seconds, Mishima Yahiko held the Japanese title with the unimpressive time of 12.0 seconds. (By 1912, the Japanese no longer credited Fujii Minoru with the time of 10.24.) Itō Kōji, the first Japanese sprinter to run 100 meters in less than 10 seconds, achieved this breakthrough in 1999, thirty years after James Hines ran the distance in 9.99 seconds.[51] The 200-meter record set in 1911 by Akashi Kazue was a very slow 25.8 seconds.[52] Japanese runners were destined to do much better in long-distance races than in the sprints. In fact, long-distance relay races have become a Japanese specialty.[53] In 1917, Tokyo's *Yomiuri shimbun* celebrated the fiftieth anniversary of the 1867 transfer of the capital from Kyoto to Tokyo by sponsoring a 508-kilometer relay race from Kyoto's Sanjō Bridge to Tokyo's Ueno Park. Still another newspaper, the *Hōchi shimbun,* invited students from Keiō, Waseda, and other universities to participate in an *ekiden* (long-distance relay race) from Tokyo to the resort town of Hakone and back, a distance of over 200 kilometers. Ten thousand spectators watched the first race on February 11, 1920.[54]

Although very few girls or women were encouraged to participate in athletics, the most successful Japanese track-and-field athlete of the early Shōwa period (1925–1930) was Hitomi Kinue. After her graduation from what is now Tokyo Women's College of Physical Education, she was hired in April 1926 as a journalist by the *Mainichi shimbun*. A month later, at the national track-and-field championships, she competed so impressively in the 100-meter dash, the long jump, the shot-put, and the baseball throw that she was chosen to be Japan's lone representative at the second quadrennial International Women's Games which the Fédération Sportive Féminine Internationale had scheduled for Gothenburg, Sweden. Traveling by the Trans-Siberian Railroad, the nineteen-year-old journeyed alone to Moscow and was then escorted to Sweden by a Moscow-based *Mainichi* reporter. Competing in six events, she won the standing and the running long jump, was second in the discus, and was third in the 100-yard dash. Her 5.5 meters in the running long jump set a world's record. She was officially honored as the outstanding athlete of the games. Four years later, when the International Women's Games were held in Prague, she competed in several events and won the long jump with a leap of 5.9 meters—despite the fact that she was suffering from a sore throat and a fever. After the games, the Japanese team went on to dual meets in Warsaw, Berlin, Paris, and Brussels. Although Hitomi was exhausted and required almost daily injections, she competed in all these meets. Returning by ship from Marseilles to Kobe, she arrived in such wretched health that her horrified father begged her to rest. She was determined, however, to fulfill all her obligations to her employer and to the national sports federation. She fulfilled her obligations, but she never recovered her health. By the spring of 1931, she had begun to cough blood. She died of respiratory failure on August 2, 1931.[55]

Fishermen and others who rowed and sailed on Japan's lakes, rivers, and coastal waters must have had informal boat races, but Western-style aquatic sports seem to have begun on September 26, 1861, when an outlandish regatta was held in Nagasaki. The participating vessels included four-oared gigs, Japanese sampans, and houseboats.[56] Rowing in the European and American style was inaugurated when foreigners residing in Yokohama imported a boat in 1866.[57] The British in Kobe founded a Regatta and Athletic Club on September 23, 1870, and constructed a boathouse and a gymnasium.[58] In 1883, the Navy held rowing races that were attended by the emperor.

A major step was taken at Tokyo University in 1884 when Frederick W. Strange, who had played such a central role in introducing track-

and-field to young Japanese, founded a boat club modeled on those at Oxford and Cambridge. The club members constructed three boats and managed to borrow a technologically advanced four-seat racing shell equipped with sliding seats. In 1885, the club's team raced against the foreigners of the Yokohama Athletic Club. In 1887, the club organized intercollegiate races on the Sumida River, which flows through Tokyo. Providing Japanese students with an equivalent to the Henley Regatta was among the last of Strange's many contributions to Japanese sports; he died of a heart attack in 1889.[59]

Rowing fever spread quickly to the Kansai area as well. In 1895, the governor of Shiga Prefecture sponsored the All-Japan Joint Rowing Meet on Lake Biwa, the biggest lake in Japan. The meet was well attended by middle-school and company crews. Although many universities and colleges in both the Kantō and the Kansai regions had crews, no regional organizations were formed before 1906.[60]

Competition was held in the water as well as on it. Since swimming was considered a useful skill for a warrior, it was taught by various schools at the end of the Tokugawa period. Native swimming styles survived into the Meiji period. Unlike practitioners of the martial arts, swimmers were not immediately challenged by imported styles that threatened to render native ones obsolete.

In addition to its military function, swimming had a recreational aspect that came into its own in the Meiji period. From 1871 until their prohibition in 1917, various schools taught traditional swimming techniques at training facilities on the Sumida River. In 1898, Tokyo University established a swimming facility in Toda in Shizuoka Prefecture. Keiō University and Tokyo Higher Normal School did likewise in Kanagawa and Chiba Prefectures, both in 1902.

The first modern swimming meet was held on August 13, 1898, in the waters of Yokohama Bay. Swimmers from the foreign settlement raced the students of a Japanese swimming school over distances of 100, 400, and 800 yards. On August 20, 1905, the *Mainichi shimbun* sponsored a 10-mile swimming race in the waters of Osaka Bay. Only seven of the twenty-eight starters finished the race. Swimming in the native style, Sugimura Yōtarō, a student in Tokyo University's Department of Law, won the contest. The arduous feat earned Sugimura 300 yen, a barrel of sake, and various other prizes. The first timed swimming competition, which was sponsored by the *Jiji shimpō* newspaper, occurred six years later, on August 28, 1911, at Shibaura in Tokyo. Ugai Yasaburō won the 220-yard race in 2 minutes, 32 seconds. Although Ugai swam then in a native style, he became known in the Taishō period (1912–1925) as the first Japanese to adopt the crawl.[61]

Although it was impossible to have predicted it in the Meiji period, golf, which was obviously even less well suited than cricket to Japanese terrain, was destined to become the preferred sport of the Japanese corporate elite. The Scottish game was planted in Japanese soil in 1901 by Arthur Hesketh Groom, the same English merchant who had led the way to formation of Kobe's cricket club. In 1903, a four-hole course was constructed at Mount Rokkō, near the port city, and the Kobe Golf Club was founded. Its Yokohama counterpart followed in 1906. The first national championship was held in 1907 and the Nihon Gorufu Kyōkai (Japan Golf Association) was founded in 1924. By 1937, there were some seventy courses, but it was not until the 1960s that golf became a prerequisite for managerial success in the corporate world.[62]

Japanese pilgrims have for centuries climbed mountains in order to communicate with the gods who made their home amid the peaks, but what Kinoshita calls *shūkyōtōzan* (religious ascent) was very different in purpose and technique from the activities of the Alpine Club (organized in London a year before the Meiji Restoration).[63] British sportsmen were the first to climb mountains in Japan simply because there were mountains to climb. The Rokkō Mountains, which loom behind Kobe, provided some initial adventures. H. E. Daunt and J. P. Warren were known as the Captain and the Lieutenant of the Kōbe Mountain Goats (and were also skilled golfers).[64] Eventually, the more challenging peaks of central Japan became a favorite venue. In time, the central range became known—in the Japanese pronunciation of the English word—as the Nihon Arupusu (Japanese Alps). Walter Weston, a British missionary, contributed to the transfer of the sport to the Japanese by publishing *Mountaineering and Exploration in the Japanese Alps* (1896) and by lending his support to the Sangakkai (Mountaineering Club) founded in 1905 by Kojima Usui (whose publications plagiarized Weston). In 1906, Watanabe Satoshi led a group of schoolgirls from Nagano and Tokyo to the top of Mount Fuji.[65]

Although the men and women of Kobe's British colony skied and skated,[66] geography dictated that winter sports were to be more popular in the snowy central mountains and on the northern island of Hokkaido than in the Kansai area. In January 1911, on snowy slopes near the town of Takeda in Niigata Prefecture, Theodor von Lerch, an Austrian military officer who had learned to ski from the famed Mathias Zdarsky, introduced the techniques of the sport to the men of the 58th Infantry

Regiment. The following year, students at the national university in Sapporo founded an Alpine club to promote their favorite activity, mountain climbing, only to discover that it was more fun to glide swiftly down a slope than to clamber laboriously up one. They seem to have been tutored by another Austrian, Egon von Kratzer. In 1916, one of the teachers at Sapporo's national university returned to Japan from study abroad and introduced the students to cross-country skiing. The university's club flourished and played a leading role in the formation, in 1925, of the Zen Nihon Sukī Renmei (All-Japan Ski Federation).[67]

Basketball and volleyball came to Japan via the Young Men's Christian Association, which was appropriate in that both games had been invented by members of that organization (basketball by James Naismith in 1891 and volleyball by William Morgan in 1896). Both sports emerged from the context of "muscular Christianity." The term refers to the efforts of Charles Kingsley and other nineteenth-century Englishmen to overcome the suspicion that had for centuries characterized Christian attitudes toward the human body. In the place of monastic asceticism, the proponents of "muscular Christianity" affirmed a robust, physically active engagement with the world. Sports were central to their program. The YMCA institutionalized and disseminated their ideals.[68] At the turn of the century, the YMCA was probably the West's most active exporter of modern sports to China, Korea, and Japan.[69]

Despite their origin in an atmosphere of fervent faith, basketball and volleyball were both exemplary products of what Max Weber termed *Zweckrationalität* (instrumental rationality). In a 1914 article published in the *American Physical Education Review* and in a short book entitled simply *Basketball* (1941), the game's inventor described his reaction to the challenge posed for him by his superiors when they asked him to create a ball game complicated enough to interest adults and spatially confined enough to be played indoors when New England winters daunted faint-hearted Christians. In his article and his book, Naismith reconstructed the sequence of logical steps he had taken as he reasoned his way to the solution to the problem. Perhaps the best indication of his instrumental approach was the placement of the basket. Fearful of potential injury from balls hurled forcefully at a ground-level vertical goal (like soccer's), Naismith elevated the goal above the players' heads and designed it so that its aperture was horizontal and narrow. Not reckoning with a team of 6′10″ slamdunkers, Naismith reasoned that the ball had to be thrown softly if its arc was to pass through the center of the basket.[70] Although the origin of volleyball was less carefully documented, the game's invention was a similar triumph of rational design.

Ōmori Heizō played YMCA basketball in the United States in the 1890s. After returning to Japan, he introduced the game at Tokyo Women's University, where he taught. Prospects for diffusion of the game diminished somewhat when Ōmori died, in the United States, on his way home from the 1912 Olympics in Stockholm, but progress resumed in 1913 when Franklin Brown fostered the sport at the Tokyo YMCA and Elwood Brown included basketball in the first YMCA-sponsored Far Eastern Games, which took place in Manila that same year. (The trials for the Far Eastern Games were subsidized, in part, by the *Mainichi shimbun,* which seems to have had a hand in every other sport event of the Taishō period.) At the first Japanese championships, which took place in 1921, the Tokyo YMCA was the easy winner.[71]

Ōmori had also observed volleyball at the Springfield YMCA. Franklin Brown introduced the game at the Tokyo YMCA in 1913.[72] There was a volleyball tournament at the Third Far Eastern Games, which were held in Osaka in 1917.[73] The game was not yet widely played in Japan, and a Japanese team was put together mostly with runners and basketball players who had the rules explained to them the day before the first game. Needless to say, they came in last among the three teams, losing by wide margins to China and the Philippines. Their losing streak at the Asian games continued until 1934, and they never managed to finish higher than last place.

Volleyball was more popular as a women's sport. At the sixth Asian Games in 1923, women's volleyball was an exhibition event, and the team from Himeji Women's Higher School won the championship, beating China. A national volleyball federation was formed in 1927 and a basketball federation in 1930. Despite the labors of Ōmori and his friends at the YMCA, neither basketball nor volleyball was widely played before the American "re-education" of Japan during the postwar Occupation. General MacArthur's influence seems to have been stronger than Franklin Brown's.[74]

Lawn tennis came to Japan in 1875 via the Yokohama Ladies Club.[75] Amherst College's George A. Leland introduced the game to Japanese students in 1878, a mere four years after it was patented by England's Major Walter Wingfield. Tennis was fashionable among the Western-oriented elite, but it was not widely played. Although students at Dōshisha Women's College took up the game in 1879,[76] the male undergraduates across the way at Dōshisha University seem not to have been inspired to do likewise. Perhaps young Japanese men scorned the sport as a "girl's game." At any rate, Kobe's socially exclusive Lawn Tennis Club was not opened until 1900. The *Mainichi Shimbun*, always eager to promote the sports events that increased its circulation, waited until 1910 to sponsor its first tennis tournament. Students and graduates of Keiō University were prominent in the diffusion of tennis as they were in the spread of baseball and many other modern sports, but their tennis team was not organized until 1913. Despite this rather hesitant acceptance of the game, Kumagai Kazuya took a silver medal in men's singles at the Olympic Games in Antwerp in 1920. Teamed with Kashio Seiichirō, he won a second silver in the doubles competition. The following year, the Japanese team advanced to the challenge round of the Davis Cup competition. In recent years, however, few Japanese players have reached the top ranks in tennis.[77]

Meiji-period participation in modern sports was not limited to college campuses and cities with a nucleus of foreign residents. Young people in smaller communities also organized clubs and built facilities to enable them to engage in modern sports. The Ryojō Youth Club, which was established in 1886 in the town of Yoshikimura in Yamaguchi Prefecture, is an example of a sports-centered voluntary association.

The original aim of the club was to stimulate the intellect of the area's youths through monthly speaking meetings, but with that agenda the club had difficulty maintaining member interest and participation. In time, verbal dexterity gave way to physical prowess. The club began to sponsor sports activities and participation increased. In March 1895 the club held a sports festival (undōkai) to commemorate Japan's victory in the Sino-Japanese War. The sports festival included footraces over 220, 330, 440, and 880 yards, baseball and soccer games, fencing, and various other events, including a three-legged race. In all, 126 young people took part. A sports committee (*undōbu*), established within the Youth Club in 1899, sponsored a number of popular activities: soccer, baseball, tennis, mountain-climbing, and long-distance footraces. Over time, use of the library declined, "public speaking" became sporadic, and sports completely dominated the calendar. Eventually, the youths devoted themselves almost exclusively to tennis, at which they were very successful in local competitions. By 1931, the club had its own tennis facilities, where—from 1934 on—it began to hold an annual tennis tournament for neighboring prefectures.[78]

In 1886, the Ministry of Education established a small number of highly selective "Higher Middle Schools," which were renamed "Higher Schools" in 1894. They served as preparatory academies for the Imperial Universities, and their headmasters were inspired by the examples of Eton, Harrow, Rugby, and other English "public schools." One of the most important of these administrators was Kinoshita Hiroji, who served from 1889 to 1897 as headmaster of Tokyo's "First Higher Middle School" (usually referred to simply as Ichikō).[79]

After graduating from Tokyo University, Kinoshita spent several years studying law in Paris, but what most impressed him during his European sojourn was the annual Oxford-Cambridge boat race at Henley on the Thames. He was especially struck by the high-minded ethos of fair play, which reminded him of what the Japanese were claiming as their own tradition of *bushidō* (the warrior's path). This ethos Kinoshita attributed to the collegians' education at Eton and other "public schools," where dedication to sports and to the humanities (in that order) seemed to produce a lifelong devotion to national service. If Ichikō was to produce a similar class of active young men eager to serve their country, sports had to be a central part of their school experience. And they were. "From sunup to sundown—before, between, or after classes—the crack of bamboo swords and baseball bats filled the air."[80]

There was no need for the masters to force sports upon recalcitrant pupils (which was then the case in India, where Hindu and Muslim boys initially resisted the efforts of English educators to bring them the joys of cricket and crew).[81] When the pupils of Ichikō founded a Society of Friends in October 1890, seven of the society's nine clubs were devoted to sports. British influence was obvious in the clubs for crew and for athletics, but indigenous traditions were strongly represented in the Japanese fencing club. There was also a baseball team.

## BASEBALL AND MODERNITY

In the world of Japanese sports, American influence was eventually dominant. In an empirical analysis of global sports participation in the 1980s and 1990s, the Dutch sociologist Maarten van Bottenburg observed that the percentage of the population that participates in sports of American origin (42%) is higher in Japan than in any European country and the percentage that participates in sports of British origin is lower than in any European country (23%). The reason is clear. "The British may have been dominant in commerce [in the Meiji period], but the Americans were more influential in the educational and cultural spheres."[82]

By the end of the Meiji period, at the very latest, baseball had become Japan's most popular modern participant sport. (One indication of this is the fact that forty-four books on baseball, and only seven on soccer, were published during the Meiji period.)[83] British observers were not happy about this. Speaking to the Japan Society of London in 1933, N. K. Roscoe revealed more than a trace of discomfort at the thought that the American game had outstripped its British rivals: "As far as popularity goes I suppose there is no sport in Japan to equal baseball. . . . If the errand-boy is late in delivering the mid-day vegetables, the probability is that he has been briefly seduced from rectitude by an impromptu baseball game on a vacant lot."[84]

Horace Wilson, a teacher at Kaisei Gakkō (later part of Tokyo University), introduced the game of baseball in 1873. Okubo Toshikazu, Makino Nobuaki, and Kido Takamasa learned the game when they studied in the United States from 1871 to 1874. Returning in 1875, they entered the Kaisei and helped popularize the game among the students. The game was also played in Tokyo at what later became Sapporo Agricultural College and at Ichikō.[85] In addition, a number of other schools had informal teams of baseball enthusiasts who enjoyed the game despite a lack of proper facilities and equipment and sometimes without a firm grasp of the rules.[86] "Informal and unskilled players," writes Kusaka Yuko, "sought only sporadically the ephemeral enjoyment of these unorganized games."[87]

Railroad engineer Hiraoka Hiroshi contributed to the establishment of baseball outside the schools. He had also learned the game during his years in America (1871–1877). While in the United States, he became acquainted with A. G. Spalding, the American businessman who was an important promoter of the game. Spalding gave Hiraoka an official baseball rulebook and some gear. After returning to Japan, Hiraoka established the Shimbashi Athletic Club at the Shimbashi Railway Bureau, in 1882, and started a baseball team.[88] The baseball diamond at the club's facility in Shibaura in Tokyo was one of the first to provide seats for spectators.[89] Among the avid players was Kabayama Aisuke, the railroad's manager. It was no accident that men engaged in modern transportation were among the first to play the game that was then, contrary to what Americans now think, the very symbol of modernity.[90] After Hiraoka left the railroad in 1887, however, the Shimbashi club died out, which suggests that secondary-school students and collegians were the game's early mainstay.[91]

In the early years of baseball, many of the spectators were unfamiliar with the game. Motivated by curiosity, they crowded on the sidelines like people gathering to watch a fire or a scuffle in the street. In the 1880s, however, students began to create more or less permanent sports clubs that received financial support from the school and were expected in return to conform to the school's educational policy. Teams that had been seen merely as boisterous young men imitating the foreigners' odd behavior were not immediately perceived as the schools' representatives. In time, however, intercollegiate rivalries transformed idle spectators into passionate fans who rooted for their representatives on the field and jeered at their opponents (whom the umpires, for unfathomable reasons, inevitably seemed to favor). In the mid-1870s, Kanō Jigorō, later famous as the founder of *Kōdōkan jūdō,* was known as captain of the hecklers, earning his reputation by furious jeering during practice games between Kaisei Gakkō and foreign teams from the settlements in Yokohama and Tsukichi.[92]

In Japan as in the United States, the existence of representative teams increased the pressure to win and this, in turn, led to the specialization of roles: captain, coach, manager, first team, second team, and—eventually—cheerleader.

The organizational history of intercollegiate baseball in Japan replicated the organizational history of American intercollegiate sports. Early in the twentieth century, the occasional challenge matches that had been characteristic of baseball's early years were replaced by the league and tournament competitions that are characteristic of modern sports. Instead of individual games that occurred at whim, whenever one team challenged another, there was a sequence of regularly scheduled encounters. In 1903, for instance, Waseda and Keiō Universities agreed to meet on a regular basis. (Their rivalry still excites emotions comparable to those aroused in the United States by the annual Harvard-Yale football game.) In time, multiteam leagues and tournaments required the creation of bureaucratic organizations to administer the system.

In 1915, the *Asahi shimbun* started a national tournament for middle schools. The local tournaments that were already in existence were transformed into preliminary rounds for *Asahi*'s grand finale. The lure of a national tournament then stimulated the creation of new preliminary rounds in other regions. At the college level, Waseda, Keiō, and Meiji formed a three-team league in 1914. The league was expanded to four, five, and eventually six teams with the addition of Hōsei (1917), Rikkyō (1922), and Tokyo (1925). The organization became the athletic equivalent of the Ivy League (upon which it was modeled). In the 1930s, intercollegiate leagues were formed in other parts of the country.

In the early years of Japanese baseball, the rules were transmitted orally by American educators and by Japanese who had lived in the United States. However, the game seemed to spread faster than a good grasp of the rules. There was ambiguity and confusion over some of the finer points. Before starting play, teams would agree on special or contingent rules for the game at hand: how many balls for a walk, etc. Some of these special rules became rather widely used, for example, the convention that the pitcher had to throw the ball where the batter wanted.

After the publication of Frederick W. Strange's *Outdoor Games* (1883), a number of Japanese handbooks appeared. These books introduced the uninitiated reader to a variety of outdoor sports—football, field hockey, and lawn tennis as well as baseball. The rules of baseball were described in some detail, but there was still a good deal of uncertainty about how the game was played. One problem was that English terminology was not adequately translated. The first attempt to create a complete set of written, unified rules for baseball was an 1895 translation of the rules in Spalding's official *Baseball Guide*. An even more detailed set of rules was published in 1897. Although it cost 40 *sen*, which was at the time a considerable sum, it had gone through seven printings by 1901. When the Japan Association of Umpires was established in February 1916, the first officially recognized set of rules went into effect, which put an end to the practice of "special" rules agreed upon between teams. These official rules were published annually with modifications from 1916 until after the end of World War II.

Rules were one problem. Equipment and facilities were another. To play baseball one needs, at the very least, a ball, a bat, and an open space. Gloves and mitts and catchers' masks, which were initially scorned by "manly" American players, were not really necessary, but baseball simply was not baseball if it wasn't played in proper uniforms. The difference between the baseball uniform and everyday dress was, of course, far greater in Japan than in the United States.

In the early years of Japanese baseball, authentic equipment had to be brought from America and only a limited number of players had access to it. When proper equipment was unavailable, players improvised. They made their own balls and bats, cleared the ground, marked the baselines, and positioned the bases, which were of various shapes and sizes. It was common, at first, for students to play in *hakama*, the split skirts they wore to school. Until the mid-1890s, the catcher, bare-headed and bare-handed, stood well behind home plate and caught the pitch on the bound, which had been the rule in the early days of American baseball. While Ichikō's catchers, wearing American-made masks and mitts, positioned themselves directly behind the plate, catchers from less prestigious (and less affluent) schools protected their hands with home-made mitts and guarded their faces with kendō masks.[93]

It was not until after the turn of the century that reliable, reasonably priced equipment was produced domestically. From 1909 on, Mizuno, Ishii Kajiyama, Tamazawa, and other manufacturers competed to mass-produce and market balls of increasingly better quality. Various woods, including cherry and magnolia, were tested for their suitability for bats. After much trial and error, manufacturers concluded that bats made of ash were ideal, and mass production began after 1905.[94]

Mitts and gloves were produced domestically as early as 1889, but their quality was poor. When the Waseda team returned from its 1905 tour of the United States, Yamagawa Shōten dissected and analyzed the mitts and gloves they had brought back from America. The company began to produce mitts and gloves of such high quality that players no longer felt the need to import them from overseas. Waseda's American tour also increased the demand for baseball uniforms, which Mizuno Rihachi was eventually able to manufacture for half the price of imported ones. By 1921, the sporting goods business was so advanced that fifty-six companies created an industrial association, the Tokyo Union of Sport Equipment Manufacturers and Distributors. By 1935, annual exports of sport equipment reached 16,851,062 yen.

For more than a decade after its construction in 1882, the Shimbashi Athletic Club's baseball field was a unique facility, but, around the turn of the century, elite schools began to construct more or less adequate baseball grounds. Ichikō constructed its first field in 1899, Keiō in 1903, Waseda in 1908, and Meiji in 1909.

In the 1920s and the 1930s, a number of large baseball stadiums were constructed: Jingū Stadium (Tokyo), Nishi Kyōgoku Stadium (Kyoto), Yokohama Park Stadium, Fujiidera Stadium (southern Osaka Prefecture), and Nishinomiya Stadium (Hyōgo Prefecture). The most famous of all Japanese ballparks is Kōshien Stadium near Osaka, completed in 1924. After renovations it now seats 55,000.

For many Japanese, the mere word "Kōshien" can induce a cloud of memories. For the true aficionado, the word "Ichikō" has the same narcotic effect. In 1886, thanks once again to the apparently ubiquitous Frederick W. Strange, a baseball club was formed at the First Higher Middle School (which became Ichikō in 1894). Initially, the rowing team, which was formed the same year, was more popular, and the springtime races on the Sumida River attracted large numbers of spectators, but the school's baseball players soon outnumbered the oarsmen. The players proudly claimed to practice harder than any other baseball team in the country and to be prepared for any sacrifice for the sake of victory. They soon became the country's dominant team. Between 1895 and 1902 they compiled a 56–10 won-lost record.

By 1891 the baseball team was ready to take on the Americans at the Yokohama Athletic Club. Their formal challenge was haughtily rejected. After five years of frustrating negotiations, William B. Mason, an English teacher at Ichikō, finally overcame his compatriots' condescension. A match was arranged. By the time the game was played, on May 23, 1896, the air crackled with emotional tension. Lingering illusions about good sportsmanship vanished when the fans of the Yokohama Athletic Club jeered the arrival of the neatly uniformed Ichikō students and taunted them as they warmed up for the game. The arrogant Americans, who had anticipated an easy rout of the impudent challengers, experienced a humiliating defeat. Wielding their bats with skill and determination, the boys smashed stereotypes and won by a lopsided score of 29–4. "While gloom pervaded Yokohama, Ichikō athletes returned home to a rousing welcome marked by *banzai* chants, choruses from the national anthem, and overflowing cups of *sake*."[95] The unexpected victory was, in fact, an occasion for national celebration.

The reaction of the foreign community was not uniformly churlish. Ichikō's captain was approached after the game by a white-haired foreigner whose name is given (in the Japanese pronunciation) as "Rarunetto." Smiling, the foreigner took the boy's hand and gave him a small sum of money, saying that he was happy and excited that "you boys" have mastered "my country's sport."[96] The *Japan Weekly Mail* found an excuse for the boastful Americans' poor performance: "School-boys with their daily opportunities for practice, their constant matches, and *sparer figures* have always the advantage over a team of grown men . . . who have not played together."[105]

There were two more games, won by Ichikō with scores of 32–9 and 22–6, and then a final rematch in which the Americans, reinforced by sailors from the cruiser *Olympia*, "whose crew members were noted for their prowess in baseball," eked out a 14–12 victory over their adolescent opponents.[98]

Kiku Kōichi, citing the rhetoric of school songs and the memoirs of former players, explains the extraordinary success of Ichikō baseball as a combination of bushidō (extreme discipline is good for the spirit) and the samurai ethos (victory is essential, defeat is a disgrace).[99] Skepticism is in order. The concept of bushidō was itself in large part a nineteenth-century product, another example of "invented tradition." The "way of the warrior" was discovered after the warriors were no more. Ironically, sports were interpreted as manifestations of the spirit of the martial arts at precisely the time that the martial arts were transformed into (more or less) modern sports. (See Chapter 6.) Symptomatic of this desire to assimilate and domesticate foreign influences was an article published by Oshikawa Shunrō in 1911. The article, which appeared in the magazine *Undō sekai* (Sports World), was entitled "Make baseball a martial art [budō]."[100]

Whether or not the spirit of Ichikō baseball derived from the ethos of the medieval samurai, its material basis was typically modern. Initially, the Ichikō baseball club relied on dues and contributions for the purchase of baseball equipment and to offset the costs of transportation. A baseman's glove cost at least 2.5 yen at a time when one *sho* (2 liters) of rice cost less than one-twentieth as much. Although lack of funds forced the team to abandon an 1893 trip to Kyoto to play Dōshisha University, the players were initially reluctant to charge for admission to their games. When over ten thousand spectators gathered on Ichikō's Tokyo field to enjoy an 1896 game against a team from the warship *Detroit*, none of them was asked to pay for the pleasure. Eventually, high-minded amateur principle gave way to economic exigency. Tickets were sold and schoolboy baseball took an important step toward becoming a typically modern spectator sport.

An important step in what Kiku calls the "monetization" of the game took place when Waseda University sent its team on the first Japanese baseball tour of the United States (April 4 to June 29, 1905).[101] The 1905 expedition was the first great test for the Japanese collegiate game. For this trip, the team secured financial support from the Morimura Bank and from Lion Toothpaste. Although the players lost nineteen games and won only seven, a record that they considered "a great defeat,"[102] the tour, which certainly allowed the players to acquire new skills and techniques, also made everyone involved more aware of the economic basis of the game.

Abe Isō, the adult in charge of the Waseda baseball club, led the 1905 American tour. Aware that American colleges charged for admission to their games, Abe explained in a newspaper article written prior to the trip that he hoped to recover some of the team's expenses from its share of the American gate receipts. While suggesting that Japanese baseball might profitably adopt some American practices, Abe also argued that the *spiritual* difference between American and Japanese baseball was not as great as some assumed. In 1909 he wrote that there was no important difference between the Anglo-American concept of fair play and the Japanese concept of bushidō. Neither ethos accepts a win-at-all-costs approach. It is no dishonor to lose, but it is unworthy to protest to the umpire or to make excuses for defeat.[103]

The first baseball game in Japan for which an admission fee is known to have been charged took place on October 31, 1907, when Keiō's team played against a team called Hawaii Saint Louis College, which despite their name appears to have been a semiprofessional team. The following year, Waseda University charged for admission to its game with Washington State University and built temporary stands to accommodate what Waseda hoped was to be a throng of spectators. As these two examples suggest, admission fees were initially charged for games with foreign teams (which might, indeed, have insisted on reimbursement for their transoceanic travel costs). The first game between two Japanese teams for which an admission fee was charged took place on October 29, 1911. The entire gate was donated to the Japanese Antarctic expedition, then in progress. When Waseda, Keiō, and Meiji Universities established their league in 1914, they agreed to charge for admission and to use the money to invite foreign teams, to cover their own travel expenses, and to improve their facilities and equipment. A rather Calvinistic proviso, which may have been intended to disarm critics, stipulated that gate receipts not be used for partying.[104]

There may also have been a whiff of Calvinism in the editorial offices of the *Asahi shimbun*. In August 1911 the newspaper published a series of articles that criticized baseball as harmful to the students and detrimental to the larger society. Baseball players skip too many classes for practice and for games, which means that their schoolwork suffers. Students should not charge admission to their games, nor should they waste money on fancy uniforms. Players are vulgar and have bad manners. Baseball breeds vanity and conceit. And, as if the indictment were still insufficient, baseball is unhealthy.[105]

Defenders rushed to publish their somewhat defensive counterarguments (mainly in newspapers other than the *Asahi*). While admitting that they must always be on guard against abuses, they testified to the physical, mental, and moral benefits of baseball. Defenders of baseball also attempted to distinguish between monetization (which they asserted was necessary for the development of the game) and commercialization (which they acknowledged must be avoided).[106]

Critics and defenders agreed that the game *was* wildly popular at the nation's secondary schools and colleges. When Nels Norgren of the University of Chicago led a collegiate team to Japan in 1922, he reported in amazement that baseball "is more the national sport of Japan than it is of America."[107] Norgren, who spent more time with Japan's educated elite than with the nation's rice farmers and factory hands, probably overstated the popular appeal of the game, but it was definitely an important part of campus life and was soon to become a national passion. Beginning in 1927, NHK made it possible for fans to hear play-by-play radio broadcasts of intercollegiate and interscholastic baseball games. By 1932, 37.5 percent of those who had radios were tuning in to sports broadcasts. Baseball games were broadcast even more often than sumō tournaments.[108] In 1938, a German visitor, using almost exactly the same words as Norgren had in 1922, commented that baseball was more popular in Japan than in the United States.[109] And twenty years after that, an American sportswriter repeated the claim: "The Japanese like baseball better than we do."[110]

Donald Roden, whose account of the Ichikō-Yokohama Athletic Club series is a classic of sports history, believes that baseball "caught on" in Japan because it "seemed to emphasize precisely those values that were celebrated in the civic rituals of state: order, harmony, perseverance, and self-restraint." That is, the Japanese adopted the game because these perceived values were familiar ones. This is also the interpretation of Tada Michitarō in *Asobi to nihonjin* (Play and the Japanese).[111] It is certainly true that the Japanese have often described baseball as if it were, indeed, the inculcator of harmony, perseverance, and self-restraint, but there was no need in the Meiji period to find these values in baseball when Japanese archery and the other martial arts were readily available. While it is certainly possible that the Japanese sought harmony in baseball, it is more likely that the Japanese seized upon the game because it seemed to embody values that were *not* traditionally Japanese. "The myth of Japan's modernization," writes William R. May, "underlines baseball's continuing popularity."[112] The American game, which Roden sees as a rather stately ceremony, Mark Twain characterized as "the outward and visible expression of the drive and push and rush and struggle of the raging, tearing, booming nineteenth century." Twain was surely right. Baseball symbolized, for both the Japanese and their American contemporaries, not tradition but modernity. Like the telegraph, the telephone, and many other technological marvels of that era, the ludic import bore the magical stamp: Made in America.[113]

## THE ROLE OF SPORTS IN PHYSICAL EDUCATION

Sports and physical education are closely related phenomena, especially in Japan, where sport is widely considered a subcategory of physical education. To understand Japanese sports, it is also necessary to attend, briefly, to the development of physical education in Japan.

During the Edo period, most domains had schools to educate the children of the samurai. Most of these schools were established toward the end of the eighteenth century.[114] The arrival of Commodore Perry's armada of "black ships" intensified the domains' previously rather desultory interest in modern methods of warfare and military training. Accordingly, many domain schools adopted gymnastics as a form of paramilitary training. Turning to European physical educators for guidance, the shogunate first adopted the Dutch version of gymnastics, then switched to the French system devised by Francisco Amoros. Different domains adopted and adapted their gymnastics from a number of different European countries: from Germany and the Scandinavian countries as well as from the Netherlands and France. Since many of these domain schools survived into the Meiji period as primary and middle schools, physical education in the late nineteenth and early twentieth centuries can best be understood as an extension of this paramilitary training.[115]

If Japan was to become a modern nation, the patchwork of local schools had to be replaced by an educational system similar to the systems developed in the United States and Western Europe. Promulgating its first major Education Ordinance in 1872, the Meiji government institutionalized physical education in the schools.[116] Meiji-period physical education was generally referred to as *taisō* (gymnastics).[117]

Implementing the Education Ordinance, the Tokyo Normal School was established in 1872 to train teachers for all subjects, including physical education. Just what activities were taught in the gymnastics classes of the day can be inferred from the response that the principal of the Osaka English School made in 1878 to a query from the Ministry of Education. According to the principal's eclectic list, the children not only marched, did calisthenics and gymnastic exercises, used Indian clubs, and played on the seesaw and the swings; they also practiced the high jump and competed in soccer games.[118]

In 1879, the National Institute of Gymnastics (Taisō Denshūjo) was established to develop methods of physical education and train instructors for the schools.[119] Minister of Education Tanaka Fujimaro traveled to the United States and hired an American advisor, George A. Leland, to teach at the institute. Although German immigrants to the United States had propagated the ideas of *Turnvater* Friedrich Ludwig Jahn, Leland favored the American gymnastic system that he had learned at Amherst College. Since this system, devised by Diocletian Lewis, required a good deal of equipment, Leland stocked the school's gymnasium with barbells, dumbbells, Indian clubs, beanbags, and wooden rings.[120]

The main program developed at the Institute under Leland's guidance came to be known as "normal gymnastics" (*futsū taisō*) or "light gymnastics" (*kei taisō*). But other forms of gymnastics were developed and taught as well. They included "heavy gymnastics" (*jū taisō*) and "outdoor activities" (*kogai undō*). Included among the latter were football, cricket, croquet, baseball, and rowing.[121]

In the published collection of his translated lectures, *Taiikuron*, Leland stated that the ultimate goal of physical education was not a strong body, but a well-developed *kokoro* (the word probably translated the English word "mind"). Imamura remarks that Leland was rational in his methodology, but spiritual (*seishinshugiteki*) in his goals.[122] This is an interesting remark because many commentators assert that seishinshugi is what makes Japanese sports uniquely Japanese.

The Institute of Gymnastics was abolished in 1886 and a special course for "gymnastic" training was offered at Tokyo Normal School (Tōkyō Shihan Gakkō). Admission to the course was restricted to army veterans of officer rank who applied within a year of their discharge from active service.[123] While it may seem odd from an American perspective to delegate the task of physical education to military personnel, many continental European educational systems also looked to the military to staff "gymnastics" programs that were, after all, essentially paramilitary.[124]

The 1887 "Course of Study for Primary Schools" (Shōgakkō Kyōsoku Taikō) specified the program for "gymnastics" classes in primary schools. In the early years of the program, classes were supposed to consist of appropriate "play and games" (*yūgi*) and "outdoor activities" (kogai undō). "Normal gymnastics" were to be introduced gradually, after which the boys were to be taught some of the simpler "military gymnastics." The guidelines did not specify what was meant by "appropriate games and outdoor activities." Tsuboi Gendō's widely read book, *Kogai yūgihō* (Outdoor Games; 1885, revised 1888), was probably used as a reference. It includes various noncompetitive games and a small number of sports: football, croquet, lawn tennis, baseball, and rowing. (Baseball and rowing were dropped from the revised edition.)[125]

After the first sports festivals (undōkai) at the Naval Academy in 1874, "sports days" spread to schools throughout the country and became a mandatory extracurricular activity. Mori Arinori, who became Minister of Education in 1885, was among the enthusiastic promoters of these undōkai, which he saw as an ideal means of improving the health and simultaneously intensifying the patriotism of the nation's schoolchildren.[126] A leading journal of education, *Dai Nihon kyōikukai zasshi*, mentioned thirty-two separate undōkai held between 1884 and 1892, mainly at the nation's primary schools. Four-fifths of these sports festivals were interscholastic in the sense that more than a single school participated. Imamura groups the events held at these undōkai into four categories. The largest category is *yūgi kyōgi*, which covers sports and noncompetitive games. Nearly 70 percent of the events fall in this category. Of the events in this category, footraces are the most popular, accounting for 32.4 percent of all events. Also included in this category are ball games (8.3%), of which soccer is the most popular (4.8%), clearly outstripping baseball (1.3%). A second large category, various kinds of gymnastics, comprises 25 percent of all events. Considering the important role assigned to the military at the Tokyo Normal School, one is surprised to discover that military gymnastics, the third category, accounted for only 3.9 percent of the undōkai events. The smallest of Imamura's four categories is *bujutsu*, the martial arts, which were a mere 1.3 percent of all events. Imamura concludes, quite plausibly, that although modern sports may have played a small part in the official curriculum, they were a major part of the children's actual physical activities (*undō seikatsu*).[127]

In 1885, at the beginning of this period, only 4 percent of middle-school pupils were girls.[128] Legislation passed in 1889 did require that every prefecture have at least one high school for girls, but the notion of using sports to prepare women for political and economic leadership remained (and to some degree still remains) foreign. Physical education was held to be a necessary part of the curriculum for girls, if for no other reason than to prepare them for their future role as healthy mothers of the boys destined to become the nation's defenders, but this eugenic motivation ran counter to traditional notions about female modesty and beauty.

Sportswear was a knotty problem. It was difficult to do calisthenics in an *obi* (the tight sash worn with kimono) and nearly impossible to run in *geta* (Japanese clogs). The long sleeves of the traditional Japanese kimono also hindered many sports activities.[129] Reform-minded Inokuchi Akuri, who had studied at Smith College in Northampton, Massachusetts, and at Boston's Normal School of Gymnastics, returned to Japan in 1903 and prescribed blouses, bloomers, and skirts for her physical education classes. In 1915, Nikaidō Tokuyo experimented with the simple tunics that she had observed while studying in England. Neither effort at dress reform was very successful. "The transition was too drastic."[130] It was not until the 1920s that Western sports clothes became standard for female physical education.

There was still another obstruction to the progress of physical education and sports at Japanese girls' schools and women's colleges. Although the Ministry of Education stipulated that female teachers should lead the girls in their exercises, few women were qualified. In 1912, there were 286 physical education teachers at the nation's 299 Women's Higher Schools—fewer than one per school. Of these 286 teachers, 150 were male and 136 female, but 128 of the men and only 12 of the women had the proper credentials. The Ferris School, founded in 1884, supplied a few reasonably qualified female teachers who—in the words of Dean Matsuda Michi of Dōshisha Women's College—had learned "ethics and gymnastics," but it was not until 1918 that Tokyo's Normal School for Female Teachers instituted a two-year physical education course for prospective teachers.[131]

The annual sports day that the Normal School inaugurated for the girls at its affiliated middle school on May 28, 1891, was a good indication of prevalent attitudes. The program for 1904 had four footraces and two tug-of-war contests, but there were six dances and ten displays of marching and doing calisthenics. The same day, the boys at the middle school affiliated with the Normal School for Male Teachers played football, wrestled, and competed in ten footraces. And they, too, had tug-of-war contests.[132]

Reporting on the Normal School's third annual celebration, journalists mentioned basketball and tennis, but the "expressive games" and the "technical games" were apparently the focus of most attention. The girls mounted bicycles, not in order to race, but rather to ride in formation "like butterflies." In time, however, the Normal School added classes in baseball to its physical education curriculum, and the students petitioned for field hockey. If they hoped to find an advocate in Inokuchi Akuri, they were disappointed. Although she was definitely an innovator when it came to dress reform, she was hardly a strong supporter of athletic competition for young women. She preferred Swedish gymnastics and the "showpiece" of the programs she devised was a "Faust Dance" to the music of Charles Gounod.[133]

At schools founded by or under the influence of Protestant missionaries, programs in female physical education were generally more ambitious. At Dōshisha Women's College, for instance, lawn tennis was played as early as 1879. Tennis was, then as now, considered an appropriately "feminine" sport, but what does one make of the appearance of kendō in the diary kept in the 1890s by a student at Meiji Girls' School? "Every day early in the morning I go to the kendō hall to practice kendō, and then attend morning service. Getting in a sweat and bracing up my spirits, I feel very refreshed. Then I find myself ready to meet my God within."[134] The surprise here is not the combination of piety and athleticism—this was, after all, the heyday of "muscular Christianity"—but rather that the girls at Meiji practiced a martial art that, until very recently, was a hallmark of the samurai. In general, however, calisthenics, taught in the not-very-strenuous manner of Dio Lewis, were more common than modern sports or the martial arts.

Whether girls played tennis, practiced the martial arts, or merely swung Indian clubs, the departure from conventional gender roles occasioned protests. In Kyoto, for instance, many parents removed their daughters from school in order to save them from the disgrace of muscular arms.[135] As Hagiwara Miyoko comments, with a bit of hyperbole, the female aesthetic ideal of the Meiji period was "a thin woman with pale skin, slender fingers and feet, and weak legs."[136] If physical debility was, indeed, the ideal, how was a basketball player to find a husband?

In April 1901, the Ministry of Education issued detailed instructions for the schedule to be followed in boys' and girls' physical education classes during each year of primary school. The instructions indicated the exact amount of time to be devoted to each of several categories of activity: gymnastics, military gymnastics, and games. Like the 1887 "Course of Study for Primary Schools," the new instructions did not specify what activities were to be considered games.[137]

The Ministry's lack of specificity was remedied by a "Detailed Plan for Primary School Instruction" (*Shōgakkō kyōjuhō saimoku*) published by the Tokyo Higher Normal School in April 1903. The plan listed no fewer than sixty-four different games, of which forty-four involved competition.[138] This was in stark contrast to a book on games, *Yūgihō,* published only nine years earlier, in which twenty-five of the forty-eight listed activities involved singing and marching.[139]

In October 1904, the Ministry of Education returned to the question of an appropriate physical education curriculum and appointed a Committee to Investigate Gymnastics and Games (Taisō Yūgi Torishirabe Iinkai). They met thirty-seven times and submitted their report in October 1905. Most of the report concerned gymnastics, but the members of the committee did list games that should be included in the curriculum for primary schools. These were divided into competitive games, marching games, and movement games. Under the first rubric, the committee recommended a broad spectrum of extracurricular sports: running and jumping; a number of Western ball games, including baseball and lawn tennis; sumō; and several of the Japanese martial arts (archery, fencing, jūjutsu). The report specifically stated, however, that there was no reason to include martial arts in the formal primary-school curriculum.[140]

During this period, games were not a part of the middle-school curriculum, but they were played as extracurricular activities. The Ministry of Education's Committee to Investigate Gymnastics and Play recommended that games become a part of the regular curriculum and that more than one-third of class time be devoted to them.[141] As these various recommendations were implemented in the decade before World War I, ordinary Japanese schoolchildren began to participate in the sports that had been introduced a generation earlier to the sons and daughters of the modernizing elite.

# 4

# The Modernization
# of Indigenous Sports

Meiji-period observer might have predicted that Japan's adoption of Western sports meant the demise—sooner or later—of the nation's traditional sports. In fact, some sporting traditions, like inuoumono, did disappear. Some, like kemari, barely managed to survive thanks to the heroic efforts of small groups of devotees. Some, like the traditional martial arts, underwent a transformation. And sumō seems—at first glance—to have continued unchanged.

## KEMARI

The social trauma that seems inevitably to accompany the transition to modernity results, just as inevitably, in an effort to preserve, revive, and revitalize traditional ways. Within the realm of sports, one of the most remarkable manifestations of this effort occurred in 1903, when kemari was played at the Fifth National Industrial Exhibition in Osaka. It was as if the Japanese wished to insist, amidst the technological spectacle, that they had not forgotten their medieval culture.[1]

A small group of aristocrats had kept the game alive in Kyoto, saving it from the extinction that had threatened it during the early years of the Meiji period. Eight disciples of the Asukai and Namba houses met for practice in 1876. The following year, Emperor Meiji viewed a performance of kemari at the Kyoto branch of the Peer's Club (the Kazoku Kaikan) and expressed his wish that the ceremonial game be preserved. A society dedicated to that worthy purpose was formed in 1884. By 1886, the

96

original group of some thirty or forty noblemen had been joined by so many new members that extra practice days had to be added. The records of the society indicate that the ball was kicked 539 times in the course of sixteen rounds, averaging more than thirty-three kicks per round. In 1887, the emperor again favored kemari with his august presence. Budding did not, however, lead to flowering. The society was apparently disbanded "for unknown reasons" in 1895.[2]

Dissolution of the society did not dissuade kemari's advocates from their work on the game's behalf. Since one obstacle to the preservation of kemari was (and continues to be) the game's expensive costumes and equipment, ranking nobles solicited the Imperial Household for financial support. In September 1901, they presented the Grand Chamberlain with an estimate of the "cost required to preserve kemari," requesting 1,153.14 yen to establish a preservation society and 360 yen a year to cover annual expenses. Although the request was not granted, the group persevered and the present Kemari Preservation Society was formed in February 1903.

The Japan Physical Education Society (Nihon Taiikukai), a private body established in 1891 to promote physical education and sports, contacted the Preservation Society and invited its members to perform at the sports meet that the physical educators were organizing for Osaka's National Industrial Exhibition. The Kemari Preservation Society agreed to send twenty-one peers and four samurai and commoners for the demonstration that was scheduled for April 22. The emperor was expected to attend the performance, but the society's desire to appear before the sovereign was thwarted when rain caused the demonstration to be postponed for a day.

Two weeks after this demonstration, a representative of the Preservation Society called on the Minister of the Imperial Household to discuss a petition that the society had submitted to the Imperial Household. (The society had repeated its earlier request for financial support and asked for the privilege of demonstrating kemari before the emperor.) The minister asked and the representative answered questions about the state of kemari, the authenticity of the costumes, and the amount of money that was needed.

The representative's answers to the next few questions presaged the course that kemari was to take in the coming decades. The minister asked why Count Asukai's name was not on the petition. The Asukai family, it will be remembered, controlled kemari throughout the Tokugawa period. The representative answered that there were rumors of some trouble in the family's affairs, and it was thought better that the count did not sign the petition. He was then asked about the society's relationship with the Japan Physical Education Society, and he replied that there was no regular relationship; the Preservation Society had merely been asked to perform at the Industrial Exhibition. When asked about the society's future plans, the representative said that the society hoped to have a member of the imperial family as president and to establish itself as a foundation.

Some aspects of this account—taken from a privately published history of the society—remain murky,[3] but it reveals quite clearly that the society, in its struggle for survival, had three options: to rely for support on kemari's traditional mainstay, the Asukai house; to strengthen its ties to the modernizers in the Japan Physical Education Society; or to seek the patronage of the Imperial Household Agency. Each option had advantages and disadvantages.

While the connection to the Asukai conferred an important aura of legitimacy, it also hindered progress. Prospective society members had no choice but to become disciples of the Asukai school, which greatly inhibited recruitment. A closer relationship with the Japan Physical Education Society might have attracted a number of new enthusiasts for the game—but only if the game were radically transformed. The society was not ready to modernize kemari by adopting new balls and costumes fabricated from more easily available materials,[4] nor were they willing to replace the traditional trees—the kakari no ki—with some functionally equivalent wooden artifact, nor were they in a mood to alter the ancient rules of the game. The Preservation Society, full membership in which was restricted to noblemen and their families, chose to cast its lot with the Imperial Household. In 1905, the society became independent of the Asukai house. In May 1907, the Imperial Household granted the society 1,535.50 yen for start-up expenses and promised to provide 700 yen a year for operating costs. The society was enabled to preserve its exclusiveness—of the thirty-one members in March 1907, nearly all were peers—and at the same time to maintain some of the forms of kemari within a changed social context.

In addition to holding five formal meets a year, the society performed kemari four times a year as an offering at shrines associated with the Asukai, Namba, and Fujiwara families. There were a few spectators at these events, but most people in Japan were probably unaware of the society's existence. In 1915, kemari was performed in Kyoto before two royal princes. Four years later, the members finally achieved one of their most cherished goals. They performed before the emperor himself. In

1922, they "went public" and performed kemari for the Prince of Wales, who was in Japan on a state visit.

The society continued to maintain a distinction between peers and commoners, but the relative representation of the two groups was gradually reversed. In 1935, there were eleven full members and nineteen associate members. In practice sessions, the more skillful members took the better positions, but at formal meets the aristocratic full members continued to occupy the important positions, those under the four trees. Associate members took the supporting positions. The society continued to be controlled by a handful of officials, and the budget was not revealed to most of the members. On the other hand, there were no membership dues. Expenses continued to be covered by the annual grant from the Imperial Household.

In the late 1930s, as the nation became more and more involved in military adventures overseas, the members of the Kemari Preservation Society found it increasingly difficult to practice and to hold meets. In the early 1940s, activity came virtually to a standstill. On April 15, 1945, the society suspended its activities.

## BUDŌ

"Budō" is usually rendered into English as "the martial arts." However, there are two other terms that are also translated as "martial arts": "*bujutsu*" and "*bugei*." The first character in these three compounds means "military" or "martial." The second characters have different nuances. Literally translated, "bujutsu" is "martial technique," "bugei" is "martial art," and "budō" is "martial way." To many people, the practice of budō means not merely the acquisition of an array of combat skills and techniques, but also a larger philosophy, a way of life. This meaning, however, is new, not more than a century old.

The term "budō" is found in documents from as early as the twelfth century, but not with the meaning that it has today. In fact, "budō" is a notoriously difficult term that means different things to different people in different historical periods. The term might mean military affairs, military preparedness, martial virtue, warfare, or training in combat skills. It might even refer to the kabuki actors who played "a loyal warrior skilled in the martial arts." In the Tokugawa period, "budō" was most often used to mean bushidō, "the way of the warrior," that is, the way a warrior should behave in a moral or ethical sense.[5]

It was not until the Meiji period, at the very earliest, that the various forms of martial arts—archery, fencing, unarmed combat—were linked to "dō" (the character for "path" or "way" in a compound like "budō"). Before the Meiji period, fencing was called "*kenjutsu*" (sword techniques), "*heihō*" (military tactics), or "*gekken*" (clashing swords); archery was "*kyūjutsu*" (bow techniques); and the many schools of unarmed combat were known generically (and rather poetically) as "*jūjutsu*" (soft techniques). Jūdō, often considered to be the most modern of the martial arts, was the first of them to become a "path" and the first to gain acceptance as an Olympic sport.

## JŪDŌ

Among the dozens of sports that now comprise the Olympic Games, jūdō is commonly perceived as the most important example of a sport whose origins are Asian rather than European or American. Jūdō's origins are unquestionably Asian, but it is important to realize that the sport was invented by a Japanese who was strongly influenced by his Western-oriented education. Kanō Jigorō (1860–1938) believed that a superior form of unarmed combat could be created through a modern synthesis of East and West. "Kanō's development of jūdō. . . . parallels the political developments of his time, for he took the largely obsolescent schools of samurai jujutsu and reinterpreted them as physical and mental culture for modern times."[6]

Like basketball, volleyball, and team handball, jūdō was a consciously *invented* sport. Its creation, like theirs, was another instance of instrumental rationality. It was, in other words, a means to an end. Jūdō's techniques were scientifically designed to enable a smaller and weaker person to overcome a larger and stronger (but less skillful) opponent. Kanō was quite aware of what he had done. Sounding almost like his contemporary, James Naismith, he explained, "Following the scientific method, I selected the best elements of older schools of *jūjutsu* and constructed a new system which is most suited to today's society."[7] Looking back in 1935, he gave credit to the scientific method for his system's "superiority to older schools."[8]

Although jūdō was an invented sport, a product of instrumental rationality, the ultimate values that it was meant to embody were ethical rather than material. Stating this interpretation in a somewhat extreme form, Jörg Möller writes, "Kanō saw jūdō first and foremost as a spiritual discipline in which Confucian virtues should dominate."[9]

Kanō Jigorō, the youngest of five children, was born in what is now Hyōgo Prefecture on October 28, 1860, seven years before Japan's feudal regime was replaced by the modernizers of the Meiji era.[10] In 1877, he entered the Literature Department at Kaisei Gakkō, a college of Western studies later to become Tokyo's Imperial University. He studied politics and economics, graduated from the university in July 1881, and completed his postgraduate education in the Philosophy Department, after which he embarked upon his long, successful career as an educator. His first teaching position was at Tokyo's Gakushūin University (where he introduced jūdō in April 1883). He was for twenty-three years headmaster of both the famed First Higher School (Ichikō) and the Tokyo Higher Normal School, later to become Tokyo University of Education (which was absorbed into Tsukuba University in 1978). During this time he also served in the Ministry of Education.

Kanō played several modern sports while an undergraduate at the Kaisei Gakkō, but he also continued his earlier study of the martial arts, seeking instruction from the masters of two of the more important schools of jūjutsu. In 1877, he enrolled as a pupil of Fukuda Hachinosuke, a representative of the Tenjin shin'yō-ryū. After Fukuda's death in 1879, Kanō continued to study with Fukada's teacher, Iso Masatomo, and then with Iikubo Tsunetoshi, a representative of Kitō-ryū.

A year after his graduation from the university, while still a student of Kitō-ryū, Kanō converted a room at Tokyo's Eishōji temple into a *dōjō* (exercise hall). There, in May 1882, he began to offer instruction in jūdō (the soft path). At first he simply combined techniques from the schools with which he was already familiar. From the Tenjin shin'yō school he took striking and strangling, and from the Kitō school he took throwing techniques. He also studied formerly secret manuals of other schools for their techniques.

The name of his own school—the Kōdōkan—was formed from three characters that can be translated as "the hall where the way is taught and learned." He called his teachings "jūdō" to distinguish them from jūjutsu. He proudly proclaimed that his martial art was "more than an art of attack and defense. It is a way of life."[11] The new name served two seemingly contradictory purposes. It attracted attention, by proclaiming to be new and different, but at the same time it appealed to tradition, since the word "jūdō" had been used by some of the old masters, in particular those of the Kitō-ryū school in which Kanō himself was licensed. In Kanō's mind, "dō" also connoted an underlying principle, of which technique (jutsu) was just one of many applications.

Writing about "the invention of the martial arts," Inoue Shun has stressed that Kanō "constructed . . . *jūdō* by modernizing *jūjutsu*."[12] Traditional notions of participation were altered. Women were accepted at the Kōdōkan and spectators were invited to the tournaments that were staged there. Traditional pedagogy was revised. "While the older schools disregarded verbal instruction in the belief that the [martial] arts were learned directly by experience and observation of the master, Kanō attached much importance to verbal explanation and comprehension."[13] In 1894, he launched the first of several Kōdōkan magazines—the *Kanō juku dōsōkai zasshi* (Kanō School Alumni Magazine). He was such a prolific lecturer and writer that his collected works extend to fourteen volumes.

A similar logic led Kanō to shift the emphasis from the repetition of kata (set forms) to the more flexible practice of *randori* (sparring). While the students of the more traditional martial arts drilled, the aspiring *jūdōka* sparred.

Kanō also revised the system of ranks that had characterized jūjutsu. In place of three stages—*mokuroku* or mastery of techniques, *menkyō* or the right to teach, and *kaiden* or initiation into the secrets of the art—he eventually introduced ten ranks, or *dan*. Justifying this innovation, Kanō argued that the division into only three stages made the transition from one to another seem intimidatingly difficult. With ten grades, however, students were rewarded for their efforts by frequent promotions, which encouraged them to improve and progress.

For Kanō himself, success came quickly, which suggests that his innovations were an appropriate response to the times. The Kōdōkan began in 1882 with only nine students. Five years later, there were nearly five hundred. One reason for the increase was that Kanō's disciples handily defeated the representatives of other schools of jūjutsu at tournaments sponsored by the Tokyo Metropolitan Police Bureau. Kanō's account of the triumph is modestly subdued:

In 1887 and 1888, as the Kōdōkan's fame spread, whenever the Police Bureau hosted big competitions, the Totsuka school and the Kōdōkan competed. At one contest in 1888, each sent fourteen or fifteen contestants. Four or five Kōdōkan students were matched against other jujutsu teams, but about ten had matches with members of the Totsuka team, which included Terushima Tarō, a great technician, and Nishimura Tadasuke, renowned for his great strength. Terushima was pitted against [the Kōdōkan's] Yamashita Yoshitsugu, and Nishimura against Satō Hōken. Surprisingly, two or three matches ended in a tie, with the Kōdōkan winning all the rest. Kōdōkan pupils had greatly improved, but I never dreamed their skills had progressed to the point that they could achieve such results.[14]

The victory was a public-relations triumph. The Metropolitan Police Bureau began to hire Kanō's students as instructors in the martial arts and the Kōdōkan began to draw students and teachers from the other schools of jūjutsu.

Thanks in part to Kanō's position as a prominent educator, jūdō spread quickly through Japan's system of military and civilian colleges and universities. In 1887, when the Naval Academy adopted Kōdōkan jūdō for its trainees, Kanō dispatched Yamashita and Satō—the two stars of the 1888 tournament at the Police Bureau—to serve as instructors. The Tokyo Imperial University and Keiō University, the civilian sector's most prestigious public and private educational institutions, followed the Naval Academy's lead. Kanō's advantageous position as headmaster of Ichikō gave additional impetus to the spread of jūdō through Japan's secondary schools. An 1898 match between Ichikō and the Second Higher School in Sendai inaugurated interscholastic jūdō competition.

Early success at home encouraged Kanō to propagate jūdō abroad. The first of his eight overseas journeys took place in 1889–1891. Yamashita Yoshitsugu, who spent the years 1903–1907 in the United States, was another of the sport's enthusiastic missionaries. Among the many Americans to be impressed by jūdō was the nation's foremost proponent of the strenuous life, Theodore Roosevelt.

Kanō's efforts to internationalize jūdō were especially successful in Europe. Led by Koizumi Gunji, a group of aspiring British jūdōka formed the Budōkai Jūdō Club in 1918. By 1929, there were enough clubs for Great Britain to have a national championship.[15] French jūdō built upon the turn-of-the-century passion for jūjutsu. In 1906, *Le Sport Universel Illustré* reported, "Jūjutsu is everything! The streets, the newspapers and magazines, the theaters, the music halls—they all sound the triumphant clarion call of this almost magic word!"[16] That same year Jules Claretie marveled in a book entitled *La Vie à Paris*, "Yes, truly, the Parisian has become jujitsu-mad. . . . He 'japanizes' himself now the way he once went crazy with anglomania."[17] Jūjutsu was not quite the same as jūdō, but Aida Hikoichi arrived in 1924 to teach the gospel according to Kanō at Le Sporting-Club de Paris. Kanō himself visited Paris in 1933 and 1936 and inspired Moshe Feldenkrais and Frédéric Joliot to found a jūdō club. (At first the French followed the version of the sport taught by Mikinosuke Kawaishi, who came to France in 1935, but they eventually joined jūdō's mainstream.) The French staged their first national championship in 1943.[18] Despite their rather slow start, the French had the strongest European team in the 1950s.[19] Germans proved to be especially keen for the new sport. Erich Rahn is even said to have established a jūdō school in Berlin in 1905, but the techniques he taught were actually jūjutsu. It is not clear exactly when authentic Kōdōkan jūdō reached Germany, but Frankfurt can claim to be the birthplace of the European Judo Federation, which was organized in 1932. Frankfurt also hosted an international tournament that same year. Dresden was the venue for the first official European championships (in 1934).[20]

## KENDŌ

In the last decades of the Tokugawa shogunate, swordsmanship flourished on the domains of Japanese feudal lords, where each daimyō had his favored version of the art, and in the urban schools that were established in Tokyo and Osaka, where followers of the different styles met and mingled. (At these urban schools, the friendships that were formed among young samurai from different feudal domains developed into political alliances that eventually undermined Tokugawa rule.)

The most famous of these schools was run by Chiba Shūsaku (1794–1855). Chiba opened his school—the Gembukan—in Tokyo in 1822 and was so successful a teacher that his establishment attracted thousands of pupils. One reason for his success was that he simplified the eight ranks of the Ittō-ryū into three, which reduced the number of fees his pupils were required to pay for each promotion. His emphasis on training the mind as well as the body had "a tremendous influence on the modernization of kendō in the Meiji era."[21]

In 1856, the shogunate established the Kōbusho (Academy for Military Training) in response to the growing foreign threat, but, reflecting the uncertainty about the proper response to that threat, there was confusion about what should be taught in the school. What was the proper balance between traditional warfare and modern military strategy and tactics? Opting for compromise, the school taught both scientific gunnery and the martial arts. While fourteen instructors taught gunnery, swordsmanship was taught by a staff of eleven (and the use of the spear by ten). Rowing was also practiced at the Kōbusho for its potential military application. The debate over the curriculum ended in 1866 when the entire school was closed.[22]

During its short existence, however, the academy had an indirect and unintended influence on the transformation of swordsmanship into modern kendō. The competitive style of practice that had become popular in the late Tokugawa era was given official approval. Students wearing protective gear fought matches with bamboo swords. Their instructors came from a variety of schools of swordsmanship, which required agreement on the rules if there was to be any sort of regular competition among the students. Standardized rules and open competition and the public display of formerly esoteric techniques all contributed to the breakup of the old schools of swordsmanship and the formation of a new, more generally understood and practiced form of swordsmanship: kendō. The academy also contributed to the diffusion of the sport by standardizing the length of the bamboo sword to 3 feet 9 inches, which remains the official length to this day.

Two years after the 1866 closure of the shogunate's Academy for Military Training, the shogunate itself ceased to exist, destroyed by rebel forces from the great southern domains of Satsuma (now Kagoshima Prefecture) and Chōshū (now Yamaguchi Prefecture). The new government, for which the Emperor Meiji (1852–1912) was the figurehead, deprived the samurai of their traditional privilege of wearing swords in public and closed the urban fencing schools. Many fencing instructors were put out of work, and the future of swordsmanship looked quite bleak.

Enter Sakakibara Kenkichi. He had been a fencing instructor at the military academy, where he so impressed Shogun Tokugawa Iemochi (1846–1866) that he was appointed as his personal instructor. After the Meiji Restoration, Sakakibara was offered a job in the newly formed Tokyo Metropolitan Police, but, ever loyal to the shogunate he had served, he declined. He wanted to do something to help revive the martial arts community. He took his cue not from Western ideals of sport and physical education, as Kanō Jigorō was to do more than a decade later, but from something closer to hand: sumō. In 1872, he formed the Gekken Kaisha (Fencing Society) and held a public demonstration of the martial arts (to which he charged admission). "Sakakibara constructed a sumo-like ring, divided the participants into two teams (an east and a west side), and had an announcer . . . call the fencers to the center of the ring, say their names, and start the matches with the ritual opening of a fan, all in imitation of sumo practice."[23]

In some ways, Sakakibara reminds one less of a sumō elder and more of Richard Kyle Fox, the American entrepreneur and publisher of the *National Police Gazette*. For his first exhibition, Sakakibara hired well-known swordsmen from various schools and lured spectators with performances by a pair of English fencers and a number of women skilled in the use of the *naginata* (halberd). (Fox often sponsored combats in which female boxers and wrestlers proved that the "fair sex" was not as frail as commonly assumed.) Sakakibara's show was such a commercial success that other swordsmen quickly imitated him. By September, Tokyo alone had twenty martial arts companies eager to offer the populace displays of swordsmanship, equestrianism, and whatever else was commercially viable and not too likely to bring about the intervention of the police. Traditionalists were, and continue to be, horrified by the unabashed commercial exploitation of what they consider to be a more dignified way of life, but the art of the sword did, undeniably, experience a revival.

The Academy for Military Training and Sakakibara Kenkichi both contributed to kendō, as we know it. The Tokyo Metropolitan Police, who were organized in 1874, also played an important role. They helped to reorganize the myriad of different styles of swordsmanship into the unified form that eventually became modern kendō. In 1879, Chief of Police Kawaji Toshiyoshi recruited a number of fencers from various schools to instruct his men in their art. Unfortunately, these prominent swordsmen did not work well together, since each of them asserted the superiority of his own style. It was clearly undesirable to have some recruits learn one style and others another. Police authorities achieved a compromise by creating a synthesis of ten *kata* (practice moves), one from each major style. This work of synthesis was carried on by Kawaji's successor, Mishima Toshitsune.

This process of unification and standardization was completed by the Dai Nippon Butokukai (Greater Japan Martial Virtue Society), which was established in 1895 to preserve and propagate the nation's traditional martial arts. It was born in the intensely nationalistic mood of turn-of-the-century Japanese imperialism, an era marked by wars of conquest waged against the Chinese and the Russians. The Butokukai had its headquarters in Kyoto, next to the Heian shrine that was erected in 1895 to celebrate the founding of the city eleven hundred years earlier. The organization's first president was Prince Komatsu Akihito, a general in the army. The chairman was the governor of Kyoto Prefecture, Watanabe Chiaki, and the vice chairman was Mibu Motonaga, chief priest of the Heian shrine.

At the Butokukai's annual tournaments, which began in 1896, there were contests not only in kendō and archery but also in naginata (the halberd), *sōjutsu* (the spear), *bōjutsu* (the cudgel), and *kusarigama* (the ball-and-chain). From 1899 on, the tournament was held at the newly constructed Butokuden (Hall of Military Virtues). This structure was a copy of the building on the grounds of the imperial palace where sumō, archery, and equestrian ceremonies were held during the Heian period. By 1906, the Butokukai claimed 1,300,000 members. Five years later, there were 1,740,000 members and the organization had ample funds with which to propagate its nationalistic vision.[24]

"The Dai Nihon Butokukai was instrumental in establishing the standardized methods of teaching and practicing kendō that we know today."[25] All matches at the annual tournament had to be refereed. (A few "distinguished" fencers were excepted.) In 1912, a special committee of twenty-five leading fencers representing all parts of the country agreed upon a standard set of kata, the Dai Nippon Butokukai kendō kata. Kanō Jigorō, who had performed a similar role in the creation of jūdō, was the vice chairman of this committee. G. Cameron Hurst III concludes, "It would be difficult, then, to overestimate the role of the Dai Nihon Butokukai in preserving Japan's fencing tradition, consolidating its varied styles into a single nationwide form of kendō, and propagating it widely both in its own tournaments and through the school system."[26]

## ARCHERY

The awesome firepower of nineteenth-century European and American military technology gave the coup de grâce to the long bow as a weapon. Archery was briefly added to the curriculum of the Academy for Military Training, and there was even a short period in which someone in love with tradition persuaded the school's administration to include inuou-mono in the curriculum, but the academy dropped these sports in 1862. When that happened, Ogasawara Kanejirō, head of the preeminent Ogasawara school of archery, lost his instructor's position and the prestige that went with it. He complained indignantly that it was shortsighted to ignore a "weapon important since the Age of the Gods."[27]

His protests were in vain. The different forms of mounted archery quickly became cultural relics in the Meiji period. Inuomono died out completely, while yabusame continued to be performed on special occasions at a few major shrines around the country, "not really a sport," as Hurst carefully explains, "not quite a religious event, but part of a long tradition of archery in Japan with social, religious, and military aspects that a few people lovingly keep alive." Standing archery, however, continued its development as a sport while maintaining "the concern for character building that was part of the art from ancient times."[28]

Honda Toshizane (1836–1917), a Tokugawa house vassal, is credited with the modernization of Tokugawa archery by contributing to its standardization. Like fencing, archery had also in the course of centuries ramified into a myriad of schools, each with its own style and rituals. As was the case with fencing, inclusion in the Dai Nippon Butokukai stimulated the sport's enthusiasts to create some unity. Toshizane "created a new form of archery combining the practical shooting techniques of his own Chikurin-ha with the ritualistic elements of Ogasawara-ryū."[29] In 1921, the Butokukai took an additional step and introduced a ranking system into archery patterned after the one Kanō Jigorō had introduced into jūdō. In 1933 and 1934, the Butokukai standardized the kata into a single set of exercises. All in all, the Butokukai played an indispensable role in the development of archery as a viable twentieth-century sport, partly traditional, partly modern, widely popular.

## SUMŌ

Sumō also suffered a decline in popularity during the early years of Meiji, when people were infatuated with foreign ways and "things Japanese" were often shunned as "uncivilized." In the eyes of many, sumō seemed "embarrassingly premodern or feudalistic (*hōkenteki*),"[30] but sumō's situation was unlike archery's or fencing's. Sumō was a thoroughly commercialized professional spectator sport with broad popular appeal. The question for sumō was: how to keep the paying customers coming? The entrepreneurs who controlled the sport accomplished their task by adopting a dual policy. On the one hand, they continued to modernize the sport. On the other hand, they found ways to emphasize its connection with Japan's traditional past. Our present concern is with the modernization of sumō; the "invention of tradition" will be discussed in Chapter 6.[31]

During the Tokugawa period and into the twentieth century, sumō was held outdoors, and temporary wooden stands were constructed for each tournament and dismantled afterwards. The day's matches were postponed in the event of rain, and there were occasions when an entire month was required to complete ten days of matches. In 1909, a permanent, roofed, ferro-concrete building, the Kokugikan (National Sports Hall) was constructed. From that point on, sumō was free from the vagaries of the weather.

The organizational changes that sumō underwent in the Meiji period were less immediately visible than the Kokugikan, but they were extremely important. They culminated, in 1926, in the establishment of a national federation to govern professional sumō (now named the Japan Sumō Association). Legally, the association is a foundation (*zaidan hōjin*) registered with the Ministry of Education. Amateur sumō was also organized on a national basis. Two federations of college wrestlers were organized in 1920, one in Tokyo and the other in the Osaka area. They merged to form the All-Japan Collegiate Sumō Federation in 1932. The Japan Sumō Federation (Nihon sumō renmei), which is also dedicated to the amateur version of the sport, was founded in 1946.[32]

The most interesting and significant aspect of the modernization of sumō is probably the development of the championship system. It has always been obvious, in Japan as elsewhere, that some athletes are better than others. The traditional way to discover who was "the greatest" was for claimants to the title to challenge one another. In chivalric terms, one "threw down the gauntlet." It was not until the nineteenth century that European and American sports evolved from such more or less impromptu challenges to modernity's rationalized format of regularly scheduled competitions specifically designed to determine the best athlete or team. Sumō, too, evolved in this way.

From the middle of the eighteenth century, four regularly scheduled tournaments per year, each lasting approximately ten days, were staged in the three cities of Edo, Osaka, and Kyoto. Before the nineteenth century, spectators attending these tournaments apparently had little interest in comparing one wrestler's past performance with another's. It was not until the Meiji period that spectators began to evince interest in a wrestler's performance over the course of an entire tournament. In fact, the word "tournament," used here to translate the Japanese term *basho*, should not be taken to mean a series of matches climaxing in a final bout to determine a single winner. In a sumō tournament, wrestlers do not advance through rounds in the manner of tennis players at Wimbledon nor do they wrestle against all the other contestants in round-robin style.

Each wrestler has only one match per day and the tournament champion is the winner of the topmost division, the *makuuchi*.

| Sumō Divisions | |
|---|---|
| Makuuchi | Jonidan |
| Jūryō | Jonokuchi |
| Makushita | Maezumō |
| Sandamme | |

| Sumō Ranks Within the Makuuchi Division | |
|---|---|
| Yokozuna | Komusubi |
| Ōzeki | Maegashira |
| Sekiwake | |

It is difficult now to imagine sumō without this championship system. Which of the previously most successful wrestlers will win the next tournament is the focus of fan and media interest. Most sumō enthusiasts are surprised, therefore, when they learn that the concept of a tournament championship is a relatively recent innovation. In fact, it did not exist at all until well into the modern period. The long, complicated, and little known development of the championship system is a fascinating case study in the modernization of sumō.

In the Tokugawa period, the focus was still on individual matches. After a particularly thrilling match, excited fans often threw money or articles of clothing into the ring. The winning wrestler kept the cash and sold or pawned the clothes. In the Meiji period, new forms of appreciation and reward appeared, forerunners of today's championship system. Like the athletes of Europe and North America, wrestlers began to receive trophies and other prizes awarded for their performance over the course of an entire tournament rather than for victory in a single match. These awards were donated by private groups, which makes the precise origins of the practice difficult to document. Newspapers, which regularly sponsored baseball and other modern sports, were often the donors.

At first, there was ambiguity about exactly what it was that the wrestler had done to deserve his reward. Initially, trophies were presented to wrestlers who were undefeated, but undefeated records were not necessarily identical because there were two different kinds of draws and absences were not recorded as losses. It was not uncommon for more than one wrestler to finish a tournament without a defeat, in which case each received a trophy. For example, after a tournament in January 1889, Konishiki (a small fellow not to be confused with his huge twenti-eth-century namesake) was awarded a trophy by the Tokyo newspaper *Jiji shinpō* despite the fact that he had not won all of his matches. He had seven victories, a draw, and a match for which the decision had been deferred. Two undefeated lower-division contestants were also awarded trophies after they wrestled to a draw on the last day of the tournament. According to the newspaper, if no wrestler went undefeated, no trophy was awarded.

A shift in the criteria for awarding trophies occurred in 1900, pro-ducing the kind of tournament champion that we now take for granted. In January of that year, Osaka's *Mainichi Shimbun* offered to award a *keshōmawashi* (ornamental apron) to an undefeated wrestler of the makuuchi division. If no wrestler survived the tournament undefeated, the apron was to be awarded to the wrestler with the fewest losses. If two or more men tied for the fewest losses, then the prize was to be given to the man who defeated the greatest number of higher-ranked opponents.[33] These new criteria provided for a single champion.

It is significant that it was a newspaper that came up with this inno-vation. Relatively few sumō fans had the opportunity actually to attend a major match. Before the advent of radio and television, they depended on newspapers and magazines for coverage of the sport. Interest in the best record over an entire tournament was reflected in and greatly stim-ulated by the modern print media. And, since the need for heroes seems to be universal, it was unquestionably sound economic strategy for news-papers and magazines to boost circulation by ostentatiously presenting trophies to larger-than-life sumō champions.[34]

Today's newspapers print a daily *hoshitorihyō*, a table containing the names of the wrestlers on one axis and the days of the tournament on the other.[35] The results of each wrestler's matches are recorded in the hoshitorihyō. From this table, one can tell at a glance who has fallen, lit-erally, out of contention and who still has a chance to become the tour-nament champion. The first version of today's hoshitorihyō appeared in 1884, at approximately the same time that American newspapers began to provide their readers with the box scores of baseball games; but it was published after the last day of the tournament, and served only to sum up a tournament that had already concluded. It was not until 1900 that newspaper readers were able to follow a favorite wrestler's ups and downs through the duration of the tournament. On May 25, the *Yorozu chōhō* published a hoshitorihyō with the following introduction:

> Results to date: the records of the main wrestlers as of the seventh day can be gleaned from this paper's daily coverage of individual matches. To summarize, Araiwa . . . is leading both sides. Hitachiyama is second, then come Umenotani, Ōzutsu, Hōō, etc. The details are as follows.

The daily hoshitorihyō was the quantified equivalent, in print, of the excited television sportscaster who shouts the names of the horses as they gallop down the home stretch.

Although the *Mainichi shimbun*'s criteria for the award of a trophy were an implicit statement about championship, it was not until 1909 that championships determined on the basis of quantified achievement were regularly designated by the press. That year, the *Jiji shinpō* began to award its trophy to the individual wrestler with the best overall record. (The newspaper also provided a large portrait to be hung in the newly opened Kokugikan.) At first, the honor accorded to the individual champion by the *Jiji shinpō* was ignored by rival newspapers. An innovation introduced that same year by the Sumō Association seemed almost designed to draw attention away from the individual champion. The association instituted competition between the two sides, the East and the West. Wrestlers from one side met only opponents from the other side, and at the end of the tournament the side with the most wins was declared the victor. That side received a flag to symbolize its victory and one of its wrestlers—the one below the top two ranks with the best record—was chosen to carry the flag in a victory parade around the city. Press coverage often emphasized the victorious side and its flag-bearer rather than the individual champion.

In 1926, the Sumō Association finally decided to recognize individual champions, and certain changes were made in the rules to eliminate ambiguity in determining outcomes. Previously, not all matches resulted in clear-cut victories and defeats. Five judges sit around the ring to monitor the matches, and any one of them (or any of the four on-deck wrestlers) can question the referee's decision. When that happens, the five judges all climb into the ring to discuss the decision. Before 1926, when the judges were unable to agree about the validity of an objection to the referee's decision, the match was declared *azukari* (no decision). If a match appeared stalemated, it could be halted and declared a *hiki-*

*wake* (draw). When one wrestler failed to appear, the match was recorded as a *yasumi* (absence) for both men. Such outcomes were not at all rare. For example, about one-third of the matches on the hoshitorihyō for May 25, 1900, were draws, no-decisions, or absences. These unsatisfactory outcomes complicated the comparison of records necessary to determine a tournament champion. Which record is better: nine wins and one loss or eight wins, one draw, and one no-decision?

Beginning with the January tournament of 1926, azukari and hikiwake were eliminated and matches with disputed outcomes were immediately refought. Those ending in a draw were rescheduled for the same day or for a later date. It is now as unthinkable for a match to be left undecided as it is for the NCAA's basketball tournament to end in a draw. If the judges cannot agree, the wrestlers grapple again and again until a clear victor can take his bows. (In May 1988, for instance, a bout in the top division required three rematches.) Finally, beginning in March 1928, "no shows" were declared forfeitures. A wrestler who withdraws from a scheduled match is now given an "uncontested loss" and his opponent can relax with an "uncontested win."

The abolition of these three outcomes meant that each match now ends in a clear-cut decision: a win for one man, a loss for the other. The wrestler with the most wins and the fewest losses over the course of the tournament strides to the fore as the undisputed tournament champion. Since the tournament is not an elimination or round-robin affair, however, two or more wrestlers may tie for the best won-loss record. When the Sumō Association first confronted this problem in 1926, it was decided to give the cup to the higher-ranked wrestler. In 1947, a "playoff" was instituted, adding drama and eliminating ambiguity.

The championship system and the hoshitorihyō are both manifestations of the desire to have objective measures of performance. This desire can also be seen in the sumō press from around 1915, when the journal *Sumō sekai* began to use statistics not merely to describe but also to evaluate a wrestler's achievement. An article discussing the wrestler Ōtori's possible promotion to the rank of *yokozuna* (grand champion) compared the statistics of his performance with those of the popular yokozuna Konishiki.[36] While it is true that sumō cannot generate baseball's plethora of statistics, sumō magazines now compile all sorts of factual information on each and every wrestler. That information includes statistics on the number of tournaments a wrestler has participated in, the percentage of his wins in the upper division, and the percentage of his wins overall.

Whenever quantification becomes pervasive, the quest for records—the ultimate characteristic of modern sports—seems to follow. Although sumō, unlike track-and-field competition, is not a precisely quantifiable "cgs" (centimeter, gram, second) sport, it does generate plenty of records, and the relative significance of these records is debated among sumō fans just as it is among fans of other sports. Citing statistics to prove their case, sumō fans can claim that their idol is the champion of champions, the greatest sumō wrestler of all time. In January 1987, for instance, the undistinguished but durable Ōshio was only twenty-three wins away from the retired yokozuna Kitanoumi's record of 951 victories. How, asked the latter's admirers, can Ōshio be said to threaten Kitanoumi's record when 804 of the great Kitanoumi's wins were in the top makuuchi division—compared to a paltry 335 by Ōshio?[37] Both wrestlers were subsequently surpassed by Chiyonofuji, who amassed 1045 wins.

If the print media have played an important role in the modernization of sumo, which they certainly have, then the electronic media have as well. When radio broadcasting began in 1925, stations expressed an immediate interest in broadcasting sumō. The leaders of the Sumō Association, however, were leery of the new medium. Like the officials of other sport bodies around the world, they were fearful of economic catastrophe. Why should fans pay good money to crowd into the Kokugikan if they are able to sit comfortably at home and listen to the radio? Broadcasters persisted and the Sumō Association reluctantly agreed to allow radio coverage on a trial basis for the January tournament of 1928. Contrary to the association's fears, radio seemed to increase rather than decrease the desire to be present at the bouts. The stadium was packed, and radio broadcasts became a regular and popular feature.[38]

To accommodate the new medium, however, there had to be adjustments in the traditional way that the matches were held. Before each match, the two wrestlers perform *shikiri*, the long ritual preparation for what often prove to be very short bouts. During shikiri, they crouch in the center of the ring, glare at one another, stand, return to their corners for another handful of salt to throw upon the ground, move back to the center of the ring, and crouch again for more baleful glaring. Traditionally, shikiri continued indefinitely, until both men were ready to charge and grapple. Radio broadcasts, however, have an allotted time frame. To ensure that the day's matches finished before the end of the broadcast, wrestlers were told to limit shikiri to ten minutes, which—with a glare at the broadcaster—they did.

In fact, it took some time for the wrestlers to become accustomed to the idea of a curtailed warm-up ritual. On the first day, anxious not to exceed the ten-minute limit, most wrestlers cut short their shikiri and started their matches so quickly that the entire program moved at a furious pace. The radio broadcast, scheduled to carry only the last and most important matches, was supposed to begin at 5:20 P.M., but the horrified promoters realized that the last wrestlers were liable to have finished their match before the broadcast even began. Although five long intermissions were hurriedly introduced, the first day of broadcasts consisted of only the last match, which ended at 5:40. On the second day of the tournament, the broadcast was started earlier. This did not solve the problem. The wrestlers soon reverted to their old ways and indulged themselves in extended shikiri. By the time the top-ranked wrestlers had stepped into the ring, the station had already moved on to its next scheduled broadcast.[39] It was some time before the wrestlers and the broadcasters were, metaphorically, on the same wavelength.

Although one might have expected that the arrival of television in the 1950s made it possible to return to longer shikiri, which are certainly more interesting to watch than to hear about, this was not the case. The time limit for the upper division has been reduced to four minutes, and the Sumō Association smoothly manages the progression of matches so that they usually end a few minutes before the 6:00 P.M. conclusion of the day's broadcast. From the fan's point of view, however, managerial efficiency has its drawbacks. Before the time limit was imposed, each shikiri was potentially the start of the match, and tension built as one shikiri followed another. In our more programmed age, the ritual has become routine, the match begins when it is supposed to, and the shikiri tends to be, for the wrestlers and spectators alike, mere posturing.

## INDIGENOUS SPORTS IN JAPANESE PHYSICAL EDUCATION

In 1883, five years after its establishment, the Ministry of Education instructed the National Institute of Gymnastics to investigate the suitability of fencing and jūjutsu for the schools. The institute convened a committee of martial artists and medical doctors who concluded after a year and a half of deliberation that jūjutsu and kenjutsu "did have physical and spiritual value" but also that "they were dangerous, violent, and detrimental to growth and health. The [committee's] recommendation was that these martial arts should not be taught in school."[40] The decision is understandable when one considers the undeveloped and fragmented state of the martial arts at the time. What respectable Meiji-era bureaucrats wanted Japan's newly established public schools to teach the nation's children techniques whose mythical source was a god in the form of a monkey? Had the nation not entered an age of "civilization and enlightenment"?

In 1896, in a period of warfare and resurgent nationalism, one year after the founding of the Butokukai, the Ministry of Education once again investigated the curricular suitability of jūdō and kendō and once again concluded that they should not be regular school subjects. They were acceptable for strong, healthy males over sixteen, but only as extracurricular activities. In 1905, the Committee to Investigate Gymnastics and Games came to the same conclusion. Western-style gymnastics and physical education "were deemed more educational and scientific."[41]

In 1908, the Diet intervened in the debate over jūdō and kendō. An act of parliament ordered the Ministry of Education to revise its regulations and to introduce the two martial arts into the middle-school and upper-school curricula. The reluctant Ministry took three years to consult with school officials nationwide, but jūdō and fencing were finally added to the "gymnastics" curriculum in 1911—as electives. "Thus the movement to have kendō (still referred to as gekken in government orders) and judo taught regularly in schools took the entire Meiji period."[42]

# 5

# Japan at the Olympics: 1912–1940

W hen Pierre de Coubertin summoned the youth of the world to appear in Athens in 1896 to participate in the Olympic Games, the call was answered by the young men of Europe and North America. No Asian nation sent its representatives to Greece to compete in the first games of the modern era, nor were Asian athletes present at the games held in Paris, St. Louis, and London. This was a cause of great concern to Coubertin, who wanted the Olympics to be a truly global phenomenon. Since he had no contacts with Japanese sportsmen, he asked the French ambassador in Tokyo to select someone to become a member of the International Olympic Committee. In 1909, Kanō Jigorō, the man who had drawn upon Japan's traditional martial arts to create the modern sport of jūdō, was chosen to "represent the IOC in Japan" (which was the formulation preferred by Coubertin).[1]

In 1910, the IOC formally invited Japan to participate in the "Games of the Fifth Olympiad," scheduled to be held in Stockholm in 1912. This was an important recognition of modern Japan's place in what John Bale and Joseph Maguire refer to as "the global sports arena."[2] In accordance with its rules, the IOC asked Kanō to establish a National Olympic Committee. Kanō consulted with the Ministry of Education about forming an NOC to select athletes and finance their journey to Stockholm, but the Ministry was uncooperative. He then approached a private body, the Japan Physical Education Society (Nippon Taiiku Kai), only to suffer a second rebuff. Ever resourceful, Kanō decided in 1911 to create his own organization, the Dai Nippon Taiiku Kyōkai (Greater Japan Physical Education Association),[3] and became its first president. The aim of Kanō's JPEA was not merely participation in the Olympics. The organization was also determined to "promote *taiiku* [sport and physical education] among the Japanese people."[4]

The first order of business, however, was preparation for Japan's Olympic debut in Stockholm. The JPEA decided to send a two-man team: sprinter Mishima Yahiko and long-distance runner Kanaguri Shizō. Traveling by the Trans-Siberian Railroad, Ōmori Heizō accompanied the pair to Stockholm as team manager.[5]

In competition with the world's fastest runners, the two Japanese athletes did poorly. In his 100-meter heat, Mishima tied his personal record but nonetheless finished last. He was last again in his 200-meter heat. He managed to finish second in his 400-meter heat, but, since there was only one other runner, this was also last place. Although this 2nd-place finish qualified him for the semifinals, he defaulted to avoid further embarassment. Kanaguri's performance was an even greater disappointment. He lost consciousness when he paused for a rest in the middle of the marathon. He was so humiliated by his failure that he hesitated to return to Japan. He brooded for decades over his "disgrace" before he discovered an appropriate way to overcome his sense of shame. He returned to Stockholm, found the exact place where he had fallen asleep, and finished the race with an elapsed time of 55 years, 8 months, 6 days, and 32 minutes.[6]

The response of the JPEA to the disappointments of 1912 was to expand its activities and to plan for better results in 1916, when the Olympics were to be held in Berlin. More attention was given to disciplines that had not been emphasized, which sometimes led to mishaps. When the javelin was first introduced at a JPEA-sponsored meet, it "flew into the military band, though fortunately no one was hurt."[7]

In 1913, Kanō was invited by Elwood Brown, an American missionary, to send a team to Manila to compete against athletes from the Philippines and China in the first YMCA-sponsored "Asian Olympic Games," but Kanō was not interested in regional competitions and he objected to the use of the word "Olympic" for an event not sanctioned by the IOC. The Japanese athletes who competed in Manila were not sent by the JPEA.[8]

World War I, which began in August 1914, forced the cancellation of the 1916 Olympics, but there was no interruption of the Asian games, which took place in Shanghai in 1915. The name of the event was officially changed to the "Far Eastern Championship Games," which presumably removed one of Kanō's objections. The JPEA joined the Far Eastern Athletic Association in 1917 and hosted the games that were held that year in Tokyo. The Japanese team had done poorly in Manila and Shanghai, but they did better with the "home-court advantage" and triumphed in the third games, which "gave a great impetus to Japanese athletics." The JPEA withdrew from the FEAA in 1919, shortly before the fourth Far Eastern Games were to begin in Manila. The probable reason for the JPEA's withdrawal was that Kanō wanted to concentrate the organization's energies on the 1920 Olympic Games. There was, however, considerable support for the Far Eastern Games within the JPEA. Members who disagreed with Kanō's leadership supported the team that went independently to Manila for the games. By 1921, the dissidents were in the majority. The JPEA rejoined the FEAA and Kanō resigned his position as JPEA president.[9]

Participation in the Far Eastern Games, which lasted only twenty years, was limited mainly to athletes from China, Japan, and the Philippines. Elwood Brown had envisioned the Far Eastern Games as a showplace for harmony among nations, but they were no more effective as a force for peace than the Olympics were. Within a few years of the tenth and final games, which were held in Manila in 1934, Japan invaded China and conquered the Philippines. The Far Eastern Games did, however, contribute to the development of sport in the participating countries. Women's sports in Japan received a significant boost when women's swimming, tennis, and volleyball were included as "open events" in the sixth games, which took place in Osaka in 1923. Men's basketball, soccer, and volleyball also profited greatly through inclusion in the Far Eastern Games.

When the Olympics resumed in 1920, Japan was represented by a fifteen-man team. The eleven track-and-field athletes who competed in Antwerp were coached by the YMCA's Franklin Brown. Most of the runners were eliminated in the initial heats, but Kanaguri Shizō did considerably better than he had done in 1912, managing to finish the marathon in 16th place with a respectable time of 2 hours, 48 minutes, 45.4 seconds. Three other Japanese marathoners came in 20th, 21st, and 24th. Neither of the two swimmers advanced beyond the first heats, but the experience of Antwerp helped popularize the crawl stroke in Japan.[10] In tennis, the picture was considerably brighter. Kumagai Kazuya reached the finals in singles and in doubles (with Kashio Seiichirō). Optimists looked upon the silver medals as an omen of future victories.[11]

If the expedition to Antwerp was a limited athletic success, it was a financial fiasco. The JPEA badly miscalculated the costs of the journey and was unable to pay for the team's return. Two industrial giants, Mitsui and Mitsubishi, provided the $15,000 necessary to bring home the stranded team. The embarrassment was so great that the Japanese government was persuaded, in 1921, to begin to subsidize the JPEA. The subsidy was increased in 1924, when the government's contribution of $28,700 was sufficient to relieve the JPEA of economic worry.[12]

That year saw many other initiatives: the inauguration of the annual Meiji Shrine Games, the creation of a national institute for research in physical education, and the proclamation of November 3 as "National Physical Fitness Day." Considering these initiatives and summarizing the results of the 1924 Olympics, which took place in Paris, Harold James Olson concluded that Japan was well on its way as "a formidable opponent in international sport."[13]

To those 1924 games Japan sent a team of twenty-eight athletes who competed in four events. Of the eight track-and-field specialists, only Oda Mikio progressed to the finals. With a triple jump of 14.27 meters, Oda had won that event at the sixth Far Eastern Games, which had been held in Osaka the year before. In Olympic competition he placed a disappointing sixth. The $4 \times 400$-meter relay team withdrew from the race as did the three runners who were supposed to compete in the 10,000-meter race. The three Japanese marathoners were among the fifty-eight who failed to finish. The swimmers were more successful. Takaishi Katsuo took fifth place in the 1500-meter freestyle with a time of 22 minutes, 10.4 seconds. He was also a member of the 800-meter relay team, which came in a very respectable fourth (10 minutes, 15.2 seconds). There was one bronze medal, secured by freestyle wrestler Naitō Katsutoshi, who was at the time a student at Pennsylvania State University.[14] Imamura Yoshio believes that the 1924 games provided a firm basis for Japan's future successes in jumping and swimming.[15] The 1924 team was equipped by the Mizuno company, which has since become one of the world's largest suppliers of sporting goods.[16]

In 1928, three years after it was founded, the Nihon Rikujō Kyōgi Renmei (Japan Amateur Athletic Federation) took over the JPEA's membership in the International Amateur Athletic Federation, the international sports federation governing track and field.[17]

In line with the liberal-democratic tendencies of the late Taishō and early Shōwa periods, a federation to promote women's sports was formed in 1926. At the Fifth Meiji Shrine Games, which took place in May 1928, two hundred female athletes competed in a wide array of sports. In addition to women's gymnastics and track-and-field, both of which were to appear for the first time in the 1928 Olympics, that year's Meiji Shrine

Games included contests in archery, riding, rowing, swimming, lawn tennis, table tennis, basketball, field hockey, and volleyball. Hitomi Kinue's performance at these games, which also served as the Olympic trials, was sensational. On May 5, she ran the 100 meters in 12.4 seconds, set an unofficial world record of 59.0 seconds for 400 meters, broke the national high-jump record with a leap of 1.43 meters, and won the javelin. The next day she reached 5.98 meters in the long jump and ran the 100 meters in 12.2 seconds; both achievements were unofficial world records.[18]

Hitomi's spectacular performance raised hopes for similar success at the 1928 Olympics. Once the Amsterdam games had begun, however, there were many gloomy moments. The inexperienced rowers, appearing at their first Olympics, did poorly. The coxed four, for instance, finished 10 lengths behind the Polish winners. Apart from Yamada Kanematsu's 4th place finish in the marathon, the runners had little reason to boast. Even Hitomi seemed outclassed. She ran 4th in the 100-meter semi-finals and was eliminated from competition. Shattered by this unaccustomed failure, she sobbed her way through a sleepless night and then surprised her teammates by announcing that she intended to compete in the 800 meters, a distance that she had almost never run. (A last-minute entry was possible in those less bureaucratic days.) She astonished everyone by sprinting to a silver medal. Her time of 2 minutes 17.6 seconds was only eight-tenths of a second behind that of the winner, Germany's Lina Radke. Japanese spectators wept tears of joy.[19]

There were other occasions for jubilation. Oda Mikio and Nanbu Chūhei, neither of whom reached the finals of the long jump, were 1st and 4th in the triple jump. Oda's triple jump of 15.21 meters was nearly a meter better than his effort at the Far Eastern Games and it brought him Japan's first gold medal in Olympic competition. A second gold came when Tsuruta Yoshiyuki swam the 200-meter breaststroke in the Olympic-record time of 2 minutes, 48.8 seconds. The swimmers garnered a second and a third medal: silver for the 800-meter relay team (which lost to an American team anchored by the future Tarzan, Johnny Weissmuller) and bronze for the veteran swimmer Takaishi Katsuo in the 100-meter freestyle.[20]

The political background of the 1932 Olympics was dark. Japan's seizure of Manchuria in 1931 and its subsequent condemnation by the League of Nations had cast a shadow over Japan's relations with the United States. Many Japanese were apprehensive about their reception in Los Angeles, where they were among the first teams to arrive. They need not have worried. In the weeks before the start of competition, the impeccable behavior of the Japanese athletes at banquets and other public occasions impressed their American hosts. Many of those whose first reaction had been to treat the athletes as representatives of a hostile nation were won over by the athletes' stellar performance once the games began.

Looking forward to 1932, a prominent American journalist, Bill Henry, had predicted, "The Japanese [swimmers] are certain to be strong."[21] His confident assertion turned out to be an understatement. Dick Schaap's account recaptures the amazement of the moment:

> The Japanese men suddenly emerged as the best swimmers in the world. Four different Japanese won individual events, and three of them broke Olympic records; their 800-meter relay quartet cracked the Olympic mark by an amazing thirty-eight seconds.[22] Even more amazing was the youthfulness of the flying fish from Japan: Kusuo Kitamura, who won the strenuous 1,500-meter free style, was only fourteen; Masaji Kiyokawa, the 100-meter back-stroke champion, was sixteen; and Yasuji Miyazaki, the 100-meter free style champion, was seventeen.[23]

In every one of the men's races, three Japanese reached the finals. The men's team won eleven of sixteen possible medals.[24] The women did less well. Wonders were expected of Maehata Hideko, who set national records while still in elementary school. She broke the Olympic record in her heat of the 200-meter breaststroke and swam even faster in the final race—only to be edged out by Australia's Claire Dennis.[25]

Although some American journalists trivialized the achievements of the "little brown men," others expressed their surprise at these unprecedented performances. Those who evinced surprise had not paid close attention to the intensive Japanese preparations for the 1932 games. The reporters were probably unaware that the Japanese had established a special camp, after the previous games, to train elite swimmers for Los Angeles. They seem also to have overlooked the results of a 1931 dual meet in which the Japanese swimmers had outscored their American opponents 40–23. And American observers failed to realize the degree of determination manifested by the early arrival of the Japanese team, which had reached Los Angeles a full six weeks before the start of the games.[26]

Other members of the 131-person team (115 men and 16 women) did well. The redoubtable jumpers Oda and Nanbu came to the games as world-record holders for the triple jump and the long jump, both records having been set at the Meiji Shrine Stadium on October 27,

1931.[27] At Los Angeles, Oda was recovering from an injury and was unable to do better than 12th place in the triple jump, but Nanbu won the event (and broke Oda's record by 14 centimeters). Nanbu also managed to win a bronze in the long jump. In the pole vault, there was a new star: Nishida Shūhei came in second to America's William Miller, who broke the world's record. Baron Nishi Takeichi, mounted on Uranus, was the popular winner of the equestrians' *Prix des Nations.* (He died in World War II; among his personal effects was a hair from Uranus.)[28]

Apart from Nanbu and Nishida, no one on the track-and-field team placed better than fourth, but even Takenaka Shōichirō, who was lapped in the 5,000-meter race, escaped the humiliation of the hapless water polo team, which gave up thirty-seven goals in three matches and failed even once to penetrate their opponents' defense.[29] The field hockey team placed second to India, but the luster of their silver medals was somewhat dimmed by the fact that the American team was the only other participant in the tournament.[30]

All in all, the Japanese had good reason to be proud of their team's achievements. Although Japanese athletes had done poorly against the Chinese in 1913 at the Far Eastern Games, they were now far superior to their mainland rivals. Indeed, the Chinese team at the 1932 Olympics consisted of four officials and a lone, far outclassed sprinter, Liu Changchun.[31]

The Japan Broadcasting Corporation, known by its Japanese acronym NHK, planned live radio broadcasts of the games in Los Angeles. They were stymied, however, because NBC and the U.S. Olympic Committee were unable to agree on a fee for broadcasting rights, and the USOC banned all live broadcasts. NHK decided to offer its listeners "lifelike" broadcasts (*jikkan hōsō*). The announcer watched the event at the stadium and was then driven by automobile to an NBC affiliate some fifteen minutes away. There he re-created the event for broadcast. His re-creation was sent by cable to San Francisco, then by short-wave transmission across the Pacific Ocean to Tokyo, where the frequency was converted and the broadcast transmitted to the rest of the country. Japan was the only country in which the games were broadcast in such a technologically impressive manner. (In the United States, radio coverage of the games was limited to regular news programs.) The Japanese broadcasts were quite popular—even when the re-creation was longer than the event itself. It is said that the announcer took nearly a minute to report the 100-meter dash, which lasted—in "real" time—less than 11 seconds.[32]

In 1933, two years after the IOC had accepted Berlin's bid to host the 1936 games, Adolf Hitler came to power as Germany's National Socialist chancellor. After brief hesitation, the IOC accepted the anti-Semitic regime's promise not to discriminate against German athletes of Jewish descent, but there was well-founded skepticism about Nazi promises and there were calls—especially in the United States—for a boycott of the 1936 Olympics. Since Japan's military leaders were then bringing their country into an alliance with Germany, the Japanese government was emphatically opposed to the idea of an Olympic boycott. The communist-sponsored "Workers' Olympics" planned for Barcelona as an alternative to the "Nazi Olympics" were hardly mentioned in the Japanese press.[33] The international boycott movement failed, but irreconcilable ideological differences remained and the months preceding the 1936 Olympics were a time of heightened political tension.

In Japan, junior army officers attempted a coup d'état on February 26, 1936, assassinating several leading political figures. The guilty officers were arrested, but they succeeded in intimidating the government and increasing the influence of the military. Martial law was declared in Tokyo and not lifted until July, the month before the games were to begin in Berlin.[34]

With Tokyo's bid to host the 1940 Olympics very much in mind, the Japanese government appropriated $87,000 to send no fewer than 161 male and seventeen female athletes to Berlin.[35] The largest and the most successful contingents were the track-and-field team and the swimmers and divers. As usual, the Japanese were better in the field events than in the races. Tajima Naoto won the triple jump with a world record of 16 meters even. Teammate Harada Masao was second. Tajima won an additional medal when he placed third in the long jump. The final moments of the pole vault were especially dramatic. The event lasted far longer than anyone expected. Summer days in northern Germany are long, but the finalists were still vaulting when night fell and the last attempts were made under artificial light. When it was over, Nishida Shūhei and Ōe Sueo finished second and third behind the American vaulter Earle Meadows. Since the two Japanese had cleared the same height, they were said to have had their silver and bronze medals cut in half and then rewelded so that each had an equal share of the two metals.[36]

For observers who were conscious of political implications, the marathon was even more dramatic. The race, which is one of the high points of Leni Riefenstahl's famed documentary film of the 1936 games, was close. When it was over, the huge electric scoreboard in Berlin's Olympic Stadium flashed the name of the winner—KITEI SON—and

Japan's rising-sun flag was hoisted to the top of the flagpole. The victor, however, resented that the German officials had been given the Japanese pronunciation of his name. Sohn Kee-Chung, as he was known in Korean, felt robbed of his identity by the Japanese annexation of his country (which had occurred in 1910). He swore never again to run under the Japanese flag.[37]

The swimming and diving team was almost as successful as it had been in 1932. In five different individual events, a trio of Japanese men reached the finals, many of them bettering the Olympic record on the way.[38] In all, the swimmers garnered four gold, two silver, and five bronze medals.[39] Hamuro Tetsuo and Terada Noboru won their races (the 200-meter backstroke and the 1,500-meter freestyle). In the 800-meter relay, Yūsa Masanori, Sugiura Shigeo, Taguchi Masaharu, and Arai Shigeo won a third gold in the world-record time of 8 minutes, 51.5 seconds. The women were less successful, but Maehata Hideko grasped the gold that had eluded her in Los Angeles. She set an Olympic record and defeated Germany's Martha Genenger in the 200-meter breaststroke.

The live broadcast of the finals of the women's 200-meter breast-stroke became a classic of Japanese sports journalism. NHK had two daily live broadcasts from Berlin, at 6:30 A.M. for 30 minutes and at 11:00 P.M. for one hour. Some of the events were covered live, and the rest were recorded for the scheduled broadcast times. The finals of the women's 200-meter breaststroke were set to start at 4:00 P.M. Berlin time, which was midnight in Japan. This, however, was the time the broadcast was scheduled to end. The announcer, Kasai Sansei, knowing that Maehata had a chance for the gold and excited by the buildup to the finals, shouted into the mike, "Don't turn off the switch! It's time for the end of the broadcast, but don't turn off the switch!" Listeners in Japan thought he meant for them not to turn off their radios, but he was really begging the technicians of NHK and the bureaucrats of the Ministry of Communication not to cut him off the air. They did not. Kasai was allowed to continue. As the race neared the finish and Maehata struggled to maintain her narrow lead, Kasai lost his composure and began rooting for her, shouting, "Maehata gambare! Gambare! Gambare! [Come on, Maehata! Come on! Come on!]" When Maehata won by six-tenths of a second, she became a national hero, and Kasai's broadcast was the talk of the country. Some of the talk was critical. The broadcast did not convey enough information about the race. What was Maehata's time? What about the other swimmers? Kasai had said Maehata was "in danger" but had not specified whether she was slowing down or her opponent was

spurting. How unprofessional! To most of those who had listened breath-
lessly, none of the criticisms mattered. The excitement created by the
broadcast was real, and the newspapers the next day lavished praise on
Kasai as well as on Maehata. He was said by the *Yomiuri shimbun* to have
become—through the broadcast of that one event—"Japan's Kasai."[40]

It was not enough for the Japanese that their Olympic athletes had
competed successfully on equal terms with the world's best. It was necessary, if Japan was to be recognized as a modern nation, that Tokyo be
entrusted to do what Paris and London and Berlin had done, namely, to
host the quadrennial festival. This was an ambition cherished by Kanō
Jigorō during his twenty-nine years on the International Olympic Committee and shared by Count Soyeshima Michimasa, who was elected to
the IOC in 1934. At the IOC's 35th Session, which took place in Berlin's
Hotel Adlon just before the start of the 1936 games, Kanō and Soyeshima
ably presented Tokyo's bid to host the 1940 games. Although Helsinki
was a strong contender, Tokyo won thirty-six of the sixty-three votes cast.
At that session, a third Japanese member of the IOC was elected, Tokugawa Iesato, the adopted son of the last Tokugawa shogun, Yoshinobu.
He became the director of the organizing committee.[41]

In the end, however, there were no games for Tokugawa to organize.
The poet Saijō Yaso had been at the 1936 games, about which he wrote
several poems for publication in Japan. In an article, he related a poignant
encounter. Just as Saijō was leaving the country, a young German poet
told him, "I'd like to be able four years from now to visit your country
for the Tokyo Olympics, traveling around and writing poetry as you have
done, but, regrettably, by that time, both your country and mine will
probably be hosting an Olympics of artillery and machine guns." Saijō
concluded his article, "I pray that these words do not come true," but, as
we now know, they did.[42]

By March 1938, when the IOC met in Cairo for its 37th Session,
Japan had already invaded China and the Chinese and British members
of the IOC were calling for a boycott of the 1940 games. The IOC, which
had accepted the Nazi regime's hypocritical promises to obey the Olympic
Charter, saw no reason to revise the decision made in Berlin. "The question of war and peace," wrote Hajo Bernett, "was seen by the IOC . . . as
a pragmatic matter, a mere organizational problem."[43] The "organizational problem" became acute when the Japanese military decided early
in 1938 that it was unwise to deflect the nation's economic resources
from the military effort in China. That spring, Soyeshima confided his
worries to IOC President Henri Baillet-Latour and suggested to the

other two Japanese members of the committee—Kanō and Tokugawa—that they accept the inevitable cancellation of their plans. Although Prime Minister Konoe Fumimaru continued to reassure the organizing committee and the IOC that the government fully expected the games to take place as scheduled, the ultimate decision was not his to make. Minister of the Army Sugiyama Hajime informed Konoe that it was inadvisable to stage the games. Konoe complied with the army's wishes and the *Japan Advertiser* revealed on July 15 that the government had decided to "request" that the organizers of the 1940 Olympics renounce the games. The organizers did as requested. Soyeshima expressed helpless regret to his colleagues and resigned from the IOC. Kanō Jigorō was spared the humiliation and the frustration of his dreams; he had died of pneumonia on May 4, 1938, on his way home from the IOC's Cairo Session.[44]

# 6

# From Taishō Democracy to Japanese Fascism

## POLITICS

In a study of Japanese physical education "under Fascism," Irie Katsumi argues that turn-of-the-century Japanese nationalism was xenophobic and imperialistic.[1] The expansionist wars against China (1894–1895) and Russia (1904–1905), the annexation of Korea (1910), and the seizure of Germany's colonies in the Pacific (1914) can certainly be cited in support of Irie's characterization. Then came what most historians, including Irie, commonly refer to as "Taishō democracy," an era characterized by relatively liberal attitudes and institutions. Political parties challenged the oligarchs who had governed Japan from the start of the Meiji period. In 1918, Hara Kei became the first prime minister to come to office from the Diet's parliamentary majority. In the 1920s, the leaders of Japan's political parties were allowed to serve in the cabinet (along with representatives of the army and navy). Restrictions on (male) suffrage were reduced and finally, in 1925, eliminated. There were cultural shifts as well. Young men expressed enthusiasm for American jazz. The *moga* (an abbreviation of the English phrase "modern girls") bobbed their hair, wore cloche hats, and followed the latest in Parisian fashion. Both sexes were entranced by Hollywood movies.[2]

The Manchurian "incident" of 1931 marked a fateful turn in Japanese history. Without the authorization or even the knowledge of the government in Tokyo, on the night of September 18, an attack was launched upon the Chinese garrison at Mukden by two colonels stationed in the Guandong Leased Territory that had passed from Russian into Japanese hands in 1905.[3] The "justification" for the attack was the claim that the Chinese had attempted to destroy the tracks of the South Manchuria Railroad, which was owned by Japanese entrepreneurs. In fact, the damage was done in secret by Japanese officers. Widening its assault, the Guandong Army ignored the appeals of Prime Minister Wakatsuki Reijirō. His liberal government fell and the somewhat more conservative Inukai Tsuyoshi became prime minister. His efforts to restrain the army and to preserve parliamentary democracy ended in his assassination on May 15, 1932. He was followed by Saitō Makoto, who accepted the army's conquest of Manchuria as a fait accompli. Whatever Japan's intellectuals might have thought, there was apparently "national euphoria over the seizure of Manchuria."[4] Condemnation of this conquest by the League of Nations in Geneva did little more than to convince Japan's political leaders that military action was, in the last analysis, the only way to secure the nation's interest.

## AMATEUR SPORTS

Imamura Yoshio has neatly summarized the two competing views of sport during the Taishō period (1912–1926). In one view, sport was an end in itself, to be pursued for its own intrinsic pleasure, and whatever positive results accrued for the body and soul (and nation) were extrinsic. In the other, sport was a means to strengthen the nation through improving the physical condition and moral character of its people. The former view was probably prevalent, but, as the nation changed course and began its march toward war, this liberal, individualistic, autotelic approach to sport was abandoned, and a militaristic, collectivist, instrumentalist view of sport became predominant.[5]

The Taishō period saw a rapid acceleration in the diffusion of modern sports. Japan's participation in the 1912 Olympics and the 1913 Far Eastern Games was one early indication of this. Another sign was the creation of an array of national federations for the governance of various sports. These included softball and rowing in 1920, soccer and the marathon in 1921, hockey in 1923, aquatic sports in 1924, skiing and track-and-field in 1925, and amateur boxing in 1926. The Japan Federation for Women's Sports was also established in 1926.[6] Between 1927 and 1936, thirteen additional national organizing bodies were established: for rugby football, volleyball, softball tennis, equestrianism, skating, gymnastics, basketball, amateur wrestling, table tennis, yachting, bicycling,

## Foundation of National Governing Sport Bodies

| Organization | Established |
|---|---|
| Japan Alpine Club | 1905 |
| Middle Schools' National Baseball Federation | 1915 |
| Japan Amateur Rowing Association | 1920 |
| The Football Association of Japan | 1921 |
| The Japan Lawn Tennis Association | 1922 |
| The Japan Equestrian Federation | 1922 |
| Japan Hockey Association | 1923 |
| Japan Amateur Swimming Federation | 1924 |
| Japan Golf Association | 1924 |
| Japan Soft Tennis Association | 1924 |
| Japan Amateur Athletic Federation [Rikujō Kyōgi] | 1925 |
| Ski Association of Japan | 1925 |
| Japan Amateur Boxing Federation | 1926 |
| Japan Volleyball Association | 1927 |
| The Japan Rugby Football Union | 1928 |
| The National Skating Union of Japan | 1929 |
| Japan Gymnastic Association | 1930 |
| Japan Amateur Basketball Association | 1930 |
| Japan Table Tennis Association | 1931 |
| Japan Amateur Wrestling Association | 1932 |
| Japan Yachting Association | 1932 |
| Japan Amateur Cycling Federation | 1934 |
| Fédération Japonaise D'Escrime [Fencing] | 1936 |
| Japan Weightlifting Association | 1937 |
| Japan Handball Association | 1937 |
| Japan Canoe Association | 1938 |
| The Amateur Rubberball Baseball Association of Japan | 1946 |
| Japan Sumo Federation | 1946 |
| Nippon Badminton Association | 1947 |
| All Japan Judo Federation | 1949 |
| Japan Softball Association | 1949 |
| The Amateur Archery Federation of Japan [Kyūdō] | 1949 |
| Japan Clay Pigeon Shooting Association | 1949 |
| National Rifle Association of Japan | 1953 |
| The Sports Arts Association of Japan | 1954 |
| The Modern Pentathlon Union of Japan | 1955 |

*Sources:* Imamura, *Nihon taiiku shi*, p. 699; Ikuo Abe, Yasuharu Kiyohara, and Ken Nakajima, "Fascism, Sport and Society in Japan," *International Journal of the History of Sport*, 9:1 (April 1992): 26–28; Kishino Yūzō, ed. *Saishin supōtsu daijiten* (Tokyo: Taishūkan shoten, 1987).

*Note:* There is a measure of uncertainty in the genealogy of today's sports federations as organizations merge, change their names, and/or revise the scope of their jurisdiction. We have chosen the earliest date that a national body of some sort was formed. We have usually (but not always) used the current name of the organization. We have deferred to the *Saishin supōtsu daijiten* when our sources differed.

weight lifting, and handball. Each of these federations sought and attained recognition by the international federation that governed its sport. At the level of individual participation, Japan—or at least Japan's urban middle class—seemed to consist of "sports maniacs."[7]

Newspapers continued to vie for the sponsorship of sports events. In April 1917, in response to the marathon races held by the *Mainichi shimbun*, Tokyo's *Yomiuri shimbun* sponsored a three-day ekiden (long-distance relay race) between Kyoto and Tokyo.[8]

In 1915, four years after it had called for the abolition of baseball, Osaka's *Asahi shimbun* decided to get on the sports bandwagon and to provide itself with a reliable supply of baseball stories. The newspaper launched a national championship baseball tournament for middle schools (the equivalent of today's high schools). To qualify for the final rounds, which from 1925 were played in famed Kōshien Stadium, teams competed in a series of local and regional tournaments. Year by year, the event attracted more teams and more spectators (and sold more newspapers). *Asahi*'s success inspired its rival, the *Osaka Mainichi shimbun*, to begin its own annual middle-school tournament in 1924. The schools whose teams participated in this tournament, which was held in the spring to avoid head-to-head competition, were chosen by the newspaper to represent their prefectures. These two competitions became—and still are—the Japanese schoolboy's most fanatically pursued extracurricular activity. Schoolgirls, who are expected to cheer themselves hoarse in support of the team, weep happy tears when their classmates win and sob uncontrollably when they lose.[9]

For the *Asahi*-sponsored tournament, Hasegawa Nyozekan, the newspaper's city editor translated the rules of baseball as published by Spalding. For a track-and-field tournament sponsored by the newspaper in 1916, Hasegawa also translated the American Amateur Athletic Union's official rules for that sport. This tournament was the first for which the term "rikujō kyōgi" (track-and-field contests) was officially used.[10]

The 1920s were also the formative years for Japan's industrial leagues. Innumerable companies institutionalized their commitment to paternalistic capitalism by sponsoring baseball teams or encouraging their employees to establish them. Although the massive Yawata Iron and Steel Works, located in northern Kyushu, was government-owned, its managers' attitudes toward labor relations were essentially the same as those in private enterprise. When Japanese industry was hit by a wave of strikes in the winter of 1920, Yawata Iron and Steel was not spared. On February 5, its 18,000-man workforce struck for the first time since the company's blast furnaces were first fired nineteen years earlier. The strike was settled when the company agreed to begin nine-hour shifts on the first of April—rather than the twelve-hour shifts that had been the rule. That October, in an effort to improve worker-management relations, which were still less than cordial, the company sponsored a baseball tournament. It was such a great success that thirty-six teams participated in the following year's tournament. A representative team was organized by the plant's workers in March 1924 and recognized by the company in 1926. In 1927 the company team began to play against teams from other companies. Crowds of seven thousand or eight thousand gathered to watch the games.[11]

At first, workers were expected to play baseball on their own time, but the experiment in social control was so successful that members of the representative team were allowed to begin their daily practice at 1:00 P.M. The entire team was transferred to Yawata Steel's main office and provided with tasks considerably less strenuous than shoveling coal into a blast furnace.

It was all worthwhile, from the company's point of view. The management was persuaded that on-the-job productivity would increase and that sports would promote harmony between capitalists and workers. They became enthusiastic (and self-interested) advocates of the ethos of fair play, good sportsmanship, teamwork, and adherence to the rules of the game—all qualities of the ideal worker.

The *Mainichi shimbun* formed a baseball team in 1920. It became Japan's most successful company team, winning 84.5 percent of its games in 1926. Well aware of the public relations possibilities, the newspaper hired a number of young men whose prowess with a bat and ball was superior to their journalistic skills. Although the players had nominal duties within the company, their real job was to play baseball. When the team did well, circulation seemed to rise. When the team's performance faltered, it was considered to have outlived its usefulness, and it was disbanded in March 1929.[12]

Kōzu Masaru, looking back from a Marxist perspective, sees these experiments in welfare capitalism as forays in social control designed to increase productivity or a sense of obligation to the company,[13] but the companies who sponsored baseball teams seem to have convinced themselves that their sports program was a benefit to their employees as well as to the firm.

Kōzu has also analyzed the place of sports in the life of a typical Japanese village in the interwar years. In 1922, 501 of the 577 families of

Shiojiri in Nagano Prefecture were engaged in agriculture. Most of these families flocked to the sumō matches that were a part of the village's Shinto festivals. The village's wealthier families preferred baseball and tennis. A baseball team was established at the prefectural normal school in 1897 and at Shiojiri's primary school in 1913. The village rejoiced when the primary school team won a local tournament in 1919.

The relationship between sports and social class was dramatically evident. Although Kōzu classified 22 percent of the village's families as "lower class," not a single player on the 1919 interscholastic team came from these families. When the village's youth club instituted a sports section, in 1920, its activities were firmly controlled by the club's middle-class members and there was the same clear correlation between sports participation and educational level that sociologists have found everywhere in the modern world. Villagers with a college education were far more likely to participate in the club's baseball games and tennis matches than their less educated neighbors.[14]

First-person accounts of sports in rural areas appear infrequently in the literature, but Kōzu Masaru has provided a few quotations from the diary of an anonymous young athlete in Yamaguchi Prefecture. In August 1929, he wrote, "Doing one's best is as beautiful as a tree in full bloom. We are deeply moved by an athlete who does his best." By October 1931, the idealism had waned and the youth lamented the "scramble for the championship flag." Despite widespread involvement in sport, other forms of recreation were even more popular. A government survey published in 1932 found that 6.4 percent of those living in the countryside participated in "sports and athletic events" while 19.5 percent of them found their amusement at the movies.[15]

Throughout the Taishō period, the Ministry of Education was whole-heartedly supportive of the diffusion of modern sports in the schools (although not to the exclusion of gymnastic exercises). The Home Ministry was equally if not more supportive. In 1924, it inaugurated the first Meiji Shrine Games at the newly completed shrine in honor of Emperor Meiji, who had died in 1912. Fourteen events were held: track-and-field, swimming, rugby, soccer, basketball, volleyball, field hockey, tennis, baseball, rowing, jūdō, kendō, kyūdō, and sumō. In subsequent years equestrian events, marksmanship, gymnastics, table tennis, aeronautics, boxing, skiing, and skating were added. The Meiji Shrine Games were clearly a major event in the sporting calendar.[16]

The first Japanese "Women's Olympics" was held in Osaka for two days in June 1924. Among the sponsors of the event were the publisher

Chuō undōsha, which had encouraged women's physical education in the pages of its magazine *Supōtsuman* (Sportsman); the research organization Kembokai, which studied women's physical education from a eugenicist's point of view; and the *Mainichi shimbun* newspaper, which provided most of the funds. In 1924, over one thousand women and girls participated in this sports competition, mainly in track-and-field. There also were lectures and films on eugenic themes. In 1926, the Japan Women's Sports Federation was established. Two years later it became a sponsor of the national "Women's Olympics." With variations in the program, the annual event survived until 1935, when changes in political climate militated against women's sports.[17] The key figure in the organization of these "Women's Olympics" was Kinoshita Tōsaka (1878–1952), a *Mainichi shimbun* sports editor who was also the head of the Kembokai and a founder of the Japanese Women's Sports Federation.

In the 1920s, radio stations began to broadcast the sports events that newspapers sponsored. When radio transmissions began, on March 22, 1925, baseball was included in the news broadcasts.[18] The first radio broadcast of an entire sports event occurred on August 13, 1927, the first day of the national middle-school baseball tournament at Kōshien Stadium. Before the sportscasters could take to the air, they had to clear a minor bureaucratic hurdle. The government strictly controlled the new medium, and the radio station had to submit to the Ministry of Communication the script of whatever it planned to broadcast. There is no prepared script for a sporting event, however, and the ministry was reluctant to allow the station to air uncensored material. Permission for the live broadcast was finally granted on the condition that an official from the ministry sat next to the announcer, ready to flick a switch and interrupt transmission as soon as the announcer uttered a politically subversive word. Since nothing that the announcer said during the eight days of the tournament threatened the safety and security of the Japanese people, the broadcasts were never interrupted.[19]

Other sports soon made their radio debuts. Track-and-field was broadcast for the first time on October 6, 1928, when a French team competed against Japanese athletes at the Meiji Shrine Stadium. A tennis match between Japan and France on October 16, 1929, was the first radio broadcast of that sport. A rugby match between Kyoto University and a "foreign team from Kobe" was broadcast from Kōshien Stadium on November 3, 1929. More collegiate sport was transmitted on September 21, 1930 (rowing), December 9, 1930 (boxing), and December 28, 1930 (soccer). The first broadcast of skiing featured the All-Hokkaido Middle

School Ski Meet in Sapporo on February 15, 1931. On July 3, 1931, the Sapporo Spring Horse Races were broadcast.[20]

## PROFESSIONAL BASEBALL

Kiku Kōichi, a scholar strongly influenced by the "figurational" sociology of Norbert Elias and Eric Dunning, has shown how the socioeconomic development of Japan between the two World Wars created a fertile field for the growth of professional baseball. A population shift from sparsely inhabited rural areas to densely settled cities provided entrepreneurs with a large market for commercialized entertainment. A rise in real wages meant more disposable income for such entertainment. The 1920s and 1930s were a period of growth for Japan's newspaper publishers and railway owners, two major sponsors of sports teams and sports events. Newspapers saw professional baseball teams as a way to increase circulation. Railways knew avid fans were likely to be frequent passengers.[21]

The Japanese were well aware that professional baseball was an American passion. As early as 1908, the sporting-goods firm A. J. Reach sent the Reach All-American Team to play a series of games in Japan, China, and the Philippines. In 1913, Chicago White Sox owner Charles Comiskey and New York Giants manager John J. McGraw were invited to bring an off-season team of major-leaguers to Japan for a series of exhibition games, but the time was not quite ripe for the Japanese to follow the American example.[22]

Japan's first professional team—now long forgotten—was formed in 1921 by the Japan Sports Association, Ltd. (Gōshi Kaisha Nippon Undō Kyōkai), a company established by former college baseball players. Graduates of Waseda University played a leading role, and one of them, a veteran of the 1905 tour to the United States, explained the rationale behind the venture. Although baseball had become Japan's national game, he wrote, the crushing defeats suffered by Japanese teams at the hands of California State University the previous spring showed that the development of collegiate baseball in Japan had reached an impasse. What Japanese baseball needed was a professional team to assume leadership and to play on equal terms with foreign professionals.[23]

The Japan Sports Association team was commonly known as the Shibaura Association team, after the stadium built in the Shibaura section of Tokyo. (This stadium seated six thousand spectators and had standing room for another fourteen thousand.) Advertisements were placed in the newspapers for candidates. Successful applicants trained for a year. The morning hours were devoted not only to English, mathematics, and other conventional areas of study but also to baseball theory. The trainees practiced baseball for three hours in the afternoon and then, for an hour or so after supper, they listened to lectures from their coach. None of the players had had college experience, and all their study and practice was in vain. The team failed to attract spectators. Commitment to the amateur code was still so strong that taking money for playing baseball was generally frowned upon.[24]

Two years after the formation of the Japan Sports Association team, the Great Kanto Earthquake of 1923 destroyed much of Tokyo and further jeopardized the team's existence. Kobayashi Ichizō, president of the Hankyū Railway, came to the rescue. He brought the team to the Kansai area in 1924 and renamed it the Takarazuka team. It was disbanded five years later, however, mainly for financial reasons, but also because there were few other professional teams playing on a regular basis and the Takarazuka players were simply not good enough to compete with the best collegiate teams.[25]

The Tenkatsu Baseball Team, which was also formed in 1921, was comprised mainly of well-known former college players. This team toured Japan with the troupe of the magician Shōkyokusai Tenkatsu. Baseball games against local teams were supposed to stimulate interest in Shōkyokusai's bag of tricks. It was apparently quite common for theatrical and other entertainment companies to have their own baseball teams, and it sometimes happened that the games were more popular than the theatrical performances. Given the general disapproval of professional teams, one has to ask why college graduates were willing to play under such conditions. The answer is fairly simple. In 1921, the postwar economy was in a slump, and the Tenkatsu team paid good money.[26]

Shibaura played Tenkatsu in Japan's first game of professional baseball—on what is now Japanese soil—on August 30, 1923. The qualification is necessary because the teams had played two earlier games in Seoul, Korea, which was then a part of the Japanese Empire. In these encounters, the Association team was an easy winner because, as Kiku has noted, the team had been formed in order to raise the level of Japanese baseball while the Tenkatsu team was merely a means of promoting an unrelated business.[27]

Japan's first professional league began with newspaper entrepreneurship rather than with magic shows. Tokyo's *Yomiuri shimbun* played a crucial role in the creation of the league. In 1931, Philadelphia Athletics

## Japan's First Professional Baseball League

| Date Established | Team Name | Financial Backer |
|---|---|---|
| December 26, 1934 | Tokyo Giants | Yomiuri Shimbun |
| December 10, 1935 | Osaka Tigers | Hanshin Railway |
| January 15, 1936 | Nagoya Squad | Shin Aichi Shimbun |
| January 17, 1936 | Tokyo Senators | Seibu Railway |
| January 23, 1936 | Hankyū Squad | Hankyū Railway |
| February 15, 1936 | Greater Tokyo Squad | Kokumin Shimbun |
| February 28, 1936 | Nagoya Golden Dolphins | Nagoya Shimbun |

owner Connie Mack was enticed by the newspaper's innovative owner, Shōriki Matsutarō, to tour Japan with an all-star team featuring Lefty Grove, who had just finished the season with a 31–4 record, and Lou Gehrig, who had shared the home run title with Babe Ruth. Mack returned in 1934 with a team that included Babe Ruth, Lou Gehrig, and Jimmy Foxx.[28] Despite the government's growing opposition to Western sports, a hundred thousand Japanese fans lined Tokyo's streets in 1934 to welcome the visiting American baseball players to the capital and tens of thousands flocked to the exhibition games they played.[29] One hundred thousand fans "pushed and shoved their way" into Tokyo's Meiji Stadium.[30]

The amateurs who were recruited to play against this second all-star team did not do very well, but they formed the nucleus of the Dai Nippon Yakyū Kurabu (the Greater Japan Baseball Club), later to become the Tokyo Giants. Since the club was "a ball team with nobody to play, [Shōriki] sent it to the United States [in 1935] for a 110-game barnstorming trip that was a sensation in the Japanese press."[31] A year later, Japan's first professional baseball league was established.

The Japan Professional Baseball League that was established on February 5, 1936, had seven teams. As the table shows, financial backing for the teams was provided by three railway companies and four newspapers.[32] It was entirely appropriate that Japan's emblematically modern sport was sponsored by enterprises symbolizing modern transportation and communication.

The newspapers had for years carried stories on baseball (and other sports). The three railroads had also been involved with the game. In the Kansai area, the Hanshin Railway Corporation, which had been founded in 1905 with fifteen miles of track, owned the grounds where Waseda University had played the University of Chicago in 1910. In 1917, the company constructed two side-by-side baseball fields in Naruo where, for several years, the *Asahi shimbun* staged its national middle-school baseball tournament. In 1923, when it became clear that these fields were too small for the crowds eager to see the schoolboys play, the railroad built Kōshien Stadium. The Kōshien Line that serviced the stadium and the surrounding sports facilities (which included a tennis court, a swimming pool, and a bathing beach) prospered, but the owners of the railroad—like all good capitalists—wanted to maximize their profits. To get more use from their stadium, which was empty through most of the year, they decided to follow Shōriki's lead and start a professional team of their own. Their earnings from the two tours by American all-stars encouraged them to venture into direct team ownership.[33]

The Hankyū Railway Company, which also served the Kansai area, soon followed suit. Founded in 1910, Hankyū had concentrated its efforts upon developing the Takarazuka area (near Osaka). They opened the Takarazuka Hot Springs Paradise in 1912 and added an all-girl theater company in 1913. One of the several golf courses built by the company was sited at the Takarazuka development. Rivalry with the Hanshin spurred Hankyū's president, Kobayashi Ichizō, to join Shōriki's new professional league and to construct a stadium of his own. Nishinomiya Stadium, between Osaka and Kobe, was ready for use in 1937, and lines were built to service it. The third railroad to enter a team in the new league, Seibu, also constructed its own stadium.[34]

Radio contributed enormously to the popular and economic success of professional baseball. A national radio network was established in October 1928, connecting stations in Tokyo, Osaka, and Nara with those in Sapporo, Sendai, Hiroshima, and Kumamoto. National broadcasts of the games of Tokyo's Six-University Baseball League, which began in 1929, contributed greatly to the sport's popularity. Shōriki and the other entrepreneurs of the new professional league were confident about radio's ability to spread—indeed, to broadcast—the word about their venture. They were correct. The broadcasts that began in July 1936 were immensely popular. According to a national survey of listener preference, 63.8 percent said they liked to tune in to baseball games. Baseball was followed by sumō with 55.5 percent, swimming with 44.4 percent (this was the year after "Maehata gambare!"), and track-and-field with 34.2 percent.[35]

Despite its great popularity, baseball suffered the stigma of foreign origins at a time when Japan's military leaders were about to lead the country into war with the United States and several European powers.

The 1930s were "a time when ultranationalism provided the political impulse for sometimes ludicrous attempts to rid Japanese culture of Western elements and reinstate social patterns of a more traditional mold."[36] Verbal opposition sometimes escalated to physical violence. Athletes training for the Far Eastern Games of 1934 were assaulted and an ultranationalist zealot was moved to stab Shōriki Matsutarō because he had arranged the 1934 baseball tour and masterminded the creation of the professional baseball league. (Shōriki survived the attack.)[37]

In 1940, the use of English terms in baseball was prohibited and the professional teams with English words in their names changed them. Instead of shouting *seifu!* (safe) the umpire announced his decision with a loud *yoshi;* unable to call a runner *auto* (out) the umpire roared *hike!* The mere substitution of Japanese words for English ones was not enough to satisfy the nation's xenophobes. Only four years after the founding of the first professional league, baseball's immediate future was grim.[38]

## SUMŌ

"From about the 1890s onwards," writes Tessa Morris-Suzuki, "many intellectuals . . . had been struggling with the problem of creating a framework for the understanding of Japanese society." The problem can be approached in two ways. One way is to stress difference. Since the West was seen as "rational, progressive, scientific, individualistic, and meritocratic," Japan was defined as "opposite but complementary," lacking in material wealth but possessing unique "spiritual qualities." The other way to approach the problem was "to argue that although surface customs might differ, the underlying qualities of the Japanese 'national character' were in fact *equivalent* to those of the west."[39]

Both of these approaches can be seen in Japanese assessments of the relative merits of imported Western sports and indigenous traditional martial arts and sumō. After a generation of modernizers whose motto was "civilization and enlightenment," a number of late-nineteenth-century Japanese thinkers called for a reassessment of traditional values and institutions. Their call "increased interest in the martial arts but at the same time set Japan upon a course that ultimately led to the warping of the traditional martial arts and attendant values into something quite different—often lumped under the ambiguous but emotionally laden label *bushidō*—designed to serve the expansionist goals of the Japanese state."[40] Nitobe Inazō popularized the term in a widely read book, *Bushidō:*

*The Soul of Japan* (1899). As his subtitle implies, Nitobe saw bushidō as an old and uniquely Japanese tradition. At the same time, writing in English for a foreign audience, he seemed to contradict his own argument by insisting that there was no essential difference between bushidō and the Western concept of chivalry. The British scholar Basil Hall Chamberlain, professor of Japanese language at Tokyo University from 1886 to 1911, was utterly unconvinced by the assertion that bushidō was a part of traditional Japanese culture. He called Nitobe's bushidō "an entirely new religion."[41] Morris-Suzuki agreed with Chamberlain's criticism. She described Nitobe's bushidō as a "mildly exoticized version of the British public school ethos."[42] Nitobe's book, in retrospect, can be seen as an original contribution to the Japanese quest for identity, to what is today known as *nihonjinron*. This effort to identify a uniquely Japanese identity is nowhere more clearly seen than in the history of sumō.

Sumō is one of the most ritualized of all Japanese sports.[43] The rituals begin long before the wrestler makes his debut in the ring. Wrestlers live and train in one of some fifty "stables." The sumō "stable" is a hierarchical organization within which everyone plays his or her traditional role. In fact, the connotations of "stable," which is the usual translation of *heya* (room), are quite unfortunate. The elder (*oyakata*) in charge of a sumō heya acts much more like a traditional Japanese patriarch than like the profit-maximizers who invest in thoroughbred horses. Indeed, the first character in the term "oyakata" means "parent." Oinuma Yoshihiro has stressed this point in a sociological analysis of the world of sumō. "Within a sumō heya," he has written, "the elder enjoys absolute authority over the heya's wrestlers. They act in accordance with their sense that they owe him complete obedience and fealty. Their thoughts and emotions are the same as those that form the moral basis of the traditional Japanese family [*ie*]."[44] In Oinuma's analysis, the sumō heya is classified as a feudal institution.

The tournament is even more ritualized than the wrestler's daily life as a member of a heya. The day before each main tournament is to begin, a special ceremony is held to bless the ring. White-robed referees acting as Shinto priests offer prayers to the gods and place wooden sticks with folded strips of white paper at the corners of the square within which the ring is located. Strips of dried squid, kelp, and other good-luck omens are blessed and buried in the center of the ring in an unglazed earthenware pot. Salt and sake are offered to the gods.

Each day of the tournament, before the upper division *makuuchi* bouts begin, the wrestlers participate in the ring-entering ceremony (*dohyōiri*).

On the odd days of the tournament, the wrestlers of the "East" are the first to enter; on the even days, those of the "West." Wearing their *keshōmawashi* (ornamental aprons) that can cost tens of thousands of dollars, the wrestlers file ponderously down the *hanamichi,* the "path of flowers" that is also a part of kabuki performance. Their names are announced over the public address system as they step up into the ring. When all are present, they face inward, clap their hands, raise their aprons slightly with both hands, throw up their hands, and file out again. They are followed by the wrestlers of the other "side," who perform the same ceremony. (Wrestlers of the second highest division, *jūryō,* also perform this ceremony before their matches start.)

The wrestlers occupying the highest rank of yokozuna have the honor of performing a solo ring-entering ceremony. A referee leads the procession of the yokozuna and his herald (*tsuyuharai* or "dew-sweeper") and *tachimochi* (swordbearer), both chosen from the ranks of makuuchi wrestlers. All three wear splendidly ornamented keshōmawashi. Knotted around the yokozuna's waist is the thick white rope from which the rank of yokozuna (literally "horizontal rope") takes its name. From the rope hang five zigzag strips of paper similar to those that hang from the rope over the main entrance of a Shinto shrine. The trio steps up to the side of the ring, where the yokozuna squats, spreads his arms as if they were wings, and brings them together in a loud clap. He then rubs his palms together, extends his arms again, turns the palms upward, and claps again. He stands, strides to the middle of the ring, and faces the front of the stadium, to where the emperor sits when he attends. Accompanied by shouts of "Yoisho!" from the audience, he then performs his ceremonial *shiko,* raising one leg high into the air and bringing it down to stamp the earth. He stamps again, then falls into a squat from which he slowly rises with his arms held out in a ritualized position. This is the high point of the ceremony, and the crowd cheers. He stamps once more, then returns to squat again between the tsuyuharai and the tachimochi. He repeats the clapping motions and strides from the ring. After each active yokozuna has performed his own ring-entering ceremony, the makuuchi bouts begin.

Appearances can be deceptive. Many of sumo's rituals are the result not of ancient tradition but rather of modern innovation. A good deal of emotional energy is invested in the conviction that sumō has always been sumō. A typical expression of this conviction appeared in a 1992 issue of *Bungei shunjū:* "All professional sports played in Japan are foreign imports except *sumō* which originated here. It has been around since time immemorial and survived centuries of tumultuous social change, preserved by devotees in more or less its ancient form."[45]

Less rather than more. Sumō's rituals are "invented traditions" in the most precise sense of the term. They represent a conscious effort to link the present to the past. By the 1880s, the Meiji government began to lose confidence in its ability to import science and technology while shunning the corrosive influence of Western culture. Enthusiasm for innovation waned and resentment of the foreigners' brash condescension grew. While there was little evidence of outright hostility to European and American sports, many of which were introduced in the late nineteenth century, there was at the same time renewed interest in native sports as representations of Japanese culture. Over the past century, sumō has assumed many of the characteristics of a modern sport, but the modernization of sumō has occurred at the same time as its "retraditionalization." The ritual elements of sumō—some old, some surprisingly new—have become more salient in the Age of Television than they were in the era of print.

The oldest of these rituals date from no earlier than the Edo period, when sumō developed as a professional spectator sport. A number of rituals were introduced by Yoshida Zenzaemon in anticipation of the first official display of sumō before Shogun Tokugawa Ienari in 1791. Yoshida also ascribed symbolic significance to each of the four pillars that supported the roof over the outdoor sumō ring, the roof that had probably been constructed simply to provide protection from rainy weather.[46]

The impetus for the "retraditionalization" of sumō intensified early in the twentieth century. The indoor sumō stadium inaugurated in 1909 is a case in point. The name of the stadium—the Kokugikan (National Sport Hall)—was a claim about the special status of sumō, which was now presented to the public as Japan's "national sport" (*kokugi*). The referees, who until that time were bareheaded and wore the *kamishimo* (the samurai's formal dress), adopted more ceremonial attire. Their new kimono and hats resembled the garb and headgear of a Shinto priest. Wrestlers who had paid no particular attention to the clothing they wore on their way to the arena were now required to wear formal *haori* and hakama. At approximately the same time, spokesmen for the sport, like Hitachiyama Taniemon, began to refer to sumō as one of Japan's traditional martial arts (budō). Hitachiyama's remarks carried weight because he was active as a yokozuna from 1903 to 1914 and because he was one of the first professional sumō wrestlers from a former samurai family. After his retirement he was chosen to lead the Sumō Association.[47]

Although the construction of the Kokugikan deprived the small roof over the sumō ring of its practical purpose, the roof was retained for its symbolic significance. In 1931, during the wave of nationalism that culminated in the seizure of Manchuria, the Sumō Association changed the shape of the roof. Originally constructed in the simple *irimoyazukuri* style, seen most often these days on ordinary farmhouses, the roof was redesigned in the *shinmeizukuri* style used for Shinto shrines. In the eyes of the Japanese spectator, the shinmeizukuri style was likely to evoke visions of the hallowed Ise shrine, the shrine of the Sun Goddess Amaterasu and the ancestral shrine of the imperial family.

Twentieth-century interpretations of sumō are often quite extreme in their claims about the religious significance of the sport's rituals. Yamaguchi Masao, for instance, observes that the ring-entering ceremony is "thought to introduce cosmic energy into the ring and hence into the world." In his view, the configuration of the dohyō symbolizes "the mandala which expresses cosmic totality in Buddhism."[48] The Sumō Association's efforts at "retraditionalization" seem to have born fruit.

The "retraditionalization" of sumō accompanied the modernization of sumō discussed in Chapter 4. It is often said that Japan has preserved or maintained its traditions while undergoing modernization, but it is more accurate to say that many of Japan's most cherished traditions were invented in response to modernization. In fact, the two concepts are interdependent; awareness of one is impossible without awareness of the other. As Itō Kimio observed in a study of the twentieth-century transformation of the image of Prince Shōtoku (574–622), "Modernization and the invention of tradition proceed together in a nested relationship."[49]

This was certainly the case for sumō. The development of the yokozuna rank, which paralleled the development of the championship system, is an instance of this nested relationship. Contrary to appearances, one of the sport's most symbol-laden traditional aspects—the rank of yokozuna— is also a modern invention. It demonstrates the complex interactions of tradition and modernity.

The conventional genealogy of yokozuna begins with Akashi Shiganosuke in the early seventeenth century, but there is no record that such a wrestler ever existed, much less that he was made a yokozuna. Instead, the institution of the yokozuna has its origins in the licenses Yoshida Zenzaemon granted to two wrestlers—Tanikaze Kajinosuke and Onokawa Kisaburō.[50] In November 1789 he authorized each of them to perform a solo ring-entering ceremony while wearing a white rope (the yokozuna) around their waists. This innovation was part of the efforts by Yoshida and the other leaders of professional sumō in Edo to increase the status of the sport, efforts that culminated with the 1791 sumō performance before Shogun Tokugawa Ienari.

Yoshida's innovation was not immediately adopted as standard practice. In fact, for nearly forty years, no further licenses to perform the solo ring-entering ceremony while wearing the decorative rope were granted. The license was revived in 1828, but by the end of the Tokugawa shogunate only nine such licenses had been awarded.[51] The institutionalization of the practice in the early twentieth century involved a series of innovations beginning in the late nineteenth century and culminating in the official recognition of the yokozuna as the highest rank in sumō.

For a century after Yoshida's grant to Tanikaze and Onokawa, the highest sumō rank continued to be *ōzeki*. During this time, the word "yokozuna" still referred merely to the rope worn by the wrestler licensed to perform a solo ring-entering ceremony. In fact, Tanikaze did not even hold the highest rank of ōzeki in the tournament after which he was awarded the yokozuna license; he was at the second-highest rank of *sekiwake*. Shiranui Dakuemon, awarded the license in 1840, was subsequently demoted to sekiwake for a tournament.

It was not until May 1890 that the word "yokozuna" appeared in the *banzuke* (the table of rankings printed before each tournament). Ironically, the motive for printing the term was to placate rather than to reward, and the consequences were entirely unintended. For the first time there were more than two ōzeki listed on the banzuke. Two new ōzeki had just been promoted, but the two reigning ōzeki were left in place. This unprecedented situation was dealt with by writing the two extra names on tabs protruding from the top sides of the printed banzuke. The ōzeki with the weakest record in the previous tournament, Nishinoumi, was one of those listed on the tabs. Since he had just been awarded a yokozuna license, he felt slighted and complained to the Sumō Association that a wrestler as honored as he deserved better treatment. To pacify him, the association put the characters for yokozuna next to his name. Once the precedent was established, it became the custom to write these characters alongside the names of ōzeki with the license, but there was still no official yokozuna rank.

Shortly after the term "yokozuna" entered the banzuke rankings, a private campaign was started to distinguish ōzeki with the yokozuna license from those without it. Jimmaku Kyūgorō had received a license, the ninth issued, in 1867. In 1895, he started a campaign to erect a monument to wrestlers who had been honored with the license. The monument was erected in 1900 without the involvement of the Sumō

Association or the Yoshida family (which still claimed sole authority to issue the yokozuna license).[52]

The Sumō Association finally recognized yokozuna as an official rank in 1909, the pivotal year in which the Kokugikan was opened, the referee's costume was redesigned, and the newspaper *Jiji shinpō* started regularly designating tournament champions. The Yoshida house, however, which continued to award the yokozuna license, refused to accept the association's interpretation of the yokozuna as a rank. It was not until 1951 that the Yoshida family finally agreed that the yokozuna was indeed a rank.[53] In short, the lofty status that is now widely perceived as the very symbol of sumō's "two-thousand-year history"[54] emerged only in the nineteenth century and was finally accepted as an official rank around fifty years ago.

The epitome of the yokozuna is probably Futabayama Sadaji, who held the rank from May 1937 to November 1945. Futabayama is most famous for his winning streak of sixty-nine bouts over the course of seven tournaments. Since the streak, which began in January 1936 and continued until January 1939, was concurrent with the very successful first phase of Japan's war with China, Futabayama was symbolically identified with the "invincible" imperial army. (As if to underscore the identification, Futabayama retired shortly after Japan's defeat in World War II.)

Futabayama's record of sixty-nine straight victories—reminiscent of Joe DiMaggio's fifty-six-game hitting streak—has never been challenged. Futabayama is the ideal to which postwar yokozuna have been held, and it is ironic but also telling that his status as the ultimate representative of a traditional role is to a large degree based on his quantified record, which is a characteristic preoccupation of modern sports.

What turned out to be the last sumō tournament before the end of the war was held in June 1945 at a Kokugikan damaged by air raids, but it was not open to the general public because of the continued danger of bombardment. Although the tournament was not broadcast on domestic radio, it was transmitted overseas by shortwave broadcasts. The purpose of the broadcasts was, presumably, to reassure Japanese forces overseas that life on the home front had not been disrupted by war. After all, if sumō was alive and well, there was still hope of ultimate victory.[55]

## KARATE

The 1920s and 1930s was also the time during which the martial art of karate established itself in Japan.[56] Karate has its roots in the present-day prefecture of Okinawa, but since the oldest written reference dates from 1867, the sport's earlier history is a matter of speculation. The most likely hypothesis, however, is that karate came from China, the hegemonic power to which the Okinawan kings had paid tribute from the fifteenth century. From the end of the fourteenth century to the beginning of the sixteenth century, Chinese from Fuchien Province immigrated to Okinawa and established a community in Kumemura, perhaps bringing a precursor of karate with them. In 1609 Okinawa was conquered by the Shimazu clan of Satsuma, in present-day Kagoshima, but the kingdom continued to pay tribute to China, which did not recognize Japan's claim to Okinawa until 1895, when China was defeated by Japan in the Sino-Japanese war.

Linguistic evidence is helpful in determining karate's origins. The word "karate" is now written with two characters that can be literally translated as "empty hand," but an earlier, phonetically identical way of writing the word used the character "tō" (also pronounced *kara* in Japanese), which refers to China—in particular T'ang-dynasty China (618–907), a period when Japan was heavily influenced by its mighty continental neighbor. Karate (then written "Chinese hand") was included in a program of performances held in Okinawa in 1867 to celebrate the recognition of the newly ascended Okinawan king by China's Ch'ing dynasty. On this occasion, karate was performed by members of the village of Chinese immigrants, Kumemura, which gives credence to the Chinese-origins hypothesis.

The first karate ("Chinese hand") dōjō in Okinawa was established in 1889 by Higashionna Kanryō, who had studied unarmed combat in China for fifteen years. His contemporary, Itosu Ankō, devised five basic kata for karate in order to systematize it for educational purposes. In 1909, he succeeded in having karate adopted for the regular curriculum at the Okinawa prefectural middle school. He joined the school's staff as karate instructor.

Karate was first performed in Tokyo in April 1922 at the Ministry of Education's first Physical Education Exhibition. Funakoshi Gichin (1868–1957) was chosen by Okinawa Prefecture to travel to Tokyo for the performance. Funakoshi, a key figure in the diffusion of the sport, had been born on Okinawa in 1868, the year of the Meiji Restoration. He had studied karate with Azato Yosutsune, who was also skilled in archery, fencing, and horsemanship, but in time Funakoshi had developed his own version of the martial art. He toured the length and breadth of the island, giving his first public demonstrations when he was nearly forty years old.[57]

The 1922 Tokyo demonstration, which occurred at the Women's College of Education, was so successful that Funakoshi moved into the Okinawan Students' Dormitory in Tokyo and started teaching karate. Mabuni Kenwa, Motobu Chōki, Miyagi Chōjun, and others followed, helping to spread karate throughout the main islands. (In October 1922, Motobu Chōki attended a boxing versus jūdō match in Kyoto and was so excited that he issued an impromptu challenge to the troupe's star boxer "George"—and knocked him down with a chop under the nose.)

Funakoshi was instrumental in starting karate clubs at Keiō University in 1924 and at Tokyo's Imperial University in 1926. Keiō students then took the lead in changing the characters used to write "karate." Before his move to the main islands, Funakoshi had called his discipline "*tōdē*," an alternate pronunciation of the characters for "Chinese hand." By the late 1920s, however, China had lost its luster in the minds of most Japanese. In March 1929, members of Keiō's karate club visited a priest of the Rinzai sect of Zen Buddhism and listened attentively as he lectured them on the Buddhist concept of emptiness. They were especially impressed by the phrase "empty hand," a phrase that can also be pronounced "karate. " The very next month, on the fifth anniversary of the founding of their club, they announced a change in the way they wrote the characters for "karate." Henceforth, "karate" was written as "empty hand" rather than "Chinese hand." The students prevailed upon Funakoshi to adopt this new appellation. In his book *Karatedō kyōhan*, published in 1935 as the Imperial Army prepared for aggression against China and amid general disdain for things Chinese, he announced the change and employed the term *karatedō* (the way of the empty hand), thereby asserting that karate was ethically comparable to jūdō and the other martial arts.

It is obvious, then, that karate as we know it today can be considered a modern innovation patterned after jūdō, the most widely practiced version of barehanded combat. "Both the uniform (*gi*) and the belt (*obi*) were taken over from Judo, and the traditional Japanese bow was introduced as a new form of greeting for *karateka*."[58] Many of the ritual elements that transformed karate from a combat sport into a "transformative experience" evolved during the 1920s and 1930s.[59] In short, karate, like sumō, is to a great extent an instance of invented tradition.

## AIKIDŌ

As jūdō and karate have become increasingly "sportified" and formally-structurally similar to modern sports, *aikidō* has moved in to occupy the ludic wavelength that they have seemingly abandoned. Aikidō, written with characters meaning "the way of harmony," is a martial art that took form in the first half of the twentieth century. In the broadest sense, aikidō refers to a number of disciplines with "aiki" in their name, all of which derive from the Daitō school of jūjutsu. The best known of these, at least in the West, is the kata-centered version of aikidō developed by Ueshiba Morihei (1883–1969).[60]

The term "*aiki*" can be found in texts from the Edo period, but it seems to have been used mostly in a negative sense: in combat as well as practice, one must guard against becoming too harmonized with one's opponent. A shift in meaning can be detected in *Budō hiketsu: Aiki no jutsu* (The Secret of the Martial Arts: The Technique of Aiki), an influential martial arts text written in 1892. Asserting that aiki was the heart of the martial arts, this text maintained that bringing one's individual *ki* (spirit) in harmony with that of the universe was the way to master oneself and one's opponents.

Takeda Sōkaku (1860–1943) revived (or, some say, created) Daitō-school jūjutsu, which he renamed Daitō-ryū Aiki Jūjutsu in 1923. In this he was probably influenced by the popularity of *Budō hiketsu: Aiki no jutsu,* which had been reissued in 1900 and was quoted in many jūjutsu and self-defense manuals. Ueshiba Morihei became Takeda's disciple in 1915. (The license he received in that year referred to the technique as "Aiki jūjutsu.") From 1920 to 1927, Ueshiba taught Daitō-ryū in Hyōgo Prefecture.

Ueshiba had been born in Wakayama Prefecture on December 14, 1883, a generation after Kanō Jigorō. In addition to his interest in the martial arts, he was fascinated by spiritual matters. In 1919, he paid his first visit to the headquarters of the religious sect Ōmoto-kyō. This sect traced its origins to a pair of mystics: the prophetess Deguchi Nao (1837–1918) and her son-in-law Deguchi Onisaburō (1871–1948). By 1921, the sect claimed several million followers, but hard times came that year when Deguchi Nao predicted that her son-in-law, who now saw himself as the reincarnation of the Buddha of the Future (Maitreya), was about to ascend to the imperial throne. The government was understandably annoyed by this and moved to repress the sect, whereupon Deguchi Onisaburō decided, in 1924, to seek further enlightenment in Mongolia. En route he announced that he was the Dalai Lama.[61]

Ueshiba was one of four disciples who followed Deguchi to the continent. There he was arrested, along with the rest of Deguchi's followers, by the Chinese government. After his release, he returned to Japan, sought wisdom in the mountains of Kumano, and—in 1925—had a mystical experience of his own. According to his account, which his faithful followers have accepted as gospel, Ueshiba was bathed in pure light. Rays darted from his eyes and he felt himself infused with ki. Ueshiba tapped the inexhaustible power of ki in order to excel in hand-to-hand combat. The force of ki enabled him to shrug off dozens of attackers and it was child's play for him to defeat Nishimura Shutarō, Waseda University's best jūdōka. He was said to have had the ability to dodge bullets. Shortly before his death, while in his late eighties, he was reputed to have subdued burly opponents with a single finger. "Ki power is never diminished and does not depend on one's physical condition."[62]

In 1931, Ueshiba opened the Kōbukan Dōjō in Tokyo and began to distance himself from Takeda Sōkaku. He experimented with several names for his new school, including Kōbukai Aiki Jūjutsu, Kōbudō, and Dai Nippon Budō. The name "aikidō" appears to have been imposed from the outside. In March 1942, the Dai Nippon Butokukai (Greater Japan Martial Virtue Society) was "transformed into a government-controlled national federation of all martial arts groups linked together to serve the war effort."[63] There were five sections: for kendō, jūdō, archery, bayonet, and marksmanship. In October, an "aikidō section" was added. This was the origin of the name "aikidō."

In 1948, a group led by Ueshiba Morihei's son Kisshōmaru established a foundation, the Aikikai, which has publicized Ueshiba as the true founder of aikidō. The goal of aikidō, according to Ueshiba and his disciples, is the harmony of the individual ki and the universal ki. The idols of science and technology, before which the modern Japanese have foolishly bowed their heads, represent little more than "the hollowness of the human spirit." Practitioners of aikidō reject rankings, weight divisions, tournaments, championships, and all the other rationalized forms characteristic of modern sports. Despite his reputed prowess in unarmed combat, Ueshiba shunned competition. "The true spirit of budō, " wrote his son and successor, "is not to be found in a competitive and combative atmosphere where brute strength dominates and victory at any cost is the paramount objective." Ueshiba's followers are explicit in their criticism of today's brands of jūdō and karate. Corrupted by blandishments of modernity, jūdō and karate have—in their view—succumbed to the ethos of competition and fallen to their lowly place in "the world of sports."[64]

There are schools of aikidō, however, that embrace the model of modern sports. After World War II, Tomiki Kenji, although he still considered himself a loyal disciple of Ueshiba, developed a competitive form of aikidō. This occurred after he became a professor at Waseda University and sought to establish an aikidō club for his students. He met initially with opposition on the grounds that aikidō had not been modernized as a sport in the manner of jūdō and kendō. As a condition for permission to establish the club, the university insisted that Tomiki develop aikidō as a sport.

Responding to this demand, Tomiki set out to systematize aikidō. He applied Kanō Jigorō's educational and ecumenical perspectives and modeled the techniques of aikidō on those that had proven successful in the case of jūdō. In 1965, he publicized a competitive form of aikidō that allowed sharp blows and pressure to joints. Since aikidō had previously been practiced mainly through kata, the form developed by Tomiki was not widely accepted by other branches of the art. Tomiki's response to criticism was to establish the Japan Aikidō Association (Nihon Aikidō Kyōkai) to propagate competitive aikidō.

In the original form of competition that he developed, both contestants were barehanded, but the matches tended to resemble jūdō. In 1966, in order to underline the uniqueness of aikidō, one of the contestants was given a rubber dagger. Formal competitions with the rubber dagger began in 1967. The annual All-Japan Student Aikidō Tournament was begun in 1970 and the semi-annual National Adult Aikidō Tournament in 1977.

The Nihon Aikidō Kyōkai is the only school to hold such tournaments. Most devotees of aikidō continue to eschew competition. Today there are many different schools of aikidō, most of which practice only kata. The person at whom the kata are directed does not resist. The advantages of this practice are that it precludes a reliance on mere strength and enables the elderly or others without great physical strength to practice. The disadvantage is that practice can become formalized and even theatrical. In the minds of many who practice noncompetitive aikido, their practice is a form of homage to the memory of Ueshiba Morihei.

## LITERARY MANIFESTATIONS

Like Ernest Hemingway, Alan Sillitoe, Henry de Montherlant, Uwe Johnson, Per Olof Enquist, and a host of other American and European authors, a number of Japanese writers have dramatized sports in their fiction. Among them are Abe Tomoji, who is little known outside Japan,

**Noriyumi.** Held at the Archery Ground Pavilion. Two archers from the Inner Palace Guards take aim while two other archers wait their turn behind them. The emperor is seated at the top of the screen. *Nenjū gyōji emaki*, fourth section of fourth scroll.

**Kemari.** The game takes place at the home of a court noble. *Nenjū gyōji emaki*, third section of third scroll.

**Gitchō.** Children and adults play in the streets of Kyoto at the New Year. The artist has drawn the trail of the ball to show its speed. *Nenjū gyōji emaki,* second section of sixteenth scroll.

**Kasagake,** ca.1295. The mounted archer draws a *hikimeya,* an arrow with a whistle at its end. The *yatori,* sitting next to the target to retrieve the arrows, blows into an arrow's whistle. *Obusuma Saburō emaki,* section two.

**Inuoumono.** Mounted archers await the release of the dog. From a pair of six-panel folding screens by Kanō Sanraku, *Inuoumono byōbu.* 16th century.

**Sumō** as a spectator sport. Performed near the Kamo River in Kyoto. There is neither a ring nor a roof and the referee, holding a fan to signal the winner, is plainly dressed. From a six-panel folding screen, *Kyōto Kamogawa tadasu no mori sumō kōgyō no zu.* Mid-17th century. Japan Sumō Association.

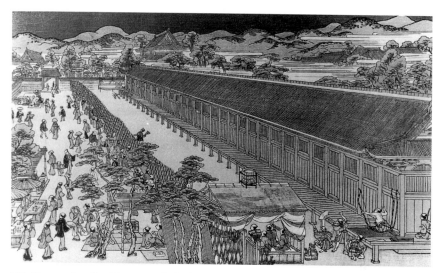

**Tōshiya** at the Sanjūsangendō in Kyoto. The archer (lower right) has released the arrow, which can be seen in the bull's eye of the target at the opposite end of the veranda.

**Tanikaze and Onokawa** at the spring tournament in Edo, 1788. Sumō now has a ring and a simple roof. From a woodblock print by Katsukawa Shunshō in the series *Edo kanjin ōzumō ukie no zu (Tanikaze Onokawa torikumi).* Japan Sumō Association.

A *gekken* (fencing) performance in Nagoya, 1878. From Shōji Munemitsu, *Kendō hyakunen* (Tokyo: Jiji tsūshin sha, 1976), p. vii.

An *undōkai* (sports day), 1885. Tokyo University and its preparatory school hold a sports day on the university's grounds in Hongō. In Nihon taiiku kyōkai, ed. *Nihon supōtsu hyakunen* (Tokyo: Nihon taiiku kyōkai, 1970), p. 38. Photo Kishimoto.

**The baseball diamond explained,** 1885. Home base is at the top of the diamond and the fielders' positions are marked by black dots. From Tsuboi Gendō and Tanaka Morigyō, *Kogai yūgihō* (Bēsubōru magajin sha, 1885).

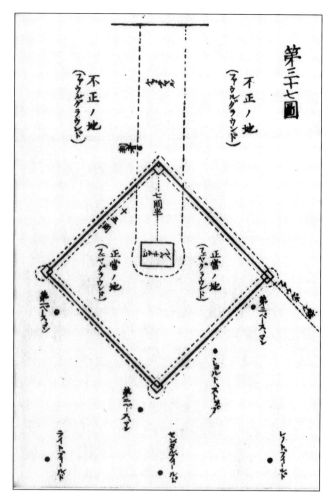

**Kōdōkan jūdō,** ca. 1888. Kanō Jigorō and his students at the new dōjō in Fujimimachi, Tokyo. Nihon taiiku kyōkai.

**Women's basketball,** 1909. Students of the Baika Women's School wearing hakama. Baika Women's College Library.

**A school kendō class,** 1930. Sixth graders practicing at Sasayama Primary School, Hyōgo Prefecture. Sasayama Primary School.

**Hitomi Kinue,** 1928. Hitomi Kinue winning her 100-meter heat at the Amsterdam Olympics. Although she lost in the semi-final, she won a silver medal in the 800-meter race.

**Crown Prince Akihito** gets an autograph. Crown Prince Akihito (the current emperor) (far right) has a ball autographed by Nankai Hawks pitcher Besshō Akira on the prince's first visit to Kōrakuen Stadium in Tokyo, November 9, 1947. Bēsubōru magajin sha.

**Professional wrestling.** Rikidōzan gives the fans what they want: his specialty, the karate chop. Asahi Shimbun sha.

**Jūdō.** Anton Geesink of the Netherlands attempting to throw Kaminaga Akio at the Third World Jūdō Championships in Paris (1961). Geesink defeated Kaminaga and repeated his victory in the unlimited division at the 1964 Tokyo Olympics. Bēsubōru magajin sha.

**Oh Sadaharu** in the "Flamingo Stance." Oh assumes his trademark stance for the first time, at Kawasaki Stadium, July 1, 1962. Bēsubōru magajin sha.

**"The Witches of the East."** The "Tōyō no Majo" upset the Soviet team for the gold medal in women's volleyball at the 1964 Tokyo Olympics. Bēsubōru magajin sha.

**Exhibition sumō.** Konishiki (left) versus Terao at Bercy Stadium, Paris, October 10, 1986. Corbis/Bettmann Archive.

**Arimori Yūko.** Marathon runner Arimori Yūko wins the bronze medal at the 1996 Atlanta Olympics. AP/Wide World.

**"Happy Harada."** Harada Masahiko triumphs in the 1998 World Cup at Ramsau, Austria. AP/Wide World.

**Professional soccer.** National team player Hirase Tomoyuki, playing against Slovakia at the 2000 Sydney Olympics, typifies the new breed of long-haired athlete.

and Mishima Yukio, who was an international celebrity at the time of his suicide in 1970. Their work can be seen as representative of Taishō democracy and of the fascism that followed it.

Abe's short story, "Nichidoku taikō kyōgi" ("The Japanese-German Track-and-Field Meet") appeared in the January 1930 issue of the avant-garde literary magazine *Shinchō*.[65] The central figure is the sexually frustrated young wife of an elderly Japanese professor of law. Together with her husband's nephew, Shibata, she watches the German team arrive at Tsuruga Bay. Accompanied by the wily Shibata, who wants to seduce her, she attends the track-and-field meet and is struck by the physical beauty of the German athletes. She is especially drawn to twenty-three-year-old Kurt Weiss, to his "auburn hair, boyish face, tanned blond skin, and . . . supple, round, resilient legs." She cannot look away from him. As he competes, "her eyes were fixed on Weiss's muscles, which were smoother and more beautiful" than those of the other athletes. She is so sexually fascinated that she goes by herself to the second day of competition and stares at the young German whose "lithe body revolved far more beautifully than any dancer's."

The next day, she encounters Weiss in the elevator of the hotel where her women's group meets. "Weiss's breath flowed through her hair." Although she does not act upon her impulses, she feels the shame of her imagined "depravity." In her thoughts, if not in her physical behavior, she succumbs to the erotic temptation. She goes to see the team's departure from Tsuruga Bay. The newspaper publishes a photograph of the team as it prepares to embark. "There, behind Wichmann's shoulder, was a Japanese woman's face, a woman who was wearing a black kimono. The face floated there, faintly white." The team's arrival awakened the heroine to the life of the senses; the team's departure dooms her to ghostly might-have-beens.

It must be noted that the story takes place before Hitler's rise to power. When Abe penned his story in 1930, Germany had a liberal-democratic government and its capital—the city of Christopher Isherwood's *Goodbye to Berlin*—had just replaced Paris as a potent symbol of sexual liberation. *Shinchō*'s readers knew this. One can assume that they saw "The Japanese-German Track-and-Field Meet" as a not-very-subtle critique of the presumably arranged and certainly loveless marriage of an older man and a younger woman. The story's implications are feminist and its acknowledgment of the erotic dimension in sports, which was a common theme in European literature, is quite radical.

Abe Tomoji was certainly unaware of the fateful consequences of

Japan's alliance with the dictatorial regime that followed the liberal-democratic Weimar Republic. Mishima Yukio, novelist and political activist, experienced the catastrophic military defeat and the postwar democratization of Japan—and longed for a more traditional, more authoritarian society. Sports, especially the martial arts, played a significant role in his art and in his life.

Born in 1925, Hiraoka Kimitake—Mishima was a pseudonym—was educated at the Gakushūin (Peers' School) in an atmosphere of chauvinistic fervor. In those years, however, he thought of himself as a poet and distanced himself from politics. The autobiographical protagonist of an early story, "Tabako" (Cigarettes; 1946), is portrayed as the sensitive victim of the school's boorish rugby team. In time, the vectors shifted and the valences were reversed. Mishima came to adore athletic virility. *Kamen no kokuhaku* (Confessions of a Mask; 1949) is the first-person narrative of a youth who is sexually excited by "death and pools of blood and muscular flesh."[66] He has visions of the martyrdom of Saint Sebastian, whose bare chest is penetrated by the phallic arrows of the Roman soldiers, and he imagines the mesomorphic young man whom he loves as another Sebastian. The pectoral development of another youth reminds the narrator of the young male swimmers who splash seductively in Walt Whitman's "Song of Myself."

Mishima did more than evoke images of homoerotic muscularity. He devoted himself to the martial arts and transformed his own body into a work of art, the physical symbol of his extreme nationalism. The most direct statement of his Weltanschauung appeared in his tract *Taiyō to tetsu* (Sun and Steel; 1970). Like the German-influenced educational theorists of the 1930s, he deplored the intellectuals' neglect of the body. "Facile optimism," he wrote, is invariably related "to feeble muscles or to obesity, while the cult of the hero and a mighty nihilism are always related to a mighty body and well-tempered muscles."[67]

Kendō was Mishima's chosen martial art. He practiced it and he placed it at the symbolic center of his short story "Ken" ("Sword"). The story concerns a group of students training for a kendō tournament. When he dons his uniform and grasps his sword, Kokubu Jirō, the idolized captain of the team, appears to the other fencers as "a god on the rampage."[68] For him, kendō is a realm apart, an island of moral purity in the morass of the modern world. "Every comparison with the mire of society . . . made the hallowed ground of sport seem more attractive."[69] The sword is described as the instrument of mystic unity. It is "a sharp-pointed crystal of concentrated, unsullied power, the natural form taken by the spirit and the flesh when they were honed into a single shaft of pure light."[70] Jiro's charismatic power over the other youths bonds the group. It is characteristic for Mishima that Jiro's power includes an element of homoeroticism: "The sides of his pleated kimono skirt gave glimpses of sleek amber thigh, alive and stirring in a way that hinted at the young body dancing within the uniform and protective gear that covered him from head to foot."[71]

Charisma is not enough. The god-like athlete fails. At a crucial moment in the story, Jiro's teammates fail to respect his authority. Unable to bear this humiliation, he puts on his uniform, with his family's crest in gold on his black-lacquered breastplate, and he kills himself.

Which is more or less what Mishima did when his appeals for a return to militaristic nationalism failed. On November 25, 1970, after he and the men of his paramilitary Tate No Kai (Shield Society) were unable to inspire the soldiers of Japan's postwar armed forces to a right-wing coup d'état, Mishima committed suicide.

## SPORTS IN PHYSICAL EDUCATION

In Japan as in Europe and the United States, the field of physical education has always been ideologically contested terrain. During the Taishō and Shōwa periods, nationalistic educators tended to be proponents of a physical-education curriculum that stressed calisthenic exercises, military drill, and the martial arts. They were likely to adopt German gymnastics as their model. More liberal educators, influenced by British and American theory and practice, tended to make modern sports the center of the physical education curriculum.[72]

After "decades of confusion" over what should be taught in physical education classes in the schools, the Ministry of Education issued the Syllabus of School Gymnastics (*Gakkō taisō kyōju yōmoku*) in 1913. The syllabus prescribed the approach of Per Henrik Ling, the Swedish proponent of "scientific" gymnastics whose system was already widely adopted in Scandinavia, Great Britain, and the United States. Although the Lingian system was to be the focus of the curriculum, it was to be supplemented by military drill and games (*yūgi*). Each district and school was supposed to devise its own curriculum, following the guidelines laid out by the syllabus.[73]

The syllabus failed to end the debate on the aims of physical education. From the promulgation of the Imperial Rescript on Education

(1890), if not earlier, the government had been concerned that Japanese schools inculcate patriotism. World War I, which began the year after the promulgation of the syllabus, convinced a number of influential politicians that Japan's national survival depended not only on patriotism but also on military preparedness. They advocated a paramilitary version of physical education in the schools. In 1917, the Diet promulgated Propositions on the Promotion of Military Gymnastics (*Heishiki taisō ni kansuru kengian*), which set forth the government's view of the objectives of physical education. The middle-school student "should be trained to be a soldier." He should be embued with patriotism and a "martial spirit." He should be obedient to authority and exhibit "toughness of mind and body."[74]

Compared to the major European powers, however, Japan played a minor role in World War I. The successful military and naval campaign against German concessions in China and German colonies in the Mariana, Caroline, and Marshall Islands was concluded before the end of 1914, but the Japanese government's concern for patriotism and military preparedness continued into the 1920s. In 1924, for instance, on the occasion of the First Meiji Shrine Games (Meiji Jingū Kyōgi Taikai), the Ministry of Education declared "National Physical Education Day" and directed all schools to observe the day as an annual event in order to inculcate "collective behavior, moral training, and . . . national spirit in the students." The following year, an Imperial Ordinance, the Order of Attachment of Military Officers to Schools (*Rikugun gen'eki shōkō gakkō haizoku rei*), was promulgated. Military drill, to be taught by army officers on active duty, became a part of the physical education curriculum at middle schools and above. The stated objective of the Imperial Ordinance was development of character. Since the total number of hours allotted to physical education was not increased, time gained for paramilitary education was time lost for sports and gymnastics.[75]

Despite this persistent governmental concern for patriotism and military preparedness, the interwar period was also the heyday of "progressive education." Educational theorists like Ono Genzō, Kinoshita Takeji, and Kawaguchi Hideaki studied Niels Bukh and John Dewey and challenged the German tradition of calisthenics and drill that had long characterized physical education at the primary and secondary levels. These educators called for "child-centered" physical education.[76] Kawaguchi, who taught at the elementary school attached to the prestigious Nara Women's Normal School, published a four-volume treatise on the topic that stressed the importance of the child's individuality and freedom of choice and urged teachers to implant the seeds of a lifelong commitment to physical education and sports.[77]

It is difficult to say how widespread this reformist mood was. The reformers were certainly a minority within their profession, but they managed to implement progressive ideas of physical education at a few experimental schools. Children fortunate enough to attend these schools were encouraged to choose their own leaders and the disorderly excitement of outdoor games replaced the dreary drill of the airless gymnasium.

Progressive educators may also have had some influence on government policy. Whether or not this was the case, officials in the Ministry of Education seem to have shared the progressive educators' worry about an over-emphasis on competition. In March 1926, the ministry issued a new directive on the proper role of sports in physical education, the "Order Concerning the Promotion of Physical Education Activities" (*Taiiku undō no shinkō ni kansuru ken*). In this document, the ministry warned local educational administrators and principals against, among other things, a win-at-all-costs attitude.[78] Two months later, in what may have been another concession to the progressive educators, the prewar Syllabus of School Gymnastics was revised to put more emphasis on games and sports.[79]

There was little evidence of any progressive influence in the sphere of physical education (or anywhere else) in the late 1920s and early 1930s. In 1928, Minister of Education Mizuno Rentarō announced that "All imported ideas were to be thoroughly 'Japanized,' abnormal thought was to be purged, and educators must firmly support the *kokutai* ["body of the nation," i.e., national polity] and truly understand its meaning."[80]

During the Meiji period, physical education, and by extension sports, had been administered under the rubric of school hygiene (*gakkō eisei*). This reflected the contemporary view of physical education, especially at the primary school level. However, as sports and the martial arts began to play an increasingly important role in the schools and in the larger society, the term "hygiene" became less and less appropriate. In May 1928 the School Hygiene Division (Gakkō Eisei Ka) of the Ministry of Education was renamed the Physical Education Section (Taiiku Ka), which more accurately reflected the nature of its work.[81]

In January 1931, in the midst of the "Manchurian incident," the regulations governing middle schools were once again revised to make jūdō and kendō required subjects in all physical education classes. The familiar reason was given: these martial arts were "recognized as useful in nurturing a resolute, determined patriotic spirit and training both the mind and the body."[82] Two years later, kyūdō too became a part of the regular school curriculum.[83]

With the continual increase of the army's influence on all aspects of Japanese life came a renewed call for *seishin kyōiku,* which might be translated as "spiritual education." In late 1932 and early 1933, Hatoyama Ichirō, who served as Minister of Education under both Inukai and Saitō, instituted a purge of educators suspected of liberal tendencies. Many were dismissed from their positions and some were arrested.[84]

As the authorities promoted military training and the martial arts in the schools, they actively discouraged sports participation. A Physical Education Council (Taiiku Undō Shingikai), established in 1929 with the Minister of Education as chairman, issued four reports before it was disbanded in 1939, all severely critical of modern sports. The council strongly influenced the Order Concerning the Control and Management of Baseball (*Yakyū no tōsei narabini shikō ni kansuru ken*) issued by the Ministry of Education in March 1932. Among other restrictions, the order required all educational institutions to obtain the ministry's permission for any and all organized baseball games.[85]

As the 1930s progressed—or regressed—American influence on Japanese physical education gave way to German. There were fewer references to the ideas of Edward Hitchcock and John Dewey and more to those of Rudolf Bode, a proponent of "rhythmic gymnastics" who wrote of *Blut und Boden* (blood and earth) as the basis of a *Nationalsozialistische Weltanschauung* (Nazi worldview).[86] Kinoshita Takeji, who had once been a leader in the movement for progressive education, sounded increasingly chauvinistic. The chilling slogan "blood and earth" began to appear in the essays and speeches of Japanese physical educators. Sophisticated intellectuals who had fled from the countryside in order to enjoy the freedom of urban life suddenly discovered that isolated villages were the true home of the descendants of the Sun Goddess.[87]

By the spring of 1936, Japan's government, ostensibly led by Prime Minister Hirota Kōki, was firmly controlled by the military. Hirota acquiesced in a policy of ever-closer co-operation with Nazi Germany. On November 25, 1936, his government officially sealed the alliance by joining Germany in the Anti-Comintern Pact.[88] When the usually compliant Hirota dared to disagree with General Terauchi Hisaichi, he was ousted from office and replaced, first by General Hayashi Senjurō and then by Prince Konoe Fumimaro. By July 1937, barely a month after Konoe assumed the office of prime minister, Japan was irrevocably at war in China.

In December 1937 the Ministry of Education issued a Circular Concerning Physical Education Activities under National Spiritual Mobilization (*Kokumin seishin sōdōin ni saishi taiiku undō no jisshi ni kansuru ken*). The nation's schools were ordered to stress patriotism and spiritual training (*seishin kunren*) as well as physical conditioning. Educational administrators were also admonished to preach the virtues of frugality.[89] ("Waste not, want not" seems to have been an adage close to the hearts of military men.) Among the contributions to Japan's "spiritual mobilization" was a variety of military gymnastics called *kenkoku taisō* ("gymnastics as the foundation of the nation").[90] Urged on by incessant references to seishin, teachers were directed not only to toughen the nation's youth by a regimen of Germanic exercises; they were also instructed to measure their students' height and weight and to examine them for any remediable physical weakness that might otherwise render them unfit for service in the army or navy. Theorists of physical education sometimes sounded like liberal-democratic advocates of individualism when they wrote of "autonomy," but they made it clear that autonomy was not to be confused with egoistic self-indulgence.[91]

Shifts in the Ministry of Education's rhetoric, which tended to become increasingly bellicose, were paralleled by changes in the personnel of the schools' physical education programs. An example of this can be seen in the history of Tokyo's Ichikō, the elite school that had since 1886 trained many of the nation's leaders. There was a shift in the ratio of conventional physical education teachers to martial arts instructors. Two of the latter were added to the eight-person physical-education staff in 1895. By 1925, each approach to physical education had six representatives. In 1939, as Japan prepared for the Pacific War, the budō instructors outnumbered their more conventional colleagues by seven to six.[92]

The schools were not the only locus of change. In January 1938, pressure from the military led to the establishment of a Ministry of Health and Welfare, within which was a Board of Physical Fitness that quickly "seized controlling power over all sports and physical activities except school gymnastics."[93] One of the new ministry's first public statements was the declaration that modern athleticism was a plague from the West.[94] Another indication of the new mood was the program at the Kantō Games of 1938. The "participants wore military uniforms and dragged sandbags in teams, dodged complex obstacles and participated in mock bayonet combat."[95] In 1939 the ministry also inaugurated compulsory fitness tests for all males between the ages of fifteen and twenty-five. The program was expanded in 1943 to include all females between the ages of fifteen and twenty-one. To motivate the participants, achievement badges were distributed. Modeled on the *Sportabzeichen* that were awarded to athletically proficient young Germans, the badges proclaimed the wearer's physical prowess. The young men and women were tested in running and jumping as well as in throwing hand grenades. After all, running and jumping are useful skills for soldiers advancing (never retreating) under enemy fire.[96]

The twenty-year history of the Meiji Shrine Games also reflects the changing power relationships. The first Meiji Shrine Games were held in 1924 under the auspices of the Home Ministry. In 1926, before the start of the third Games, there was a dispute between the Home Ministry and the Ministry of Education over student participation. The Ministry of Education, believing that the Home Ministry was infringing upon its jurisdiction by taking students from their classes, issued a directive prohibiting student participation. A compromise was reached by taking jurisdiction for the games away from the Home Ministry and creating a new private body to run them, the Meiji Shrine Athletic Association (Meiji Jingū Taiiku Kai). Then, from 1939 until their cancellation in 1943, the Meiji Shrine Games were administered by the newly established Ministry of Health and Welfare.[97]

The change in the dominant view of the purpose of physical education and sports was reflected in the name changes undergone by these national games. The first two games were called the Meiji Jingū Kyōgi Taikai (Meiji Shrine Sports Meet). From 1925 to 1937 they were called the Meiji Jingū Taiiku Taikai (Meiji Shrine Physical Education Meet). "*Taiiku*" is broader than "*kyōgi*" and emphasizes educational aims. In 1939, when jurisdiction over the games was transferred to the Ministry of Health and Welfare, the word "*Kokumin*" (people of the nation) was added to the title of the games. In 1942, the name was changed yet again. "*Rensei*" (training, drill) replaced the word "taiiku" and the final result was Meiji Jingū Kokumin Rensei Taikai, that is, the Meiji Shrine National People's Training Games. The name was appropriate to the event, which had become completely militaristic, including martial arts, mass gymnastics, anti-air raid drills, and army combat exercises.[98]

The militarization of Japanese physical education that began in the 1930s intensified during the course of the Pacific War. There were two important manifestations of this in 1941. In March, the National People's School Order (Kokumin Gakkō Rei) was promulgated, influenced by the German concept of the *Volksschule*. Elementary schools were to be reorganized into "national people's schools" and the purpose of compulsory education was proclaimed to be training "loyal subjects of the emperor." From its inception, physical education in the schools had been called *taisō*, gymnastics in its broader, classical Greek or German sense. Under the new system, gymnastics was renamed *tairen* (physical discipline). In December, the Ministry of Education created the Greater Japan Society for the Promotion of Physical Education for Students (Dai Nippon Gakutō Taiiku Shinkōkai) as an extradepartmental body whose purpose was to reorganize all student sport organizations into a unitary administration under the Ministry of Education.[99]

The war with China had already been dragging on for four years when General Tōjō Hideki became prime minister in October 1941. Less than two months later, Japan was at war with the United States and Great Britain. Four months after that, in April 1942, the Greater Japan Physical Education Association (Dai Nihon Taiiku Kyōkai) was reorganized to become the Dai Nippon Taiiku Kai, an extra-governmental organization headed by Prime Minister Tōjō. All the affiliated sport bodies were dissolved and became divisions of the new association. "Thus, all sporting activities were absorbed into the Imperial Rule Assistance regime for the Pacific War." And by the next year the government had banned most sports.[100]

In March 1942, the regime called for an even greater emphasis on the martial arts. Physical education was now to center on archery, jūdō, kendō, and rifle practice, and the approach to these sports was hardly playful. "The use of real swords on the battlefield affected the technique of kendo, and in 1943 its rules were changed to revert to the art of real sword fighting."[101] When the tide of war turned against the Japanese, total military mobilization became necessary and most Western sports were "prohibited by a series of government orders."[102] The *Mainichi shimbun*-sponsored middle-school baseball tournament had already been suspended in 1941.[103] In March 1943, the Ministry of Education called a halt to all collegiate sports except archery, kendō, and jūdō. Professional baseball, which had already switched to khaki uniforms, abjured the use of English terms. In 1942, games began to feature "attractions" in which players threw hand grenades at targets inscribed "Annihilate England and America." Professional baseball ceased to function in November 1944.[104] "The fire of sports cannot be extinguished," proclaimed Kinoshita Hideaki in his account of these years,[105] but the "fire of sports" was much less evident in 1945 than the flames that consumed

Japan's cities. As the war approached its dreaded end, teachers and students no longer had time for physical education of any sort. Together—as if they were dutiful students of Martin Heidegger—they experienced *"absolute Einsamkeit"* (absolute loneliness) and faced the prospect of life as a march toward death. This, at least, was the view of Hata Takao, who quoted Heidegger in the original German.[106]

# Part III

## Postwar Sports

# 7

# Rising from the Ashes

## PLAY BEGINS AGAIN: SPORTS

Apart from Kyoto, which had not been bombed, Japan's urban centers were a postwar wasteland. Despite the devastation, children played among the ruins and adults began, tentatively, to rebuild the organizations and the material infrastructure of Japanese sports. Like their grandparents in the Meiji period, they wanted not only the opportunity to participate in traditional and modern sports but also international recognition of their athletic achievements. For the leaders of Japanese sports, if not for rank-and-file athletes, readmission into the global sports arena was an enormously important goal.

During the Occupation, kendō and other traditional martial arts were banned and the Dai Nippon Butokukai was abolished, but sumō, whose practical military application was less obvious, was allowed to resume before the end of 1945. General Douglas MacArthur's advisors actively encouraged participation in baseball and other modern sports.[1]

On September 23, 1945, barely three weeks after Japan's political leaders boarded the U.S.S. *Missouri* and signed the documents that formally acknowledged their nation's defeat in war, the students of Tokyo University had their first postwar rugby game. Younger boys had already begun to play baseball and a National Students' Baseball Organization was quickly organized. That autumn the Japan Basketball Association was resurrected.[2]

On January 21, 1946, the *Asahi shimbun* carried a notice announcing the revival of the national middle-school baseball tournament. While recognizing the dire straits the country was in, the newspaper asserted its belief that "baseball will help mend young souls twisted by war, and

**163**

contribute to the development of democratic spirit . . . and the reconstruction of Japan."[3] Ideology changed; rhetoric did not: sport was for the good of the nation.

In January 1946, the Japan Physical Education Association (Nihon Taiiku Kyōkai) was reestablished as a private entity whose task was to supervise amateur sports. By 1999, this entity, which now calls itself (on its English-language home page) the Japan Amateur Sports Association, included fifty-four sports federations and had forty-seven prefectural sports associations as additional affiliated members.[4] One of the most important goals of the JPEA's revived or newly founded national federations was to gain acceptance by their respective international sports federations in order to be eligible to participate in the Olympic Games and other international competitions. Some member nations of the international sports federations were initially reluctant to welcome back their wartime foes, but the basketball and volleyball federations voted for readmission in 1950 and 1951 and the other federations followed.

With the coming of spring 1946, the horses began to race again at Japanese tracks (and gamblers once again rushed to bet on them).[5] Speedy horses shared the headlines with human runners. In 1946, the *Mainichi shimbun* resumed its prewar role as a sponsor of sports events; the newspaper staged a footrace around historic Lake Biwa (near Kyoto). The *Mainichi*'s longtime rival, the *Asahi shimbun*, responded in 1947 with the Fukuoka Marathon, which ranks today as one of the world's most important road races.[6]

In light of Japan's prewar enthusiasm for baseball and General MacArthur's belief that the game instilled a democratic ethos in its players, it was hardly a surprise that the professional game was also revived in 1946. In their first season eight teams played a total of 105 games.[7]

In order to raise money for postwar urban reconstruction, the government enacted a law in 1948 that allowed "local public bodies" to hold bicycle races (and to sell tickets to spectators eager to bet on the outcomes). The first races were held that November at the Ogura City Race Track in Kyushu. Observing that Ogura City took in nearly 20 million yen during the first four days of racing, other local governments scrambled to organize their own races and *keirin* (cycling competition) soon rivaled horse races in popularity.[8]

During the first days of November 1946, barely a year after the surrender, a national sports meet was held in Kyoto and at facilities in the surrounding prefectures. This was the first Kokumin Taiiku Taikai, the official English translation for which is "National Sports Festival" (showing once again how the term "taiiku" can mean "sports" as well as "physical education"). Unlike the Meiji Shrine Games, which the new national meet was meant to replace, the National Sports Festival changes its venue every year as different prefectures take turns hosting the event.[9]

They also vie for the national championship. During the festival's first ten years, Tokyo, the prefecture with the largest population and the most colleges, won both the men's and women's all-around championship. As the games increased in cost as well as in prestige, the host prefectures began to make special efforts to win. How else were they to justify the expense that hosting the meet involved? In 1956, at the eleventh annual meet, the host prefecture, Shizuoka, managed to win the men's championship. (Shizuoka's women's team came in third.) Tokyo's men and women were unbeatable from the thirteenth to the eighteenth meets, but the host prefecture almost always placed second. From the nineteenth meet, held in Niigata in 1964, the host prefecture has won almost every time.[10]

Victory at the National Sports Festival is undoubtedly sweet, but it does not mean that the level of sport in the winning prefecture has been permanently raised. With the exception of Tokyo, the performance of the host prefecture almost always falls dramatically at the following year's meet. Behind this strange phenomenon is something more tangible than the "home-court advantage." To each meet come "gypsy athletes" who are induced annually to change their legal residence to the host prefecture. The practice has long been criticized, but is apparently as difficult to eradicate as under-the-table payments to intercollegiate athletes in the United States. An eligibility rule was passed to prohibit an athlete who has competed for one prefecture from competing for a different prefecture the next year, but the rule has been ineffective.

Although newspapers had been publishing stories on modern sports events from 1883, when the *Tōkyō nichi nichi shimbun* reported on a boat race on the Sumida River, the sports pages of the post-1945 daily press were no longer enough to sate the Japanese appetite for sports news. Entrepreneurs took advantage of this thirst for information. They launched the *Nikkan supōtsu* on March 6, 1946. Three more sports dailies followed in the next four years. By 1960, Japan had no fewer than seven daily newspapers devoted to sports. (In time, these newspapers added gossip, serial novels of an erotic nature, pornographic photographs, and advertisements for sexual services.)[11]

Like most European countries, Japan had long relied on state-run radio, but privately owned stations began to broadcast on September 1,

1951, when CBC (in Nagoya) and NJB (in Osaka) took to the airwaves. The first sports broadcast by a commercial station was the very next day, when NJB broadcast an exhibition game between the Hawaii Red Sox and Waseda University. Six stations were broadcasting by the end of 1951, and eighteen by the end of 1952. In January 1952, a consortium of commercial stations began to broadcast sumō meets, in competition with NHK's coverage.[12]

Japan's exclusion from the London Olympics of 1948 was painful but hardly unexpected. That Japan was chosen by the International Olympic Committee to host the 1964 Olympics, which took place in Tokyo, was celebrated as a symbol of Japan's acceptance within the community of nations. (See Chapter 8.) It was the final realization of a dream deferred.[13] En route to the moment when the Japanese played host to the world's athletes there were several milestones, each of them carefully noted by patriotic sportswriters. Since China, Korea, the Philippines, Burma, and most other nations of Southeast Asia all had bitter memories of wartime occupation by the Japanese, it was a real breakthrough when a Japanese team was invited to the inaugural Asian Games, which took place in New Delhi in March 1951. Japan's seventy-seven athletic representatives returned home in triumph, having won twenty-four gold medals, twenty of them in the thirty-three track-and-field events. Radio coverage of the games was provided by NHK.[14]

Admission to the 1952 Olympics, celebrated in Helsinki, was welcomed as proof that Japan was no longer a pariah in Western eyes. (It had been a full ten years after the end of World War I before a German team was allowed once again to compete in the Olympics.) In 1958, the Third Asian Games were celebrated in Tokyo, and Japan won fifty-nine of the ninety-nine events.[15]

Sugimoto Atsuo maintains that the special characteristic of Japanese sports has always been the role played by business enterprise.[16] This characteristic is hardly unique, but it is certainly prevalent. The postwar years saw the reconstitution of the industrial and commercial leagues that had offered the prewar Japanese opportunities to continue to participate in sports after the end of their formal education. For most men, and for many of the women in the workforce, it was the company's sports program that provided the facilities for ball games and the martial arts. The small city of Kōriyama, located in Fukushima Prefecture, exemplified the situation in the first postwar decades. In 1962, 10,000 of the city's 138,000 citizens (7.2%) were members of sports clubs, mostly those at school or at their place of employment. For students, the most popular sports were jūdō, baseball, and table tennis. For adults, they were kendō, baseball, and mountain-climbing. Membership in sports clubs was correlated, as it tends to be everywhere, with social class. Kōriyama's more affluent and highly educated citizens were more likely to be members of sports clubs and to participate in the clubs' activities. To encourage wider participation, the city sponsored or authorized over forty separate sports events, including folk dances, that involved 14,380 participants from the city and from nearby towns.[17]

To complete the resurrection of Japanese sports, it was necessary for Japanese athletes to prove that they were once again able to hold their own against the best American and European athletes. For this to be accomplished, in order to "beat them at their own game," it was essential that Japanese victories be in modern sports and not just in sumō or the martial arts.

Among the first of the postwar athletic heroes was the swimmer Furuhashi Hironoshin. In less than two years, competing in the United States as well as in Japan, pushed to his limits by his rival Hashizume Shirō, he set no fewer than twenty-three free-style world records over distances from 400 to 1,500 meters. The first of them—4:38.4 for 400 meters—came in 1947, when he was still a student of economics at Nihon University. Two years later, at the American championships in Los Angeles, he won the 400-meter and 800-meter titles and set a world record of 18:19.0 in the 1,500-meter race. (American sportswriters nicknamed him the "Flying Fish of Fujiyama.") The race was broadcast live in Japan, the first live overseas sports broadcast since the war, and the whole country celebrated, as it did when Yukawa Hideki received the Nobel Prize in Physics the same year, the first Japanese to be so honored. Although Furuhashi failed to win a medal at the 1952 Olympics in Helsinki, his athletic achievements and the fame they generated sufficed for him to be made director of the Japan Olympic Committee in 1990.[18]

Many Japanese hoped for similar success in professional boxing. In 1950, they looked eagerly to thirty-five-year-old Horiguchi Tsuneo, better known as "the Piston." Horiguchi—in the famous phrase from *On the Waterfront*—might indeed have been "a contenda." He had fought 176 times and won 138 of his bouts, 82 of them by knock-outs. After Horiguchi was killed in a train accident, hopes were centered on Shirai Yoshio. On May 19, 1952, fighting in the flyweight division, he became Japan's first world champion in boxing.[19]

There had also been good news in 1951, when Tanaka Shigeki became the first Japanese runner to win the Boston Marathon.[20] Two years later,

Yamada Keizō won the classic race and thereby overcame the humiliation of his 26th-place finish at the 1952 Olympics.[21] Tanaka and Yamada were followed by six other Japanese winners, the last of whom took the title in 1987.[22] By that time, most Japanese seem to have recovered from whatever blows to their collective self-esteem that they might have suffered as a result of World War II. According to survey data reported in 1981, they thought Japan—all things considered—superior to other nations; Germany came in second, the United States third, and India last.[23]

The first postwar television broadcast of a sports event was a test broadcast of two professional baseball games at Kōrakuen Stadium on June 3, 1951. The transmission was picked up at the Mitsukoshi Department Store in the Nihonbashi section of Tokyo, where the "new medium" was being featured in a special exhibition. NHK began regular broadcasting on February 1, 1953, and the first privately owned, commercial television station, Nihon Television (NTV), followed a few months later, on August 28, 1953. Both stations responded to the viewers' preferences, measured by surveys, and supplied frequent sports coverage, especially baseball, boxing, and—from 1954 on—professional wrestling (known by the Japanese abbreviation "*puroresu*").[24]

When television coverage was impractical, radio provided celebratory words and music. In 1956, when a group of Japanese mountaineers led by Maki Yūkō successfully scaled Mount Manaslu, an 8,000-meter Himalayan peak that rises to more than twice the height of Japan's tallest mountain (Mount Fuji), NHK's proud report of the feat was accompanied by a rendition of the national anthem. The airwaves crackled with similar enthusiasm fourteen years later when Uemura Naomi and Matsuura Teruo became the first Japanese to reach the summit of Mount Everest.[25]

Triumphs such as these were savored, but the patriotic public hungered for more regular (and more visible) fare. Wrestling matches in which Japanese grapplers mauled hapless foreigners were especially popular. Wrestling quickly became television's most popular attraction for men (and the third most popular for women). In a November 1957 survey by the advertising agency Dentsū, professional wrestling enjoyed the highest ratings of any TV genre. Another survey, taken in March 1961, found that the matches were watched by 60.5 percent of the viewers (compared to 37.4 percent for American detective series). The unchallenged superstar of professional wrestling was the former sumō wrestler Rikidōzan. Over a ten-year period, more than half of the 450 *Mainichi shimbun* articles on wrestling named him in the headline (and the next-most-popular grappler was named a mere thirty-one times). At the peak of his popularity, Rikidōzan drew a million fans a year to ringside. Fans who were unable to purchase tickets waited impatiently for his weekly appearance on NTV's Saturday evening "Fightmen Hour" (sic), during which the indomitable Rikidōzan used his famed "karate chop" to defeat a number of villainous foreign challengers—usually Americans—who were paid to submit to enormous amounts of real and simulated violence. Viewers were thrilled as they received jolts of vicarious self-esteem. "Through professional wrestling," commented NTV's Komatsu Nobuyasu, "Rikidōzen physically expressed the revival of the spiritual confidence of the Japanese." There was great distress in 1963 when Rikidōzen was murdered by a petty gangster. He was only thirty-nine. Few of the reporters who mourned him mentioned that this potent symbol of national pride was an ethnic Korean.[26]

With Japan scheduled to host the Olympics in the year 1964, the Ministry of Education decided in the late 1950s to renew its efforts to promote active participation in sport. The ministry created a special Bureau for Physical Education and sponsored its first postwar National Sports Day in May 1958. By August, over twenty thousand professional and volunteer coaches and trainers were at work in Japan's cities, towns, and villages.[27] The government's campaign to increase active sports participation included the passage in 1961 of the Sports Promotion Act, which broke new ground by citing improvements in Japan's "quality of life" as its raison d'être. Communities of every size became increasingly committed to providing public facilities and sponsoring sports festivals. According to a survey by the Ministry of Education, between 1963 and 1968 the number of public "community sports" facilities outside the schools nearly doubled, from 2,519 to 4,659. Gymnasiums increased from 163 to 420; baseball fields from 468 to 703; tennis courts from 321 to 482; volleyball courts from 128 to 240; playing fields from 116 to 419; and swimming pools from 426 to 899.[28] Some thought that the government's programs were *too* successful. By 1962, two years before the Olympics came to Japan, the *Japan Times* was already lamenting the neglect of tradition symbolized by the widespread passion for Western sports.[29]

## BASEBALL

Three months after the end of the war, representatives of seven professional baseball teams met in Tokyo to discuss the future of the sport. They managed to gather enough former players for two teams. The first postwar professional baseball game was an East–West contest held at the Jingū Stadium in Tokyo on November 23, 1945, in front of a crowd of 5,878.[30] In 1946, eight teams participated in a full season of 105 games. Over the next four years there were many mergers, new teams, and name changes. In 1948, a new professional baseball federation was established, and a former public prosecutor general was named the first baseball commissioner in 1951.

One league became two in 1950. In the summer and fall of 1949 several newly established teams had requested to join the federation. The existing teams split over whether or not to allow this expansion. Their disagreement resulted in the creation of two leagues, the Pacific League (composed of the teams favorable to expansion) and the Central League (composed of the teams opposing expansion). The Central League, with the Yomiuri Giants and the Hanshin Tigers, has always been more popular.

On November 13, 1951, a Pacific League all-star team beat a team of American League players 3–1 in a postseason game in Okayama. This was the first time that a Japanese team defeated an American team in a professional baseball game, and the victory created a sensation.

Professional baseball also had its dark moments. Near the end of the 1969 season, two newspapers reported that a pitcher for the Seitetsu Lions had cooperated with a criminal organization to "fix" certain games. The pitcher was expelled from professional baseball for life. This scandal became known as the "Black Mist" incident, a reference to the insidious and corrupting influence of organized crime. The revelations and expulsions continued for two years. A number of players were suspended or expelled for fixing baseball games and automobile races and for illegally betting on horse races.[31]

Like the "Black Sox" scandal of 1920, the "Black Mist" incident may have briefly dampened public enthusiasm for baseball, but the demand for sports heroes is insatiable. Heroes there had to be, and Japan's counterpart to Babe Ruth was Oh Sadaharu, who played for Tokyo's Yomiuri Giants, the team that dominated postwar Japanese baseball the way the New York Yankees had dominated the American scene.[32] The man, the team, and the game were taken, collectively, as symbols of the Japanese spirit. The names on the uniform were in the Roman alphabet rather than in Chinese characters, but Oh Sadaharu and his teammates were perceived by their admirers to embody *konjō*, an attitude that combines "passive, stoic endurance with active, all-out drive."[33] The way of the warrior—bushidō—was said to have shaped the game and inspired its players, modern samurai all.

This legend of "samurai baseball" was skillfully propagated by Robert Whiting. His two books on the game, *The Chrysanthemum and the Bat* (1977) and *You Gotta Have Wa* (1989), were accepted as gospel not only by foreigners, whose knowledge of Japanese baseball was limited to what they read in Whiting's books, but also by the Japanese, who were delighted to hear a foreigner tell the stories they told about themselves. After all, if baseball Japanese-style is a continuation of bushidō, if the players can be perceived as samurai in pin-striped uniforms, then Japan has made the transition to modernity without the sacrifice of its (allegedly) ancient traditions.[34]

Innumerable academic and nonacademic authorities have argued that the Japanese have always subordinated the individual to the group. "Where Westerners may at least put on a show of independence and individuality," writes Edwin O. Reischauer, "most Japanese will be quite content to conform in dress, conduct, style of life, and even thought to the norms of their group."[35] Whiting's version of this generalization refers to Japan as "a paternalistic society with values deeply rooted in Confucianism and agrarian tradition."[36] The word "feudal" might just as well have expressed Whiting's convictions about Japanese baseball. Team managers seemed to treat their players as daimyō treated their serfs. Managers insisted that there was only one correct way to swing a bat or run the bases and coaches drilled the players obsessively until they got it right (or collapsed from exhaustion). Hirōka Tatsurō's demand that his players practice for nine hours a day was seen not as madness but as proof of true dedication. It was hardly a surprise when an NHK survey found that *doryoku* (effort) was the favorite word of those polled.[37] Of the Yomiuri Giants' training camp, Warren Cromartie commented, "I'd come to Japan to play baseball and discovered that I'd joined the Marines instead."[38]

Individual careers were sacrificed for the good of the team. Sugiura Tadashi of the Nankai Hawks pitched forty-two games in 1959, winning thirty-eight of them, and he then pitched four games against the Yomiuri Giants in the Japan Series, winning all of them. By the age of twenty-six, he had ruined his arm. Why did Sugiura ignore his body's signals and trudge meekly to the mound? "The Japanese pitcher simply has no choice."[39]

Managers exercised the same tight control of the team's off-the-field behavior. Unmarried players lived in barracks, to which they obediently returned as the hour of the curfew approached. If a player wished to marry, he sought permission from his manager, whose approval or disapproval of a bride was as final as his decision if and when to lay down a bunt. The Hiroshima Carp's star shortstop Takahashi Yoshihiko was sent to the minor leagues in the middle of a pennant race because he balked at attending a rally. Clearly, he lacked the spirit necessary to become a champion.[40] Criticism of managers by players was anathema. When Emoto Takenori violated the tabu in 1981, the Hanshin Tigers sent him into premature retirement (where he increased the volume of his criticism).[41]

Total loyalty was also expected of the managers. In their relationship to the owners of the team, which were almost invariably corporations, they were expected to be models of humility and self-abasement. When their teams did well, they modestly disclaimed credit; when their teams played badly, they apologized. In return for such loyalty, managers were spared the publicly abusive treatment for which George Steinbrenner has become famous. Managers were seldom fired. They were simply granted a much-deserved *kyūyō* (rest), which was sometimes of indefinite duration. If Don Blasingame's experience with the Hanshin Tigers and the Nankai Hawks is any indication, however, Americans who manage Japanese baseball teams are treated with less deference by the players and less civility by the owners.

Although Whiting's influential characterization of the game emphasized humility, subservience, and respect for authority, Whiting did acknowledge the existence of a *shinjinrui* (new breed) of players who behaved outrageously, broke the rules, gleefully violated ethical norms, and avoided sanctions. Play has grown rougher, more aggressive. In the 1950s, Japanese sportswriters criticized American players for "murder sliding." Today, Japanese base runners routinely slide into the second baseman in order to break up the double play.[42] Whether there has been a similar decline in standards for off-the-field conduct is unclear, but Cromartie's autobiography painted a bleak picture of dismally provincial players addicted to S/M films in which helpless women are ripped to shreds. "Real life for them was that night's game and their favorite comics."[43]

Cromartie's memoir of his years in Japanese baseball is one of many books and essays that tell the tale of mutual miscomprehension.[44] American players have not always displayed the dedication and humility expected of them. Some have been arrogant and disdainful of Japanese culture. Many have not made the effort to learn enough of the language to ride the subway or order their own lunch. For their part, the Japanese have not always been sympathetic to foreigners bewildered by cultural differences. American players are paid more than their Japanese team-mates but more is expected of them. If their performance falls short of expectations, they are exposed to excoriation in the press and obscene racist jeers from the fans. "You're an outcast no matter what you do," complained Cromartie, "You go five-for-five and you're ignored. You go zero-for-five and it's 'Fuck you, Yankee go home.'" In 1987, Takeuchi Juhei, the commissioner of baseball, asked if any foreign player had ever taught the Japanese anything of value.[45]

Randy Bass, who won the Central League triple crown in 1985 and led the Hanshin Tigers to their first victory in the Japan Series, seemed like an ideal person to overcome the prejudice against *gaijin* (outside people, i.e., foreigners). He managed to combine athletic prowess with modesty and an admirable appreciation for Japanese culture. This was not enough, however, to win unqualified acceptance. Toward the end of the 1985 season, when his 54 home runs threatened Oh Sadaharu's record, he was repeatedly walked and the record survived. On October 24, at Kōrakuen Stadium, the Hanshin Tigers played the Yomiuri Giants, who at that time were managed by Oh. The Giants' pitchers didn't throw Bass one strike in five at-bats. (Oh contended later that he had not directed his pitchers to behave in such an unsportsmanlike way.)[46]

Bass received adulation as well as invective, but the final assessment was that he failed to exhibit the proper spirit. His career in Japan came to an end when he left in midseason to take his son to the United States for a brain-tumor operation that saved his life. The Tigers denied that Bass had received permission to stay with his son—until he produced hard evidence to the contrary. One of Japan's greatest players, Harimoto Isao, concluded from the brouhaha over Bass that foreign players "are just not a good example for young people."[47]

Who *was* a good example? Oh Sadaharu, star of the Waseda High School team, for whom he pitched in four straight tournament games despite his blistering, bleeding hands, star also of the Yomiuri Giants, whom he joined in 1959. From 1962 to 1974, Oh led the league in home runs. He won two successive triple crowns; in 1973, he hit 51 home runs, batted .355, and drove in 114 runs; in 1974, it was 49, .332, and 197. His lifetime total of 868 home runs eclipsed Hank Aaron's 755. (Japanese ballparks are smaller than American stadia, but this factor is balanced by the fact that the Japanese season lasts for only 130 rather than 162 games.)[48]

The only baseball player to rival, and perhaps even surpass, Oh as a national hero was his teammate Nagashima Shigeo. Whiting, who was not given to understatement, called him "the best loved, most admired, and most talked about figure in the history of sport."[49] The *Asahi shimbun* agreed: "Without question [Nagashima] was the brightest star of postwar sports."[50] He joined the Giants in 1958, a year before Oh, and had his grandest moment on June 26, 1959, when the emperor attended his—the emperor's—first baseball game. Playing against the Yomiuri Giants' archrivals, the Hanshin Tigers, Nagashima won the game with a bottom-of-the-ninth *sayōnara* (game-winning) home run. He also earned three straight batting crowns and contributed immensely to the Giants' unprecedented streak of nine consecutive championships (from 1965 through 1973).

Nagashima, however, lacked Oh's highly public identification with Japanese tradition. Most Japanese fans seem to have forgiven Oh the fact that he had a Chinese father. His mixed ancestry may even have been an attraction in the eyes of those whose sense of identity was "learned, incomplete, painful, vulnerable."[51] Except for the most xenophobic fans, the nationality of Oh's biological father was less salient than the guidance of his spiritual father, Arakawa Hiroshi, who introduced him to the mysteries of Zen Buddhism and the equally esoteric doctrines of aikidō.[52] In 1962, while he and Oh were learning from Ueshiba Morihei, aikidō's venerable founder, how to tap the power of ki, Arakawa had the epiphany that transformed his protégé's career. To perfect his batting, to become infused with ki, Oh needed to raise his right foot and adopt a "flamingo stance." It may have seemed foolish, and Oh certainly looked odd in comparison to all the other batters who had been drilled in the "correct" stance, but it worked. What Zen and Noh and aikidō had begun, kendō concluded. Arawaka studied that discipline too, and he instructed Oh to practice the swordsman's moves, but Arawaka decided that real kendō matches were too risky. It was Oh's destiny to wield the bat rather than the bamboo sword.[53]

William W. Kelly has rightly criticized Whiting's account of Japanese baseball. One of Kelly's criticisms is that Whiting ignored the attractions of baseball as a kind of bittersweet comic drama of the *dys*functions of corporate life. Like the serial stories in Japanese comic books, baseball games can be enjoyed as sardonic narratives exposing "the drudgery of day-to-day work" and expressing the vicissitudes of "life under pretentious, unreasonable, uncaring bosses."[54] A second criticism is that Whiting exaggerates the "Japanese-ness" of the players. In fact, over three hundred of the postwar players have been from North America and many of the "Japanese" have been ethnically Koreans, Chinese, or men of mixed ancestry. Whiting also erred when he took the rhetoric of the Yomiuri Giants at face value and wrote as if the authoritarian leadership of Kawakami Tetsuharu, who managed the Giants in their heyday, were the norm for all of Japanese baseball.[55] The critique is just, but Whiting *was* an excellent guide to what most Japanese fans wanted to believe: that baseball was a microcosm of Japanese culture, that the Giants were an epitome of baseball, that Oh Sadaharu was the embodiment of the necessary spiritual qualities, the "right stuff." It may have been a fantasy, but the combination of quantified achievement and spiritual enlightenment was irresistible. Oh Sadaharu had the "stats" required to gain entry into the record books and he embodied the spirit of the samurai. He symbolized modernity and he symbolized tradition. Small wonder that he became a hero.

Early in the century, Tobita Suishū dreamed of the day when Japanese baseball players might meet their American mentors on equal terms. No student of the game thinks that that day has arrived, but Nomo Hideo is its harbinger. His 1995 acquisition by the Los Angeles Dodgers and his subsequent success may signal a new trend in Japanese-American sports relations. Nomo, playing for the Los Angeles Dodgers and then for the New York Mets, seems to have adjusted on the town as well as on the mound. (Nomo's American success may be explained, in part, because he has spoken flatteringly of the United States as the home of the "real" major leagues).[56] Nomo—along with golfer Aoki Isao, Formula I driver Nakayama Akihiko, and tennis player Date Kimiko—is part of the international migration in athletic talent. He may pitch, literally, in Yankee Stadium, but he plays in the global sports arena.[57]

## TRADITIONAL SPORTS

### *The Martial Arts*

As part of the war effort, kendō and jūdō had been "distorted into a means of spiritually transforming Japanese schoolboys into willing volunteers for the imperial armed forces."[58] Both sports suffered the consequences of that distortion after Japan's defeat. In 1945, the new Ministry of Education, under the direction of the Supreme Commander for the Allied Powers, banned martial arts training from the school curriculum, forbade it as a student club activity, and even prohibited kendō practice on school properties. Archery had not played a central role in the prewar educational system, but it too was associated with bushidō and banned along with the other martial arts.

To subvert the ban, kendō enthusiasts created a new, rationalized form of the sport which they called *shinai kyōgi* (bamboo sword competition). The equipment was revised, and the rules and judging made clearer. This apparently mollified the American authorities as well as the Ministry of Education, and this new form of kendō was allowed into the regular middle-school and high-school curricula in 1952. The Occupation ended that year, and kendō was reinstated in middle and high schools in 1953. Merging then with shinai kyōgi, it became "school kendō" (in 1957). The short history of shinai kyōgi indicates that it was mainly a euphemism to ensure the survival of kendō, but many of the changes made in the name of shinai kyōgi remained long after the demise of the subterfuge.[59]

In October 1952, the All Japan Kendō Federation was established, followed in 1961 by the All Japan School Kendō Federation and the All Japan Kendō Federation for Industrial Organizations. It was not until 1964, however, that the Budōkan (Hall of Martial Arts) was established. Since that time, the number of participants has soared. In 1969, some 30,000 fencers a year achieved the first of kendō's ten ranks, but the total number between 1976 and 1991 was 883,544, of which 27 percent were female. In the kendō clubs that have proliferated through the secondary schools, 40 percent of the membership is now female, a remarkable deviation from the stereotype of the subservient Japanese woman.[60]

Like jūdō, kendō has gone global. The International Kendō Federation was established in 1970 and a world championship has been held every three years. By 1992, the fifteen founding nations of the IKF had become thirty and the non-Japanese membership had grown to over 260,000.[61]

What all of this means, of course, is that kendō—and the other martial arts—continued to modernize and to undergo what German scholars call *Versportlichung* (sportification). For many practitioners, this tendency for the martial arts to blur the line separating them from modern sports is subversive and transgressive. "It is patent," writes Donn Draeger, "that no sport can ever be a true classical dō form; no classical dō form can ever house a sport entity." Draeger's argument is awkwardly expressed, but his position is clear enough. Sports involve not only competition, which some versions of the martial arts seek to avoid, they also involve "records or championships," which "traditionalists" regard as totally foreign to the spirit of budō.[62]

The modernization of kendō accelerated after the creation of the International Kendō Association in 1970, but the sport continued to be seen by many if not by most of its devotees as an embodiment of tradition. This is the case for foreign as well as for Japanese practitioners. John J. Donohue, for instance, is quite lyrical about the sport's traditions: "The sight of a long line of *kendōka* donning equipment with roots in the feudal past has an effect of timelessness. As they put on their equipment, *kendōka* also put on the tradition of *kendō:* its form, its purpose."[63]

The appearance of the kendō fighter is certainly imposing. Dressed in a black hakama that reaches to his or her bare feet, masked, mittened, padded, armored, wielding a sword made from four shafts of split bamboo bound with a leather grip and leather thongs, the kendō fighter looks to Western eyes like the medieval warriors of Kurosawa Akira's films. The irony, of course, is that the equipment is *not* timeless. It was developed over the years as part of the "sportification" of kendō.

While many men, women, boys, and girls look to kendō for morality and character building, for others the competitive motive seems to have become dominant. In any case, kendō's format now resembles that of other combat sports. Matches take place in rectangular "rings" and winners are decided on the basis of points scored. Three judges supervise the five-minute contests. In the case of a draw, there is a two-minute "overtime" period. National tournaments are staged in Tokyo's huge Budōkan, which is also used for rock concerts and other popular events.[64]

Kendō, of course, was not the only martial art to experience a postwar revival. The Japan Kyūdō Federation was formed in 1949, and archery was included in the fourth annual National Sports Festival held in the fall of that year. The federation started its own national tournament in 1950, which continues to the present. In 1951, kyūdō became part of the school curriculum once again.[65] The Sanjūsangendō in Kyoto, which was once the site of the ōyakazu contests, is today the host of an archery meet held annually on Coming-of-Age Day (January 15).[66] The forty-ninth national meet, in 1999, was attended by 1,670 participants, including 930 "new adults" from all over the country. The veranda of the temple is no longer used for archery contests; the archers shoot at targets set up behind the building, and the course is only 60 meters long. (The veranda once used for ōyakazu measures 112 meters.)[67]

Jūdō was banned during the first years of the postwar occupation of Japan by the United States, but the authorities allowed a new national

association—the Zen Nihon Jūdō Renmei (All Japan Jūdō Federation)—
to form in 1950. That year, the sport was allowed back into the schools
and colleges. Two years after that, representatives from seventeen
nations founded the International Jūdō Federation and elected Kanō
Jigorō's son Risei as its first president. In 1956, Tokyo hosted the first
world championships.[68]

One of Kanō Jigorō's most cherished dreams was finally realized in
1964, when jūdō made its Olympic debut. Two men deserve most of the
credit for the International Olympic Committee's acceptance of the
sport: Azuma Ryōtarō, president of the Japan Physical Education Association, and Avery Brundage, the American president of the IOC, who
strongly supported Azuma's efforts to bring the 1964 games to Tokyo.
Once Tokyo had won the right to host the games, the IOC's acceptance
of the organizing committee's request for jūdō's inclusion in the program was a foregone conclusion.[69]

At the games, it was definitely an unpleasant shock to Japanese
chauvinists when a Dutch jūdōka, Anton Geesink, defeated Japan's star,
Kaminaga Akio, thereby winning the coveted open championship. On
the other hand, Kanō's spirit, which must have hovered over the city during the 1964 games, was presumably pleased that medals were garnered
by athletes from seven different countries. Kanō's spirit might, however,
have been troubled by the fact that the sport contested in 1964 was not
exactly the sport that he had invented some eighty years earlier. Jūdō,
which Kanō had created as a balanced synthesis of modern and traditional elements, had become markedly more modern. This has meant, in
part, that the trend toward increasing rationalization, specialization,
bureaucratization, and quantification has continued. One sign of this is
the elaborate system of colored belts, an English innovation dating from
1927.[70] Progression through the hierarchy of grades is now on the basis
of quantified achievement. "The criteria for promotion are . . . public,
explicit, and rule-governed rather than implicit."[71]

Weight classes, which provide a degree of equality in the conditions
of competition, are one of the hallmarks of modern combat sports.
Although there were no weight classes at the International Jūdō Federation's first world championships in 1956, the organization introduced
them at its fourth championship in 1965—over the opposition of the All
Japan Jūdō Federation.[72] Another sign of modernization is the recasting
of the instructor's role. The instructor may still be addressed as *sensei*
(teacher), but his authority is now based more on his demonstrable technical expertise than on his personal charisma. With the modernizing

trend has come a change in values. "For a significant number of practitioners, Dr. Kano is venerated less than successful tournament competitors, and his philosophical ideals . . . are dismissed as 'mumbo jumbo' that add nothing to the sport." Inevitably, the "virtually exclusive emphasis on tournament competition"[73] has led to an increasingly intense rationalization of the sport. Judō has undergone the "routinization of charisma."[74] In the West, and to some degree even in Japan, young competitors are now likely to approach a match as if they were inspired by Vince Lombardi rather than by Kanō Jigorō.

In a study that compared seventeen black-belt British jūdōka active before 1960 with fourteen who were active after 1960, two sociologists found that eight of the former had made a serious study of Zen Buddhism while none of the latter had. Similarly, eight of the older men were able to speak Japanese "reasonably well" while only one of the younger men had a serious interest in the language. "In recent years," concluded the authors, "jūdō has become increasingly Westernized and oriented towards international competition."[75] The French situation is no different: "Modern jūdō has little resemblance to the jūdō of [the sport's] founder, Kanō Jigorō. . . . Its traditions have retreated in the face of modernity."[76] In the somewhat exaggerated words of an American authority, the spiritual aspect of jūdō has been crushed by "that unstoppable force called modernization." Kanō's cherished beliefs are scoffed at as "philosophical malarky."[77]

The modernization of the sport has also transformed its governance. Despite its dismal reputation, bureaucratic organization, which Max Weber identified as a hallmark of modernity, is actually the most rational way to administer complex enterprises. Unfortunately, bureaucracies are not immune from internal squabbles. In the 1980s, the world of Japanese jūdō was disrupted by a struggle for power. On January 25, 1983, the All Japan Student Jūdō Federation, which had been established in 1953, seceded from the parent organization, the All Japan Jūdō Federation. The main bone of contention was the series of international tournaments that the former organization had begun to sponsor—with the approval of the International Jūdō Federation—in the face of the AJJF's strong disapproval. The AJJF responded to the students' secession by creating the All Japan University Jūdō Federation (on September 21,1983). In the compromise that ended the schism in 1989, the dissident and the loyal student organizations merged to form the Japan Jūdō Student Federation. The headquarters of the reconstituted AJJF was transferred from its traditional site in Kanō Jigorō's Kōdōkan to a new location in Kishi Memorial

Hall, the headquarters of the Japan Physical Education Association and many other national sports bodies.[78] This move symbolizes the further "sportification" of judo.

There have also, inevitably, been controversies at the international level. They were exacerbated when the Japanese ceased to be the taken-for-granted leaders of the International Jūdō Federation. Conflicts have arisen between the Japanese bodies, who see themselves as the legitimate heirs of jūdō, and the jūdō organizations of other countries. Differences have developed between international rules and the ones used in Japan.[79] In October 1993, the European Jūdō Union announced that it was considering the use of colored uniforms at international tournaments held in Europe. To help the spectators distinguish between the two wrestlers, one of the contestants in a match would wear blue. The Japanese federation initially announced its intention to boycott those tournaments if colored outfits were required, but the federation relented and indicated in December 1996 its willingness to continue to participate in tournaments in Europe—on a test basis.[80]

To what degree has "sportification" also characterized jūdō as practiced in Japan? The question cannot be answered with quantified precision, but no observer doubts that many younger men and women see jūdō as simply another modern sport rather than as the repository of uniquely Japanese values. Japanese jūdō's center of gravity has definitely moved in the direction of out-and-out competition.

Karate has also taken on more and more of the characteristics of modern sports. In 1957, the year of Funakoshi's death, the Nihon Karate Kyōkai (Japan Karate Association) was founded and the first national championships were held. Within the association, however, there were many different schools of karate, based on differences in technique. The 1964 Tokyo Olympics gave impetus to unification, and in October of that year the All Japan Karatedō Federation was established. It became a foundation in 1969, and a member organization of the Japan Physical Education Association in 1972. In 1970 the World Union of Karatedō Organizations was established, and thirty-three countries participated in the sport's first world championships. By June 1985, when the WUKO was recognized as an International Federation by the International Olympic Committee, it had ninety-six member countries.[81] Karate continues, however, to be associated in the popular mind with deadly strikes, thrusts, and kicks, and there is "a growing demand for full-contact fighting techniques."[82]

## *Sumō*

One of the Sumō Association's first acts after the war demonstrates the flexibility and variation in use of the term "tradition." During the war, the Kokugikan had been requisitioned by the military. During the Occupation, it was taken over by the American forces. The Sumō Association petitioned to have the facility returned to them, claiming that it was a "tradition" for sumō to be held in the Kokugikan.[83] Since sumō had moved indoors only thirty-six years earlier, in 1909, the leaders of the association were actually trying to avoid the "good old days" of outdoor sumō, when they had to worry about bad weather and the economic costs of cancelled matches.

Sumō continued to develop after the war, both as a sport and as a representative of Japanese tradition. In 1947, another obstacle to open competition for the individual championship was removed. Before 1947, competition had been limited to matches between two wrestlers from opposite "sides." Wrestlers on the West side faced only wrestlers on the East side. This restriction greatly limited competition and lessened the legitimacy of the individual champion. If wrestlers from the same side were never matched against one another, how was it possible to know which of them was the best? The elimination of the restriction in 1947 increased the importance of the individual championship.

The association took another important step toward open competition in 1965 when it abolished the rule preventing tournament matches between wrestlers from the same family of stables. To this day, however, wrestlers from the same stable do not wrestle one another, which creates problems when one stable dominates the upper ranks. In March 1993, for instance, ten of the top forty wrestlers belonged to the Futagoyama stable. A year later, the stable had three of the five most highly ranked wrestlers. There was no chance for one of them to inflict a loss on his stable mates, which gave all three of them an advantage vis-à-vis their rivals from other stables.

The championship system and the yokozuna rank are two different ways of recognizing supremacy in the performance of sumō. The first is modern in the sense that the format of the competition has been rationalized in order to determine an undisputed champion on the basis of unambiguous quantified achievement. The second is traditional in the sense that ascription also plays a role. The yokozuna is sumō's representative man. To embody the ethos of sumō—and by implication the ethos of Japan—physical prowess is clearly necessary, but it is just as clearly not sufficient. A wrestler can rise to the rank of ōzeki mainly on the basis of objectively determined achievements, but promotion to the exalted status of yokozuna requires subjective judgments on the part of the elders of the Sumō Association.

This means that the tournament championship system and the yokozuna rank are basically in tension. A yokozuna cannot win every tournament and yet he is expected to do so. Quantitative evaluation of performance, which is the necessary basis of the championship system, reveals the yokozuna's vulnerability. This tension between expectations and performance is an important source of excitement in sumō, as can be seen from the roar of the crowd when a lower-ranked wrestler scores an upset. The discrepancy between ascription and achievement is most crass when a yokozuna cannot validate the honor of his rank with a superior record. At that juncture, a kind of cognitive dissonance occurs and the institution of sumō is open to criticism.

In the fall tournament in Osaka in 1949, for instance, the yokozuna Maedayama won his first match but lost the next five. After the fifth defeat, he withdrew from the tournament, ostensibly with colitis, and returned to Tokyo. The very next day, however, he appeared at an exhibition baseball game between the Yomiuri Giants and the San Francisco Seals. His appearance was reported in the press and a great fuss ensued. The enraged executive board of the Sumō Association forced Maedayama to retire.[84]

At the time of this incident, which took place during the postwar Occupation, sumō's popularity was in a slump and baseball's was on the rise. The symbolic significance of a yokozuna abandoning his duties in the ring to watch a baseball game was potentially devastating. The incident also shows how the expectations surrounding yokozuna had changed with the development of the tournament champion system. In the late Meiji period, the great yokozuna Hitachiyama did not wrestle 131 of his 320 scheduled matches in the upper division, an absentee rate of 40 percent, without harm to his reputation. (We do not know how many of those *yasumi* were due to Hitachiyama's absence, and how many were the fault of his opponents.)[85]

The dissonance between the championship system and the yokozuna rank caused still another crisis the year after the Maedayama Affair. After a series of humiliating defeats, all three reigning yokozuna dropped out of the January tournament. Clearly disgusted by this debacle, the executive board of the Sumō Association was ready to scrap the unwritten rule that says a yokozuna cannot be demoted. Some of the members objected, however, on the grounds that the prestige of the yokozuna goes back three hundred years to the (legendary) Akashi Shiganosuke. After further discussion, they decided to form a Yokozuna Review Board, consisting of representatives from outside the association, to recommend and evaluate yokozuna. If greater care were taken in selecting ōzeki for promotion to yokozuna, future embarrassments might be avoided. The committee, which was formed in May 1950, consisted of scholars, businessmen, and politicians.

One of the first questions to come before the new committee was what to do about the ōzeki Chiyonoyama, who had won two tournaments in a row. The furor over the poor performances of the three reigning yokozuna gave pause to the committee, which delayed Chiyonoyama's promotion until after he won a third tournament in the summer of 1950. His performance occasioned further problems during the March tournament of 1953. He lost four of his first five bouts and seemed unlikely to finish the tournament with a winning record. On the sixth day he petitioned the director of the Sumō Association to be allowed to give up the rank of yokozuna and start over from ōzeki. This request was leaked to the media. Pressed by them for an explanation, the director retorted that for a yokozuna to give up his position would make the association and the Yokozuna Review Board look like fools. If Chiyonoyama had doubts about his ability to perform as a yokozuna, the director admonished, he should have declined the promotion. Chiyonoyama struggled on to a winning record and the crisis passed.[86]

On January 6, 1958, the Yokozuna Review Board announced the following bylaws for recommending the promotion and retirement of yokozuna:

1. Candidates for yokozuna shall be of outstanding character and ability.
2. In principle, future candidates for yokozuna recommended by the Yokozuna Review Board shall have two consecutive tournament championships at the rank of ōzeki.
3. A unanimous vote is required to recommend a wrestler with a record equivalent [but not equal] to the criteria of Article 2.
4. Under the following conditions, the Yokozuna Review Board may conduct an investigation of a yokozuna and, by a vote of two-thirds of its members, take such action as issuing a warning or recommending retirement:

    a. He has numerous absences. However, when extended absence is due to injury or illness, the possibility of recovery can be taken into consideration and a sufficient treatment period granted.

    b. He dishonors the rank of yokozuna.

    c. He has an extremely poor record for a yokozuna, one judged not deserving of the rank.[87]

The contradictions of the yokozuna system can be seen in these bylaws. The first article implies that yokozuna is not a mere rank attained on the basis of achievement, but Article 2 establishes precise quantified criteria for the promotion of yokozuna. These criteria are then undermined by Article 3, which provides a sumō-sized loophole. The key word is *junzuru,* which can be translated as "next best" as well as "equivalent." In the past, this has been interpreted to mean that a wrestler can be promoted if he had the second best record of the tournament before or after the tournament he won. If one examines the records of the twenty-seven yokozuna from Chiyonoyama to Musashimaru, one discovers that very few of the first twenty-two were promoted simply on the basis of Article 2. Indeed, many seem not to have fulfilled the criteria as spelled out in Article 3. In other words, promotion to the rank of yokozuna continued to be partially subjective despite the elaboration of ostensibly objective criteria.

During the January tournament of 1958, the first one after the announcement of the new bylaws, the yokozuna Yoshibayama and Kagamisato both announced their voluntary retirement. It was the first time that two yokozuna had retired during a single tournament. Three years later, in September 1961, Kashiwado and Taihō were chosen for promotion to yokozuna. Messengers were sent to their respective stables, where they both accepted the honor, pledging to strive to do their utmost not to defile the exalted rank: "I will do my best as yokozuna not to disgrace the rank."[88] This is the first reference in the official history of modern sumō to messengers dispatched to the stables and to the reply of the new yokozuna. This procedure is now standard.

Solemn pledges, however, are not enough to resolve the tension between achievement and ascription, which continues to cause problems—and none more dramatic than an incident involving Futahaguro. Although Futahaguro had never won a tournament, he was promoted in July 1986, at the age of twenty-three. There was great pressure on him to win a tournament and thus to justify his promotion, but, although he was

## Sumō Promotion
### Records in three tournaments prior to promotion to Yokozuna

| Name | 3rd Tournament Prior | 2nd Tournament Prior | Prior Tournament |
|---|---|---|---|
| Chiyonoyama | 11–4 | 8–7 | C14–1 |
| Kagamisato | 11–4 | R12–3 | C14–1 |
| Yoshibayama | R14–1 | 11–4 | C15–0 |
| Tochinishiki | 9–6 | C14–1 | C14–1 |
| Wakanohana I | 11–4 | R12–3 | C13–2 |
| Asashio | C14–1 | R11–4 | R13–2 |
| Kashiwado | 10–5 | 11–4 | T12–3 |
| Taihō | R11–4 | C13–2 | C12–3 |
| Tochinoumi | 11–4 | C14–1 | 13–2 |
| Sadanoyama | R13–2 | R13–2 | C13–2 |
| Tamanoumi | C13–2 | 10–5 | T13–2 |
| Kitanofuji | R12–3 | C13–2 | C13–2 |
| Kotozakura | 9–6 | C14–1 | C14–1 |
| Wajima | R11–4 | R13–2 | C15–0 |
| Kitanoumi | 10–5 | C13–2 | T13–2 |
| Wakanohana II | R13–2 | T13–2 | T14–1 |
| Mienoumi | 10–5 | R13–2 | T14–1 |
| Chiyonofuji | R11–4 | R13–2 | C14–1 |
| Takanosato | R12–3 | R13–2 | C14–1 |
| Futahaguro | 10–5 | R12–3 | T14–1 |
| Hokutoumi | 11–4 | C12–3 | R13–2 |
| Ōnokuni | C15–0 | R12–3 | R13–2 |
| Asahifuji | 8–7 | C14–1 | C14–1 |
| Akebono | 9–6 | C14–1 | C13–2 |
| Takanohana | 11–4 | C15–0 | C15–0 |
| Wakanohana III | 10–5 | C14–1 | C12–3 |
| Musashimaru | 8–7 | C13–2 | C13–2 |

(C = Champion; T = Tied for championship but lost play-off; R = Runner-up)

*Passed over for promotion (some examples)*

| | | | |
|---|---|---|---|
| Wakanohana I | R13–2 | T12–3 | C12–3 |
| Asahifuji (1988) | 11–4 | C14–1 | R12–3 |
| Konishiki (1992) | C13–2 | 12–3 | C13–2 |
| Takanohana (1993) | R11–4 | C14–1 | T13–2 |
| Takanohana (1994) | C14–1 | 11–4 | C15–0 |

always in contention, the tournaments came and went without the coveted title. He was criticized in the press and within the sumō world, and was finally drummed out of the sport after an altercation with his stablemaster in the last days of 1987.[89]

A year after Futahaguro's promotion, Ōnokuni was elevated to yokozuna although he too had a questionable record. Ōnokuni's failure was equally dismal. Although it was an almost unthinkable disgrace for a yokozuna to have a losing record in a tournament, he finished a tournament with seven wins and eight losses. He sat out six of the next ten tournaments and retired in 1991 at the early age of twenty-eight.

In 1987, Hokutoumi was also promoted without the supposedly necessary qualifications. He acquitted himself better than his immediate predecessors had, but their early departure forced him to linger on as the only yokozuna. In the only tournament he finished in his last year, his record of nine wins and six losses was far from outstanding.

Behind the premature promotions and postponed retirements of the 1980s lurked a foreign threat. In the 1960s and 1970s, when the Hawaian-born Jesse Kuhaulua wrestled under the name of Takamiyama, he was nicknamed *kurobune* (black ship), an obvious allusion to Commodore Matthew Perry's unwelcome arrival in Japanese waters.[90] Takamiyama never achieved the rank of ōzeki, but he defeated yokozuna on twelve separate occasions, which is something no other wrestler below the two top ranks had ever done. Another Hawaian-born wrestler, the massive Konishiki (Salevaa Atisanoe), posed an even greater danger to Japanese pride. Futahaguro, Hokutoumi, and Ōnokuni may have been promoted prematurely to "fill" the yokozuna rank and thus to make it more difficult for the rapidly rising Konishiki to achieve the highest honor in Japan's "national sport." Suspicions that this was indeed the case were intensified when a member of the Yokozuna Review Board published an article in which he maintained that it would be difficult for a foreigner to meet the requirements of Article 1 because of a lack of *hinkaku* (dignity, character).[91] Whether the Sumō Association had intended to stack the rank or not, the chairman announced, after the disappointing performance of the three previous yokozuna, that the criteria for promotion would be more strictly enforced in the future. That meant, in effect, that Konishiki had to clear a higher bar than the others had.

At the age of twenty, with only two years of experience, Konishiki had defeated the yokozuna Takanosato and Chiyonofuji.[92] By March 1992, he had compiled a record that certainly seemed to warrant promotion. He had won two of the previous three tournaments, which was obviously a better record than Futahaguro's, but his objective achievements were not enough to overcome a presumed deficit in hinkaku. Soon after what must have been a great disappointment for him, Konishiki passed his peak and his performances began to decline.

The lame duck yokozuna Hokutoumi retired in May 1992 and the banzuke was without a yokozuna for the first time in sixty years. This situation lasted for six months until the Hawaii-born Chadwick Rowan, who wrestled under the name Akebono, won two consecutive tournaments. Since no wrestler since Chiyonoyama had ever been denied the rank of yokozuna after two consecutive championships, any doubts about Akebono's hinkaku were quietly set aside and he was promoted in January 1993. He was the first obviously foreign yokozuna.

The promotion of Akebono, whose name means "dawn," must have seemed like symbolic darkness to the officials and fans who desperately wanted an authentically Japanese yokozuna. For several years, however, the Sumō Association had publicly insisted on a strict application of the quantified criteria for promotion. While it was an embarrassment that there was no Japanese yokozuna, there was understandable hesitation to promote a native-born wrestler without consecutive championships (and thereby to revive accusations of favoritism).

The strongest candidate for promotion was Takanohana, a member of the famous Hanada family of wrestlers. Takanohana's father, a former ōzeki, ran the Futagoyama stable to which Takanohana and his brother, Wakanohana III, belonged. (His uncle, the original Wakanohana, was a former yokozuna and former chairman of the Sumō Association.) The problem was that Takanohana's performances in Tokyo were much better than his performances in the alternating tournaments in Nagoya, Osaka, and Fukuoka. On the basis of three consecutive wins in Tokyo, the chairman of the Sumō Association recommended Takanohana to the Yokozuna Review Board in September 1994. The Review Board, which had for twenty-five years accepted every nomination of the Sumō Association, surprised everyone and rejected Takanohana. The majority of six in favor and five opposed was less than the two-thirds required.[93] It was just as well. Takanohana was undefeated in the November tournament in Fukuoka and was then promoted without the stigma of special favor.

As one commentator remarked at the height of the controversy over Takanohana's promotion, "The yokozuna is an illogical sort of thing. And that's what gives it the essence of a uniquely Japanese traditional performing art."[94] Quite aside from the unintended irony of the word "traditional" for a nineteenth-century innovation, one can see that the tensions between the achievement-oriented championship system and the ascriptive aspect of the yokozuna make the rank inherently problematic. Within the context of the championship system, the rank of yokozuna is an anomaly that has more to do with the "retraditionalization" of sumō than with the sport's modernization. The "traditional" yokozuna is in large measure a product of the modern championship system. The image of the mighty yokozuna represents security and assurance—and an element of mystery—in the face of the impersonal objectivity of quantifiable achievement.

There is another irony. The need to preserve the image and mystique of sumō seems to have made the Sumō Association allergic to accusations about the corruption that seems to be an inescapable aspect of commercialized sports. When the retired wrestler Itai Keisuke claimed that many bouts, including one of his against Akebono, were fixed, the association dismissed his accusations and Japan's major newspapers gave them "scant attention." After all, explained a writer for *Shūkan bunshun,* sumō is "the national sport."[95]

## KEMARI

The survival of the traditional sport of kemari had been severely threatened by the drastic social changes that followed the Meiji Restoration, but by the early years of this century it had achieved a stable, if much reduced, existence as a pastime for a small number of aristocrats. They were supported, as we have seen, by an annual stipend from the Imperial Household. They had their headquarters and a practice court at the Kyoto branch of the Peer's Club.

Japan's defeat in World War II renewed the threat to kemari's survival. Under the Occupation, the Peer's Club was requisitioned for American use and the society lost its practice court. There was great confusion in the rush to move the costumes, equipment, and records to a safe place. The society was forced to begin a "life in exile" that continues to this day. Another blow came in 1947 when the prewar peerage system itself was abolished, officially eliminating the class around which the preservation society was organized.[96]

On the brighter side, kemari had never been associated with militarism or the war effort. It not only escaped prohibition; it was presented at the first National Sports Festival held in Kyoto in 1946. An article from the *Kyōtō shimbun* (November 3, 1946) reported that kemari was held on a tennis court as the climax of the festival. The newspaper listed the team and individual winners.[97]

Kemari was shown on television for the first time in summer of 1956 and was performed at the imperial palace in Kyoto on January 2, 1963. (This performance was broadcast live by NHK.) In 1964, negotiations were conducted with the Japan Olympic Committee to include a demonstration of kemari at the Tokyo Olympics, but the initiative failed because of the JOC's alleged "lack of funds." On their own, twenty members of the society went to Tokyo and performed kemari at a temporary court at the Meiji shrine a week before the Olympics.[98]

Women were allowed to join the society in 1963. There were members of the society who wanted to include women earlier, but the president, who had held office for nearly twenty-five years, had been opposed. A month after his death, in January 1963, the new board of directors voted to allow female members. In 1965, the society, which at one point had been reduced to thirty-one members, grew to number forty-eight, of which seven were women (and only nine were former peers).

At about that time, the society began to receive invitations to give demonstrations of kemari. The first overseas exhibition of kemari took place in Paris in 1986 at the Festival of Traditional Japanese Arts and Crafts. In 1992, the society participated in the World Festival of Traditional Sports that was celebrated in Bonn, Germany. In January 1992, members of the Kemari Society performed for George Bush during his presidential visit to Kyoto. *Time* magazine published an account written by Michael Duffy:

> Last week, Bush watched eight men in brightly colored robes demonstrate an ancient Japanese game called *kemari*, in which players use their feet to keep a large deerskin ball inside their small circle without ever letting it touch the ground. The object of the 1,300-year-old game is not so much to win as to display proper form and correct etiquette. The President watched the less-than-riveting spectacle for a while, then impulsively threw himself into the contest. Without regard for the players' harmony, or *wa*, Bush entered the circle (strike 1), hit the ball with his head, soccer-style (strike 2), and kicked it out of the circle completely (strike 3). At the game's end, while the Japanese players politely tried to mask their dismay, he shouted, 'We won! We won!'[99]

Whether or not the Japanese players were as dismayed as Duffy imagined, Bush may have established a precedent. That summer, when kemari was performed for the crown prince, that exalted personage borrowed a pair of shoes from one of the members and joined the fun.

The Kemari Society may enjoy the favor of princes and presidents, but it continues to face long-term problems. A 1997 publication lists five of them. The first is that the society's meager budget does not allow for much publicity. The second problem, which has become acute as the present membership grows older, is recruitment. Over the previous ten years, the society had gained eleven new members and lost four old ones. A third problem is the supply of balls. Kemari balls must be "overhauled" after they have been used for ten to twenty hours. The process is arduous. Members must pour three kilograms of barley into the ball, a few grains at a time, through a hole that is only 2 centimeters in diameter. And the balls cannot be replaced. Over the decades, members have tried and failed to make their own kemari balls. In the Edo period there were craftsmen who specialized in the manufacture of kemari balls, but no one makes them now, and the few balls that remain are about two hundred years old. Another serious problem the society faces is the lack of its own practice court. Currently, the members practice on the grounds of shrines and temples and other sites in Kyoto. The fifth problem is the costume. A proper kemari costume is expensive, and the materials and the craftsmen are harder and harder to find. A complete outfit (headgear, jacket, divided skirt, shoes, and fan) costs as much as a million yen and can be worn no more than about forty times.[100]

Kemari's future is unclear. Confronted with problems of such severity, the game is not likely ever to be played by more than a few hundred devotees, but their devotion is probably strong enough for the game to survive as a precious relic of the past.

## SPORT IN PHYSICAL EDUCATION

During the Occupation, the Ministry of Education, influenced by American educators associated with the Civil Information and Education Section, issued a series of directives intended to "demilitarize" education. The Prospectus for Teaching Physical Education in the Schools (Gakkō Taiiku Shidō Yōkō), promulgated in June 1947, called for the cultivation of a "proper attitude" toward winning and losing.[101] In February 1949, the Ministry of Education's Committee on the Promotion of Physical Education (Taiiku shinkō iinkai), while expressing its pleasure at the popularity of sports, recommended that appropriate measures be promptly taken against the evils that can accompany them. As antidotes to these evils, the report mentions good sportsmanship and the ethos of amateurism, rational management of sports, and concern for the athletes' health.

The Physical Education edition of the Prospectus for Primary School Education (Shōgakkō gakushū shidō yōryō taiikuhen), which appeared in September 1949, specified the aims and objectives of primary-school physical education. Although this prospectus—like the one published in 1947—was unclear about the materials and methods by which those aims and objectives were to be realized, sports and noncompetitive games seemed to be the preferred means of personality development. In 1951, the Ministry of Education published guidelines for the teaching of physical education in middle and high schools. Among the recommended activities for boys' and/or girls' physical education classes were basketball, soccer, volleyball, softball, touch football, swimming, and track-and-field. Sumō was listed as a "main activity" for middle-school boys and jūdō as an elective activity. Paramilitary drill was not recommended.

Some scholars, like Imamura Yoshio, believe that there was an overreaction to the war years. During and immediately after the Occupation, education became excessively student-centered. Teachers were reluctant to offer the guidance necessary to resist the hedonism that spread with postwar prosperity. Physical education that stressed play failed to develop children's skills and actually contributed to a decline in their ambition. As proof, critics of postwar physical education cited the poor performance of Japanese athletes at the Olympics of 1952 and 1956. This was the background for the 1958 revision of the Prospectus for Primary-School Education. This revision eliminated references to student-centered education and emphasized social responsibility. A revision of the middle-school curriculum, issued on the same day, reintroduced sumō and the martial arts to the curriculum and gave more emphasis to *taisō* (gymnastics). These reforms were expected to produce better results at the Rome Olympics in 1960.

Japanese physical educators and bureaucrats distinguish between *gakkō taiiku* (physical education in the schools) and *shakai taiiku* (physical education in society at large). The latter includes amateur sports and the martial arts. The question then arises: Should gakkō taiiku and shakai taiiku be administered together within a single ministerial bureau or should the two be administered separately? In January 1946, the integrated approach was chosen. Administration of shakai taiiku was moved from the Ministry of Health and Welfare and integrated into the Physical Education Bureau of the Ministry of Education, becoming the Division for the Promotion of Physical Education.

In June 1949, however, the Physical Education Bureau was abolished in a reform of the Ministry of Education, and its areas of jurisdiction were divided among three new entities: the Bureau of Primary and Secondary Education, the Bureau of College Education, and the Bureau of Community Education. It was ten years before this fragmented structure, which was unpopular among physical educators, was replaced by the reestablished Physical Education Bureau. During these ten years two committees played important roles in the administration of physical education and sports. The first, the Sports Promotion Council (Supōtsu Shinkō Kaigi), was established in May 1949 with thirty-nine permanent members drawn from the Diet, business, labor, and the media. Two months later, the Health and Physical Education Commission (Hoken Taiiku Shingikai) was established as an advisory body to the Ministry of Education.

In 1955, the chairman of the Health and Physical Education Commission submitted a proposal to the Minister of Education calling for the reunification of the administration of health, physical education, school lunches, sports, and recreation, asserting that the dismantling of the Bureau of Physical Education and the distribution of its jurisdiction among other bureaus had led to the neglect and decline of physical education. Fragmentation had also led, in this view, to the contamination of the concept of physical education from areas outside the field of education. Physical education, including sports, must always be promoted from an educational perspective. A similar proposal was submitted in June 1956.

Planning for the Tokyo Olympics, which were to be held in 1964, had a profound effect on the administration of Japanese physical education and sports. The prospect of the games gave impetus to the call for the reunified administration of school and community physical education within the Ministry of Education. In January 1958, four months after the Committee to Prepare for the Tokyo Olympics held its first meeting, the Physical Education Bureau was reestablished and the role of sports within the sphere of physical education was enhanced. As 1964 approached, the goal of Olympic glory, like the dream of a truly democratic society, seemed increasingly attainable.

# 8

# Japan at the Olympics:
# 1952–1998

A year had not passed after Japan's surrender before the Japan
Physical Education Association began to work for the country's
return to international sporting competition. The first step was
to rejoin the nongovernmental sports organizations that administer
international sports. A committee to investigate that possibility was set
up in July 1946. An "Olympic Preparation Committee" was established
in January 1947, with an eye to the first postwar Olympics, which were to
be held in London the following year. In May 1948, the Olympic Preparation Committee was renamed the Olympic Committee and given the
status of a National Olympic Committee. The JPEA then submitted documents to the International Olympic Committee and requested recognition of the newly established NOC. In compliance with IOC regulations,
the JPEA also sought to have Japan's national sports federations reinstated
in the Fédération Internationale de Football Association (FIFA) and other
international sports federations.[1]

The British hosts of the first postwar Olympics refused to invite the
Japanese to London. In 1948, the wounds of war had barely begun to
heal. It was a painful exclusion, especially for the Japanese swimmers,
whose times were often better than those recorded in London.[2] Two
years later, there was bitter controversy when Avery Brundage, then IOC
vice president, nominated Azuma Ryōtarō to become Japan's third IOC
member. As head of the JPEA, Azuma was obviously well qualified for
membership. His nomination was, moreover, endorsed by General Douglas MacArthur, commander of the Occupation. When the IOC met in
Copenhagen, in May 1950, there was adamant opposition to Brundage's

move. The Marquis of Exeter, the influential senior British IOC member who was also president of the International Amateur Athletic Federation, pointed out that Japan already had two members (Nagai Matsuzō and Takaishi Shingorō, both elected in 1939). Sir Harold Luxton of Australia reminded his colleagues of the Japanese mistreatment of prisoners of war. At the crucial moment, Sigfrid Edström, the Swedish president of the IOC, intervened in the debate. He had fought successfully to prevent the ouster of former Nazis and Fascists from the committee. Now he informed his colleagues on the IOC that he had already asked Azuma to come to Copenhagen to attend the session. The controversy was resolved when Nagai, whose health was poor, resigned. Azuma was named not as a third but merely as the second member from Japan.[3]

In November 1951, Japan signed a peace treaty with the forty-eight nations against which it had been at war, which led to the end of the Occupation on April 28, 1952. Anticipating this event, the IOC, meeting in Vienna in May 1951, finally recognized Japan's NOC. The way was open for Japan's participation in the 1952 Olympics, which took place in Helsinki.[4] The main focus of the world's mass media was on the rivalry between the United States and the Soviet Union (competing for the very first time in the "bourgeois" games), but the Japanese were understandably more concerned to follow the fortunes of their own team, participating for the first time in sixteen years. Japan sent a contingent of 102 athletes and officials, but the athletes had minimal success, reflecting the difficult conditions at home, where most people were still struggling to overcome the ravages of war.[5] Ishii Shōhachi wrestled his way to a gold medal and Kitano Hirohide to a silver. The swimmers, who had been the stars of the last two prewar teams, performed well. Hashizume Shirō and Suzuki Hiroshi won silver medals in the 1,500-meter and 100-meter freestyle races. Suzuki teamed with Hamaguchi Yoshihiro, Gotō Tōru, and Tanikawa Teijirō to garner a second silver medal in the 800-meter freestyle relay. Ethnically Japanese swimmers competing for Brazil (Okamoto Tetsuo) and the United States (Oyakawa Yoshinobu) brought medals home to their adopted countries.

Furukawa Masaru, who had broken several world records in 1954 and 1955, was first in the 200-meter breaststroke in Melbourne in 1956 (with Yoshimura Masahiro two-hundreths of a second behind him). Furukawa's time, 2:34.7, was an Olympic record. That year, two other swimmers—Ishimoto Takashi and Yamanaka Tsuyoshi—accounted for three more silver medals.[6]

The Japanese, who sent nearly two hundred athletes and officials to

Melbourne, expected to do well in track-and-field as well as in the Olympic pool, but their victories were in gymnastics and wrestling (as they tended to be at later Olympics).[7] Led by Ono Takashi, who was first on the horizontal bar, second on the pommel horse, and third on the parallel bars, the Japanese team won a silver medal.[8] Eugene Wettstone, the manager of the American gymnastics team, thought that the Japanese had actually outperformed the Soviet team. Competing in the early morning hours, the Japanese "never were credited with the high scores which they deserved and which were more liberally awarded teams performing in the evening."[9] In the individual competition, Ono lost to the Soviet Union's Viktor Shukarin. The freestyle wrestlers managed to win two golds (Sasahara Shōzō, featherweight; Ikeda Mitsuo, welterweight) and a silver (Kasahara Shigeru, lightweight).[10] It is noteworthy that all three medals went to men who weighed less than 75 kilograms. The Japanese have always done better in the lighter weight classes, not only in freestyle and Greco-Roman wrestling but also in boxing, jūdō, and weightlifting.

The 1956 Winter Olympics at Cortina d'Ampezzo in the Italian Alps were the first to be shown on Japanese television. NHK bought a film summary of the games and edited it for the scenes with Japanese athletes.[11] Igaya Chiharu placed second in the men's slalom, earning Japan's first Olympic medal in the seven winter competitions that had taken place since 1924—and the only one for another sixteen years. The economic boom that provided the wherewithal to put millions of Japanese on skis and skates was not to come for another generation.

Japan had initially hoped to bring the "Games of the XVII Olympiad" to Tokyo. In May 1952, the Tokyo Metropolitan Assembly passed a unanimous resolution to seek the 1960 games, and Tokyo sent its formal bid to the IOC on July 2. On a visit to Japan in May 1955, Avery Brundage, who had become president of the IOC in 1952, suggested that Tokyo seek to host the 1964 games instead. Brundage explained that the countries of Europe, which made up the majority of IOC members at the time, were reluctant for geographical and financial reasons to undertake the arduous journey only four years after having gone to Melbourne. Brundage suggested that Tokyo act as host for the IOC's 54th Session, in 1958. That would allow the IOC members to observe the state of sports in Japan and to form their own—presumably favorable—opinion. In addition, the Third Asian Games were scheduled for Tokyo in 1958, and they would be an opportunity for Japan to demonstrate that it had the ability to stage a major international sports festival.

Brundage was persuasive. In October 1955, the Tokyo Metropolitan Assembly officially approved a bid for the 1964 games. The governor of Tokyo, Yasui Seiichirō, presented the city's bid at the IOC's 52nd Session, which took place in Melbourne in November and December 1956. Azuma Ryōtarō and Takaishi Shingorō attended the session as regular IOC members. Tokyo was, indeed, chosen as the site of the 54th Session. The government forged ahead with its preparations. In February 1957, a Council for the Promotion of Sport (Supōtsu Shinkō Shingikai) was created within the Prime Minister's Office. On January 22, 1958, the Preparatory Committee for the Tokyo Olympics (Tōkyō Orimpikku Jumbi Iinkai) held its first meeting at the prime minister's official residence. The committee, which was chaired by Prime Minister Kishi Nobusuke, had over one hundred members, including Diet members, government officials, the two IOC members, and representatives from the JPEA, the Tokyo metropolitan government, and the worlds of business, journalism, and education. The committee's budget for the fiscal year 1958, 4.35 million yen, was supplemented by a 950,000 yen grant from the national government.[12]

The 54th IOC Session was opened in Tokyo with an address from the emperor. The Asian Games, which took place concurrently, were a success, but the IOC's final decision on awarding the "Games of the XVIII Olympiad" was deferred until the next IOC Session.[13]

At the International Olympic Committee's 55th Session, which took place in Munich in May 1959, Azuma proposed again to his IOC colleagues that Tokyo host the 1964 games. Brundage strongly supported the proposal, and Tokyo prevailed over Detroit by a vote of 34–10. While Brundage's support for the Japanese rather than the American venue was extremely unpopular in the United States, he captured and held the esteem of Japanese sportsmen and sportswomen. As for Azuma, his crucial role in Tokyo's bid had helped him win the city's governorship.[14]

Before Tokyo enjoyed its day in the (rising) sun, there were the games celebrated in Rome in the summer of 1960. Host-to-be Japan sent a contingent of 218. The country was disappointed once again by the performance of its swimmers and track-and-field athletes. There were no gold medals for the swimmers, but Yamanaka Tsuyoshi repeated his second-place finish in the men's 400-meter race and won another silver medal with the 4 × 200-meter relay. Bronze medals came for Ōsaki Yoshihiko in the 200-meter breaststroke, for the Japanese quartet in the 4 × 100-meter relay, and for Tanaka Satoko in the women's 100-meter backstroke. There were also silver and bronze medals in boxing, wrestling, and weightlifting, but the great triumph came in men's gymnastics.[15]

The contest between Ono Takashi and the Soviet Union's Boris Shaklin was intensely dramatic. (The site—the ruins of the ancient baths of Caracalla—added to the drama.) In the vault, they tied for first place with identical scores. Shaklin won gold on the parallel bars and Ono bronze. On the pommel horse, Shaklin tied for first with Finland's Emil Ekman while Ono was far behind in 6th place. In the floor exercise, which was won by Aihara Nobuyuki, Ono managed a 4th-place finish while his Russian rival did poorly. Ono then won the competition on the high bar and Shaklin fell to 3rd place. The two men differed in the order in which they moved through the six events and Ono was actually ahead when he came to the rings for his final effort. On the rings, Shaklin had a score of 19.500 and Ono was right behind him with 19.425, but that was not quite good enough. In the final tally, Ono trailed Shaklin by a score of 115.90 to 115.95, but he had a second gold medal to add to the one awarded for his performance on the high bar. His teammates had placed 4th, 5th, 6th, 7th, 9th, and 10th in the final standings, which was enough to propel them past the Soviet team.[16]

Preparations for 1964 were on schedule. The Preparatory Committee for the Tokyo Olympics had been dissolved in June 1959, and the Organizing Committee for the Tokyo Olympics was formed in September. In July 1961, the organizing committee was reorganized as a foundation (*zaidan hōjin*) authorized by the Ministry of Education. In consultation with the IOC, which was the final authority on the program, the committee decided on twenty events: track-and-field, rowing, basketball, volleyball, boxing, cycling, canoeing, fencing, soccer, gymnastics, hockey, modern pentathlon, swimming and diving, equestrian events, marksmanship, water polo, weightlifting, wrestling, jūdō, and yachting. The Tokyo metropolitan government granted the organizing committee 1.55 billion yen to subsidize the games and also constructed the necessary sports facilities. The government invested additional funds to expand and improve the area's transportation system. It was in the context of preparing for the Olympics that the Physical Education Bureau was reestablished in the Ministry of Education on June 14, 1958. On November 4, 1960, a "preparatory office" for the Olympics was established in the bureau. It later became the Olympic Division.[17]

The 1964 games, beautifully filmed by Ichikawa Kon in *Tōkyō Orimpikku* (1965), were the zenith of Japan's Olympic trajectory. With sixteen gold, five silver, and eight bronze medals, the hosts placed third in the unofficial standings. More important than the quantitative results was the simple fact that the International Olympic Committee had honored

Japan with its trust and that the Japanese were able to glory in their reputation "for internationalism and modernity."[18] Innumerable Japanese sportswriters produced dithyrambs of prose describing the "Tokyo Olympiad" as a symbol of their country's definitive return to the community of nations.

Like other Olympic hosts, Japan reaped the benefits of the "home court advantage." Japan fielded the third most successful team, harvesting a total of twenty-nine medals.[19] Only one of them, Tsuburaya Kōkichi's bronze in the marathon, came in track-and-field. No fewer than five of Japan's sixteen gold medals were awarded to the wrestlers, all of them for victories in the lighter classes. Yoshida Yoshikatsu, Uetake Yōjirō, and Watanabe Osamu won the freestyle flyweight, bantamweight, and featherweight divisions while Hanahara Tsutomu and Ichiguchi Masamitsu were victorious in the misnamed Greco-Roman flyweight and bantamweight categories.[20] While Japan's wrestlers took five of the sixteen gold medals awarded for their sport, the jūdō team accounted for three-quarters of the victories in their sport, which appeared for the first time on the Olympic program. National pride soared as Nakatani Takehide, Okano Isao, and Inokuma Isao defeated their opponents in the lightweight, middleweight, and heavyweight classes, but pride took a fall when—after 9 minutes and 22 seconds of struggle—Kaminaga Akio was upset by Anton Geesink of the Netherlands in the open class. Japanese spectators were said to have felt "a kind of collective sorrow,"[21] but those who had followed the sport should not have been surprised; three years earlier, Geesink had taken first place at the International Jūdō Federation's third world championships in Paris.[22]

The shock and disappointment of this defeat were offset by the unexpected victory of the women's volleyball team, which vanquished their highly touted (and much taller) rivals from the Soviet Union. (The men's volleyball team had to be content with bronze medals.) The final set of the women's tournament was intensely dramatic. Behind by a score of 8–14, the Soviet women scored 5 points and seemed unstoppable—until one of them reached over the net and inadvertently ended the drive. The Japanese press exulted in this triumph of the *Tōyō no Majo* (Witches of the East) and commentators invariably attributed their victory to their exceptional determination. Critics deplored what they saw as the fanaticism and brutality of the women's coach, Daimatsu Hirofumi—who seemed to think that the young women had to endure deprivation and pain comparable to what he had endured as a soldier in Burma at the end of World War II—but they were in the minority. The players themselves expressed tearful gratitude at the time and gathered together after his death to honor his memory.[23]

In gymnastics, it was the other way around. The women's team managed to place third without a single medal in the individual events while the men garnered four individual golds (Endō Yukio, parallel bars and all-around; Yamashita Masahiro, vault; Hayata Takuji, rings) and four silvers (Endō Yukio, floor; Tsurumi Shūji, pommel horse, parallel bars, and all-round) en route to the team's second victory over the Soviet Union.[24]

There were tickets for only a small fraction of the millions of Japanese who applied for them. The vast majority watched the competition on television. In the five years preceding the Olympics, the number of television owners paying reception fees to NHK zoomed from 2 million to 16 million.[25] Many acquired their first sets to be able to watch the games. Many who had already become addicted to the black-and-white images bought their first color sets to watch the broadcasts that were truly *tasai* (colorful).[26]

NHK had prepared very well for the Tokyo Olympics. In 1959, it had moved its sports division from the educational department to the news department. A huge staff of 2,548 covered the games, including 42 announcers, 195 directors and producers, 146 reporters and cameramen, and 598 broadcast technicians. They used an array of equipment to create the broadcasts: 74 black-and-white TV cameras, 6 color TV cameras, 46 videotape recorders, 600 audiotape recorders, 18 black-and-white TV broadcast cars, 2 color TV broadcast cars, 17 generator cars, and 8 videotape recording cars.[27]

The station broadcast Olympic events for ten hours each day. The entire marathon was carried live for the first time in Olympic history. For more than two hours, a helicopter flew above the broadcast car in order to relay its signal. Ethiopia's Abebe Bikila won the race, and Japan's Tsuburaya Kōkichi came in third, overtaken by Great Britain's Basil Heatley in the last 200 meters. For much of the race, however, Tsuburaya was not to be seen on the television screen. Since there was only one broadcast car, it had to stay with Abebe, who was more than a kilometer ahead of Tsuburaya. Angry viewers called NHK to complain, but the broadcast provided coverage for stations all over the world. NHK felt obliged to show the leader rather than the local hero.[28]

Of Japanese households with TV sets, 87.4 percent watched the opening ceremony of the Olympics; 85 percent watched the women's volleyball final between Japan and the Soviet Union; and 83.1 percent watched the marathon. According to NHK surveys, 97.3 percent of all households in Japan watched at least some of the Olympics on TV.[29] "The Tokyo Olympics were an opportunity to extend television throughout Japan. When they were over, television and sports events had forged an unbreakable bond."[30] Finally, it should be noted that satellite transmission made it possible for Japanese viewers to be joined by viewers from around the world. In fact, the success of these "televised Olympics" created a global market for the sale of television rights and rescued the International Olympic Committee from its endemic economic crisis.[31]

Japan sent 215 athletes and officials to Mexico in 1968.[32] The male gymnasts repeated their 1964 triumph. In fact, in the thin air of Mexico City, their supremacy was more striking than it had been four years earlier on their home ground. In the floor exercises, for instance, Katō Sawao—the victor—was followed by teammates who finished in 2nd, 3rd, 4th, and 6th place. Nakayama Akinori, who took the silver medal for this event, won gold medals on the rings and the parallel bars. Katō defeated the Russian Mikhail Voronin for the all-around title and Nakayama came in third. In fact, four of the five best all-around performances were by the Japanese team.

The wrestlers did almost as well as they had done in Tokyo. In the freestyle bouts, Nakata Shigeo, Uetake Yōjiro, and Kaneko Masaaki earned the gold medals for the flyweight, bantamweight, and featherweight divisions while Munemura Shūji added a fourth gold in the Greco-Roman lightweight category. The weightlifters, who had picked up a gold and two bronzes in 1964, increased their haul to a gold, a silver, and a bronze. The gold and the bronze medals went to a pair of brothers—Miyake Yoshinobu and Miyake Yoshiyuki—who competed in the featherweight class. There were no medals to be garnered in jūdō because the IOC had dropped the sport from the program.

The female volleyball players were unable to duplicate their 1964 achievement, but they managed to win the silver medal and their male counterparts did the same. There was also a surprising bronze medal in soccer. In track-and-field, the marathon was—as usual—the one bright spot for the Japanese team. Kimihara Kenji arrived at the finish some 3 minutes behind the winner, Ethiopia's Mamo Wolde.[33]

In 1972, Japan played the role of Olympic host for the second time. The winter games took place in or near Sapporo on the northern island of Hokkaido. Some of the luster of the games was dimmed by the controversy that followed the disqualification of the Austrian skier Karl Schranz, who had repeatedly and blatantly violated the rules that did not allow amateur athletes to receive endorsement money. It was nonetheless immensely gratifying that the Japanese team did well. Kasaya Yukio, Konno Akitsugu, and Aochi Seiji placed 1st, 2nd, and 3rd in the 70-meter ski-jump. Not since 1956 had a Japanese won a medal at the winter games.[34]

Like the games in Mexico City, those celebrated in Munich were preceded by political controversies. The South Africans were banned in 1968 because their racial policies violated the Olympic Charter. The Rhodesian team was sent home, in 1972, for the same reason. The games themselves were overshadowed by the murder of Israeli athletes by Palestinian terrorists. Despite their horror at the desecration of the Olympic Village, Japanese officials and athletes supported the International Olympic Committee's controversial announcement—in the words of IOC President Avery Brundage—that "the games must go on." The decision was firmly supported by the Japanese media and by Japanese public opinion.[35]

In the sports events, Japan's men's gymnastic team continued to dominate their opponents. The five best performances on the high bar and the three best on the parallel bars were all by Japanese gymnasts. In the competition for the individual championship, Katō Sawao, Kemmotsu Eizō, and Nakayama Akinori were first, second, and third. Karamatsu Shigeru was fifth. En route to his triumph, Katō won a gold medal on the parallel bars and silver medals on the high bar and the pommel horse. He was also fourth on the rings and in the vault. Seldom, if ever, has a gymnast been as dominant. He was as celebrated in Japan as swimmer Mark Spitz was in the United States.

Other gold medals went to the flyweight and bantamweight freestyle wrestlers (Katō Kiyomi and Yanagita Hideaki) and to the lightweight, welterweight, and middleweight jūdōka (Kawaguchi Takao, Nomura Toyokazu, Sekine Shinobu). In the Olympic pool, Japanese swimmers recovered a bit of their former glory. Aoki Mayumi was first in the women's 100-meter butterfly, but she was overshadowed (or outsplashed) by Taguchi Nobutaka, who won the men's 100-meter breaststroke and took a bronze in the 200-meter breaststroke. At the 1968 Olympics, the seventeen-year-old Taguchi had been disqualified. In the intervening years, he experimented with new ways to plunge into the water, to kick, and to turn. His reward for perseverance and inventiveness was an upset victory over England's favored David Wilkie. Taguchi was hailed in the media as a symbol of the "New Japanese."[36]

The men's volleyball team defeated East Germany to win their first Olympic title. The women were frustrated by their familiar adversaries, the Soviet team. Although the Japanese swept two of the sets by scores of 15–9 and 15–4, they lost three sets at 15–11.

They had their revenge four years later in Montreal, when they won the first two sets by scores of 15–7 and 15–8 and then held the demoralized Soviet women to a mere 2 points in the final set. There were other successes in Montreal. For the third time in a row, Katō Sawao led the gymnasts to the team title in Montreal. He and Tsukahara Mitsuo won their second gold medals on the parallel bars and the high bar, but none of the Japanese dazzled the judges as did the Russian star Nikolai Andrianov. His victories in the floor exercise, the vault, and the rings pushed Katō and Tsukuhara to second and third place in the overall rankings. The women's team continued to lag behind the world's best. None of them was able to leap and swing with the likes of Nadia Comaneci (Romania) or Ludmilla Tourisheva, Nelli Kim, and Olga Korbut (all three from the Soviet Union).[37]

As had been the case since the end of World War II, the wrestlers and the jūdōka continued to be much more successful than the swimmers, the rowers, and the track-and-field athletes (none of whom was among the top six in his or her event). Freestyle wrestlers Takada Yūji and Date Jiichirō won the flyweight and the welterweight divisions. In jūdō, Sonoda Isamu (middleweight), Ninomiya Kazuhiro (light-heavyweight), and Uemura Haruki (open) were triumphant.

These victories may have been enough to maintain the public's pride in its athletic representatives, but the ambitious men in charge of Japanese sports were not satisfied. In the aftermath of the 1976 Olympics, the government allocated new money to improve the "international competitiveness" of the country's athletes. In 1978, the Japan Physical Education Association decided that victory was better than purity. The JPEA began to accept corporate sponsorship and to advertise its benefactors' products. In 1979, it joined with other national sports federations to create the *Gambare Nippon* (Fight On, Japan!) program under which corporations were matched with sports disciplines whose elite athletes they were expected to support. The giant advertising firm Dentsū, which was soon to become a premier fund-raiser for the International Olympic Committee, coordinated the effort to hitch multinational corporations to Japan's athletic bandwagon. Old-timers devoted to the amateur ethic asked ironically if the national sports federations were to become *geisha okiya* (geisha houses) for Japan's CEOs.[38]

The best laid plans of mice and sports administrators can go awry. There were no Olympic triumphs for the Japanese in the summer of

1980 because no Japanese athletes competed in the Moscow games. Once President Jimmy Carter presented his ultimatum—if the Soviet Union failed to withdraw its invading army from Afghanistan, the United States would boycott the summer Olympics—the result was easily foreseeable. As Carter must have realized, control of Afghanistan was far more important to the Soviet Union than the presence or absence of American athletes in Moscow. And no astute observer of the international scene doubted that the Japanese government, militarily dependent on American power, would acquiesce in Carter's demand that Japan follow the American lead.[39] Nor did the astute observer of Japanese society doubt that the Japan Olympic Committee would do exactly what the U.S. Olympic Committee had done—protest against the government's interference in its statutory independence and then abjectly comply with the government's wish.

The controversy was protracted and bitter. According to Ono Akira of the *Mainichi shimbun,* the Japan Olympic Committee was pressured by the government to observe the boycott. On January 29 and 30, the head of the Ministry of Education's Physical Education Bureau called representatives of the JOC, the JPEA, and the two IOC members (Kiyokawa Masaji and Takeda Tsuneyoshi) to a secret meeting at the Imperial Hotel in Tokyo. Two days later, the government and the JOC issued separate statements, leaving open the question of Japan's participation. Public opinion was apparently divided. A late February survey done for the *Yomiuri shimbun* found that 52 percent thought a nation at war should not be allowed to host the Olympic Games, but the *Asahi shimbun* found 55 percent against a boycott and 75 percent for a strict separation of sports and politics. Confusion in the public's mind mirrored confusion within the JOC. When the *Mainichi shimbun* conducted a telephone poll on April 17, the newspaper found six JOC members supporting the government's call for a boycott, fourteen disagreeing, and nine urging that each of the national sports federations decide for itself (which was not allowed under IOC rules). May 24 was the deadline to enter the national team. A general meeting of the JOC was held that afternoon to vote on whether or not Japan would send a team. It was attended by bureaucrats of the Ministry of Education, including the head of the Physical Education Bureau, who threatened that the JOC's budget would be cut if it did not comply with the government's decision to boycott the games in Moscow. Although Kiyokawa and Takeda advocated an independent course for the committee, in the end, the majority bowed meekly to the government's wishes. The final vote to boycott was 31–13.[40] Looking back on this decision, many scholars consider it to have placed a "stain" on Japan's Olympic history.[41]

In his subsequent account of this bitter disappointment, Kiyokawa stubbornly maintained that the 1980 games were a huge success. The atmosphere was peaceful, the mood was amiable. If that was the case, which is doubtful, Japanese TV viewers were offered limited opportunity for vicarious enjoyment of all the peace and amity. Asahi Television reduced its coverage of the games from 240 hours to 40. Even so, Asahi behaved more generously than NBC, which canceled rather than curtailed its plans for the Olympics.[42]

There was another shock in the fall of 1981. In 1979, Nagoya was the acknowledged front runner in the race to host the 1988 Summer Olympics, but Japan's decision to boycott the Moscow games undermined its support in the Soviet Union, which was understandably miffed that the JOC had joined the United States Olympic Committee as a spoil sport. Nagoya's bid, which was backed by the city's political and economic elites, was also undermined by a determined group of environmentalists who collected signatures to petitions and staged protest demonstrations in Baden-Baden, where the IOC met to make the decision for 1988. Although Japanese newspapers had already prepared headlines announcing the good news, the IOC chose to award the prize to Seoul.[43]

All the more reason to look forward to Los Angeles. In the eyes of Kiyokawa Masaji, who returned as an IOC member to the scene of his greatest triumph as an Olympic swimmer, these highly commercialized games were "uniquely" organized but a "huge success."[44] That seems to have been the impression of most of the Japanese spectators. They were delighted at the many occasions to shout "*banzai!*" and to wave the rising-sun flag and watch their representatives collect their medals. The Japanese team won ten gold medals and ranked sixth among the 140 nations that ignored the Soviet Union's call for a retaliatory boycott.

Although they did not have to compete against the Soviet Union's perennially powerful gymnastics team, Gushiken Kōji and his teammates confronted some remarkably strong opposition from the United States and China. Gushiken tied for 1st place on the rings (with China's Ning Li), tied for 2nd place on the pommel horse (with Mitch Gaylord of the United States), and was third on the horizontal bar (on which his teammate Morisue Shinji was first). Gushiken's performance was enough to win him the individual championship, but the team finished third.[45] The women's team, which has never been as strong as the men's team, had to be satisfied with 7th place on the uneven parallel bars and in the floor exercises (and an 8th place in rhythmic gymnastics).[46]

During the wrestling and the jūdō matches, there were additional moments of glory. In addition to Tomiyama Hideaki's gold in freestyle wrestling (bantamweight) and Miyahara Atsuji's in Greco-Roman style (flyweight), the wrestlers won five silver and two bronze medals. The Japanese jūdōka won the two lightest and the two heaviest of the eight weight divisions in their sport. In addition to these victories by Hosokawa Shinji, Matsuoka Yoshiyuki, Saitō Hitoshi, and Yamashita Yasuhiro, there was a bronze for the middleweight Nose Seiki. (Yamashita went on to a spectacular career. After nine national championships and a string of 203 victories, he retired in 1985 at the peak of his fame.)[47]

A tenth gold medal went to Kamachi Takeo for rapid-fire pistol-shooting, and there were additional bronze medals in archery, cycling, synchronized swimming, women's volleyball, and weightlifting.

Although 6th place in the Los Angeles games was quite respectable, especially in light of Japan's perennial weakness in track-and-field, the Japan Olympic Committee was dissatisfied by the meager results of the winter games in Sarajevo (a silver medal for speed-skater Kitazawa Yoshihiro in the 500-meter event) and shocked by the outcome of the 1986 Asian Games, which were held in Seoul as a kind of trial run for the 1988 Olympics. Japan had easily dominated the Asian Games in their early years, winning more than half of the events in 1951, 1954, 1958, and 1962.[48] In 1986, however, the Japanese team was able to do no better than a distant 3rd place. It was especially humiliating that the South Koreans, who enjoyed the "home court advantage," won six of the eight weight classes in jūdō.[49] The poor showing caused repercussions within the government. The Minister of Education summoned the leaders of the JOC and told them to try harder to obtain financial support from the private sector.[50]

It was too late to expect an infusion of financial aid to produce dramatic results in 1988. At the winter games, which took place in Calgary, Japanese speed-skaters managed to win a bronze medal, but the games continued to be dominated by the Europeans and North Americans. At the summer games in Seoul, the Japanese wrestlers and gymnasts had to cope with the return of their rivals from the Soviet bloc.

Although the Soviet Union took eight of the sixteen gold medals in wrestling (and their allies added four more to the count), the Japanese did almost as well as they had in Los Angeles. There was gold for Kobayashi

Takashi and Satō Mitsuru (freestyle paperweight and flyweight) and a pair of silver medals. The gymnastic results, however, were disheartening. Vladimir Artemov won three gold medals and led his team to a fourth. The Japanese had to be content with a bronze for Iketani Yukio's floor exercises and a bronze for the team's performance. For poolside supporters of the Japanese swimming team, there was a victory to celebrate. Suzuki Daichi's win in the 100-meter backstroke race stirred memories of Japan's once-dominant swimmers. Jūdō, however, was another disaster. In only one of the seven divisions was a Japanese the victor. Saitō Hitoshi won the "open" division.[51]

With four golds, three silvers, and seven bronzes, Japan fell to 14th place in the unofficial ranking. There was consolation in Pierre de Coubertin's idealistic reminder that participation is what matters most, but the Japan Olympic Committee was not to be consoled by mere idealism. In order to facilitate raising funds from big business, the JOC was incorporated in 1989, freeing itself institutionally from the JPEA. According to Ono Akira of the *Mainichi shimbun,* the "new" JOC was controlled by wealthy businessmen. The new chairman was Tsutsumi Yoshiaki, whom *Sports Illustrated* described as "the reclusive, richer-than-Buddha president of the Japan Ski Association and owner of the gargantuan Seibu corporation, whose holdings include the Prince Hotel chain and baseball's Seibu Lions."[52] One result of the shift in leadership seems to have been the IOC's choice of Nagano as the site of the 1998 Winter Olympics. With the enthusiastic backing of Nagano's millionaire entrepreneur Yoshida Soichirō,[53] who courted IOC members in eighty countries, Tsutsumi promised—among other things—to pay the travel expenses of foreign athletes and to donate generously toward fulfillment of IOC President Juan Antonio Samaranch's dream: an Olympic Museum adjacent to IOC headquarters in Lausanne. In all, the quest for the games is said to have cost Nagano's organizers $20 million. The games themselves were said to have cost over a billion dollars, but most of that was for infrastructure that remains in place. Salt Lake City, the runner-up, was asked to wait until 2002.[54] (Salt Lake City's determination not to fail in its next bid led to the greatest bribery and corruption scandal in Olympic history.)

Before Nagano there was Barcelona, where the gymnasts of the "Unified Team" from the former Soviet Union took a lion's share of the medals. Thanks largely to 3rd-place performances by Iketani Yukio in the floor exercises and Matsunaga Masayuki on the parallel bars, the Japanese team was able to place 3rd (behind the Chinese). The wrestlers were reduced to a single bronze medal, but there was a come-back of sorts in jūdō. Koga Toshihiko and Yoshida Hidehiko won the lightweight and the half-middleweight divisions and Ogawa Naoya took the silver in the heavyweight division. In addition, there were three silver medals and two bronzes in the first-ever women's jūdō competition. The spirit of Kanō Jigorō might also have been pleased to see the prowess of the French and Spanish women (who won two gold medals each). In their quest for heroes and heroines, many Japanese fixed upon the silver medalists in the men's and women's marathon—Morishita Kōichi and Arimori Yūko.

The winter games celebrated in Albertville, France, in 1992, were followed in quick succession by those in Lillehammer, Norway, in 1994, because the International Olympic Committee had decided to alter the sequence that had been established at the first winter games in 1924 (in which the winter and summer games took place in the same "Olympic" year). In Albertville and Lillehammer, Japan's skaters and skiers finally achieved the success that had eluded them for decades.

The brightest of the hibernal stars was Itō Midori. After finishing in 5th place in Calgary in 1988, the 4-foot-9-inch-tall figure skater revised her style. She de-emphasized her ballet-like moves and concentrated on athleticism. Her jumps became spectacular. In 1989, she was the first woman to complete a triple axel in competition, and she won that year's world championship. Many expected her to ascend the victor's podium in Albertville, but, according to one story, she was unnerved during a practice session when France's Surya Bonaly cut in front of her and executed an illegal backflip. Itō continued to practice, but she missed seven of her ten attempts at a triple axel and dropped that jump from her compulsory program. Her last hopes for a gold medal vanished when she fell while executing the triple lutz that she had substituted for the triple axel. She recovered her composure and did well enough in the free skating to finish behind Kristi Yamaguchi but ahead of Nancy Kerrigan (both of the United States).

Fast rather than fancy skating was Hashimoto Seiko's forte. In 1988, she was fifth in both the 500-meter and the 1,000-meter sprints. In the 1,500-meter event, she rose from 6th place in 1988 to 3rd in 1992—and became the first Japanese woman ever to win a medal at the winter games.[55] (Subsequently, she sped on to become a member of the Japanese parliament.) At the Lillehammer games in 1994, Hashimoto was unable to do better than 6th place (over 3,000 meters), but her teammate Yamamoto Hiromi won a bronze medal (over 5,000 meters).

Albertville was a breakthrough for the men just as Lillehammer was for the women. As early as 1936, when the winter games were celebrated at Garmisch-Partenkirchen, Ishihara Shōzō had placed 4th in the 500-meter sprints. Kuroiwa Akira was expected to win in 1984 and was pilloried in the press when he did not. On the other hand, Kitazawa Yoshihiro skated to a silver medal in that event (he was more than 2 seconds faster than Ishihara had been in 1936). In 1992, Kuroiwa Toshiyuki and Inoue Jun'ichi were 2nd and 3rd over 500 meters, while bronze medals went to Miyabe Yukinori for the 1000-meter race and to the short-track 5,000-meter relay team.

At Albertville and Lillehammer, the members of the ski-jump and the Nordic-combined teams also joined the world's elite. The jumpers moved from 4th place in 1992 to 2nd in 1994. In the combined event (jumps plus a 10-kilometer relay), Japanese teams won the gold medal in 1992 and 1994. When to these achievements one added Kōno Takanori's silver medal in the 1994 individual Nordic combined, it was clear that the Japanese skiers had to be among the favorites when the winter games returned to Japan in 1998.

At Atlanta's "Centennial Games" of 1996, at which gold medals were won by fifty-three different teams, Japan's athletes received three gold medals, six silver, and five bronze, which put them in 24th place.

Half of these fourteen medals, including four of the six silver medals and all three of the gold, were earned by the jūdōka. On the men's team, Nomura Tadahiro and Nakamura Kenzō won the extra-lightweight and the lightweight divisions; on the women's team, Emoto Yūko was the best of the half-middleweights. Silver medals went to Nakamura Yukimasa (half-lightweight), Koga Toshihiko (half-middleweight), Tamura Ryōko (extra-lightweight), and Tanabe Yūko (half-heavyweight). Half-lightweight Sugawara Noriko won a bronze.

In the early rounds of the baseball tournament, Japan romped to easy victories over the Netherlands (12–2), Guyana (13–6), Korea (14–4), and Italy (12–1), but lost to Cuba (7–8), Australia (6–9), and the United States (5–15). In the semifinal, the Japanese upset the Americans by a score of 11–2 and went on to face the Cubans in the final game, in which they scored 6 runs to the Cubans' 9.

Patriotic Japanese were doubtless proud that their representatives also won a silver medal in yachting and bronze medals in cycling, free-style wrestling, and synchronized swimming, but there was euphoria when the immensely popular marathoner Arimori Yūko added a bronze to the silver she had earned in Barcelona. She, rather than one of Japan's gold-medal winners, graced the cover of a special Olympic issue of *Asahi Graphic* magazine.

The Nagano games opened on February 7, 1998, with a complex orchestration of national and international themes. Among the elements providing a "representation of 'Japaneseness'" were a Buddhist temple bell, a sumō wrestler exorcising evil spirits, and a chorus of schoolchildren performing a Shinto ritual dance. Internationalism reached a climax when interactive television made it possible for Seiji Ozawa[56] to conduct five orchestras on five continents in a rendition of the choral movement from Beethoven's *Ninth Symphony*.[57]

In the course of the games, the erstwhile hapless skier whom American sportscasters now called "Happy Harada" became the center of an intense drama. At the Albertville games, Harada Masahiko and his teammates had the fourth-best combined score in the large-hill ski-jump competition. At the Lillehammer games, after the seventh of their eight jumps, the Japanese quartet had an apparently insurmountable lead of 54.9 points. Then the last German jumper—Jens Weissflog—soared 133.5 meters, which tied the record for the longest jump in Olympic history. Harada, who needed a mere 105 meters to ensure victory for the Japanese team, mistimed his take-off and touched down at 97.5 meters. He and his teammates—Okabe Takanobu, Nishikata Jin'ya, and Kasai Noriaki—had to be content with silver medals. Four years later, history threatened to repeat itself. Harada and Okabe, joined now by Saitō Hiroya and Funaki Kazuyoshi, were engaged in another close contest with the German team. Stretching forward, holding his body nearly parallel to the *V* of his skis, Harada flew, redeemed himself, and wept with joy as the team took the gold medal.

There were other triumphs. In the individual competition, Funaki won a gold medal on the 120-meter hill (Harada took the bronze) and added a silver on the 90-meter hill. Satoya Tae bumped and jumped her way to victory in the first-time-ever women's moguls. Among the skaters, who sped to a flurry of five world's records on their newly introduced "clap skates," the Japanese were almost as strong as the Dutch (who won five gold medals). Shimizu Hiroyasu was first in the men's 500-meter sprint and third over 1,000 meters. In the short-track 500-meter race, Nishitani Takafumi and Uematsu Hitoshi were first and third. A fifth medal went to Okazaki Tomomi for her 3rd-place finish in the women's 500-meter sprint.

If we consider only the number of medals won as a percentage of all the medals awarded, we have to conclude that the Japanese contingent in Nagano had far surpassed the achievements of their counterparts in Atlanta. This reversal of the historical pattern may reflect Japan's postwar affluence and the resulting transformation of its leisure. A vacation in the Alps or a series of weekends on the slopes and trails of Nagano Prefecture is obviously more expensive than a daily stint on the 400-meter track or in the swimming pool, but the Japanese who can afford winter sports are increasingly numerous and they form the critical mass from which world-class athletes emerge. Or if we wanted to be more cynical, we might speculate on the role of billionaire Tsutsumi, who headed both the Japan Ski Association and the JOC. He played a crucial role in obtaining the winter games for Nagano, and his resorts and properties will profit from the popularity generated by the games.

When the accountants had finished their work, it seemed that Tsutsumi was not alone in profiting from the games. Although huge sums had been spent for new sports facilities—the luge and bobsled venue was said to have cost over 10 billion yen (roughly $100,000,000)—the organizing committee was able to announce that it had paid its bills and still had over 5 billion yen with which to promote the Olympic movement. Of that sum, 90 percent was allotted to Nagano Prefecture for the promotion of winter sports. The rest was to go to the Japan Olympic Committee.[58] A great deal had changed since 1920, when Japan's stranded Olympians had had to beg for help from industry in order to pay the return fare from Antwerp.

# 9

# New Directions

Japan's political, economic, social, and cultural institutions are by definition unique, but it is undeniable that they have become increasingly similar to those of the United States and Western Europe. This similarity has provoked a reaction from a small army of writers busy with the production of *Nihonjinron* (theories about Japanese uniqueness). The content of these theories—for instance, that Japanese brains are constructed differently from American and European brains[1]—is less significant than what they tell us about the feeling, widespread among traditionalists, that Japanese society is under siege, threatened by an invasion from overseas. Although traditionalists often speak as if modern Japan were simply the result of "Americanization" or "Westernization," such terms obscure Japan's own innumerable contributions to modernity at home and abroad. The global diffusion of ideas, institutions, and material products has never been unidirectional. Even in the early Meiji period, when the Japanese were busily importing everything Western, from locomotives to ballet slippers, there were American and European artists—Whistler and Van Gogh, for instance—who were strongly influenced by Japanese woodblock prints. Today, Japanese automobiles, electronic equipment, sushi bars, and shiatsu specialists can be found in every modern city.

There are martial arts centers, too, like Cologne's Budōkan, and the distinctively Japanese sport of kendō is now promoted by an International Kendō Federation (founded in 1970) that claims over a quarter of a million non-Japanese members. Nonetheless, when we examine the balance of trade in sports, we find that the Japanese continue to import much more than they export. Among the most striking recent examples of this is the vogue of golf, skiing, soccer, and a miscellany of activities whose most obvious common characteristic is that they seem all to have arrived from California.

## GOLF

As we have seen, the game was known in the late nineteenth century, when British consular officials and businessmen played it in Kobe and Yokohama, but it did not become popular until the 1960s. By the early 1990s, golf had moved from the margins to the center of Japanese sports. Today, corporate executives and even the ordinary *sararīman* ("salary man," i.e., white-collar employee) are said to have become "golf crazy," and it is a boardroom commonplace that a modicum of ability with driver and putter is essential for advancement in the corporate hierarchy. In 1990, Japan had 1,718 golf courses, some 300 more were under construction, and 955 were planned. Although some 1.25 percent of the nation's land is used for golf courses, it seems impossible for the supply to keep up with the demand generated by an estimated 12 million golfers.[2]

Although the corporate executive and the sararīman whom he employs are the stereotypical golfers, women too have taken to driving and putting. If it is true—as some have alleged—that 15 percent of Japan's golfers are female, then some 1,800,000 women participate in this expensive and prestigious sport.[3] In 1995, the Japanese Golf Association estimated that 23.6 percent of all Japanese men and 2.6 percent of all women, some 13 million in all, played the game. Even by this more modest calculation, nearly 1,600,000 women have taken to golf.[4]

The boom in golf has come despite the fact that Japan's mountainous terrain has always limited the space available for agriculture, urban development, and recreation. Golf courses require extensive tracts of level or moderately hilly land and the supply-demand equation makes the acquisition of such land extremely expensive (as well as environmentally destructive). Ironically, the scarcity of usable land in Japan makes golf especially attractive to those who can afford to play the game because "the sheer physical size of the space this sport occupies may be seen as a measure of the social space occupied by its players."[5] Confronted by this shortage of suitable space, golf clubs scramble to rent or buy space wherever they can. On the northwest edge of Kyoto, monks in their *kesa* and *geta* (Buddhist robes and wooden sandals) share the temple grounds of Shōdenji with businessmen nattily attired in their imported golfing togs. (The space has also been shared with occasional joggers from Amherst,

Massachusetts.) Another solution to the lack of space has been to purchase or construct golf courses in Scotland, the United States, and Australia. Examples of this trend are Japanese ownership of Turnberry (Scotland), the Riviera Country Club (California), and Riverside Oaks (New South Wales). The last facility is also the headquarters of Australian Professional Golfers Association.[6]

Wherever the game is played, it requires a hefty commitment in time and money. Golfers who insist on a full eighteen-hole course must "book rounds months in advance, often drive for several hours to get to the courses, pay heavy user fees, and purchase memberships at prices commonly in excess of . . . $400,000."[7] To become a member of the socially exclusive Koganei Country Club, near Tokyo, affluent golfers allegedly paid $3 million. At this and similar clubs, the fee for a single round of golf was as much as $300.[8] Although these were the extreme figures, average costs in the early 1990s were still formidable. According to a 1991 report by the Economic Planning Agency, Tokyo's least expensive club charged its members 6,760 yen a round (over $60). Visitors paid 25,670 yen (over $200). At Tokyo's public courses, a round cost 9,920 yen (over $90) while Londoners and New Yorkers paid approximately $20 for an equivalent day of urban golfing.[9] In Thorstein Veblen's terms, golfing in Japan is a form of conspicuous consumption. Those who cannot afford club membership can, of course, even in downtown Tokyo, stand shoulder to shoulder with dozens of other enthusiasts and drive a bucket of balls into a net, but the accrued prestige is hardly worth the effort.

For the most part, executives can rely on the corporation to subsidize a day on the links—just as the corporation does when managers invite their subordinates to an evening at a high-priced hostess bar. Ironically, the better one is at driving off the tee, the greater the risk of another cost that the corporation does *not* underwrite. Custom dictates that a hole-in-one be celebrated by the entire club—at the "lucky" golfer's expense.

The corporate expense account is a global phenomenon, but the Japanese executive may be in a class of his own when it comes to tender, loving, corporate care. "They are picked up at their homes in hired cars, play all day at private golf courses where membership is both exclusive and exorbitantly expensive, have their own caddies and locker-room attendants, are served exquisite lunches in magnificent dining rooms, and are returned home in the hired cars that have been waiting all day."[10] Another example of golf-related corporate largesse is the Suntory Golf Tournament in Chiba prefecture, to which Suntory—a whisky manufacturer—invited its customers and clients for "a week-long bacchanal."[11]

This *gorufu* bash was as much a part of corporate culture during the "bubble" economy of the 1980s as the sponsorship of the tournament (which cost from $1.5 million to $3 million.)[12]

When a Japanese corporation sends Tanaka-san abroad, to Singapore, for instance, his corporate superiors are likely to inform him—and it is almost invariably "him"—that the Singapore Island Country Club is a fine organization and a membership has been purchased in his name. If he neglects, in the rush to depart, to pack his clubs, no matter; a new set can be purchased at the Singapore branch of Takashimaya or Daimaru, two of Japan's most prestigious department stores. When Tanaka-san chats with Yamamoto-san at the clubhouse bar after his first time on the links, he may be told how lucky he was to have had his membership approved. So many Japanese applied to Singapore's twelve private golf clubs that some the clubs placed a quota on Japanese members—no more than 30 percent of the total membership. As a result of this restrictive policy, many of the Japanese who live in Singapore travel once or twice a week to Malaysia or Indonesia, where new golf courses have been constructed to accommodate them.[13]

A combination of enthusiasm and affluence has made Japan into a regular stop on the professional golfers' global tour. Thirty-seven foreigners were among the eighty-four players who competed in 1994 on the links of the Phoenix Country Club in Miyazaki City. Seventy-two sponsors, divided into five categories, provided the prize money and bragged about their products and services to the viewers reached by more than a dozen over-the-air and cable TV stations at home and abroad. And the Phoenix Country Club tournament was only one of the thirty-eight annual events on the Japanese part of the men's international tour. (The women's international tour scheduled thirty-nine Japanese events.)[14]

## MOUNTAIN SPORTS

With the exception of Sapporo on the northern island of Hokkaido, few of Japan's major urban centers are situated in close proximity to "snow country." Before the 1960s, few Japanese had the economic means to ski in the mountains of Nagano Prefecture, and most of those who were wealthy enough to afford a winter vacation were too obsessed with their careers to indulge in a week away from their work. The relative affluence of the 1970s and the 1980s and some small alterations in the sararīman's attitude toward leisure have sent millions of Japanese to the ski slopes. These slopes now include American resorts owned by Japanese entrepreneurs. Two of Colorado's busiest ski resorts, Steamboat and Breckenridge, are owned by Japanese corporations, and Alaska's Mount Alyeska was purchased nearly twenty years ago.[15]

In Japan, isolated mountain villages have been transformed into busy tourist resorts. Typical of the pattern is the town of Hanasaku. The terrain where Minamoto Yoritomo hunted in the twelfth century is now the site of the Olympia Hotel. Initial efforts to lure skiers from Tokyo, in the 1950s, failed, but, in 1964, the villagers entered into an agreement with Tokyo Tower Kankō, a firm that specializes in tourism. Tokyo Tower provided the capital and the expertise; Hanasaku provided the land and the workforce. Skiers came in such numbers that the new hotel was not able to accommodate them. *Gasshuku* (lodges) proliferated. Families that had in the past farmed or raised silkworms enlarged their homes and rented rooms to the vacationers. One family, for instance, began with accommodations for twenty guests, added rooms for fifty more, drained their paddy fields in order to construct three tennis courts, and began in 1981 to expand their facility to take in another eighty guests.[16]

The anthropologist who studied the town sees the turn from agriculture to tourism as a "positive adaptive strategy" and she subtitled her book "The Revitalization of Tradition in Japanese Village Life."[17] The argument is based largely upon the revival of moribund local festivals like the *saruoi matsuri,* which commemorates the miraculous moment when flowers sprang from the stone upon which the warrior Hotaka was seated. A skeptic might counter that the exploitation of festivals as tourist attractions, like the commercial development of the ski slopes, is an indication of the village's modernization rather than a sign of the revitalization of tradition. Japanese tourists photographing the saruoi matsuri are very much like Japanese tourists photographing picturesque Alpine inns, and it seems improbable that tradition plays a significant role in the sporting lives of either group.

During summer months, railroad lines and highways bring mountain-climbers to Hanasaku and similar villages. Mountain-climbing, which in the Taishō period had been the risky passion of a small number of upper-class youths in their twenties and thirties, has become a not-particularly-dangerous recreational sport for tens of thousands of older men and women. (The majority of the members of the Nihon Sangaku Kyōkai [Japan Mountaineering Association] are forty years old or older and nearly 40 percent of the members are female).[18]

For urbanites too busy to venture to Nagano Prefecture or to Colorado or to Switzerland, Japan's cities offer artificial cliffs for rock-climbers and indoor slopes for skiers. Some of the latter have been constructed on the upper floors of downtown skyscrapers. At the Sayama facility in suburban Tokyo, for instance, a fleet of trucks brings in thousands of tons of glacial ice in 300-pound blocks to be ground into bits to provide a 14-inch base of "snow" that guarantees the busy sararīman easy access to a 300-meter slope.[19] No doubt his active imagination supplies images of bright sun on distant snow-capped peaks.

## SOCCER

Like golf, soccer was introduced by the British in the Meiji era and remained a marginal sport until the 1960s. The apogee of prewar achievement was reached when Japan defeated Sweden 3–2 at the 1936 Olympics. At the 1964 Olympics, the national squad, coached by Germany's Dettmar Cramer, managed to upset Argentina's formidable team by the same score. A men's amateur league, composed of company teams, was established in 1965. Only three years after that, a Japanese team was the surprise winner of an Olympic medal (bronze). In 1986 and 1987, Japanese players won the Asian Champion Teams' Cup. The national team won the Asian Cup in 1992 and the Asian Football Conference Marlboro Dynasty Cup in 1995. The team has not yet done well in World Cup competition, but the Japanese will play at home in 2002, when they and the South Koreans will jointly host the tournament. Following the unexpected French victory in the 1998 World Cup, Philippe Troussier was named as manager of Japan's national team. In preparation for the 2002 tournament, fifteen Japanese cities are planning to construct 40,000-seat stadia.[20]

By the early 1990s, the game was widely played at Japanese universities, where baseball had formerly reigned supreme. The game was especially popular among female students. In general, soccer's popularity among Japanese teenagers was second only to baseball's and commercial entrepreneurs were eager to exploit that popularity. Suntory and eleven other major corporate sponsors decided to invest in the Japan Professional Football League (familiarly known in Japanese English as the "J. League"). Three major corporations—Mazda, Mitsubishi, and Nissan—became team owners. Kawabuchi Saburō, who had played on Japan's 1964 Olympic team, was selected to head the organization and provide the technical expertise. The first ten franchises were distributed to smaller cities, like Kawasaki, which won the first two championships, and the teams bore the city's name rather than the corporate sponsor's. In Japan soccer was sold to institutional investors as a focus for communal identity.[21] The professional soccer league also departed from the baseball model in that the income from the sale of tickets, merchandise, and television rights goes directly to the league. (Teams, however, have the right to sell the advertisements that appear on the players' uniforms.) In their recruitment policy, the league followed the example of Japanese baseball. Each team was allowed to acquire foreigner players and to field three of them at a time. While doing its best to promote home-grown heroes like Maezono Masakiyo, the league brought in European stars like Gary Lineker and Pierre Littbarski and dozens of South Americans. By 1995, the league had more than thirty Brazilians, including seven who had played on Brazil's national team.[22]

The formula seemed to work. In its initial season, 1993, the league drew 4 million spectators and some of its games were sold out four months in advance. The second season brought over 5 million fans to the soccer stadiums. The television audience was far larger than the league's promoters had expected. The J. League was so popular that Chiba Television responded to the viewers' demand and added soccer matches to its program. Sales soared for products bearing the league's logo. Calbee, for instance, sold 200 million packages of its J. League potato chips and Fuji Bank attracted 820,000 new customers with its J. League bankbook.

Soccer was shrewdly marketed.[23] "We set out to make soccer like a disco," commented an executive of the league's advertising agency, "lots of vivid color, lights, fashion, music."[24] Players like twenty-eight-year-old Miura Kazuyoshi, who "breaks into a frenzied dance after every goal,"[25] were treated like rock stars and young people flocked to the game. Accompanied by five friends, Kawami Atsuko drove four hours to a game for which she had purchased her ticket two months in advance. The game seems to have been worth the eight hours on the road. "Baseball," explained Kawami, "is boring. There aren't any interesting players to look at. Soccer is entertaining."[26]

Her assessment of baseball is obviously not shared by most Japanese, but it does underscore the results of surveys that indicate that soccer is most popular with males and females aged fifteen to twenty-five while baseball is most popular with males fifty and over.[27] These data raise a question: Why does soccer entertain large numbers of young people, especially young women, whom baseball bores? It is certainly not simply because of some intrinsic difference discovered for the first time in 1960 (and still undetected in the United States). A number of explanations are possible.

Sociologists have surveyed soccer spectators and asked about their motives, but the responses are not very helpful. Men say that they want to support their team and women say that they appreciate the players (which may or may not indicate a sexual interest); both say they are learning about the game and both deny that they are simply doing what is fashionable.[28] These responses do not explain their interest in soccer rather than baseball.

One possible explanation is that young people perceive a different ethos in soccer. Baseball and its collective virtues—teamwork, self-discipline, self-sacrifice—may be less attractive to young people than the freer spirit of a soccer match. Some of the freedom is in the rules. Baseball's prescribed offensive and defensive positions restrict the players' movements (don't step out of the batter's box, don't stray too far from first base) while the spatial configuration of a soccer game, with players constantly in motion, is a continual flux. The contrast can also be seen at the level of personality. Baseball's heroes have always tended to be admired for their self-discipline and their contribution to team harmony.[29] The J. League has allowed its players somewhat more leeway to express their individuality with long hair and short tempers, with fashionable clothes and fast cars. The contrast between Oh Sadahara and Miura Kazuyoshi is hard to miss, and it is somewhat generational.

Since there is a strong positive correlation between sports participation and sports spectatorship, some portion of professional soccer's extraordinary appeal can be attributed to the fact that millions of young Japanese now play the game. In junior high school and high school, however, baseball continues to be more widely played than soccer (at least among boys).

Perhaps the most convincing explanation emphasizes the state-of-the-art strategies adopted by the J. League's directors in their effort to market their product. If younger fans are more susceptible to clever promotional campaigns than their presumably more jaded elders, the package may count for more—with them but not with their parents—than the product. This explanation is similar to one put forth by Uesugi Masayuki. He has argued that young people are socialized into a consumer rather than a producer society. It doesn't matter that they don't know the rules of the game because their active spectatorship—face paint, balloons, noise-makers—is a form of individualistic self-expression quite unlike the statement of collective loyalty made by the rigidly disciplined fan clubs of professional baseball.[30]

A highly speculative article by Takahashi Hidesato on the chants of baseball fan clubs can be read as support for this possibility. Many observers of Japanese baseball have commented on the tightly organized fan clubs whose faithful members dress in team uniforms and travel long distances to cheer—in unison, as directed—for the team. Takahashi analyzed the rhythmic pattern of the baseball fans' collective chants. He concluded that the drums, bells, trumpets, and whistles reproduce the standard rhythm of music associated with traditional Japanese agricultural festivals. Baseball, which was and still is taken by most observers as a sign of Japan's modernity, is also, Takahashi claims, an occasion for the spectators to participate in medieval ritual.[31]

Takahashi's implausible speculations are another instance of something we have seen many times in our investigation of Japanese sports: appeal to an imagined traditional past. The speculations do lead, however, to an intriguing question. If baseball has in fact become an anachronism in the eyes of many young Japanese, is it simply that the game dates from the early Meiji period (which must seem like antiquity to teenaged soccer fans)? Looking back on the history of Japanese sports from the Meiji era to the present, one has to wonder if one reason for soccer's popularity is simply that baseball now seems too familiar, too old-fashioned, too traditional.

At any rate, soccer's popularity has proved to be fleeting. The average attendance at J. League games peaked in its second year, 1994, at 19,600. Average attendance fell to 10,000 by 1997 and then rebounded somewhat to 12,000 in 1998, ranging from 7,686 for Kobe to 22,705 for Urawa.[32] The age of the fans has also increased about one year annually, indicating that the teams may just be maintaining the fan base that they captured in the first years of the "*sakkā*" boom.[33]

Even as attendance has fallen, however, the league kept to its plans for expansion. Starting with ten teams in 1993, it expanded to twelve in 1994, fourteen in 1995, sixteen in 1996, seventeen in 1997, and eighteen in 1998. In 1999, the league split into two divisions. The upper division, J1, has sixteen teams; the lower division, J2, has ten.[34]

Falling attendance and the recession of the 1990s forced many companies to reconsider their commitment to the teams they sponsor. In 1999, the league instituted a rule limiting the number of players earning salaries of 4.8 million yen or more to 25 per team.[35] Many teams restructured to bring down expenses. By December 15, 1998, 181 players in the

J. League and its subsidiary, the Japan Football League (JFL), had been dismissed by their teams, twice as many as the year before. That was 23 percent of players with professional contracts. The new salary-cap rule made it difficult if not impossible for released players to find a new team.[36]

The Yokohama Flugels, whose name meant "wings" in German, were sponsored by All Nippon Airways. The team's annual expenses were around 3 billion yen, but only half of that was covered by gate receipts and the sale of team-related goods. The deficits had to be paid by the parent company (ANA), which reluctantly concluded that the game was not worth such a costly candle. At the end of October 1998, it was announced that the Flugels were to merge with the Yokohama Marinos. The end did not come without some consolation. Two months after their sad fate was announced, the Flugels won the 78th All-Japan Championship Emperor's Cup, reaching that pinnacle of Japanese soccer in their final game.[37]

Barely a week after the imminent demise of the Flugels was announced, the *Yomiuri shimbun* announced that it was withdrawing from the management of its team, Verdy Kawasaki. This was a hard blow because the team had for years been a power in Japanese soccer. In 1993 and 1994, Verdy Kawasaki had led the league in average attendance, drawing 25,200 and 24,900 fans. By the end of the 1998 season, however, average attendance had fallen to 10,900. That year, together with its sister company, Nihon Television (NTV), the newspaper had invested 2.5 billion yen in the team, but it had decided that such an investment no longer made economic sense. The *Yomiuri shimbun*'s 49 percent share in the club was transferred to NTV, which became the sole owner of the team (and the sole entity ultimately responsible for its financial fortunes). The head of NTV explained that he, too, had considered dropping the team, but he had finally decided to keep it because the station needed programming in the coming years as it expanded into multichannel broadcasting. Even as he announced his decision to continue to support the team, he warned the J.League that corporate sponsorship of professional sports was not a form of charity.[38]

The bad news kept coming. Newspapers reported that the construction company Fujita wanted to sell its 69.88 percent share in Bellmare Hiratsuka because it was no longer able to put 500 million yen per year into the team. Itoh Ham, a main sponsor of Vissel Kobe, cut its financial support for 1999 in half from the previous year, and removed its name from the front of the players' jerseys.[39]

The recent decline in soccer's fortunes hasn't deterred politicians from trying to cash in on the sport's popularity. As early as the 1960s there had been talk of instituting a soccer lottery like those in European countries (e.g., Italy's *toto calcio*). The funds raised could be used to "promote sports." Although the sporting establishment in Japan has always scrupulously avoided any connection with gambling, in 1998 the Diet passed a euphemistically entitled Promotion of Sports Ticket Bill (Supōtsu Shinkō Tōhyō Hōan). The lottery tickets are expected to go on sale from March 2001.[40]

## WOMEN'S SPORTS

Until very recently, Hitomi Kinue's extraordinary achievements at the 1926 International Women's Games in Gothenburg and at the 1928 Olympics in Amsterdam seemed isolated episodes in the otherwise unimpressive story of women's track-and-field sports. In the 1980s and 1990s, worthy successors have appeared. This has been especially true in the marathon. Arimori Yūko became a national heroine when she won the silver medal at the 1992 Olympics in Barcelona. It was fitting that Arimori was awarded Okayama Prefecture's Hitomi Prize because Arimori took Hitomi as her role model.[41] In turn, Arimori has inspired younger Olympic marathoners like Takahashi Naoko, who won the event at the 2000 Olympics in Sydney, the first Japanese woman ever to win Olympic gold in track-and-field.[42]

Girls and women have also begun to excel as jūdōka and, more recently, as Western-style wrestlers. They have actually encountered less hostility than one might have expected. We have long been familiar with the obsessed father who encourages his son to become a sports star in order to recover his own athletic past. Now we have a feminist variant of the story. The remarkable success of wrestler Yamamoto Miyū—a tough young girl with a passion for stuffed dolls—has enabled her proud father, Yamamoto Ikuei, to overcome the disappointment of his 7th-place finish in the 1972 Olympics.[43]

In the 1970s, Japan's most famous female athlete may have been Hisano Eiko, a mountain climber whose accomplishments included an expedition to the top of Mount Everest. Tabei Junko, one of the all-female group whom Hisano led to the top, responded with understatement to queries from the press: "Men are stronger, it's true. But we women have lots of endurance. It just takes us a little longer."[44]

### Male and Female Sports Participation
#### *Percent Involved in Sports*

| Age | Male | Female |
| --- | --- | --- |
| 20–24 years | 75.0 | 62.5 |
| 45–49 years | 66.9 | 25.2 |

If one comes down from the heights of elite sports and asks about the "woman on the street," the picture is darker. Japanese men have always been much more athletically active than Japanese women and they continue to be more involved as participants and as spectators. A 1961 survey indicated 16.9 percent of adult men were involved in organized sports, mostly through Japan's renascent industrial leagues, while a mere 3.3 percent of adult women were members of an organized sports group. As late as 1976 1.6 million Japanese men and only 116,860 women were enrolled as members of the Japan Amateur Athletic Association. In other words, this national sports federation had 10 times as many male members as female members.[45]

A 1981 study of sports participation found a gender gap in every age group. The difference was fairly small for those in their early twenties, quite large for those in their late forties.[46] These data are no surprise. In every modern society, as players and as spectators, men have been and still are more involved in sports than women. (Empirical studies, like the one done by Tatano Hideo for Fukuoka, have shown that the "gender gap" is especially large for poorly educated women with young children.)[47]

Differences in rates of participation are not the only problem. As late as 1999, in a generally optimistic book entitled *The Mountain Is Moving*, Patricia Morley reported in dismay on "the type of activity undertaken by some high school girls in aid of male sports teams. The girls . . . call themselves team managers but their work consists of preparing food and drinks for players, cleaning the dressing room, and even washing players' socks and uniforms."[48]

There are, however, encouraging signs. The gender gap has narrowed. In 1989, Saeki Toshio published the good tidings that some 55 percent of all Japanese women were involved in sports (as compared to about 65 percent of men), but one must bear in mind his definition of sports. Saeki informed his readers that the most popular Japanese sport was "stretching," which attracted 37.8 million people. By doing some considerable stretching of his own, Saeki was able to claim that 24.2 percent of all Japanese women (and 56.6 percent of girls aged fifteen to nineteen) are joggers or marathoners.[49] Stricter definitions lead to somewhat less sanguine conclusions, but it is undeniable that Japanese women have made real gains in the extent of their sports participation.

They are, in fact, participating in unprecedented numbers. The most dramatic increases in participation came in the 1970s and 1980s, during the economic boom, rather than in the first two postwar decades.

The gold medals presented to the Japanese women's volleyball team at the 1964 Olympics were earned—literally—by the players' blood, sweat, and tears, but the game can be played recreationally as well as competitively and it was (and still is) possible for novices to enjoy the game and imagine themselves as teammates of the heroic "Witches of the East." If the women of Nara Prefecture were typical, volleyball continued into the 1980s to be the most popular sport for female members of sports clubs. In 1981, 60 percent of Nara's clubs for women's sports offered their members a chance to play volleyball while only 17 percent of the clubs had softball teams.[50] Nationally, volleyball is popular among schoolgirls, 63.2 percent of whom are said to play the game,[51] among college-age women, and also among older players, many of whom are active in "Mama-San" leagues. By the late 1970s, 10 percent of Japan's 5 million female volleyball players were in these leagues specifically designed for older women.[52] By the early 1990s, the number enrolled in "Mama-San" leagues had risen to an estimated 2 to 3 million.[53]

In the 1980s and 1990s, in Japan as in every other modern society, the number of male sports participants has grown more slowly than the number of female participants. Statistically, this has meant that the ratio of male-to-female sports participation has moved from 10.0 or higher in the 1960s to 1.5 in the 1990s (i.e., women are now approximately two-fifths rather than one-tenth of all those actively involved in sports). On a comparative basis, however, the data still indicate that the ratio of male-to-female participation continues to be more skewed in Japan than elsewhere, a result that some scholars attribute to a residual commitment to Confucianism.[54]

Confucianism may or may not be the explanation, but there is indeed evidence of resistance to women's sports. Many men, especially those who are themselves athletic, *say* that they approve of women's sports,[55] but there is reason to suspect that their support comes from the head rather than the heart. Many men continue to be ambivalent if not distraught by any departure from the conventional female role of wife and mother. In a study of contemporary husbands, Yuzawa Yasuhiko came across an example of this ambivalence. Of one of the men whom he inter-viewed, Yuzawa writes,

> One day he happened to look out the window of his office and saw his wife playing tennis. They'd been married for eight years and had no children and she had asked him if he'd mind her playing tennis once in a while. He'd said no, go ahead. Yet when he saw her playing tennis that one day, sweat started pouring out of him and he had a reaction of disheartenment.[60]

There are doubtless millions of Japanese men who have experienced the same conflict between what they say and what they feel.

The hostility of some men and the ambivalence of others surely explains the fact that Japanese women who are physically active in their teens and early twenties are more likely than Western women to aban-don sports once they marry. A study of 128 Japanese and foreign partic-ipants in the All-Japan College Women's Ekiden[57] confirmed this. While 24 percent of the Japanese runners intended to continue to do sports after their marriage, 82 percent of the foreign participants expressed the same intention. Clearly, for these collegians, who were certainly more educated than the average Japanese woman, "marriage is a social factor of the utmost importance."[58]

Women have also begun, slowly, to assume other sports-related roles. The first female referee to work a Japan Basketball League first division game appeared on September 9, 1998. Two months later, eight women referees were to be found in the JBL (along with the 160 men).[59]

In March 1998, Takahara Sumiko became the first female league chairperson in professional baseball in Japan when she was appointed *kaichō* of the Central League. Takahara had been a pioneer in other posi-tions. She was the first female cabinet minister selected from the private sector, one of Japan's first female ambassadors (she served in Finland), and the first female chairperson of the Japan Physical Education Associa-tion. Takahara's appointment seems, however, to have been an expression of gender stereotypes rather than a repudiation of them. The previous league chairman, whose promotion to baseball commissioner created the vacancy, commented that, as over half of the professional sport's fans are women, he expects Takahara to come up with new ideas to attract them. The chairman of the Pacific League echoed those sentiments, expecting Takahara to bring a woman's perspective to professional base-ball. Takahara herself was quoted in much the same vein, saying that she hoped to think up new attractions, from her woman's point of view, to appeal to the many women and children among the sport's fans.[60]

Unfortunately for Takahara and others who are striving to bring more Japanese women into sports as spectators and as participants, women's sports are as susceptible as men's sports to fluctuations in the economic sector. The "Dream Ladies," the women's soccer team sponsored by Nikkō Securities, is a sad example of this susceptibility. The team was a pet project of the company's president, who wanted a sports team for public relations. Women's soccer seemed a good bet. A women's soccer federation had been established in 1979, and a national tournament was begun 1980. In 1989, a six-team Japan Ladies Soccer League was formed, expanding to ten teams by 1991. (In 1994 the name was changed to "L. League" in imitation of J. League, the "L" standing for "ladies.") Nikkō Securities formed its team in 1991, recruiting athletes from all over the country and excusing them from office work during the playing season. With an annual budget of 200 million yen, the Dream Ladies produced the desired results, winning the Japan Championship in their very first season and repeating their triumph in 1996 and 1997. Despite their success on the pitch, however, the team failed to survive to the end of the decade. Hard hit by the economic recession, in fiscal year 1998, Nikkō Securities sold some of its properties and cut its workforce by two thousand. The team was disbanded after the 1998 season. The Dream Ladies and their thirty-five-year-old (male) manager were on their own and he, at least, was glum about his prospects: "It's too late for me to learn the securities business."[61]

A similar fate befell the women's volleyball team sponsored by the giant retailer Daiei. The team finished the 1997–1998 season in first place, but the parent company, in grave financial straits, announced its intention to cut its losses. The team members and management decided to try to survive by turning professional. They launched Japan's first professional volleyball team, the "Orange Attackers," with limited support from a subsidiary of the parent company, Daiei Communications.[62]

## *LES SPORTS CALIFORNIENS*

The phrase is French, but the cosmopolitan Japanese is likely to know exactly what is meant. Whatever the actual origins of "pop sports," young Asians and Europeans think of them as typically Californian. More often than not, they are right.

By the Twenties, Californians had imported surfboarding from Hawaii. By the mid-Fifties, adventurous souls had mounted masts and sails on their surfboards and thus invented windsurfing, a sport that quickly moved from the water to the boardwalk and streets. Californians were soon accustomed to having their cars serviced by roller-skating gas-station attendants. The mania for rolling along spread, and the skateboard was invented, eventually to be followed by the now ubiquitous rollerblades.[63]

Surfboarding came to Japan in 1965, windsurfing in 1973. Neither of these sports nor skateboarding and rollerblading are as common in Japan as they are in the United States, but the popularity of these and other risky recreations among young Japanese sends an unmistakable signal to middle-aged stick-in-the-muds.[64]

To this short list of "new sports" one can add many others that are also products of modern technology. California's cyclists "were no more confined to bike paths than skiers were to ski trails. Mountain bikes were invented."[65] These bikes are now almost as popular in Fukuoka and Sapporo as they are in San Francisco. "Although it is impossible to roller-skate through snow drifts," comments Peter Kühnst, "clever Californians designed snowboards." The origins of hang-gliding are less obviously Californian, but adventurous young Japanese have taken to that sport as if they were soaring above the Sierra Nevada range.[66]

Not all of these "Californian sports" require as much physical strength and dexterity as surfboarding does. For men and women in their thirties and forties, the internal combustion engine substitutes nicely for muscle power. Kühnst, who is an expert in the depiction of sports in the visual arts, has vividly described the arrival of California's "motorized pop sports":

> Thanks to the alternatively wild and "laid-back" culture of the "easy rider," motorcycles joined with other innovatively powered vehicles as the newest symbols of unlimited freedom. Propeller-driven boats glided across lakes and swamps. Dune buggies traversed coastal wastelands. Airplanes no bigger than the Wright brothers' first constructions took to the air . . . In this atmosphere of quasi-religious fanaticism, the most striking and imaginative products of California's multicultural pop sports were those that took place on, in, or under the water. Whether driven by motors or by wind or by human muscles, water-borne craft jostled bathers, swimmers, snorkelers, divers, and surfers.[67]

Motor boats and privately owned airplanes are much less common in Japan than in the United States, and dune buggies are as rare as snowmobiles, but a glance at vehicles parked on the campus of any Japanese university should be enough to convince the observer that motorcycles are the Japanese undergraduate's preferred mode of transportation. Although these chromium-coated marvels of modern technology can be as expensive as an automobile, they are more suited to Japan's crowded streets and narrow roads. And the noise they make is probably as attractive to the "easy riders" of Tokyo and Osaka as it is to motorcyclists on the Los Angeles freeways. It is safe to assume that most of the motorcycles one sees are used for recreation as well as for utilitarian purposes.

Southern California is perceived—and not just by young Japanese—as the holy land from which the hedonistic cult of physical fitness has been disseminated. Fitness centers, which spread through Japan during the 1980s, were associated with Hollywood, thanks in part to the film *Perfect* (1985) and to Jane Fonda's immensely popular exercise book. There were 246 such centers in 1980. By 1992, an estimated 3 million Japanese, most of whom were female, had memberships in some 1,564 fitness studios. Dancing aerobically and working with lightweight dumbbells, they created for themselves what the Japanese called, in English, the "fashionable lifestyle image." The geisha's kimono had revealed the nape of her neck; the aerobic dancer's miniskirt displays legs shaped by her "body work." Kawahara Kazue suggests that Madonna's blatantly entitled book, *Sex* (1992), contributed to the fitness boom by calling attention to the fashionable appeal of the toned body.[68] The book certainly contributed to the association of fitness and Hollywood.

In Japan as elsewhere, many "Californian" sports began as countercultural activities popular among rebels with or without a cause, but there has been an apparently inevitable tendency for them to submit to the imperatives of modern sports and to establish national and international associations that formalize rules and regulations, stage championships, and—*horrible dictu!*—ratify records. Once established, these associations send their executive officers to Lausanne to knock on the doors of the International Olympic Committee. With the backing of NBC television, always on the look-out for new sports to cover, beach volleyball and mountain biking became Olympic events. Freestyle skiing (mogul and aerial) and snowboarding (half-pipe and "daikaiten") were on the program of the Nagano Olympics, and Satoya Tae took the gold medal in the women's moguls.

Neither convergence in organizational structure nor elevation to Olympic status means that "Californian" sports are identical in their ethos to track-and-field or the array of modern ballgames. The mood among enthusiasts for "Californian" sports is not Puritanical. Conspicuous among those enamored of surfing and gliding is a turn away from the austere asceticism characteristic of the martial arts and "samurai baseball." Interscholastic and intercollegiate sports have become ruthlessly competitive and fewer young people want to subject themselves to the kind of spartan discipline demanded to represent their schools.[69] Of rugby, for instance, Richard Light has observed that "far fewer young men are now prepared to put up with traditional hard training, hazing and the strict hierarchy that has characterized the way [the game] has been conducted in the strong rugby playing schools and universities."[70] Rather than endure the "involuntary labor" of interscholastic and intercollegiate sports, young people are increasingly turning to out-of-school recreations like motocross and scuba diving.[71] For athletes, wrote physical educator Sugawara Rei in 1984, "there are neither rainy days nor windy days. When the cold wind stabs their skin, they venture forth with bare feet. Calmly, with dedication, they carry on."[72] Rugby players may agree, but skateboarders and windsurfers are likely to dissent.

In a world where the members of fitness clubs describe themselves as "exercise-averse,"[73] hedonism might seem to have gained the upper hand, at least among the young, but asceticism has not wholly disappeared. Zealots have turned the cult of physical fitness into an internationally organized competition (for which they have vainly sought the International Olympic Committee's stamp of approval). Bodybuilders trace their heritage back to Eugen Sandow and the "physical culturists" of nineteenth-century Europe, but the Japanese who "pump iron" are much more likely to have fantasies of Steve Reeves on "Muscle Beach" in the 1940s or of Arnold Schwarzenegger at Gold's Gym in the 1970s. In those years, southern California supplanted central Europe as the "mecca of professional bodybuilding."[74] From their offices in Los Angeles, Joseph and Benjamin Weider control the affairs of the International Federation of Bodybuilding, which they established in 1946. The Weiders also publish *Muscle and Fitness*, which appears in a Japanese edition. Male bodybuilders are a marginal group in Japan as elsewhere, but their exaggerated musculature can be likened to that of the sumō wrestlers depicted in nineteenth-century woodblock prints by Utagawa Kunisada and other popular artists. Aggressively competitive female bodybuilders like Nishiwaki Michiko have found it hard to win acceptance in the "home of the geisha and other forms of the subdued woman,"[75] but dozens of young women do flex and strut at the annual Miss Tokyo contest. There have been as yet no Japanese names among the winners of the Mr. Olympia and the Ms. Olympia contests, both of which are sponsored by the Weiders' International Federation of Bodybuilding, but one can always dream.

## NEW SPORTS INVENTED IN JAPAN

In sports as in literature, music, and the visual arts, the Japanese were never passive borrowers of Western culture. They adopted and adapted, and in the early years it was often out of necessity. George Leland brought a tennis racket and balls with him and started teaching the game when he came to Japan to teach at the National Institute of Gymnastics in 1878, the year after the first tournament at Wimbledon. The balls were expensive to import, however, and Japanese manufacturers were at first unable to duplicate them. A rubber ball was produced as a substitute, and soon a new form of tennis developed using this softer ball. The game became known as *nanshiki tenisu* (softball tennis). This version of the game uses a slightly different racket, which is gripped differently, and the main form of competition is doubles play. The court and dress code are like those in "hardball" tennis.[76]

In 1904, students from four colleges gathered to draw up the first rules. In 1923, the Tokyo Softball Tennis Association was formed and the first national championships were held. The Tokyo Association became the Japan Softball Tennis Association in 1924, and softball tennis became an event at the Meiji Shrine Sports Games in 1925. In 1939, the JSTA joined the Japan Physical Education Association. Today, many universities have softball tennis clubs and the game is widely played at the community level as well. Several courts have been constructed in the southeast corner of the park surrounding the imperial palace in Kyoto. National tournaments are held annually for men and women on high-school, middle-school, and company teams.[77]

Following the pattern of the diffusion of Western sports, "softball tennis" spread to Japan's colonies of Taiwan, Korea, and Manchuria in the first half of the twentieth century. After the war, the sport traveled abroad with Japanese businessmen. In 1955, the Asian Softball Tennis Federation was formed, and the first Asian Championships were held the next year. By 1999, the International Soft Tennis Federation [sic], which was established in 1973, consisted of thirty-four countries with over a million players. An international championship tournament has been held biannually since 1975.[78]

One of the demographic markers of modernity is a population skewed toward the elderly. Longevity increases, fertility decreases, and no society demonstrates this phenomenon more clearly than the Japanese. The "graying" of Japanese society means a decline—among men—in the percentage of those actively involved in sports, but the same seems not to be true for women. In fact, there are data to suggest that women in their sixties are *more* actively involved in sports than younger women are. For many of the elderly, sports are a form of socialization into new lives without their deceased partners.[79]

The sports of the elderly are, of course, different from those of younger men and women. With age comes a shift from strenuous, highly competitive sports like basketball toward less physically demanding recreational sports.[80] Elderly Japanese play shuffleboard, croquet, and all the other sports popular with their peers in other modern societies, but the favorite, for men and for women, is gateball.

Like softball tennis, gateball is the offspring of a preexisting Western sport. Like basketball, it was invented by a single person, Suzuki Kazunobu. In 1947, he became concerned about the lack of healthy recreational opportunities for young people. At the time, there was still a severe shortage of the rubber needed to make the balls used in many sports. Suzuki, working in the lumber industry on the northern island of Hokkaido, realized that there was a ready supply of the wood used to make croquet balls and mallets. He revised the rules of croquet and created gateball. His invention received some national attention when it was introduced at the Seventh National Recreation Meet in Nikkō, Ibaraki Prefecture, in 1951, but the mainstream recreation movement showed little interest in the game.[81]

Then, in the late 1950s a physical education instructor introduced gateball to the women's societies and senior citizens' clubs of Kumamoto City (on the southern island of Kyūshū). There, at the other end of the archipelago from Hokkaidō, the game became quite popular. The Kumamoto Gateball Association, which was formed in 1962, developed a local set of rules and their version of the game became known nationally when it was demonstrated at a national fitness meet in Kumamoto in 1976. It was presented as a sport uniquely suited for the elderly. Local government officials and representatives of senior citizens' organizations introduced the sport around the country, and its popularity exploded.

The game, which is subsidized by many local governments, is played by two teams who take turns knocking the ball through three gates (one point each) to a stake in the ground (2 points). "Play continues," according to Kathleen Kalab, who studied the game as it was played in Osaka, "until all members of the one team have hit the center pole or thirty minutes, whichever comes first." The group whom Kalab observed consisted of eight men and nine women in their sixties. They begin to play at about 8:30 in the morning, stop at around 10:00 for coffee or tea, and continue to play until lunchtime. They dress in slacks or sweatsuits and wear caps or hats. The constant flow of friendly banter that accompanies the game is typical of all sports where sociability is more important than competition. All the players whom Kalab interviewed agreed that the game promoted physical and mental fitness.[82] Responses from a survey conducted by other sociologists suggest that older women value sports participation more highly than do older men. The reason may be that they are, on the whole, in better health.[83] Cynics may adduce another reason: these older women have outlived the husbands who constrained them to physically inactive domesticity.

The explosive popularity of gateball gave rise to several national organizations, each promoting its own version of the game. In 1984 the Japan Gateball Alliance (Nihon Gētobōru Rengō) was founded, the rules and forms unified, and a national meet was held. The number of people playing the sport around 1990 was estimated at 3 million, most of them in their sixties and seventies.[84]

The media responded to this "gateball fever" by first lauding the positive aspects of this new pastime for the elderly, and then by giving prominence to some of the curious and unpleasant aspects of the boom, which usually involved problems that do not fit the popular image of the elderly. In the heat of competition, fights sometimes break out among the players. The old folks have also been known to take over a park for gateball and not let children in to play.[85]

The invention of new sports in Japan continues along with the adoption of each and every modern sport invented in the West. If the past is a good predictor of the future, these new sports will, sooner or later, acquire the formal-structural characteristics of other modern sports. At the same time, however, Japanese (and foreign) observers will detect in these new sports manifestations of Japanese tradition or—at the very least—signs of the samurai spirit.

# Notes

## Introduction

1. The bullfight has survived in Spain, side by side with soccer football, but one is hard pressed to find other examples of traditional sports that remain widely popular.

2. On the mix of tradition and modernity in a Japanese wedding, see Ofra Goldstein-Gidoni, *Packaged Japaneseness* (Honolulu: University of Hawaii Press, 1997).

3. Edwin O. Reischauer, *The Japanese* (Cambridge, Mass.: Harvard University Press, 1977), p. 228.

4. Ian Reader has recently published a very astute review of several studies of Japanese modernization, including Eisenstadt's; see "Studies of Japan, Area Studies, and the Challenges of Social Theory," *Monumenta Nipponica,* 53:2 (Summer 1998): 237–255.

5. Masao Miyoshi, "Against the Native Grain," in *Postmodernism and Japan,* ed. Masao Miyoshi and H. D. Harootunian (Durham: Duke University Press, 1989), p. 146.

6. John Whitney Hall, "Changing Conceptions of Modernization in Japan," in *Changing Japanese Attitudes toward Modernization,* ed. Marius B. Jansen (Princeton: Princeton University Press, 1965), pp. 40–41.

7. Allen Guttmann, *From Ritual to Record: The Nature of Modern Sports* (New York: Columbia University Press, 1978); Lee A. Thompson, "The Modernization of Sumo as a Sport" (Ph.D. dissertation, University of Osaka, 1989).

8. The next eight paragraphs are a revised version of Allen Guttmann, *A Whole New Ball Game* (Chapel Hill: University of North Carolina Press, 1988), pp. 5–11. Those pages are, in turn, a condensation of the argument put forth in Guttmann, *From Ritual to Record.* See also Eric Dunning, "The Structural-Functional Properties of Folk-Games and Modern Sports," *Sportwissenschaft,* 3:3 (1973): 215–232; Eric Dunning, "The Figurational Dynamics of Modern Sport," *Sportwissenschaft,* 9:4 (1979): 341–359.

9. Guttmann, *From Ritual to Record,* pp. 54–55.

10. Max Weber, *Wirtschaft und Gesellschaft,* 2 vols. (1920; Cologne: Kiepenheuer & Witsch, 1964), 1:15.

11. Colin D. Howell, "On Metcalfe, Marx, and Materialism," *Sport History Review*, 29:1 (May 1988): 96, 100.

12. For a more detailed response, to which we subscribe, see Melvin L. Adelman, "Modernization Theory and Its Critics," in *Encyclopedia of American Social History*, ed. Mary Cupiec Cayton et al., 3 vols. (New York: Scribner's, 1993).

13. Richard D. Brown, *Modernization* (New York: Hill & Wang, 1976), p. 19.

14. Peter N. Stearns, "Modernization and Social History," *Journal of Social History*, 14:2 (Winter 1980): 189.

15. See the papers in Steven Vlastos, ed., *Mirror of Modernity: Invented Traditions of Modern Japan* (Berkeley: University of California Press, 1998).

16. Pierre Bourdieu, *La Distinction* (Editions de minuit, 1979).

17. Joseph Strutt, *The Sports and Pastimes of the People of England*, 2nd ed. (London: Thomas Tegg, 1838), pp. xvii–xviii.

## Chapter 1. Sumō, Ball Games, and Feats of Strength

1. Carl Diem, *Weltgeschichte des Sports*, 3rd ed., 2 vols. (Frankfurt/Main: Cotta, 1971), 1:3.

2. Wolfgang Eichel, quoted in Horst Ueberhorst, "Ursprungstheorien," in *Geschichte der Leibesübungen*, ed. Horst Ueberhorst, 6 vols. (Berlin: Bartels & Wernitz, 1972–1989), 1:17; see also Dieter Voigt, *Soziologie in der DDR* (Cologne: Verlag Wissenschaft & Politik, 1975), pp. 29–31.

3. Research into the origins of these rituals is especially difficult because the Japanese had no written language before the sixth century A.D., when Chinese characters (kanji) began to be widely used.

4. P. L. Cuyler, *Sumo: From Rite to Sport* (New York: Weatherhill, 1979), p. 21.

5. Jörg Möller, *Sumō: Kampf und Kult* (Sankt Augustin: Academia, 1990), p. 37.

6. These issues are discussed in Lee A. Thompson, "The Modernization of Sumo as a Sport" (Ph.D. dissertation, Osaka University, 1989). The most widely referenced standard history of sumō is Sakai Tadamasa, *Nippon sumō shi*, 2 vols. (Tokyo: Baseball Magazine, 1956, 1964). See also Ikeda Masao, *Sumō no rekishi* (Tokyo: Heibonsha, 1977); Cuyler, *Sumo;* Lora Sharnoff, *Grand Sumo*, rev. ed. (New York: Weatherhill, 1993).

7. Jörg Möller, *Spiel und Sport am japanischen Kaiserhof* (Munich: Iudicium, 1993), p. 38; *Nihongi*, trans. W. G. Aston, 2 vols. (Rutland, Vt.: Charles E. Tuttle, 1972), 1:173–174.

8. *Nihongi*, 1:361–362.

9. Wakamori Tarō, *Sumō ima mukashi* (Tokyo: Kawade shobō shinsha, 1963), p. 22.

10. Cuyler, *Sumo*, pp. 28–30.

11. Ibid., pp. 30–32; Harold Bolitho, "Frolicking Dragons: Mythic Terror and the Sumō Tradition," *ASSH Studies in Sports History*, 2 (1987): 14.

12. When Japanese scholars insist that religious origins are what distinguishes sumō from European sports, they seem unaware of Carl Diem's assertion—quoted above—that *all* sports have cultic origins.

13. Nitta Ichirō, *Sumō no rekishi* (Tokyo: Yamakawa shuppansha, 1994), pp. 45, 55, 60, 62, 128–129.

14. Eiko Kaneda, "Trends in Traditional Women's Sumo in Japan," *International Review of the History of Sport*, 16:3 (September 1999): 113–119.

15. Nitta, *Sumō no rekishi*, 60, 64, 129–130.

16. The Tanabata Festival occurs when the stars Vega and Altair seem to converge. They are said to be lovers allowed to meet once a year.

17. Louis Frédéric, *Daily Life in Japan at the Time of the Samurai*, trans. Eileen M. Lowe (Tokyo: Charles E. Tuttle, 1973), p. 28.

18. Möller, *Spiel und Sport am japanischen Kaiserhof*, pp. 34–41.

19. *A Tale of Flowering Fortunes (Eiga monogatari)*, trans. William H. and Helen Craig McCullough, 2 vols. (Stanford: Stanford University Press, 1980), 1:391–392.

20. Our main source for this and the next six paragraphs is Obinata Katsumi, *Kodai kokka to nenjū gyōji* (Tokyo: Yoshikawa kōbunkan, 1993), pp. 91–93, 96, 109, 113–115.

21. John Whitney Hall, *Japan: From Prehistory to Modern Times* (Tokyo: C. E. Tuttle, 1971), pp. 65–66. See also G. Cameron Hurst III, *Insei: Abdicated Sovereigns in the Politics of Late Heian Japan, 1086–1185* (New York: Columbia University Press, 1976).

22. Obinata, *Kodai kokka to nenjū gyōji*, p. 126.

23. Ibid., pp. 126–127.

24. Scharnoff, *Grand Sumo*, p. 40; Gordon Daniels, "Japanese Sport," in *Sport, Culture and Politics*, ed. J. C. Binfield and John Stevenson (Sheffield: Sheffield Academic Press, 1993), p. 171; Imamura Yoshio, *Nihon taiiku shi* (Tokyo: Fumaidō, 1970), p. 97.

25. Sharnoff, *Grand Sumo*, p. 40.

26. Nitta, *Sumō no rekishi*, pp. 168, 184–185.

27. On the evolution of soccer and rugby, see Eric Dunning and Kenneth Sheard, *Barbarians, Gentlemen and Players* (Oxford: Martin Robertson, 1979).

28. Nitta, *Sumō no rekishi*, pp. 93–95.

29. Ibid., pp. 158, 165–169, 193–195.

30. Ikeda, *Sumō no rekishi*, pp. 94–97.

31. Takahashi Yoshitaka, *Ōzumō no jiten* (Tokyo: Sanseidō, 1985), p. 37.

32. Nitta, *Sumō no rekishi*, p. 185.

33. Cuyler, *Sumo*, p. 59.

34. Suzuki Toshio, "Tokugawa bakufu shohōrei ni mirareru shomin no yūgi tōsei ni tsuite," *Nihon taiiku gakkai dai 30 kai taikai gō*, 1979, p. 86.

35. The diminution of expressive (as opposed to instrumental) violence is at the core of what Norbert Elias refers to as "the civilizing process." For this process as it relates to sports, see Dunning and Sheard, *Barbarians, Gentlemen and*

*Players;* Norbert Elias and Eric Dunning, *Sport im Zivilisationsprozeß* (Münster: LIT, 1983); Norbert Elias and Eric Dunning, *Quest for Excitement* (Oxford: Basil Blackwell, 1986); Eric Dunning et al., *The Roots of Football Hooliganism* (London: Routledge, 1988); Eric Dunning, *Sport Matters* (London: Routledge, 1999).

36. Nitta, *Sumō no rekishi,* pp. 190–192.

37. Ibid., pp. 198–99.

38. Ibid., p. 202.

39. Cuyler, *Sumo,* pp. 89–90.

40. Oinuma Yoshihiro, "Ōzumō ni okeru heyaseido no rekishi," *Tōkai daigaku taiikugakubu kiyō,* 10 (1980): 12–13. For the role of the Jockey Club in English horse-racing, see Wray Vamplew, *The Turf* (London: Allen Lane, 1976); Mike Huggins, *Flat Racing and British Society, 1790–1914* (London: Frank Cass, 2000).

41. Nitta, *Sumō no rekishi,* pp. 229–232.

42. Cuyler, *Sumo,* p. 81.

43. Nitta, *Sumō no rekishi,* pp. 246, 255–256.

44. Hall was also upset by a match at a temple festival "between a girl twelve or fourteen years old and a boy of similar age, both naked except [for] a narrow strip of cloth that barely saves the last outrage in [sic] decency"; Francis Hall, *Japan through American Eyes,* ed. F. G. Notehelfer (Princeton: Princeton University Press, 1992), pp. 127, 285, 422, 500. (Not in this order.)

45. Basil Hall Chamberlain and W. B. Mason: quoted in Bolitho, "Frolicking Dragons," pp.15–16.

46. Ibid., pp. 17–19. Many such prints can be seen in Lawrence Bickford, *Sumo and the Woodblock Print Masters* (Tokyo: Kodansha International, 1994).

47. Hall, *Japan through American Eyes,* pp. 124–28, 262, 500.

48. Soon Hee Wang, "Bunka to shite no shintai: rikishi no ba'ai," *Supōtsu shakaigaku kenkyū,* 4 (1996): 23–33; Soon Hee Whang, "The Body as Culture: The Case of the Sumo Wrestler" (paper presented at a conference on "Sports and Body Culture in Modern Japan," Yale University, March 31–April 2, 2000). Our comments are not meant to imply that Edo-period Japanese thought in terms of "Japanese culture."

49. Nitta, *Sumō no rekishi,* pp. 222–225. For the concept of "invented tradition," see Eric Hobsbawm and Terence Ranger, eds., *The Invention of Tradition* (Cambridge: Cambridge University Press, 1983).

50. Watanabe Tōru and Kuwayama Kōnen, *Kemari no kenkyū* (Tokyo: University of Tokyo Press, 1994), pp. 5–6, 125.

51. Möller, *Spiel und Sport am japanischen Kaiserhof,* p. 87.

52. Watanabe Tōru, "Kemari no tenkai ni tsuite no ichikōsatsu: Edo jidai no sōron wo chūshin to shite, kemari ni okeru iemoto sei ni tsuite," *Taiikugaku kiyō,* 3 (1966): 13–22.

53. Watanabe in Watanabe and Kuwayama, *Kemari no kenkyū,* pp. 7–8.

54. Kuwayama adds that the religious explanation for the calls made when

passing the ball was a later addition to kemari lore. See Kuwayama in Watanabe and Kuwayama, *Kemari no kenkyū*, pp. 153–154.

55. Watanabe in ibid., p. 19.

56. Ibid., pp. 8–13.

57. Möller, *Spiel und Sport am japanischen Kaiserhof*, p. 92.

58. Watanabe in Watanabe and Kuwayama, *Kemari no kenkyū*, pp. 13–15.

59. Ibid., pp. 16–17.

60. On court tennis, see Heiner Gillmeister, *Tennis* (Leicester: Leicester University Press, 1997).

61. Möller, *Spiel und Sport am japanischen Kaiserhof*, p. 89.

62. Ibid., pp. 90–91.

63. Players other than the principal eight also sometimes participated. These were called *nobushi*. Nobushi were either assigned to a position or to a player. Those assigned a position covered areas that were difficult for the main eight to reach, for example, open areas outside the square. Or they were assigned to elder or noble players whose skills were no longer equal to the challenge. A nobushi stood behind the player he was assigned to and helped him with balls too difficult for him to handle. This took as much tact as it did skill. *Kabeshiro* refers to a practice by which a lower-status player was allowed into a game to which he might not normally be invited. An especially skillful player of lower status might be invited to play at the palace or some other venue not normally accessible to someone of his social class. In this case, a nobleman of appropriate standing was the nominal player while the lower-status player took his place under the tree. See Watanabe in Watanabe and Kuwayama, *Kemari no kenkyū*, pp. 29–30.

64. Möller, *Spiel und Sport am japanischen Kaiserhof*, p. 88.

65. This and the next two paragraphs are based on Watanabe in Watanabe and Kuwayama, *Kemari no kenkyū*, pp. 19–22.

66. *The Confessions of Lady Nijō*, trans. Karen Brazell (Stanford: Stanford University Press, 1976), pp. 92–95.

67. Watanabe in Watanabe and Kuwayama, *Kemari no kenkyū*, pp. 24–25.

68. Ibid., pp. 21–23.

69. Möller, *Spiel und Sport am japanischen Kaiserhof*, p. 87.

70. Watanabe in Watanabe and Kuwayama, *Kemari no kenkyū*, pp. 37–38. On the concept of the sports record, see Richard Mandell, "The Invention of the Sports Record," *Stadion*, 2:2 (1976): 250–264; Allen Guttmann, *From Ritual to Record* (New York: Columbia University Press, 1978), pp. 52–55.

71. Watanabe in Watanabe and Kuwayama, *Kemari no kenkyū*, pp. 27–28.

72. Ibid., pp. 28–29.

73. Sei Shōnagon, *Makura no sōshi*, ed. Ikeda Kikan, Kishigami Shinji, and Akiyama Ken, NKBT 19 (Tokyo: Iwanami shoten, 1958), p. 249.

74. Murasaki Shikibu, *Genji Monogatari*, trans. Edward Seidensticker (New York: Knopf, 1976), p. 581.

75. Watanabe in Watanabe and Kuwayama, *Kemari no kenkyū*, pp. 43–44.

76. Ibid., pp. 46–49.

77. Watanabe, "Kemari no tenkai," p. 14.

78. Fujiwara Narimichi: quoted in Möller, *Spiel und Sport am japanischen Kaiserhof,* p. 105.

79. Watanabe in Watanabe and Kuwayama, *Kemari no kenkyū,* pp. 46–50; Watanabe Tōru, "Kemari no tenkai ni tsuite no ichikōsatsu: Edo jidai no sōron o chūshin to shite, kemari ni okeru iemoto seido ni tsuite," *Taiikugaku kiyō,* Tōkyō daigaku kyōyōgakubu, 3 (1966), p. 14.

80. Watanabe in Watanabe and Kuwayama, *Kemari no kenkyū,* p. 51.

81. Kuwayama in Watanabe and Kuwayama, *Kemari no kenkyū,* p. 132.

82. This and the next four paragraphs are based on Watanabe in Watanabe and Kuwayama, *Kemari no kenkyū.* pp. 51–72.

83. Ibid., pp. 76–77; Imamura, *Nihon taiiku shi,* 102. Over seven centuries later, the novelist Mishima Yukio, himself an advocate of the martial tradition, used kemari as a metaphor for the fatal indecisiveness of the aristocratic class. In *Spring Snow,* the fictional Count Ayakura, upon hearing that his daughter, the fiancée of an imperial prince, is pregnant by another man, does nothing. His response, writes Mishima, "had a great deal in common with *kemari,* the traditional sport of the Ayakuras. No matter how high one kicked the ball, it would obviously come down to earth again at once. . . . Since all the solutions left something to be desired in terms of good taste, it was better to wait for someone else to make the unpleasant decision. Someone else's foot would have to stretch out to intercept the falling ball. . . . The Count was never one to be long vexed by worries, and as an inevitable consequence, his worries always ended up by vexing others." See Yukio Mishima, *Spring Snow,* trans. Michael Gallagher (Tokyo: Charles E. Tuttle, 1972), pp. 294–295.

84. Watanabe in Watanabe and Kuwayama, *Kemari no kenkyū,* pp. 84–86.

85. Kuwayama in Watanabe and Kuwayama, *Kemari no kenkyū,* pp. 126–127. The authority to issue licenses to followers (*monjin*) was a significant source of income. In particular, the licensing of costume according to social status gave the pastime an aristocratic atmosphere. Issuing licenses was also a way for the aristocrats, who had lost political power to the samurai, to enjoy a sense of superiority. See Watanabe Tōru, "Kemari no tenkai ni tsuite . . . ," *Taiikugaku kiyō,* pp. 20–21.

86. Watanabe in Watanabe and Kuwayama, *Kemari no kenkyū,* pp. 77–79, 81.

87. Our description of the early history of kemari is derived mostly from the *Naige sanjisho,* which has two chapters on practice, or training, for kemari. The first is devoted to individual practice. It starts with advice on the proper mental approach or attitude toward training. Between the discussion of posture and footwork and the discussion of the various kicks there is a section that explains how to deal with the trees. The chapter concludes with a summary. The second chapter on practice is about application of the techniques learned in the first.

It discusses team play and how to handle various situations that arise during the game. Summarizing the book seven hundred years after its first appearance, Watanabe marvels at the systematic and rational presentation of its topic. Another remarkable characteristic of the *Naige sanjisho* is that it presents its teachings in stages. Watanabe comments that, to the best of his knowledge, this is the only kemari treatise that does so. See Watanabe and Kuwayama, *Kemari no kenkyū*, pp. 8, 97, 100, 103.

88. Ibid., p. 7.

89. Ibid.

90. Machida Ryōichi, "Shinano ni okeru kemari no ryūkō," *Shinano*, 3:12 (1951): 45–46, 49.

91. Ibid.

92. Vivienne Kenrick, *Horses in Japan* (London: J. A. Allen, 1964), pp. 107–109. Kenrick also points out that modern polo did not arrive in Japan until 1952, when the Hawaii Polo Association invited Keishi Hamano to visit Hawaii.

93. Möller, *Spiel und Sport am japanischen Kaiserhof*, p. 80.

94. Iwaoka Toyoma, "Dakyū," *Saishin supōtsu daijiten*, ed. Kishino Yūzō (Tokyo: Taishūkan shoten, 1987), pp. 752–754.

95. On medieval folk-football, see Francis P. Magoun, *History of Football* (1938; Bochum-Langendreer: Kölner Anglistische Studien, 1966).

96. Sōgawa Tsuneo, "Gitchō," in *Saishin supōtsu daijiten*, pp. 201–203.

97. Itō Akira, "Tōkyōto Suginamiku Ōmiya Hachimangū no chikaraishi no kenkyū," *Taiikushi kenkyū*, 2 (March 1985): 6–11; Itō Akira, "Tōkyōto Daitōkunai no chikaraishi no chōsa-kenkyū," *Taiikushi kenkyū*, 4 (March 1987): 1–10; Itō Akira, "Chikaraishi," *Saishin supōtsu daijiten*, pp. 782–83; Itō Akira, "Tōkyōto Itabashikunai no chōsa-kenkyū," *Taiikushi kenkyū*, 5 (March 1988): 34–40.

98. Arnd Krüger and Akira Ito, "On the Limitations of Eichberg's and Mandell's Theory of Sports and their Quantification in View of Chikaraishi," *Stadion*, 3:2 (1977): 244–252.

99. For specific replies to Krüger and Ito, see Henning Eichberg, "Recording and Quantifying Is Not Natural," *Stadion*, 3:2 (1977): 253–256; Thompson, "The Modernization of Sumō as a Sport, " p. 71.

## Chapter 2. Pre-Meiji Sports

1. G. Cameron Hurst III, *Armed Martial Arts of Japan* (New Haven: Yale University Press, 1998), p. 103.

2. Jörg Möller, *Spiel und Sport am japanischen Kaiserhof* (Munich: Iudicium, 1993), p. 41; Koyama Takashige, "Nihon kyūdō gairon," in *Gendai kyūdō kōza*, ed. Uno Yōzaburō (Tokyo: Yūzankaku, 1970), pp. 11–12.

3. Hurst, *Armed Martial Arts*, pp. 105, 107.

4. Ibid., p. 104.

5. Ibid., p. 110.

6. Möller, *Spiel und Sport am japanischen Kaiserhof,* p. 10, citing Michael Charlier, *Das Dairi-Shiki* (Wiesbaden, 1975), pp. 100–105.

7. Ibid., pp. 41–45. Members of the nobility also used light bows for *suzume koyumi* (sparrow shooting).

8. Ibid.; Imamura Yoshio, *Nihon taiiku shi* (Tokyo: Fumaidō, 1970), pp. 36–37.

9. Obinata Katsumi, *Kodai kokka to nenjū gyōji* (Tokyo: Yoshikawa Kōbunkan, 1993), pp. 17–19; Imamura, *Nihon taiiku shi,* pp. 36–37.

10. Obinata, *Kodai kokka to nenjū gyōji,* pp. 23–24.

11. Ibid.

12. Möller, *Spiel und Sport am japanischen Kaiserhof,* pp. 45, 129; Imamura, *Nihon taiiku shi,* pp. 37–38; Yamanaka Yū, "Noriyumi,"in *Heibonsha's World Encyclopedia* (Tokyo: Heibonsha, 1988), 22:265. In later times, the number of rounds was reduced to three or five.

13. Obinata, *Kodai kokka to nenjū gyōji,* pp. 25–27.

14. Ibid., pp. 29–30.

15. Ibid., pp. 73–75.

16. Imamura, *Nihon taiiku shi,* pp. 38–39.

17. Obinata, *Kodai kokka to nenjū gyōji,* pp. 40–47.

18. Möller, *Spiel und Sport am japanischen Kaiserhof,* p. 48.

19. This arrangement was akin to the hierarchical distinction between jarai and noriyumi.

20. Obinata, *Kodai kokka to nenjū gyōji,* p. 63. This three-day cycle, consisting of preparation on the twenty-eighth, the main event on the fifth, and entertainment and a display of superior skills on the sixth, was paralleled in court sumō from the end of the ninth century. Before the main event, *meshiawase,* an open practice called *uchitori* was held, and after the main event the wrestlers were gathered once again for a less formal competition called *nukide* (p. 47).

21. Obinata, *Kodai kokka to nenjū gyōji,* pp. 80, 83.

22. Hurst, *Armed Martial Arts,* p. 111; Masukawa Kōichi, "Supōtsu to kake," in *Saishin supōtsu daijiten,* ed. Kishino Yūzo (Tokyo: Taishūkan shoten, 1987), p. 626.

23. *Ōkagami,* trans. Helen Craig McCullough (Princeton: Princeton University Press, 1980), p. 197.

24. *Tale of the Heike,* trans. Kitagawa Hiroshi and Bruce Tsuchida (Tokyo: Tokyo University Press, 1975), p. 660.

25. Gordon Daniels, "Japanese Sport," in *Sport, Culture and Politics,* ed. J. C. Binfield and John Stevenson (Sheffield: Sheffield Academic Press, 1993), p. 171.

26. Hurst, *Armed Martial Arts,* pp. 23–24.

27. Imamura, *Nihon taiiku shi,* pp. 88–89; Hayasaka Shōji, "Kasagake," in *Saishin supōtsu daijiten,* pp. 164–165; Hurst, *Armed Martial Arts,* p. 116.

28. Möller, *Spiel und Sport am japanischen Kaiserhof,* pp. 53–54.

29. Hayasaka Shōji, "Yabusame," *Saishin supōtsu daijiten,* pp. 1261–1263; Imamura, *Nihon taiiku shi,* p. 88.

30. Hurst, *Armed Martial Arts,* p. 116.

31. Imamura, *Nihon taiiku shi,* p. 89. According to Hurst, the targets were erected some 50 yards apart and approximately 6.5 feet from the track; *Armed Martial Arts,* p. 116.

32. Ibid., p. 118.

33. Ibid., p. 119.

34. Imamura, *Nihon taiiku shi,* p. 90.

35. Möller, *Spiel und Sport am japanischen Kaiserhof,* pp. 72–78; Imamura, *Nihon taiiku shi,* pp. 90–91; Hayasaka Shōji, "Inuoumono," *Saishin supōtsu daijiten,* pp. 81–82.

36. Hagenaer: quoted in Reinier H. Hesselink, "The Warrior's Prayer: Tokugawa Yoshimune Revives the Yabusame Ceremony," *Journal of Asian Martial Arts,* 4:4 (1995): 40–49.

37. Ibid.; Imamura, *Nihon taiiku shi,* p. 182.

38. Allen Guttmann, *A Whole New Ballgame* (Chapel Hill: University of North Carolina Press, 1988), pp. 16–22.

39. Yoshimune: quoted in Hesselink, "The Warrior's Prayer," pp. 40–49.

40. Hayasaka, "Inuoumono," pp. 81–82; Möller, *Spiel und Sport am japanischen Kaiserhof,* p. 131.

41. Karl F. Friday and Seki Humitake, *Legacies of the Sword* (Honolulu: University of Hawaii Press, 1997), p. 18; Hurst, *Armed Martial Arts,* pp. 112, 120–121.

42. Nishiyama Matsunosuke, *Edo Culture,* trans. Gerald Groemer (Honolulu: University of Hawaii Press, 1997), p. 32.

43. Hurst, *Armed Martial Arts,* pp. 123, 128.

44. Ibid., p. 117.

45. The emphasis on Zen Buddhism was abetted by Eugen Herrigel's famous *Zen in der Kunst des Bogenschießens* (1948; Tübingen: Otto-Wilhelm Barth, 1975). The tendency to see Zen Buddhism everywhere in Japanese culture was given an additional boost by Roland Barthes in *L'Empire des signes* (Paris: Editions d'Art Albert Skira, 1970).

46. E. J. Harrison, *The Fighting Spirit of Japan* (Woodstock, N.Y.: Overlook, 1982), p. 141. Quoted in Hurst, *Armed Martial Arts,* p. 175.

47. Ibid., p. 174.

48. Ibid., p. 127. The following description of tōshiya is from Shuku Homma, "Archery as a Contest," in *Proceedings of the 1991 ISHPES Congress,* ed. Roland Renson, Teresa Gonzalez Aja, Gilbert Andrieu, Manfred Lämmer, and Roberta Park (Madrid: Instituto Nacional de Educación Fisica de Madrid, 1993), pp. 106–113; Oscar Ratti and Adele Westbrook, *Secrets of the Samurai* (Rutland, Vt.: Charles E. Tuttle, 1973), p. 238; Hurst, *Armed Martial Arts,* pp. 135–140; Imamura, *Nihon taiiku shi,* pp. 169–181.

49. Hurst, *Armed Martial Arts,* p. 138.

50. Richard Mandell, "The Invention of the Sports Record," *Stadion,* 2:2 (1976): 250–264; Guttmann, *From Ritual to Record,* pp. 52–55.

51. Kohsuke Sasajima, "History of Physical Education and Sport in Japan," in *Geschichte der Leibesübungen,* ed. Horst Ueberhorst, 6 vols. (Berlin: Bartels & Wernitz, 1972–1989), 4:199.

52. Inazo Nitobe, *Bushido* (1905; Rutland, Vt.: Charles E. Tuttle, 1969), p. 131.

53. Donn F. Draeger and Robert W. Smith, *Asian Fighting Arts* (Palo Alto: Kodansha International, 1969), p. 95; Winston L. King, *Zen and the Way of the Sword* (New York: Oxford University Press, 1993), p. 70; Hurst, *Armed Martial Arts,* pp. 103–104.

54. Ibid., pp. 28–29.

55. Ibid., pp. 33–37.

56. Noel Perrin, *Japan Gives Up the Gun* (Boston: Godine, 1979).

57. Hurst, *Armed Martial Arts,* p. 84.

58. Friday and Humitake, *Legacies of the Sword,* p. 137.

59. Hurst, *Armed Martial Arts,* pp. 61–62.

60. Ibid., p. 45.

61. The school's claim of primacy has been challenged by Ellis Amdur in "Maniwa Nen-Ryu," *Journal of Asian Martial Arts,* 4:3 (1995): 10–25.

62. Ellis Amdur, "Divine Transmission Katori Shrine Ryu," *Journal of Asian Martial Arts,* 3:2 (1994): 49–61; Hurst, *Armed Martial Arts,* pp. 46–47; Friday and Humitake, *Legacies of the Sword,* pp. 24–28.

63. Nyle C. Monday, "The Ryu-Ha System," *Journal of Asian Martial Arts,* 3:1 (1994): 76.

64. Donn F. Draeger, *The Martial Arts and Ways of Japan,* 3 vols. (New York: Weatherhill, 1973–1974): 1:21.

65. Hurst, *Armed Martial Arts,* pp. 47–48; Ratti and Westbrook, *Secrets of the Samurai,* p. 175; Friday and Humitake, *Legacies of the Sword,* pp. 27–28; Minoru Kiyota, *Kendō* (London: Kegan Paul International, 1995), p. 45.

66. Hurst, *Armed Martial Arts,* pp. 48–49; Friday and Humitake, *Legacies of the Sword,* pp. 24–31.

67. Ibid., pp. 27–32; Hurst, *Armed Martial Arts,* pp. 49–50.

68. Ibid., pp. 50–52. Quotation from p. 51.

69. Ibid., pp. 55–57, 62; Quotation from p. 62. Imamura, *Nihon taiiku shi,* p. 150; "Tenshinshō-den shintō ryū," *Nihonshi kōjien,* p. 1485.

70. Hurst, *Armed Martial Arts,* p. 57.

71. Ibid., pp. 57–58; Friday and Humitake, *Legacies of the Sword,* p. 76.

72. Musashi Miyamoto, *A Book of Five Rings,* trans. Victor Harris (Woodstock, N.Y.: Overlook Press, 1974), pp. 46, 95.

73. Hiroaki Sato, *The Sword and the Mind* (Woodstock, NY: Overlook Press, 1986), p. 17.

74. Ibid., p. 118.

75. Ibid., p. 60.

76. Hurst, *Armed Martial Arts,* p. 60.

77. Ibid., p. 53.

78. Imamura, *Nihon taiiku shi,* pp. 142, 150.

79. Hurst, *Armed Martial Arts,* pp. 70–71.

80. Minoru, *Kendō,* pp. 2–5; Hurst, *Armed Martial Arts,* p. 74, n. 56; pp. 212–213.

81. As the name implies, the "muscular Christianity" advocated by Charles Kingsley and other Victorian moralists was an attempt to imbue athleticism with Christian virtues and simultaneously to create a more "masculine" version of Christianity.

82. Hurst, *Armed Martial Arts,* p. 75; Imamura, *Nihon taiiku shi,* pp. 163–166.

83. Hurst, *Armed Martial Arts,* p. 73.

84. Ibid.

85. Imamura, *Nihon taiiku shi,* p. 111.

86. Hurst, *Armed Martial Arts,* p. 80.

87. Ibid., pp. 82–83.

88. Ibid., pp. 83–86, quotation from p. 83; Imamura, *Nihon taiiku shi,* p. 161.

89. Draeger, *Martial Arts and Ways,* 2:82–83; Ratti and Westbrook, *Secrets of the Samurai,* p. 286; Hurst, *Armed Martial Arts,* p. 84.

90. Ibid., pp. 87–95.

91. Ibid., p. 98.

## Chapter 3. The Arrival and Diffusion on Western Sports

1. Imamura Yoshio, *Nihon taiiku shi* (Tokyo: Fumaidō, 1970), p. 329.

2. Tanaka Tokuhisa and Yoshikawa Kumiko, *Supōtsu* (Tokyo: Kondō, 1990), pp. 72–73; Imamura, *Nihon taiiku shi,* p. 330.

3. Donald Keene, *The Japanese Discovery of Europe, 1720–1830* (Stanford: Stanford University Press, 1969); W. G. Beasley, *Japan Encounters the Barbarian* (New Haven: Yale University Press, 1995).

4. George. B. Sansom, *The Western World and Japan* (New York: Knopf, 1950), pp. 277–280.

5. Francis L. Hawks, *Narrative of the Expedition of an American Squadron to the China Seas and Japan* (New York: D. Appleton, 1857), p. 432; quoted from Francis Hall, *Japan through American Eyes,* ed. F. G. Notehelfer (Princeton: Princeton University Press, 1992), p. 127, n. 24.

6. P. L. Cuyler, *Sumo* (New York: Weatherhill, 1979), p. 11.

7. Hugh Cortazzi, *Victorians in Japan* (London: Athlone Press, 1987), p. 7.

8. Sansom, *The Western World and Japan,* p. 285.

9. Marius B. Jansen, *Japan and Its World* (Princeton: Princeton University Press, 1980), p. 64. Between 1862 and 1868, that is, even before the Meiji Restoration, more than one hundred Japanese students were sent abroad to study; see Beasley, *Japan Encounters the Barbarian,* p. 119.

10. Eugene Soviak, "On the Nature of Western Progress: The Journal of the Iwakura Embassy," in *Tradition and Modernization in Japanese Culture,* ed. Donald H. Shively (Princeton: Princeton University Press, 1971), pp. 7–34.

11. Donald Keene, "The Sino-Japanese War of 1894–95 and Its Cultural Effects in Japan," in *Tradition and Modernization in Japanese Culture,* p. 170; Sansom, *The Western World and Japan,* p. 371.

12. Motoda: quoted by Donald H. Shively, "The Japanization of the Middle Meiji," in *Tradition and Modernization in Japanese Culture,* p. 87.

13. H. Paul Varley, *Japanese Culture,* 3rd ed. (Honolulu: University of Hawaii Press, 1984), p. 208.

14. Ernest Satow, *A Diplomat in Japan* (1921; New York: ICG Muse, 2000), pp. 46–51.

15. Shively, "The Japanization of the Middle Meiji," in *Tradition and Modernization in Japanese Culture,* p. 88.

16. Eric Hobsbawm and Terence Ranger, *The Invention of Tradition* (Cambridge: Cambridge University Press, 1983). By the term "invented tradition," Hobsbawm and Ranger mean consciously invented tradition, of which the Imperial Rescript was certainly an example. In the sense that all traditions are socially constructed, they could be said to be invented, whether consciously or not, but it is useful to make a distinction. See also Marilyn Ivy, who observes in her study of Japanese modernity, "To say that all tradition is invented is still to rely on a *choice* between invention and authenticity, between fiction and reality, between discourse and history"; see *Discourses of the Vanishing* (Chicago: University of Chicago Press, 1995), p. 21.

17. Herschel Webb, "The Development of an Orthodox Attitude toward the Imperial Institution in the Nineteenth Century," in *Changing Japanese Attitudes toward Modernization,* ed. Marius B. Jansen (Princeton: Princeton University Press, 1965), pp. 167–191.

18. Donald H. Shively, "Nishimura Shigeki," in *Changing Japanese Attitudes toward Modernization,* ed. Marius B. Jansen (Princeton: Princeton University Press, 1965), pp. 193–241.

19. S. N. Eisenstadt, *Japanese Civilization* (Chicago: University of Chicago Press, 1996), p. 78.

20. Sansom, *The Western World and Japan,* p. 383.

21. Toshio Saeki, "Sport in Japan," in *Sport in Asia and Africa,* ed. Eric A. Wagner (Westport: Greenwood Press, 1989), p. 54.

22. Sociological research suggests that Japanese schools continue to play a larger role in the socialization into sports than schools in the West; Yasuo Yamaguchi, "A Comparative Study of Adolescent Socialization into Sport," *International Review of Sport Sociology,* 19:1 (1984): 63–82.

23. Ikuo Abe, Yasuharu Kiyohara, and Ken Nakajima, "Fascism, Sport and Society in Japan," *International Journal of the History of Sport,* 9:1 (April 1992): 6.

24. On this, see Allen Guttmann, *Games and Empires* (New York: Columbia University Press, 1994).

25. Adoption of the *shūkyūsei* (weekly holiday system) facilitated regular participation in weekend sports. See David W. Plath, "Land of the Rising Sunday," *Japan Quarterly*, 7:3 (1960): 357–361.

26. Roger F. Hakett, "The Meiji Leaders and Modernization," in *Changing Japanese Attitudes toward Modernization*, ed. Marius B. Jansen (Princeton: Princeton University Press, 1965), pp. 243–273.

27. Kinoshita Hideaki, *Supōtsu no kindai Nihonshi* (Tokyo: Kyōrin shoin, 1970), pp. 3–7.

28. Shinsuke Tanada, "Diffusion into the Orient: The Introduction of Western Sports in Kobe, Japan," *International Journal of the History of Sport*, 5:3 (December 1988): 372–376; Wolfram Manzenreiter, *Die soziale Konstruktion des japanischen Alpinismus* (Vienna, Abteilung für Japanologie/Institut für Ostasienwissenschaften, 2000), p. 53.

29. Cortazzi, *Victorians in Japan*, p. 293.

30. Edward Seidensticker, *Low City, High City* (New York: Alfred Knopf, 1983), p. 167.

31. Cortazzi, *Victorians in Japan*, p. 298.

32. Tanada, "Diffusion into the Orient," pp. 372–376; Kinoshita, *Supōtsu no kindai Nihonshi*, p. 9.

33. Imamura, *Nihon taiiku shi*, p. 331.

34. Haruo Nogawa and Hiroka Maeda, "The Japanese Dream," in *Football Cultures and Identities*, ed. Gary Armstrong and Richard Giulianotti (Houndsmill: Macmillan, 1999), p. 223.

35. Kinoshita, *Supōtsu no kindai Nihonshi*, p. 85.

36. Gareth Williams, "Rugby Union," in *Sport in Britain*, ed. Tony Mason (Cambridge: Cambridge University Press, 1989), p. 338.

37. Tanaka and Yoshikawa, *Supōtsu*, pp. 42–47; Kinoshita, *Supōtsu no kindai Nihonshi*, p. 87. Richard Light dates the national federation from 1926; see, "A Centenary of Rugby and Masculinity in Japanese Schools and Universities," *Sporting Traditions*, 16:2 (May 2000): 87–104.

38. Ibid., p. 93.

39. N. K. Roscoe, "The Development of Sport in Japan," *Transactions and Proceedings of the Japan Society*, 30 (1933): 65.

40. On Kobe's string of championships, see Hayase Keiichi, *Hirao Seiji, hengen jizai ni* (Osaka: Mainichi Shimbunsha, 1997). Many members of the championship team had played for Dōshisha, which is still a rugby power.

41. Imamura, *Nihon taiiku shi*, p. 332.

42. *Ichikō* is simply the abbreviation of the Japanese for "First Higher Middle School."

43. Teijirō Muramatsu, *Westerners in the Modernization of Japan* (Tokyo: Hitachi, 1995), p. 224.

44. Roscoe, "The Development of Sport in Japan," p. 54.

45. Imamura, *Nihon taiiku shi,* p. 334.

46. Ibid., pp. 337, 424.

47. *Asahi Shimbun,* January 28, 1999; Imamura, *Nihon taiiku shi,* p. 424.

48. Ibid., p. 423.

49. *Asahi Shimbun,* January 20, 1999.

50. William R. May, "Sports," in *The Handbook of Japanese Popular Culture,* ed. Richard Gid Powers and Hidetoshi Kato (Westport: Greenwood Press, 1989), p. 173. Gordon Daniels gives Fujii's height as 3.424 meters and the world record as 3.427 meters, but vaulting records were not ordinarily measured to the millimeter; see "Japanese Sport," in *Sport, Culture, and Politics,* ed. J. C. Binfield and John Stevenson (Sheffield: Sheffield Academic Press, 1993), p. 178. Imamura Yoshio gives Fujii's record as 3.66 meters; Imamura, *Nihon taiiku shi,* p. 423.

51. Masujima Midori, *Samenai yume* (Tokyo: Za masada, 2000), p. 36.

52. Tanaka and Yoshikawa, *Supōtsu,* pp. 144–145.

53. The fondness for relay races supports Joy Hendry's comment about a predilection for cooperative sports; see *Understanding Japanese Society* (London: Croom Helm, 1987), p. 47. On the other hand, sumō, kendō, kyudō, and the other sports that developed from the martial arts are all individual.

54. Kinoshita, *Supōtus no kindai Nihonshi,* pp. 56–60; Tanaka and Yoshikawa, *Supōtsu,* p. 168; Mombushō kyōgi supōtsu kenkyūkai, ed., *"Miru supōtsu" no shinkō* (Tokyo: Baseball Magazine, 1996), pp. 174–180.

55. Ohara Toshihiko, *Hitomi Kinue monogatari* (Tokyo: Asahi shimbunsha, 1990).

56. Cortazzi, *Victorians in Japan,* p. 19.

57. Imamura, *Nihon taiiku shi,* p. 331.

58. Cortazzi, *Victorians in Japan,* p. 164.

59. Muramatsu, *Westerners in the Modernization of Japan,* pp. 219–225; Kinoshita, *Supōtsu no kindai Nihonshi,* pp. 21–22, 122–123; Imamura, *Nihon taiiku shi,* pp. 425–426.

60. Ibid.

61. Sugimura later became deputy secretary-general of the League of Nations and a member of the International Olympic Committee. See Imamura, *Nihon taiiku shi,* p. 434; Kinoshita, *Supōtsu no kindai Nihonshi,* p. 66; Mombushō kyōgi supōtsu kenkyūkai, ed., *"Miru supōtsu" no shinkō,* p. 33; *Asahi shimbun,* January 26, 1999.

62. Tanaka and Yoshikawa, *Supōtsu,* pp. 80–81; Tanaka Yoshihisa, *Gorufu to Nihonjin* (Tokyo: Iwanami shinsho, 1992), pp. 70–73.

63. Manzenreiter, *Die soziale Konstruktion des japanischen Alpinismus,* pp. 45–51; Kinoshita, *Supōtsu no kindai Nihonshi,* p. 40.

64. Manzenreiter, *Die soziale Konstruktion des japanischen Alpinismus,* p. 53.

65. Ibid., pp. 56–69, 84.

66. Shinsuke Tanada, "Introduction of European Sport in Kobe," *Civilization in Sport History*, ed. Shigeo Shimizu (Kobe: Kobe University, 1987) pp. 68–76.

67. Franz Klaus, "Gedenken an Generalmajor Theodor von Lerch," *Zdarksy-Blätter*, 35 (March 1986): 11–13; Sasase Masashi, "Hokkaidō Teikoku Daigaku Sukī-bu ni okeru tōzan to kyōgi," *Taiikushi kenkyū*, 11 (1994): 41–54; Manzenreiter, *Die soziale Konstruktion des japanischen Alpinismus*, p. 90.

68. Bruce Haley, *The Healthy Body and Victorian Culture* (Cambridge, Mass.: Harvard University Press, 1978); Elmer L. Johnson, *The History of YMCA Physical Education* (Chicago: Follett, 1979).

69. Guttmann, *Games and Empires*, pp. 100–103.

70. James Naismith, "Basketball," *American Physical Education Review*, 19:5 (May 1914): 339–351; James Naismith, *Basketball* (New York: Association Press, 1941).

71. Ibid., pp. 153–154; Kinoshita, *Supōtsu no kindai Nihonshi*, pp. 87–88; Tanaka and Yoshikawa, *Supōtsu*, pp. 60–61.

72. Alan Trevithick, "Volleyball," in *Encyclopedia of World Sport*, ed. David Levinson and Karen Christensen, 3 vols. (Santa Barbara: ABC-CLIO, 1996): 3:1142.

73. The Far Eastern Games are discussed in Chapter 5.

74. Tanaka and Yoshikawa, *Supōtsu* pp. 64–65; Kinoshita, *Supōtsu no kindai Nihonshi*, pp. 184–185; *Asahi shimbun*, February 19, 1999.

75. Cortazzi, *Victorians in Japan*, p. 292.

76. Yoshie Hata, "The Influence of Protestantism of [sic] Modern Physical Education in Japan," in *Civilization in Sport History*, pp. 77–86.

77. Tanaka and Yoshikawa, *Supōtsu*, pp. 66–67.

78. Matsumoto Junko, "Yamaguchi Ken Yoshikimura no Ryojō Seinenkai 'Undōbu' (1886–1937) ni kansuru shiteki kōsatsu . . . ," *Taiikushi kenkyū*, 10 (1993): 29–42

79. Donald Roden, *Schooldays in Imperial Japan* (Berkeley: University of California Press, 1980).

80. Ibid., p. 113.

81. Guttmann, *Games and Empires*, pp. 34–36.

82. Maarten van Bottenburg, *Verborgen Competitie: Over de Uiteenlopende Populariteit van Sporten* (Amsterdam: Bert Bakker, 1994), pp. 132–133.

83. Ikuo Abe and J. A. Mangan, "The British Impact on Boys' Sports and Games in Japan," *International Journal of the History of Sport*, 14:2 (August 1997): 189.

84. Roscoe, "Development of Sport in Japan," p. 63.

85. Before reaching its permanent site, the agricultural college was located in Tokyo.

86. Kiku Kōichi, *"Kindai puro supōtsu" no rekishi shakaigaku* (Tokyo: Fumaidō shuppan, 1993), p. 57.

87. Yuko Kusaka, "The Development of Baseball Organizations in Japan," *International Review of Sport Sociology*, 22:4 (1987): 266.

88. Imamura, *Nihon taiiku shi*, pp. 331–332.

89. Kiku, *"Kindai puro supōtsu" no rekishi shakaigaku*, p. 238.

90. Roscoe, "Development of Sport in Japan," p. 63; Watanabe Tohru, "The Why of the Japanese Choice of Baseball," in *Civilization in Sport History*, pp. 113–128. Details of the earliest period of Japanese baseball differ from account to account.

91. Kinoshita, *Supōtsu no kindai Nihonshi*, pp. 44–45.

92. This and the next five paragraphs are from Kiku, *"Kindai puro supōtsu" no rekishi shakaigaku*, pp. 58–70, 238–239.

93. Kinoshita, *Supōtsu no kindai Nihonshi*, p. 45.

94. This and the next four paragraphs are from Kiku, *"Kindai puro supōtsu" no rekishi shakaigaku*, pp. 71–90.

95. Donald Roden, "Baseball and the Quest for National Dignity in Meiji Japan," *American Historical Review*, 85:3 (June 1980): 524.

96. Kiku, *"Kindai puro supōtsu" no rekishi shakaigaku*, pp. 86–87.

97. Roden, "Baseball and the Quest for National Dignity," p. 525.

98. Ibid., pp. 524–528.

99. Kiku, *"Kindai puro supōtsu" no rekishi shakaigaku*, pp. 91–93.

100. Ibid., p. 103.

101. Ibid., pp. 86–87, 115.

102. Tanaka and Yoshikawa, *Supōtsu*, p. 126.

103. Kiku, *"Kindai puro supōtsu" no rekishi shakaigaku*, pp. 104–105. Abe was a proponent of socialism from a Christian humanist perspective, a founder of the Fabian Society of Japan (1924), a member of the Lower House of the Diet (1928), and a post-World War II advisor to the Socialist Party.

104. Ibid., pp. 111, 115–116.

105. Imamura, *Nihon taiiku shi*, pp. 493–496.

106. Ibid., pp. 497–500; Kiku, *"Kindai puro supōtsu" no rekishi shakaigaku*, pp. 118–119.

107. Norgren: quoted in Robert J. Sinclair, "Baseball's Rising Sun: American Interwar Baseball Diplomacy and Japan," *Canadian Journal of History of Sport*, 16:2 (December 1985): 48.

108. Kōzu Masaru, *Nihon kindai supōtsushi no teiryū* (Tokyo: Sōbun kikaku, 1994), pp. 244–250.

109. Arthur S. Grix, *Japans Sport* (Berlin: Limpert, 1938), p. 63.

110. Herbert Warren Wind, "The Bouncing Ball," *Sports Illustrated*, 8 (February 24, 1958): 57.

111. Roden, "Baseball and the Quest for National Dignity," p. 519; Tada Michitarō, *Asobi to Nihonjin* (Tokyo: Chikuma shobō, 1974), p. 76.

112. May, "Sports," p. 181.

113. Mark Twain: quoted in Harry C. Palmer, "The 'Around the World'

Tour," *Athletic Sports in America, England, and Australia,* ed. Harry Clay Palmer (Philadelphia: Hubbard Bros., 1889), p. 447.

114. Imamura, *Nihon taiiku shi,* p. 204.

115. Ibid., p. 216.

116. Ibid., p. 306.

117. Abe, Kiyohara, and Nakajima, "Fascism, Sport and Society in Japan," p. 4. "Taisō" referred both to gymnastic exercises and to physical education in general, which could include other forms of exercise such as sports.

118. Imamura, *Nihon taiiku shi,* pp. 327–329

119. Ibid., pp. 341–343.

120. Abe and Mangan, "The British Impact on Boys' Sports and Games in Japan," p. 198; Norbert Mosch, "Die politische Funktion des Sports in Japan und Korea" (Ph.D. dissertation, University of Vienna, 1987), p. 93.

121. Imamura, *Nihon taiiku shi,* pp. 343–345.

122. Ibid., p. 375.

123. Ibid., p. 349.

124. Pierre Arnaud, *Le Militaire, l'écolier, le gymnaste* (Lyon: Presses universitaires de Lyon, 1991).

125. Imamura, *Nihon taiiku shi,* pp. 399–401.

126. Shun'ya Yoshimi, "Body, Festivity and Modernity" (paper presented at a conference on "Sports and Body Culture in Modern Japan," Yale University, March 31–April 2, 2000).

127. Imamura, *Nihon taiiku shi,* pp. 410–416.

128. Hiroko Seiwa and Chieko Onishi, "Women and Athletic Meetings in Japan" (unpublished paper, 1997).

129. Imamura, *Nihon taiiku shi,* pp. 416–417.

130. Miyoko Hagiwara, "Japanese Women's Sports and Physical Education under the Influence of Their Traditional Costumes," in *Civilization in Sport History,* p. 266.

131. Nishimura Ayako, "Zenkoku kōtō jogakkōchō kaigi ni mirareru kōtō jōgakko no taiiku mondai," *Taiikushi kenkyū,* 5 (March 1988): 7–21; Yoshie Hata, "The Influence of Protestantism of [sic] Modern Physical Education in Japan," in *Civilization in Sport History,* p. 82.

132. Seiwa and Onishi, "Women and Athletic Meetings in Japan."

133. Ibid.

134. Hata, "The Influence of Protestantism of [sic] Modern Physical Education in Japan," p. 79.

135. Ibid., p. 83.

136. Miyoko Hagiwara, "Japanese Women's Sports and Physical Education," in *Civilization in Sport History,* p. 263.

137. Imamura, *Nihon taiiku shi,* pp. 475–477.

138. Only one ball game was listed: football.

139. Imamura, *Nihon taiiku shi,* p. 478.

140. Ibid., pp. 459–466.

141. Ibid., p. 482.

## Chapter 4. The Modernization of Indigenous Sports

1. Kinoshita Hideaki, *Supōtsu no kindai Nihonshi* (Tokyo: Kyōrin shoin, 1970), p. 41.

2. Kemari Preservation Society, *Kemari hozonkai kyūjūnen shi* (Kyoto: Kemari hozonkai, 1997), pp. 24–26, 32–48. Our account of "modern" kemari is drawn mainly from this invaluable privately published source.

3. The murkiness may have been in order to avoid offending the descendants of some of the principals, many of whom are still involved with kemari.

4. The traditional kemari costume, consisting of headwear, garments for the upper and lower body, shoes, stockings, and accessories such as a fan, was preserved. As in the past, each of these articles came in a hierarchy of different styles, patterns, and colors. Promotion to a higher-grade costume was based on skill, attendance at practice and meets, and social rank; Kemari Preservation Society, *Kemari hozonkai kyūjūnen shi*, pp. 47–48.

5. G. Cameron Hurst III, *Armed Martial Arts of Japan* (New Haven: Yale University Press, 1998), pp. 7–12.

6. Kevin Grey Carr, "Judo," in *Encyclopedia of World Sport*, ed. David Levinson and Karen Christensen, 3 vols. (Santa Barbara: ABC-Clio, 1996), 2:528.

7. Kanō: quoted by Inoue Shun, "Budō," in *The Culture of Japan as Seen through its Leisure*, ed. Sepp Linhart and Sabine Frühstück (Albany: SUNY Press, 1998), p. 85. Inoue offers a slightly different translation in "The Invention of the Martial Arts," in *Mirror of Modernity*, ed. Stephen Vlastos (Berkeley: University of California Press, 1998), p. 165. Except where otherwise noted, our account of Kanō's career is drawn from these two essays and Kanō's own *Kodokan Judo* (Tokyo: Kodansha International, 1986).

8. Kanō: quoted by Inoue, "Invention of the Martial Arts," p. 165.

9. Jörg Möller, "Der deutsche Arzt Erwin von Bälz und die Entwicklung von Körperkultur und Sport in Japan," *Stadion*, 16:1 (1990): 136.

10. Although some historians object to the use of "feudal" to characterize the Tokugawa regime, the system of lords and peasants was similar enough to the institutions of medieval Europe to warrant the term.

11. Kanō, *Kodokan Judo*, p. 16.

12. Inoue Shun, "Budō," p. 84.

13. Ibid., p. 85.

14. Kanō: quoted by Inoue, "Invention of the Martial Arts," p. 166.

15. B. C. and J. M. Goodger, "Judo in the Light of Theory and Sociological Research," *International Review of Sport Sociology*, 12:2 (1977): 5–34; Michel Brousse and David Matsumoto, *Judo* (Seoul: International Judo Federation, 1999), p. 97.

16. *Le Sport Universel Illustré:* quoted in Michel Brousse, *Le Judo: son histoire, ses succès* (Geneva: Liber, 1996), p. 33.

17. *La Vie à Paris:* quoted in Michel Brousse and Jean-Paul Clément, "Le judo en France," *Histoire des sports,* ed. Thierry Terret (Paris: L'Harmattan, 1996), p. 140.

18. Brouse, *Le Judo,* pp. 64–97.

19. Michel Brousse, "Du Samouraî à l'Athlète: L'Essor du Jûdô en France," *Sport/Histoire,* 3 (1989): 11–25; Brousse and Clément, "Le judo en France," pp. 135–158.

20. Norbert Mosch, "Die politische Funktion des Sports in Japan und Korea" (Ph.D. dissertation, University of Vienna, 1987), p. 59; Brousse and Matsumoto, *Judo,* pp. 99–100.

21. Hurst, *Armed Martial Arts,* p. 89.

22. Imamura Yoshio, *Nihon taiiku shi* (Tokyo: Fumaidō, 1970), pp. 220–240, 331; Hurst, *Armed Martial Arts,,* pp. 148–153. Except where otherwise noted, our account of kendō is drawn mainly from these two sources.

23. Hurst, *Armed Martial Arts,* p. 155. Sumō matches, however, are not started with "the ritual opening of a fan."

24. Ikuo Abe, Yasuhara Kiyohara, and Ken Nakajima, "Fascism, Sport, and Society in Japan," *International Journal of the History of Sport,* 9:1 (April 1992): 8–9; Sakaue Yasuhiro, "Taishōki ni okeru Dai Nippon Butokukai . . . ," *Taiikushi kenkyū,* 7 (1990): 37–51; Kinoshita, *Supōtsu no kindai Nihonshi,* pp. 97–102.

25. Hurst, *Armed Martial Arts,* p. 160.

26. Ibid., p. 161.

27. Quoted in ibid., p. 152.

28. Ibid., pp. 169–70.

29. Ibid., pp. 170–171.

30. Roderic Kenji Tierney, "Performing for the Nation: Sumō Becomes the 'National Sport'" (paper presented at a conference on "Sports and Body Culture in Modern Japan," Yale University, March 31–April 2, 2000).

31. In addition to personal experience and newspaper reports, our account of modern sumō is drawn largely from the following sources: Wakamori Tarō, *Sumō ima mukashi* (Tokyo: Kawade shobō shinsha, 1963); Nihon sumō kyōkai hakubutsukan un'ei iin, ed., *Kinsei Nihon sumō shi,* 5 vols. (Tokyo: Baseball Magazine, 1975–1981); Ikeda Masao, *Sumō no rekishi* (Tokyo: Heibonsha, 1977); P. L. Cuyler, *Sumo: From Rite to Sport* (New York: Weatherhill, 1979).

32. Tōno Takeo, "Amachua sumō,", in *Saishin supōtsu daijiten,* ed. Nihon taiiku kyōkai (Tokyo: Taishūkan shoten, 1987), pp. 34–35.

33. *Mainichi shinbun,* January 21, 1900.

34. Tsuganezawa Toshihiro, "Ōsaka Mainichi Shimbunsha no 'jigyō katsudō' to chiiki seikatsu bunka," in *Kindai Nihon no media ibento,* ed. Tsuganezawa Toshihiro (Tokyo: Dōbunkan, 1996), pp. 217–248.

35. *Hoshi,* the first kanji of the compound, means "star."

36. "Ōtori Tanigorō no yokozuna ni tsuite," *Sumō sekai*, 35 (February 1915): 2.

37. *Asahi shimbun*, January 22, 1987.

38. Since the first sumō announcers were new to the sport and not familiar with the moves, a sports reporter from a newspaper sat next to the announcer at the stadium and quickly wrote up a simple summary of each match, which the announcer would then read; Hashimoto Kazuo, *Nihon supōtsu hōsōshi* (Tokyo: Taishūkan shoten, 1992), pp. 35–36.

39. Ibid., p. 36.

40. Hurst, *Armed Martial Arts*, p. 162; Imamura, *Nihon taiiku shi*, pp. 346–347.

41. Ibid., pp. 393, 466; Hurst, *Armed Martial Arts*, pp. 162–163.

42. Ibid., p. 163; Imamura, *Nihon taiiku shi*, pp. 455–456.

## Chapter 5. Japan at the Olympics: 1912–1940

1. Allen Guttmann, *The Olympics* (Urbana: University of Illinois Press, 1992), p. 31.

2. John Bale and Joseph Maguire, eds., *The Global Sports Arena* (London: Frank Cass, 1994).

3. The Nippon Taiiku Kyōkai is sometimes translated as "Japan Amateur Athletic Association," but this translation invites confusion with the Japan Amateur Athletic Federation, which governs track-and-field. Another translation is Japan Amateur Sports Association, which the organization itself currently uses. We have opted for a literal translation.

4. Imamura Yoshio, *Nihon taiiku shi* (Tokyo: Fumaidō, 1970), pp. 500–503, quotation from p. 520.

5. Higashi Michio, *1912 nen orimpikku, ano natsu no otokotachi* (Tokyo: Shinchōsha, 1996), pp. 20–21, 117–120.

6. Ibid., pp. 121, 132–141; Hartmut Gabler, "Olympische Sieger und Siegerinnen," in *Olympischer Sport*, ed. Ommo Grupe (Schorndorf: Karl Hofmann, 1997), p. 181.

7. N. K. Roscoe, "The Development of Sport in Japan," *Transactions and Proceedings of the Japan Society*, 30 (1933): 57.

8. Imamura, *Nihon taiiku shi*, p. 504.

9. Ibid., pp. 537–541; Ikuo Abe, Yasuharu Kiyohara, and Ken Nakajima, "Fascism, Sport and Society in Japan," *International Journal of the History of Sport*, 9:1 (April 1992): 9–10.

10. Imamura, *Nihon taiiku shi*, p. 536.

11. Harold James Olson, "Japan at the Olympic Games, 1909–1938" (M.A. thesis, California State Polytechnic University, 1991), p. 50.

12. Ibid., p. 47; Guttmann, *The Olympics*, p. 40.

13. Olson, "Japan at the Olympics," p. 64.

14. Tanaka Tokuhisa and Yoshikawa Kumiko, *Supōtsu* (Tokyo: Kondō, 1990), pp. 126–127; Olson, "Japan at the Olympics," pp. 58–64.

15. Imamura, *Nihon taiiku shi*, p. 537.

16. "Mizuno," *Olympic Magazine*, No. 11 (November 1996): 28–30.

17. Tanaka and Yoshikawa, *Supōtsu*, p. 143.

18. Ohara Toshihiko, *Hitomi Kinue monogatari* (Tokyo: Asahi shimbunsha, 1990), pp. 136–137.

19. Ibid., pp. 161–172.

20. Tanaka and Yoshikawa, *Supōtsu*, pp. 161, 221; Olson, "Japan at the Olympic Games," pp. 75–76.

21. *Los Angeles Times*, August 10, 1928.

22. The four swimmers were Miyazaki Yasuji, Yūsa Masanari, Toyoda Hisa-kichi, and Yokoyama Takashi.

23. Dick Schaap, *An Illustrated History of the Olympics*, 3rd ed. (New York: Knopf, 1976), p. 204. Schaap gives the names in the Western order. The fourth individual gold medalist was Tsuruta Yoshiyuki in the 200-meter breaststroke.

24. The number of possible medals was not divisible by three because all four members of the winning relay team received medals. In all, twenty-four medals were awarded, but it was of course not possible for the relay team to win any of the eight medals awarded for 2nd and 3rd places.

25. Esashi Shōgo, *Josei supōtsu no shakaigaku* (Tokyo: Fumaidō, 1992), p. 221; Olson, "Japan at the Olympic Games," pp. 106–110.

26. David B. Welky, "Viking Girls, Mermaids, and Little Brown Men," *Journal of Sport History*, 24:1 (Spring 1997): 24–49; Masaji Kiyokawa, "'Swimming into History,'" *Journal of Olympic History*, 5:3 (Fall 1997): 10–14.

27. Kinoshita Hideaki, *Supōtsu no kindai Nihonshi* (Tokyo: Kyōrin shoin, 1970), p. 179.

28. Olson, "Japan at the Olympic Games," pp. 97–104, 118–21; Tanaka and Yoshikawa, *Supōtsu*, pp. 159, 261.

29. Olson, "Japan at the Olympic Games," pp. 94–97, 112.

30. Roscoe, "Development of Sport in Japan," p. 68.

31. Hai Ren, "China and the Olympic Movement," in *Sport and Physical Education in China*, ed. James Riordan and Robin Jones (London: E and FN Spon, 1999), p. 204.

32. Hashimoto Kazuo, *Nihon supōtsu hōsōshi* (Tokyo: Taishūkan shoten, 1992), pp. 45–49.

33. Kawanari Yō, *Maboroshi no Orimpikku* (Tokyo: Chikumashobō, 1992), pp. 47–98; Seki Harami and Karaki Kunihiko, *Supōtsu wa dare no tame ni* (Taishūkan shoten, 1995), pp. 32–67 [section written by Ueno Takurō].

34. Shortly before the 1936 games began, a reporter at the *Yomiuri shimbun* is said to have come up with the Japanese term for the Olympics. Then, as now, the word was transcribed into *kana* (phonetic syllables). Since the word in kana required six characters, a copyreader asked the reporter if he could think of a shorter term. He suggested a two-character substitute: *gorin* (five rings), which refers to the five circles on the Olympic flag and at the same time alludes to *Gorin*

*no sho* (*The Book of Five Rings*) by the famous seventeenth-century swordsman Miyamoto Musashi. See *Asahi shimbun,* June 18, 1996.

35. Olson, "Japan at the Olympic Games," p. 139.

36. Ibid., pp. 139–147; Tanaka and Yoshikawa, *Supōtsu,* pp. 159, 161, 261.

37. Richard D. Mandell, *The Nazi Olympics* (New York: Macmillan, 1971), pp. 215–220. At the opening ceremony of the Olympic Games in Seoul in 1988, Sohn Kee-Chung was the next to the last runner in the torch relay. See Hashimoto, *Nihon supōtsu hōsōshi,* p. 73.

38. The Japanese finalists were Yūsa Masanori, Arai Shigeo, and Taguchi Shōji (100-meter freestyle); Kiyokawa Masaji, Yoshida Kiichi, Kojima Yasuhiko (100-meter backstroke); Hamuro Tetsuo, Koike Reizo, Itō Saburō (200-meter breaststroke); Utō Shumpei, Makino Shōzō, Negami Hiroshi (400-meter freestyle); Terada Noboru, Utō Shumpei, Ishiharada Sunao (1,500-meter freestyle).

39. Olson, "Japan at the Olympic Games," pp. 154–161; Tanaka and Yoshikawa, *Supōtsu,* pp. 221.

40. Hashimoto, *Nihon supōtsu hōsōshi,* pp. 74–77.

41. Kunihiko Karaki, "Die aufgegebenen Olympischen Spiele in Tokio 1940," *Hitotsubashi Journal of Arts and Sciences,* 23 (December 1982): 60–70; Hajo Bernett, "Das Scheitern der Olympischen Spiele von 1940," *Stadion,* 6 (1980): 252–253; Junko Tahara, "Count Michimasa Soyeshima and the Cancellation of the XII Olympiad [sic] in Tokyo," *International Journal of the History of Sport,* 9:3 (December 1992): 467–472.

42. Hashimoto, *Nihon supōtsu hōsōshi,* p. 79.

43. Bernett, "Das Scheitern der Olympischen Spiele von 1940," p. 254; Karaki, "Die aufgegebenen Olympischen Spiele in Tokio 1940," pp. 60–70.

44. Japanese teams had competed in many other international competitions between 1927 and 1936. Counting only the more "prominent" cases, Imamura says thirty-two overseas trips were made while foreign teams or individuals visited Japan twenty-five times, but such international competition was almost completely halted after 1936. See his *Nihon taiiku shi,* p. 558.

### Chapter 6. From Taishō Democracy to Japanese Fascism

1. Irie Katsumi, *Nihon fashizumu ka no taiiku shisō* (Tokyo: Fumaidō, 1986).

2. Edwin O. Reischauer and Albert M. Craig, *Japan* (Tokyo: Charles E. Tuttle, 1978), p. 207.

3. The Chinese had been coerced by the Russians to lease to them this area on the Liaodong Peninsula.

4. Edwin O. Reischauer, *The Japanese* (Cambridge, Mass.: Harvard University Press, 1977), p. 99.

5. Imamura Yoshio, *Nihon taiiku shi* (Tokyo: Fumaidō, 1970), pp. 566–567.

6. Ibid., pp. 543–544.

7. Irie, *Nihon fashizumu ka no taiiku,* p. 86; Imamura, *Nihon taiiku shi,* pp. 558–559.

8. Ibid., p. 545.

9. Tanaka Tokuhisa and Yoshikawa Kumiko, *Supōtsu* (Tokyo: Kondō, 1990) pp. 26–27; Mombushō kyōgi supōtsu kenkyūkai, ed., *"Miru supōtsu" no shinkō* (Tokyo: Baseball Magazine, 1996), pp. 32–33; Imamura, *Nihon taiiku shi*, pp. 545–546; Kiku Kōichi, *"Kindai puro supōtsu" no rekishi shakaigaku* (Tokyo: Fumaidō, 1993), pp. 200–203; William W. Kelly, "An Anthropologist in the Bleachers," *Japan Quarterly*, 44:4 (October–December 1997): 66.

10. Imamura, *Nihon taiiku shi*, pp. 545–546.

11. For this and the next two paragraphs, see Kozonoi Masaki, "Senzen no Kitakyushu chihō ni okeru kigyōnai supōtsu no kenkyū . . . ," *Taiikushi kenkyū*, 9 (1992): 33–43.

12. Kiku, *"Kindai puro supōtsu" no rekishi shakaigaku*, pp. 143–145.

13. Kōzu Masaru, *Nihon kindai supōtsushi no teiryū* (Tokyo: Kamokado yoshio, 1994), pp. 51–52.

14. Ibid., pp. 79–177.

15. Masaru Kōzu, "The Development of Sports in Japanese Agricultural Districts," *Hitotsubashi Journal of Arts and Sciences*, 21:1 (1980): 46–48.

16. Imamura, *Nihon taiiku shi*, pp. 541–542.

17. Raita Kyōko, "Nihon Joshi Orimpikku Taikai to josei kyōgi supōtsu," *Taiikushi kenkyū*, 13 (1996): 39–52; Kyoko Raita, "The Movement for the Promotion of Competitive Women's Sport in Japan, 1924–35," *International Journal of the History of Sport*, 16:3 (1999): 120–34.

18. Kiku, *"Kindai puro supōtsu" no rekishi shakaigaku*, p. 230.

19. Hashimoto Kazuo, *Nihon supōtsu hōsōshi* (Tokyo: Taishūkan shoten, 1992), pp. 20–21.

20. Ibid., p. 37.

21. The railroad industry experienced especially rapid growth early in this century. At the end of 1905, there were 2,562.4 kilometers of railway lines in operation, which carried a total of 31.027 million passengers. By the end of 1935, there were 17,138.2 kilometers of railway, which carried 999.181 million passengers; Kiku, *"Kindai puro supōtsu" no rekishi shakaigaku*, pp. 190–194, 214.

22. Robert Obojski, *The Rise of Japanese Baseball Power* (Radnor, Pa.: Chilton, 1975), pp. 7–14.

23. Kiku, *"Kindai puro supōtsu" no rekishi shakaigau*, pp. 125–131.

24. Ibid., pp. 127–135; *Asahi shimbun*, September 30, 1921.

25. Kiku, *"Kindai puro supōtsu" no rekishi shakaigaku*, pp. 136–137.

26. Ibid., pp. 140–142.

27. Ibid., pp. 142–143.

28. Ibid., pp. 205–207.

29. Richard C. Crepeau, "Pearl Harbor: A Failure of Baseball?" *Journal of Popular Culture*, 15:4 (Spring 1982): 68–69.

30. Edward Uhlan and Dana L. Thomas, *Shoriki* (New York: Exposition Press, 1957), p. 109.

31. Ibid., p. 111.

32. Kiku, *"Kindai puro supōtsu" no rekishi shakaigaku,* p. 189.

33. Ibid., pp. 221–226.

34. Ibid., p. 228–230.

35. Only 8.6 percent of those surveyed said they enjoyed broadcasts of soccer and rugby football; Hashimoto, *Nihon supōtsu hōsōshi,* p. 30; Kiku, *"Kindai puro supōtsu" no rekishi shakaigaku,* pp. 233, 237–238.

36. George O. Totten, "Collective Bargaining and Works Councils as Innovations in Industrial Relations in Japan during the 1920s," in *Aspects of Social Change in Modern Japan,* ed. R. P. Dore (Princeton: Princeton University Press, 1967), p. 204.

37. Kiyokawa Masaji, *Supōtsu to seiji* (Tokyo: Baseball Magazine, 1987), p. 206; Crepeu, "Pearl Harbor," p. 69.

38. Tanaka and Yoshikawa, *Supōtsu,* p. 37.

39. Tessa Morris-Suzuki, "The Invention and Reinvention of 'Japanese Culture,'" *Journal of Asian Studies,* 54:3 (August 1995): 765.

40. G. Cameron Hurst III, *Armed Martial Arts of Japan* (New Haven: Yale University Press, 1998), p. 159.

41. Ibid., p. 223, n. 35.

42. Morris-Suzuki, "The Invention and Reinvention of 'Japanese Culture,'" p. 765.

43. Except where otherwise indicated, our discussion of sumō is drawn from Nihon sumō kyōkai hakubutsukan un'ei, ed., *Kinsei Nihon sumō shi,* 5 vols. (Tokyo: Baseball Magazine, 1975–1981); Ikeda Masao, *Sumō no rekishi* (Tokyo: Heibonsha, 1977); P. L. Cuyler, *Sumo: From Rite to Sport* (New York: Weatherhill, 1979); Lora Sharnoff, *Grand Sumo,* rev. ed. (New York: Weatherhill, 1993); Nitta Ichirō, *Sumō no rekishi* (Tokyo: Fumaidō, 1994).

44. Oinuma Yoshihiro, *Sumō shakai no kenkyū* (Tokyo: Fumaidō, 1994), p. 322.

45. *Bungei Shunjū:* quoted in T. J. Pempel, "Contemporary Japanese Athletics," in *The Culture of Japan as Seen through Its Leisure,* ed. Sepp Linhart and Sabine Frühstück (Albany: SUNY Press, 1998), p. 129.

46. Harold Bolitho, "Sumō and Popular Culture: The Tokugawa Period," in *The Japanese Trajectory: Modernization and Beyond,* ed. Gavan McCormack and Yoshio Sugimoto (Cambridge: Cambridge University Press, 1988), pp. 26–28.

47. Nitta, *Sumō no rekishi,* p. 224.

48. Yamaguchi Masao, "Sumo in the Popular Culture of Contemporary Japan," in *The Worlds of Japanese Popular Culture,* ed. D. P. Martinez (Cambridge: Cambridge University Press, 1998), p. 20.

49. Itō Kimio, "The Invention of *Wa* and the Transformation of the Image of Prince Shōtoku in Modern Japan," in *Mirror of Modernity: Invented Traditions of Modern Japan.* ed. Stephen Vlastos (Berkeley: University of California Press, 1998), p. 38.

50. According to the conventional list, Tanikaze and Onokawa were the fourth and fifth yokozuna, but the legendary Akashi Shiganosuke and the two wrestlers who followed him all predate Yoshida's first yokozuna license.

51. By comparison, between 1868 and 1999, fifty-five were awarded—one for every 2.38 years compared to one for every 8.77 years before 1868.

52. Ikeda, *Sumō no rekishi*, p. 126.

53. Nihon sumō kyōkai hakubutsukan un'ei iin, ed., *Kinsei Nihon sumō shi*, 3:18.

54. The reference to two thousand years of history is from a director of the Sumō Association, the former yokozuna Kasugano, quoted in the magazine *Sumō* (February 1988), p. 158.

55. Hashimoto, *Nihon supōtsu hōsōshi*, pp. 164–165.

56. The following account is based mainly on Michihara Shinji, "Karatedō," in *Saishin supōtsu daijiten*, ed. Kishino Yūzō (Tokyo: Taishūkan shoten, 1987), pp. 186–191.

57. Gichin Funakoshi, *Karate-Dō* (Tokyo: Kodansha, 1975).

58. Benny Josef Peiser, "Karate," in *Encyclopedia of World Sport*, ed. David Levinson and Karen Christensen, 3 vols. (Santa Barbara: ABC-CLIO, 1996), 2:543.

59. John J. Donahue, "The Ritual Dimension of *Karate-Dō*," *Journal of Ritual Studies*, 7:1 (Winter 1993): 105–124.

60. Shishida Fumiaki, "Aikidō," in *Saishin supōtsu daijiten*, pp. 1–3. Except where otherwise noted, the following account relies mainly on Shishida.

61. On *Ōmoto-kyō*, see Emily Groszos Ooms, *Women and Millenarian Protest in Japan* (Ithaca: Cornell University Press, 1993).

62. This paragraph is based on John Stevens and Shirata Rinjiro, *Aikido: The Way of Harmony* (Boston: Shambhala, 1984). Quotation from p. 9.

63. Hurst, *Armed Martial Arts*, p. 165.

64. Ueshiba Kisshōmaru, *Spirit of Aikidō*, trans. Unno Taitetsu (Tokyo: Kodansha International, 1984), pp. 12, 14–15, 19.

65. Abe Tomoji, *"Nichidoku taikō kyōgi" Shinchō*, 27:1 (1930): 17–26. Quotations are from an unpublished translation by Matsumura Misako.

66. Yukio Mishima, *Confessions of a Mask*, trans. Meredith Weatherby (New York: New Directions, 1958), p. 35.

67. Yukio Mishima, *Sun and Steel*, trans. John Bester (New York: Grove Press, 1976), p. 41.

68. Yukio Mishima, *Acts of Worship*, trans. John Bester (Tokyo: Kodansha, 1989), p. 75.

69. Ibid., p. 58.

70. Ibid., p. 45.

71. Ibid., p. 37.

72. Nowhere was the conflict between British sports and German gymnastics more dramatic than in the Netherlands, located geographically and culturally between Great Britain and Germany. See Ruud Stokvis, *Strijd over Sport* (Deventer: Van Loghum Slaterus, 1979).

73. Abe, Kiyohara, and Nakajima, "Fascism, Sport and Society in Japan," p. 5.

74. Ibid.; Imamura, *Nihon taiiku shi,* pp. 528–530.

75. Ibid., pp. 509, 530–533; Abe, Kiyohara, and Nakajima, "Fascism, Sport and Society in Japan," pp. 5, 11, quotation from p. 11.

76. Ōtsuka Mieko, "Ono (Hatakeyama) Genzōron," *Taiikushi kenkyū,* 8 (1991): 31–42; Suzuki Akisato, "Taishō jiyūkyōiku ni okeru taiiku ni tsuite," *Taiikushi kenkyū,* 8 (1991): 43–54.

77. Suzuki Akisato, "Nara joshi kōtō shihan gakkō fuzoku shōgakkō jidai no Kawaguchi Hideaki no taiiku ni kan suru ichi kōsatsu," *Taiikushi kenkyū,* 9 (1992): 19–32.

78. Imamura, *Nihon taiiku shi,* pp. 561–564.

79. Ibid., pp. 533–535.

80. Richard H. Mitchell, *Thought Control in Prewar Japan* (Ithaca: Cornell University Press, 1976), p. 92.

81. Imamura, *Nihon taiiku shi,* p. 510.

82. Ibid., p. 573; quotation from Hurst, *Armed Martial Arts,* p. 164.

83. Ibid., p. 172.

84. Irie, *Nihon fashizumu ka no taiiku shisō,* p. 90.

85. Imamura, *Nihon taiiku shi,* pp. 565–566; Abe, Kiyohara, and Nakajima, "Fascism, Sport and Society in Japan," p. 12; Kōzu, "The Development of Sports in Japanese Agricultural Districts," pp. 40–51. On Nazi physical education, see Hajo Bernett, *Nationalsozialistische Leibeserziehung* (Schorndorf: Hofmann, 1966).

86. Rudolf Bode, *Bewegung und Gestaltung* (Berlin: Weidekind Verlag, 1936), p. 39.

87. Irie, *Nihon fashizumu ka no taiiku shisō,* pp. 36, 123, 130–132, 219–221; Suzuki Akisato, "Shōwa senzenki ni okeru Kinoshita Takeji no taiikuron no henyō ni tsuite," *Taiikushi kenkyū,* 11 (1994): 27–39.

88. "Comintern" was the standard abbreviation for the Communist International created in 1919 by the Soviet Union.

89. Abe, Kiyohara, and Nakajima, "Fascism, Sport and Society in Japan," pp. 21–22; Imamura, *Nihon taiiku shi,* pp. 581–583.

90. Irie, *Nihon fashizumu ka no taiiku shisō,* p. 142.

91. Ibid., pp. 157–158.

92. Watanabe Tōru, "Dai ichi kōtō (chū) gakkō no taisō kyōin ni tsuite," *Taiikushi kenkyū,* 3 (March 1985): 16–25. Of the fifty public middle schools in the Kantō region (which includes Tokyo) that responded to a 1936 survey, 100 percent had kendō clubs and only 76 percent had baseball teams. Kōzu, *Nihon kindai supōtsushi no teiryū,* p. 271.

93. Abe, Kiyohara, and Nakajima, "Fascism, Sport and Society in Japan," p. 18.

94. Ibid., p. 21.

95. Gordon Daniels, "Japanese Sport," in *Sport, Culture, and Politics,* ed. J. C. Binfield and John Stevenson (Sheffield: Sheffield Academic Press, 1993), p. 184.

96. Abe, Kiyohara, and Nakajima, "Fascism, Sport and Society in Japan," pp. 18–19; Imamura, *Nihon taiiku shi,* pp. 600–604.

97. Ibid., pp. 510, 541–543.

98. Ibid., p. 568; Abe, Kiyohara, and Nakajima, "Fascism, Sport and Society in Japan," p. 21.

99. Imamura, *Nihon taiiku shi,* pp. 577, 585; Abe, Kiyohara, and Nakajima, "Fascism, Sport and Society in Japan," pp. 14, 22.

100. Ibid., p. 22; Imamura, *Nihon taiiku shi,* pp. 607–608.

101. Yasuhiro Sakaue, "Kendo," in *Encyclopedia of World Sport,* ed. David Levinson and Karen Christensen, 3 vols. (Santa Barbara: ABC-CLIO, 1996), 2:549.

102. Abe, Kiyohara, and Nakajima, "Fascism, Sport and Society in Japan," p. 22.

103. Tanaka and Yoshikawa, *Supōtsu,* p. 27.

104. Kōzu, *Nihon kindai supōtsushi no teiryū,* pp. 327–328; Nakamura Toshio, Izuhara Yoshiaki, and Todoriki Kenji, *Gendai supōtsu ron* (Tokyo: Taishūkan, 1988), pp. 202–203.

105. Kinoshita Hideaki, *Supōtsu no kindai Nihonshi* (Tokyo: Kyōrin shoin, 1970), p. 222.

106. Hata Takao, *Nihon taiikudō* (1943), quoted in Irie, *Nihon fashizumu ka no taiiku shisō,* p. 229.

## Chapter 7. Rising from the Ashes

1. Kinoshita Hideaki, *Supōtsu no kindai Nihonshi* (Tokyo: Kyōrin shoin, 1970), pp. 224–229.

2. Yuko Kusaka, "The Development of Baseball Organizations in Japan," *International Review of Sport Sociology,* 22:4 (1987): 272.

3. Hashimoto Kazuo, *Nihon supōtsu hōsōshi* (Tokyo: Taishūkan shoten, 1992), pp. 182–183.

4. Http://www.japan-sports.or.jp/english/index.html.

5. In 1948 the national government took over the management of horseracing. The five major events of the Japanese racing calendar, which includes a Tokyo Derby, were modeled on England's classic races. See Kinoshita, *Supōtsu no kindai nihonshi,* p. 254; Nobuhiro Nagashima, "Gambling and Changing Japanese Attitudes toward It," *The Culture of Japan As Seen Through Its Leisure,* ed. Sepp Linhart and Sabine Frühstück (Albany: SUNY Press, 1998), pp. 355–356; Tanaka Tokuhisa and Yoshikawa Kumiko, *Supōtsu* (Tokyo: Kondō, 1990), pp. 119–120.

6. Ibid., p. 155.

7. Itō Kazuo, "Puro yakyū," in *Saishin Supōtsu daijten* (Tokyo: Taishūkan shoten, 1987), pp. 1126–1135.

8. Tanaka and Yoshikawa, *Supōtsu,* pp. 208–209; *Asahi shimbun,* evening edition, Osaka, December 16, 1998.

9. The example of the National Sports Festival was followed in 1947 by the newly formed Japan Recreation Association. Its first national festival was held in

Kanazawa from October 27 to November 2. (The objective of this organization was to provide opportunities and leadership for sports for workers.) See Imamura Yoshio, *Nihon taiiku shi* (Tokyo: Fumaidō, 1970), pp. 696, 727–728, 738.

10. Ibid., pp. 727–728.

11. William R. May, "Seishin" (unpublished paper, 1988).

12. Hashimoto, *Nihon supōtsu hōsōshi*, pp. 197–200.

13. James L. McClain, "Cultural Chauvinism and the Olympiads of East Asia," *International Journal of the History of Sport*, 7:3 (December 1990): 388–404.

14. Hashimoto, *Nihon supōtsu hōsōshi*, p. 202.

15. Imamura, *Nihon taiiku shi*, p. 723. Japan's Olympic Committee continues to take great pride in its ability to stage the Asian Games, which they did again, at Hiroshima, in 1994; Hironoshin Furuhashi, "The Hosting of International Sports Events," *Japan Twenty-First*, 39:6 (June 1994): 14–15; Mombushō kyōgi supōtsu kenkyū kai, ed. *"Miru supōtsu" no shinkō* (Tokyo: Baseball Magazine, 1996), pp. 140–147.

16. Sugimoto Atsuo, *Supōtsu bunka no hen'yō* (Kyōto: Sekai shisōsha, 1995), p. 186.

17. Sugawara Rei, *Taiiku to supōtsu no shakaigaku* (Tokyo: Fumaidō, 1984), pp. 95–113.

18. Tanaka and Yoshikawa, *Supōtsu*, pp. 221–222; Yomiuri shimbun Osaka honsha undōbu, ed., *Za hīrō: sengo supōtsu no yonjūnin* (Tokyo: Yomiuri shimbun, 1996), pp. 8–13; Hashimoto, *Nihon supōtsu hōsōshi*, pp. 190–192.

19. Tanaka and Yoshikawa, *Supōtsu*, pp. 133–134; Toshio Saeki, "Sport in Japan," in *Sport in Asia and Africa*, ed. Eric A. Wagner (Westport: Greenwood Press, 1989), p. 55; Yomiuri shimbun, *Za hīrō: sengo supōtsu no yonjūnin*, pp. 20–25.

20. William R. May, "Sports," *Handbook of Japanese Popular Culture* (Westport: Greenwood Press, 1989), p. 175.

21. Yomiuri shimbun, *Za hîrō: sengo supōtsu no yonjūnin*, pp. 44–48.

22. Hamamura Hideo (1955), Shigematsu Morio (1965), Kimihara Kenji (1966), Unetani Yoshiaki (1969), Seko Toshihiko (1981 and 1987), Gorman Miki (1974 and 1977).

23. Ardath W. Burks, *Japan* (Boulder: Westview, 1981), p. 214.

24. Hashimoto, *Nihon supōtsu hōsōshi*, pp. 211, 216–218.

25. Fukata Kyūya, "After Manaslu: Postwar Japanese Alpine Expeditions," *Japan Quarterly*, 12:3 (1965): 357–364; Wolfram Manzenreiter, *Die soziale Konstruktion des japanischen Alpinismus* (Vienna: Abteilung für Japanologie/Institut für Ostasienwissenschaften, 2000), pp. 126, 134.

26. Lee Austin Thompson, "Professional Wrestling in Japan: Media and Message," *International Review of Sport Sociology*, 21:1 (1986): 65–80; Yomiuri shimbun, *Za hîrō: sengo supōtsu no yonjūnin*, pp. 14–19.

27. Norbert Mosch, "Die politische Funktion des Sports in Japan und Korea" (Ph.D. dissertation, University of Vienna, 1987), p. 90.

28. Imamura, *Nihon taiiku shi*, pp. 743–744.

29. The journal also lamented the passion for Western art, drama, music, and architecture; see John W. Bennett, "Japanese Economic Growth," in *Aspects of Social Change in Modern Japan,* ed. R. P. Dore (Princeton: Princeton University Press, 1967), p. 442.

30. This and the next three paragraphs are based on Itō, "Puro yakyū," pp. 1126–1135.

31. Ishii Tsuneo, ed., *Puro yakyū no jiten* (Tokyo: Sanseidō, 1986), pp. 120–128.

32. A business executive explained to Robert Whiting, "Those who are not Giants fans are rated low in Japanese society"; see *You Gotta Have* Wa (New York: Macmillan, 1989), p. 237.

33. William W. Kelly, "Blood and Guts in Japanese Professional Baseball," in *The Culture of Japan as Seen through Its Leisure,* ed. Sepp Linhart and Sabine Frühstück (Albany: SUNY Press, 1998), p. 104.

34. Sugimoto, *Supōtsu bunka no hen'yō,* pp. 194–202.

35. Edwin O. Reischauer, *The Japanese* (Cambridge, Mass.: Harvard University Press, 1977), p. 127.

36. Robert Whiting, *The Chrysanthemum and the Bat* (New York: Dodd, Mead, 1977), p. 20. See also Reischauer: "Almost no one considers himself a Confucianist today, but in a sense almost all Japanese are" (*The Japanese,* p. 214).

37. Whiting, *You Gotta Have* Wa, p. 61.

38. Warren Cromartie and Robert Whiting, *Slugging It Out in Japan* (1991; New York: Signet Books, 1992), p. 104.

39. Whiting, *The Chrysanthemum and the Bat,* p. 71.

40. Whiting, *You Gotta Have* Wa, p. 72.

41. Ibid., pp. 72–73.

42. Nakamura Toshio, *Nihonteki supōtsu kankyō hihan* (Tokyo: Taishūkan shoten, 1995), p. 59.

43. Cromartie and Whiting, *Slugging It Out in Japan,* p. 249.

44. American players in Japan are a favorite topic for journalists; see, for instance, Donald S. Connery's article on Joe Stanka of the Nankai Hawks: "A Yank in Japan," *Sports Illustrated,* 16 (October 29, 1962): 60–69.

45. Whiting, *You Gotta Have* Wa, pp. 264, 276.

46. *Asahi shimbun,* September 1, 1998.

47. Whiting, *You Gotta Have* Wa, pp. 302–304. Ironically, Harimoto is ethnically Korean.

48. Oh Sadaharu and David Faulkner, *Sadaharu Oh* (New York: Times Books, 1984), pp. 278–279.

49. Whiting, *The Chrysanthemum and the Bat,* p. 100.

50. *Asahi shimbun,* Sunday Supplement, March 14, 1999.

51. Kelly, "Blood and Guts in Japanese Professional Baseball," p. 102.

52. See Chapter 6 for our attempt to understand aikidō.

53. William W. Kelly, "Learning to Swing: Oh Sadaharu and the Pedagogy

and Practice of Japanese Baseball," in *Learning in Likely Places*, ed. John Singleton (New York: Cambridge University Press, 1998), pp. 265–285.

54. William W. Kelly, "'Men at Work': What Does Professional Baseball Demonstrate in Contemporary Japan" (paper presented at a conference on "Sports and Body Culture in Modern Japan," Yale University, March 31–April 2, 2000).

55. "Blood and Guts in Japanese Baseball," pp. 95–111.

56. David Tokiharu Mayeda, "From Model Minority to Economic Threat," *Journal of Sport and Social Issues*, 23:2 (May 1999): 203–217.

57. John Bale and Joseph Maguire, eds., *The Global Sports Arena: Athletic Talent Migration in an Interdependent World* (London: Frank Cass, 1994). Nomo was not the first Japanese to play major league baseball in the United States. Murakami Masanori pitched successfully for the San Francisco Giants during the 1964 and 1965 seasons. He returned to Japan when the Nankai Hawks offered him twice the salary paid by the Giants; see Robert Obojski, *The Rise of Japanese Baseball Power* (Radnor, Pa.: Chilton, 1975), pp. 80–88.

58. G. Cameron Hurst III, Armed Martial Arts of Japan (New Haven: Yale University Press, 1998), p. 148.

59. Ibid., pp. 165–169, 172–173.

60. Yasuhiro Sakaue, "Kendo," in *Encyclopedia of World Sport*, ed. David Levinson and Karen Christensen, 3 vols. (Santa Barbara: ABC-CLIO, 1996), 2:549.

61. Ibid., p. 550.

62. Donn F. Draeger, *Martial Arts and Ways of Japan*, 2 vols. (New York: Weatherhill, 1973), 2:125.

63. John J. Donohue, "Dancing in the Danger Zone," *Journal of Asian Martial Arts*, 1:1 (January 1992): 89.

64. Sakaue, "Kendo," p. 549.

65. Hurst, *Armed Martial Arts*, p. 173.

66. Coming-of-Age Day (*Seijin no Hi*) is celebrated annually in honor of all those who have reached the age of twenty.

67. *Asahi shimbun*, Osaka, January 16, 1999.

68. Mosch, "Die politische Funktion des Sports in Japan und Korea," pp. 59–62.

69. "Procès-Verbale de la Session de Copenhagen," May 15–17, 1950; "55th Session of the International Olympic Committee, May 25–28, 1959," *Bulletin du C.I.O.* (August 15, 1959).

70. Michel Brousse, "Du Samouraî à l'Athlète," *Sport/Histoire*, 3 (1989): 17.

71. B. C. and J. M. Goodger, "Jūdō in the Light of Theory and Sociological Research," *International Review of Sport Sociology*, 12:2 (1977): 20.

72. Mosch, "Die politische Funktion des Sports in Japan und Korea," pp. 62, 67.

73. Kevin Gray Carr, "Judo," in *Encyclopedia of World Sport*, 2:529.

74. B.C. and J.C. Goodger, "Jūdō in the Light of Theory and Sociological Research," p. 20.

75. B. C. and J. M. Goodger, "Organizational and Cultural Change in Post-War British Jūdō," *International Review of Sport Sociology*, 15:1 (1980): 37, 42–43.

76. Brousse, "Du Samouraî à l'Athlète," pp. 12, 21.

77. Kevin Gray Carr, "Making Way: War, Philosophy and Sport in Japanese *Jūdō*," *Journal of Sport History*, 20:2 (Summer 1993): 181.

78. Toshio Saeki, "The Conflict between Tradition and Modernization in a Sport Organization," *International Review of Sport Sociology*, 29:3 (1994): 301–13.

79. Agemizu Ken'ichirō, "Jūdō no supōtsu kindaika" (paper delivered March 27, 1999, at the 8th Conference of the Japan Society of Sport Sociology, Hiroshima).

80. *Asahi shimbun*, December 11, 1996.

81. Michihara Shinji, "Karatedō," in *Saishin supōtsu daijiten*, p. 188.

82. Benny Josef Peiser, "Karate," in *Encyclopedia of World Sport*, p. 544.

83. Nihon Sumō Kyōkai Hakubutsukan Un'ei Iin, ed., *Kinsei Nihon sumō shi*, 3:3–9.

84. Ibid., 3:13,123. Maedayama continued, however, to run his own stable after his retirement as an active wrestler.

85. Hatano Ryō, Koike Kenichi, and Mizuno Naofumi, *Meiji Taishō Shōwa zen makuuchi rikishi meikan* (Tokyo: Yūhō Shoten, 1985), p. 7.

86. Nihon Sumō Kyōkai Hakubutsukan Un'ei Iin, ed., *Kinsei Nihon sumō shi*, 3:3–25.

87. Ibid., 4:18.

88. Ibid., 5:12.

89. Ian Reader, "Sumo: The Recent History of an Ethical Model for Japanese Society," *International Journal of the History of Sport*, 6:3 (December 1989): 285–298. For this and the next eight paragraphs, see Lee Thompson, "The Invention of the *Yokozuna* and the Championship System," in *Mirror of Modernity*, ed. Stephen Vlastos (Berkeley: University of California Press, 1998), pp. 183–187.

90. William Wetherall, "Striking Sensitivities in Sumo's Inner Sanctum," *Far Eastern Economic Review*, 126 (November 8, 1984): 51. On Takamiyama's career, see Jesse Kuhaulua and John Wheeler, *Takamiyama* (Tokyo: Kodansha International, 1973).

91. Kojima Noboru, "'Gaijin yokozuna' wa iranai," *Bungei shunjū*, 70:4 (April 1992): 372–378.

92. Chujo Kazuo, "Sumo Enters a New Age," *Japan Quarterly*, 32:1 (January–March 1985): 40–45.

93. The bylaws had been revised to allow promotion upon the recommendation of a two-thirds majority.

94. Kosaka Shūji, "Sumō tankyū 80," *Ōzumo*, 40:11 (November 1994): 61.

95. Mark Mravic, "Scorecard: Say It Ain't Sumo!" *Sports Illustrated*, 92:7 (February 21, 2000): 24. Allegations of corruption in sumo are nothing new. See, for example, the alleged expose by the former elder Ōnaruto, *Yaochō*, (Tokyo: Rokusaisha, 1996).

96. Kemari Preservation Society, ed., *Kemari hozonkai kyūjūnen shi* (Kyoto:

Kemari hozonkai, 1997), pp. 25–26, 49, 52. Except where otherwise indicated, our discussion of kemari is based on this source (pp. 52–73).

97. In 1952, kemari was designated an Intangible Cultural Asset by the Ministry of Education, but apparently subsequently lost this designation. In 1984, Kyoto City made kemari an Intangible Folk Cultural Asset.

98. The Kemari Society had its financial difficulties too. For a period in the 1960s the society had stooped to perform for tourists on an indoor stage.

99. Michael Duffy, "Mission Impossible," *Time,* January 20, 1992, p. 10. This was the same trip during which the president threw up in the lap of Prime Minister Miyazawa Kiichi at a state dinner.

100. The Kemari Preservation Society is not the only kemari society in Japan. Reflecting the history of kemari in that prefecture, the Shinano Kemari Society was established in Ueda, Nagano Prefecture, in 1996. The society has a kemari museum and something the Kyoto society lacks: an indoor practice area; *Asahi shimbun,* evening edition, October 26, 1996.

101. This section on postwar physical education is based mainly on Imamura, *Nihon taiiku shi,* pp. 621–663.

## Chapter 8. Japan at the Olympics: 1952–1998

1. Imamura Yoshio, *Nihon taiiku shi* (Tokyo: Fumaidō, 1970), p. 700.

2. Kiyokawa Masaji, *Supōtsu to seiji* (Tokyo: Baseball Magazine, 1987), pp. 30–31.

3. "Procès-Verbale de la Session de Copenhagen," May 15–17, 1950 (Avery Brundage Collection, University of Illinois, Box 76).

4. Imamura, *Nihon taiiku shi,* p. 700.

5. Ibid., p. 702.

6. Ishimoto's silver was in the 200-meter butterfly, Yamanaka's were in the 400-meter and 1,500-meter freestyle. Tanaka Tokuhisa and Yoshikawa Kumiko, *Supōtsu* (Tokyo: Kondō, 1990), pp. 261–262; Yomiuri shimbun Ōsaka honsha undōbu, ed., *Za hīrō: sengo supōtsu no yonjūnin* (Tokyo: Yomiuri shimbun, 1996), pp. 210–215; Sase Minoru, *Orimpikku hīrōtachi no nemurenai yoru* (Tokyo: Sekai bunkasha, 1996), p. 55. For the performance of Japanese athletes in the summer games through 1976, see Korube deitamu henshūshitsu, ed., *Orimpikku deita bukku* (Tokyo: Kolbe Publishing, 1984).

7. Imamura, *Nihon taiikushi,* pp. 702–703.

8. Yomiuri shimbun, ed., *Za hīrō: sengo supōtsu no yonjūnin,* pp. 26–31.

9. *United States 1956 Olympic Book* (New York: United States Olympic Association, 1957), p. 187.

10. Tanaka and Yoshikawa, *Supōtsu,* p. 262.

11. Hashimoto Kazuo, *Nihon supōtsu hōsō shi* (Tokyo: Taishūkan shoten, 1992), p. 231.

12. Imamura, *Nihon taiiku shi,* pp. 704–705.

13. Ibid., p. 706.

14. "55th Session of the International Olympic Committee, May 25–28, 1959," *Bulletin du C.I.O.* (August 15, 1959).

15. Imamura, *Nihon taiikushi,* p. 703; Tanaka and Yoshikawa, *Supōtsu,* pp. 189, 262.

16. The Japanese women, who had been 5th in 1952 and 6th in 1956, climbed to 4th place but won no individual medals. Heinz Maegerlein, *Olympia 1960* (Frankfurt: Wilhlem Limpert, 1960), pp. 150–163.

17. Imamura, *Nihon taiiku shi,* pp. 706–710, 721.

18. Gordon Daniels, "Japanese Sport," in *Sport, Culture, and Politics,* ed. J. C. Binfield and John Stevenson (Sheffield: Sheffield Academic Press, 1993), p. 187.

19. This 3rd-place finish, repeated in 1968, has never been surpassed. See Willi Könning, *Spitzensport in Japan* (Bonn: Dieter Born, 1990), pp. 101–112.

20. Tanaka and Yoshikawa, *Supōtsu,* p. 127.

21. John Lucas, *The Modern Olympic Games* (New York: A. S. Barnes, 1980), p. 184.

22. Norbert Mosch, "Die politische Funktion des Sports in Japan und Korea" (Ph.D. dissertation, University of Vienna, 1987), p. 68.

23. Tanaka and Yoshikawa, *Supōtsu,* p. 262; Yomiuri shimbun, ed., *Za hīrō: sengo supōtsu no yonjūnin,* pp. 154–159; Sase, *Orimpikku hīrōtachi no nemurenai yoru* (Tokyo: Sekai bunkasha, 1996), pp. 15–44.

24. Yomiuri shimbun, ed., *Za hīrō: sengo supōtsu no yonjūnin,* pp. 204–209; Imamura, *Nihon taiiku shi,* p. 717.

25. Hashimoto, *Nihon supōtsu hōsō shi,* p. 279.

26. Mombushō kyōgi supōtsu kenkyūkai, ed., *"Miru supōtsu" no shinkō* (Tokyo: Baseball Magazine, 1996), pp. 41–44.

27. Hashimoto, *Nihon supōtsu hōsō shi,* pp. 249, 274.

28. Ibid., pp. 275, 280–283.

29. Ibid., pp. 272, 287; Imamura, *Nihon taiiku shi,* p. 716.

30. Kaneyoshi Yasuyuki and Matsumoto Yoshiaki, *Gendai seikatsu to supōtsu bunka* (Tokyo: Taishūkan shoten, 1997), p. 98.

31. Mombushō kyōgi supōtsu kenkyūkai, ed., *"Miru supōtsu" no shinkō,* pp. 43–44.

32. Imamura, *Nihon taiikushi.,* p. 648.

33. Yomiuri shimbun, ed., *Za hīrō: sengo supōtsu no yonjūnin,* pp. 146–151.

34. Tanaka and Yoshikawa, *Supōtsu,* p. 267; Yomiuri shimbun, ed., *Za hīrō: sengo supōtsu no yonjūnin,* pp. 128–133.

35. Allen Guttmann, *The Games Must Go On* (New York: Columbia University Press, 1984), pp. 249–255; Sase, *Orimpikku hīrōtachi no nemurenai yoru,* pp. 279–287.

36. Tanaka and Yoshikawa, *Supōtsu,* pp. 222, 263; Yomiuri shimbun, ed., *Za hīrō: sengo supōtsu no yonjūnin,* pp. 92–96; Sase, *Orimpikku hīrōtachi no nemurenai yoru,* pp. 45–68.

37. Ibid., pp. 69–96.

38. Ono Akira, *Gendai supōtsu hihan* (Tokyo: Taishūkan shoten, 1996), pp. 34–37.

39. The German government, which was equally sheltered by the American "nuclear umbrella," put the same kind of pressure on its National Olympic Committee and with the same deplorable results. See Willi Knecht, *Der Boycott* (Cologne: Verlag Wissenschaft und Politik, 1980); Günter R. Müller and Dieter Kühnle, *Moskauer Spiele* (Gütersloh: Bertelsmann, 1980).

40. Kiyokawa, *Supōtsu to seiji*, pp. 71–143; Ono, *Gendai supōtsu hihan*, pp. 125–147; Nakamura Toshio, Izuhara Yoshiaki, and Todoriki Kenji, *Gendai supōtsu ron* (Tokyo: Taishūkan, 1988), pp. 211–213. Nakamura, Izuhara, and Todoriki give the final vote as 29–13 (p. 213). For a Western perspective, see Baruch Hazan, *Olympic Sports and Propaganda Games* (New Brunswick: Transaction Books, 1982); Derick L. Hulme, Jr., *The Political Olympics* (New York: Praeger, 1990).

41. Nakamura, Izuhara, and Todoriki, *Gendai supōtsu ron*, p. 212.

42. Kiyokawa, *Supōtsu to seiji*, pp. 135–143; Hazan, *Olympic Sports and Propaganda Games*, p. 165.

43. Ono, *Gendai supōtsu hihan*, pp. 147–155.

44. Kiyokawa, *Supōtsu to seiji*, pp. 148–150.

45. There was also a silver medal for Kajitani Nobuyuki on the parallel bars and two bronzes in addition to Gushiken's (Sotomura Kōji in the floor exercises and Morisue Shinji on the horse).

46. Tanaka and Yoshikawa, *Supōtsu*, pp. 205, 263; Yomiuri shimbun, ed., *Za hīrō: sengo supōtsu no yonjūnin*, pp. 62–67.

47. T. J. Pempel, "Contemporary Japanese Athletics," in *The Culture of Japan as Seen through Its Leisure*, ed. Sepp Linhart and Sabine Frühstück (Albany: SUNY Press, 1998), p. 124.

48. Imamura, *Nihon taiiku shi*, p. 723.

49. Pempel, "Contemporary Japanese Athletics," p. 122.

50. Ono, *Gendai supōtsu hihan*, pp. 175–179.

51. Tanaka and Yoshikawa, *Supōtsu*, p. 222.

52. Steve Rushin, "Planet Nagano," *Sports Illustrated*, 88:5 (February 9, 1998): 87. For an account of Tsutsumi and his family background, see Lesley Downer, *The Brothers: The Saga of the Richest Family in Japan* (London: Chatto & Windus: 1994).

53. *Sports Illustrated* credited Yoshida with ownership of sixty-six gas stations, thirty-four Kentucky Fried Chicken franchises, and a 1954 Mercedes-Benz that once belong to Konrad Adenauer; see Rushin, "Planet Nagano," p. 84.

54. Ono, *Gendai supōtsu hihan*, pp. 99–114; Rushin, "Planet Nagano," pp. 85–86.

55. In Squaw Valley in 1960, the first winter games that included female speed skaters, Takamizawa Hatsue reached 5th place and 4th place in the 500-meter and 3,000-meter races. Between then and 1992, a number of Japanese women placed 5th, 6th, or 7th, but Hashimoto was the first to attain 3rd place.

56. We give Ozawa Seiji's name in the Western order because he became internationally famous as the conductor of the Boston Symphony Orchestra.

57. Takayuki Yamashita, "The Nagano Olympics: Inventing Japaneseness in a Global Imaginary" (paper presented at a conference on "Sports and Body Culture in Modern Japan," Yale University, March 31–April 2, 2000).

58. *Asahi shimbun,* October 27, 1998; March 1, 1999.

## Chapter 9. New Directions

1. Tadanobu Tsunoda, *The Japanese Brain: Uniqueness and Universality,* trans. Yoshinori Oiwa, (Tokyo: Taishūkan shoten, 1985).

2. Ono Akira, *Gendai supōtsu hihan* (Tokyo: Taishūkan shoten, 1996), p. 94; Nelson H. H. Graburn, "Work and Play in the Japanese Countryside," in *The Culture of Japan as Seen through Its Leisure,* ed. Sepp Linhart and Sabine Frühstück (Albany: SUNY Press, 1998), p. 202.

3. Ibid..

4. John Horne, "The Politics of Sport and Leisure in Japan," *International Review of Sport Sociology,* 33:2 (June 1998): 175.

5. Eyal Ben-Ari, "Golf, Organization, and 'Body Projects'" in *The Culture of Japan as Seen through Its Leisure,* p. 154.

6. Brian Stoddart, "Wide World of Golf," *Sociology of Sport Journal,* 7:4 (1990): 382; Peter J. Rimmer, "Japanese Investment in Golf Course Development," *International Journal of Urban and Regional Research,* 18 (1994): 234–255.

7. Ben-Ari, "Golf, Organization, and 'Body Projects,'" p. 143.

8. Stoddart, "Wide World of Golf," pp. 381–382.

9. Tanaka Yoshihisa, *Gorufu to nihonjin* (Tokyo: Iwanami shoten, 1992), p. 32. Figures from Keizai kikaku chō, "Rejā sābisu ryōkin no naigai kakakusa chōsa," 1991; Gavan McCormack, "The Price of Affluence: The Political Economy of Japanese Leisure," *New Left Review,* 188 (1999): 121–34.

10. Anne Allison, *Nightwork: Sexuality, Pleasure, and Corporate Masculinity in a Tokyo Hostess Club* (Chicago: University of Chicago Press, 1994), p. 57.

11. Carl Goldstein, "The Corporate Pitch," *Far Eastern Economic Review,* 151 (February 28, 1991): 66.

12. Golf tournaments are a bonanza for advertising agencies like Dentsū and Hakuhōdō, which controlled forty-two of them in the early 1990s; see Carl Goldstein, "Japan's Spoilsports," *Far Eastern Economic Review,* 151 (February 28, 1991): 67–68.

13. Ben-Ari, "Golf, Organization, and 'Body Projects,'" pp. 141–146.

14. Mombushō kyōgi supōtsu kenkyūkai, ed., *"Miru supōtsu" no shinkō* (Tokyo: Baseball Magazine, 1996), pp. 107–113.

15. Bruce Newman, "Japan: Coming on Strong," *Sports Illustrated,* 71 (August 21, 1989): 51.

16. Okpyo Moon, *From Paddy Field to Ski Slope* (Manchester: Manchester

University Press, 1989), pp. 78–93. See also Kazunori Matsumura, "Sport and Social Change in the Japanese Rural Community," *International Review of Sport Sociology*, 28:2–3 (1993): 135–142.

17. Moon, *From Paddy Field to Ski Slope*, p. 176.

18. Wolfram Manzenreiter, *Die soziale Konstruktion des japanischen Alpinismus* (Vienna: Abteilung für Japanologie/Institut für Ostasienwissenschaften, 2000), pp. 75–86, 150, 214–215.

19. Newman, "Japan: Coming on Strong," p. 61.

20. Our discussion of soccer is drawn mainly from the following sources: Haruo Nogawa and Hiroka Maeda, "The Japanese Dream," in *Football Cultures and Identities*, ed. Gary Armstrong and Richard Giulianotti (Houndsmill: Macmillan, 1999), pp. 223–233; John Horne, "'Sakka' in Japan" *Media, Culture and Society*, 18:4 (October 1996): 527–547; Kathleen Morris, "How Japan Scored," *Financial World*, 164 (February 14, 1995): 82–85; Maezono Masakiyo, *Doriburu* (Tokyo: Baseball Magazine, 1996); John Horne, "Soccer in Japan," *Culture, Sport, Society*, 2:3 (Autumn 1999): 212–229.

21. Jonathan Watts, "Soccer *Shinhatsubai:* What Are Japanese Consumers Making of the J. League?" in *The Worlds of Japanese Popular Culture*, ed. D. P. Martinez (Cambridge: Cambridge University Press, 1998), p. 189.

22. Horne, "'Sakka' in Japan," pp. 527–547; Maezono, *Doriburu*.

23. Horne, "'Sakka' in Japan," p. 542.

24. Quoted from Watts, "Soccer *Shinhatsubai:* What Are Japanese Consumers Making of the J. League?" p. 193.

25. Morris, "How Japan Scored," p. 83.

26. Horne, "'Sakka' in Japan," p. 542.

27. Jonathan Friedland, "Japan Shoots for Goal," *Far Eastern Economic Review*, 156 (June 17, 1993): 48–50.

28. Kisanuki Hisayo and Esashi Shōgo, "Sakkā no kansen dōki ni mirareru seisa no kentō," *Supōtsu shakaigaku kenkyū*, 4 (1996): 106–114.

29. A study of the "lifestyles" and sports preferences of university students found that those who prize harmony are strongly drawn to baseball; see Yamamoto Norihito, "Daigakusei no raifusutairu to supōtsu no katsudōsenkō," *Supōtsu shakaigaku kenkyū*, 3 (1995): 13–25.

30. Uesugi Masayuki, "Shōhi shakai ni okeru supekuteitā supōtsu," *Supōtsu shakaigaku kenkyū*, 3 (1995): 1–11.

31. Takahashi Hidesato, "Hiroshima shimin kyūjō ni okeru puroyakyū no shūgōteki ōen ni kan suru kenkyū," *Supōtsu shakaigaku kenkyū*, 2 (1994): 53–66; Hidesato Takahashi, "Fan Clubs of Japanese Professional Baseball Teams" (paper presented at a conference on "Sports and Body Culture in Modern Japan," Yale University, March 31–April 2, 2000); William W. Kelly, "An Anthropologist in the Bleachers," *Japan Quarterly*, 44:4 (October–December 1997): 66–79.

32. *Asahi shimbun*, December 12, 1998.

33. Ibid., February 20, 1999.

34. Ibid., November 17 and 26, 1998.

35. Ibid., October 31, 1998.

36. Ibid., December 27, 1998.

37. Ibid., November 7, 1998; October 31, 1998; January 3, 1999.

38. Ibid., November 13, 1998.

39. Ibid. The bursting of the economic bubble in the 1990s affected not only the fledgling soccer league. As a quick means of cutting expenses, many companies withdrew or curtailed their sponsorship of sports events. Eighteen major events suffered in 1992 and eleven in 1993. Many companies simply abolished their company teams. In the five years from 1994 to 1998, sixty-four company teams in thirteen different sports were disbanded. See *Asahi shimbun*, November 16, 1992; March 2, 1999.

40. Ibid., March 6, 1999.

41. Ise Akifumi, *Hashiru!* (Tokyo: Futabasha, 1996), p. 67; Masajima Midori, *Samenai yume* (Tokyo: Za masada, 2000), pp. 30–32.

42. Ibid., pp. 10–17.

43. Yamamoto Ikuei, *Musume to watashi* (Tokyo: Kiyomizu shoin, 1996).

44. Tabei: quoted in Joyce Lebra, Joy Paulson, and Elizabeth Powers, *Women in Changing Japan* (Stanford: Stanford University Press, 1976), p. 262.

45. Ibid.

46. Esashi Shōgo, *Josei supōtsu no shakaigaku* (Tokyo: Fumaidō, 1992), p. 51. The data are from Nara Prefecture.

47. Tatano Hideo, *Supōtsu shakaigaku no riron to chōsa* (Tokyo: Fumaidō, 1997), pp. 196–221.

48. Patricia Morley, *The Mountain Is Moving: Japanese Women's Lives* (New York: New York University Press, 1999), p. 65.

49. Toshio Saeki, "Sport in Japan," in *Sport in Asia and Africa*, ed. Eric A. Wagner (Westport: Greenwood Press, 1989), pp. 52, 69.

50. Esashi, *Josei supōtsu no shakaigaku*, p. 232.

51. Saeki, "Sport in Japan," p. 72.

52. Lebra et al., *Women in Changing Japan*, pp. 257–258.

53. Tanaka Tokuhisa and Yoshikawa Kumiko, *Supōtsu* (Tokyo: Kondō, 1990), p. 65.

54. For comparative data, see Allen Guttmann, *Women's Sports* (New York: Columbia University Press, 1991), pp. 231–243.

55. Yoshiro Hatano, Ayako Ota, and Noriko Sudo, "Cross-Cultural Comparison of Public Image on Female Participation in Sport," in *Proceedings of FISU/CESU Conference* (Kobe: Kobe kokusai kōryū kaikan, 1985), pp. 186–192.

56. Yuzawa: quoted in Allison, *Nightwork*, p. 111.

57. An ekiden is a long-distance relay race.

58. Yoshiko Tanaka, "The Role of the University in Women's Athletics in Japan," in *Proceedings of the FISU/CESU Conference*, pp. 342–343.

59. *Asahi shimbun*, September 15, 1998.

60. Ibid., February 17, 1998.

61. Ibid., March 2–6, 1999; Haruo Nogawa and Hiroka Maeda, "The Japanese Dream," pp. 223–233.

62. *Asahi shimbun*, October 20, 1998. The structure of Japanese volleyball makes it especially difficult for a team to survive without substantial corporate support. Television income goes to the Japan Volleyball Association, and is not distributed to the individual teams. Even gate receipts go to the JVA and the local volleyball associations.

63. Peter Kühnst, *Sports*, trans. Allen Guttmann (Dresden: Verlag der Kunst, 1996), pp. 345–347.

64. Tanaka and Yoshikawa, *Supōtsu*, pp. 232–233. Tanaka and Yoshikawa estimate surfboarders at a million and windsurfers at 400,000. The numbers seem doubtful.

65. Kühnst, *Sports*, p. 347.

66. Ibid.

67. Ibid.

68. Kawahara Kazue, "'Fittonesu' genshō e no shiten," *Supōtsu shakaigaku kenkyū*, 3 (1995): 44.

69. Willi Könning, *Spitzensport in Japan* (Bonn: Dieter Born, 1990), p. 72; Nakamura Toshio, *Nihonteki supōtsu kankyō hihan* (Tokyo: Taishūkan shoten, 1995), pp. 91–104.

70. Richard Light, "A Centenary of Rugby and Masculinity in Japanese Schools and Universities," *Sporting Traditions*, 16:2 (May 2000): 101.

71. Nakamura, *Nihonteki supōtsu kankyō hihan*, pp. 156–168.

72. Sugawara Rei, *Taiiku to supōtsu no shakaigaku* (Tokyo: Fumaidō, 1984), p. 141.

73. Laura Ginsberg, "The Hard Work of Working Out," *Journal of Sport and Social Issues*, 24:3 (August 2000): 260–281.

74. Anne Bolin, "Bodybuilding," in *Encyclopedia of World Sport*, ed. David Levinson and Karen Christensen, 3 vols. (Santa Barbara: ABC-CLIO, 1996), 1:129.

75. Maggie Kinser, "Body Beautifuls," *Tokyo Journal*, 7:6 (September 1987): 37.

76. Tanaka and Yoshikawa, *Supōtsu*, pp. 66–67, 70–71

77. Fujiyoshi Hisanori and Tawara Takehiro, "Nanshiki Tenisu, " in *Saishin supōtsu daijiten*, ed. Kishino Yūzō (Tokyo: Taishūkan shoten, 1987), pp. 920–924.

78. Tanaka and Yoshikawa, *Supōtsu*, pp. 70–71; International Soft Tennis Federation, http://village.infoweb.ne.jp/~fwgj4139/soft-tennis/inter-national.htm. The ISTF translates the name of the sport as "soft tennis," an unfortunate choice because it is the ball that is soft, not the tennis.

79. Esashi, *Josei supōtsu no shakaigaku*, p. 111; Makoto Chogahara and Yasuo Yamaguchi, "Resocialization and Continuity of Involvement in Physical Activity among Elderly Japanese," *International Review of Sport Sociology*, 33:3 (September 1998): 277–89.

80. Kaneyoshi Yasuyuki and Matsumoto Yoshiaki, *Gendai seikatsu to supōtsu bunka* (Tokyo: Taishūkan shoten, 1997), pp. 27–32.

81. Tanaka and Yoshikawa, pp. 58–59. Sonoda Sekiya, "Geitobōru," in *Saishin supōtsu daijiten, pp. 275–276.*

82. Kathleen A. Kalab, "Playing Gateball," *Journal of Aging Studies,* 6:1 (1992): 23–40.

83. Kawanishi Masashi, Kitamura Takahiro, and Tomiyama Kōzō, "Chūkōnen supōtsu sankasha no seikatsu manzokudo—zenkoku supōtsu-reku matsuri sankasha ni tsuite," *Supōtsu shakaigaku kenkyū,* 4 (1996): 93–105.

84. Tanaka and Yoshikawa, *Supōtsu,* p. 59.

85. Ibid. Gateball has spread to Korea, Taiwan, Thailand and China. In the city of Xi'an in China, for example, it was first played around 1985, according to the Shanxi Province Gateball Association. There were only five teams in Shanxi Prefecture in 1986, but as of 1997 there were five thousand teams with eighty thousand players, some of which do well at the national tournament. Teams from Shanxi Prefecture have played "friendlies" in Japan in 1993 and 1994, and an Asian gateball tournament is scheduled to be held in Xi'an in the year 2000; *Asahi shimbun,* evening edition, June 7, 1997.

# Bibliography

Abe, Ikuo. "A Study of the Chronology of the Modern Usage of 'Sportsmanship' in English, American and Japanese Dictionaries." *International Journal of the History of Sport,* 5:1 (May 1988): 3–28.

Abe, Ikuo, Yasuharu Kiyohara, and Ken Nakajima, "Fascism, Sport and Society in Japan." *International Journal of the History of Sport,* 9:1 (April 1992): 1–28.

Abe, Ikuo, and J. A. Mangan. "The British Impact on Boys' Sports and Games in Japan." *International Journal of the History of Sport,* 14:2 (August 1997): 187–199.

Abe Tomoji. "Nichidoku taikō kyōgi." *Shinchō,* 27:1 (1930): 17–26.

Acker, William R. B. *Japanese Archery.* 3rd ed. Rutland: Charles Tuttle, 1965.

Adams, Andrew, and Mark Schilling. *Jesse! Sumo Superstar.* Tokyo: Japan Times, 1985.

Adelman, Melvin L. "Modernization Theory and Its Critics." In *Encyclopedia of American Social History,* ed. Mary Cupiec Cayton et al. 3 vols. New York: Scribner's, 1993.

Agemizu Ken'ichirō. "Jūdō no supōtsu kindaika." Unpublished paper; 8th Conference of the Japan Society of Sport Sociology, 1999.

Ahn Changkyu and Fujiwara Kengo. "Supōtsu shōhisha kōdō kenkyū no shakaigakuteki shiza." *Supōtsu shakaigaku kenkyū,* 4 (1996): 63–78.

Allison, Anne. *Nightwork.* Chicago: University of Chicago Press, 1994.

Amdur, Ellis. "Divine Transmission Katori Shinto Ryu." *Journal of Asian Martial Arts,* 3:2 (1994): 48–61.

———. "Maniwa Nen-Ryu." *Journal of Asian Martial Arts,* 4:3 (1995): 10–25.

———. "The Role of Arms-Bearing Women in Japanese History." *Journal of Asian Martial Arts,* 5:2 (1996): 10–35.

Arnaud, Pierre. *Le Militaire, l'écolier, le gymnaste.* Lyon: Presses universitaires de Lyon, 1991.

*Asahi shimbun.* September 30, 1921; January 22, 1987; November 16, 1992; June 18, 1996; October 19, 1996; December 11, 1996; June 7, 1997; February 17, 1998; September 1, 1998; September 15, 1998; October 20, 1998; October 27, 1998; October 31, 1998; November 7, 1998; November 13, 1998; November 17, 1998; November 26, 1998; December 12, 1998; December 20, 1998; January 3, 1999; January 16, 1999; January 26, 1999; January 28, 1999; February 19, 1999; February 20, 1999; March 2–6, 1999; March 14, 1999.

**273**

Bale, John, and Joseph Maguire, eds. *The Global Sports Arena*. London: Frank Cass, 1994.

Barthes, Roland. *L'Empire des signes*. Paris: Editions d'Art Albert Skira, 1970.

Beasley, W. G. *Japan Encounters the Barbarian*. New Haven: Yale University Press, 1995.

Bellah, Robert. *Tokugawa Religion*. New York: The Free Press, 1957.

Ben-Ari, Eyal. "Golf, Organization, and 'Body Projects.'" In *The Culture of Japan as Seen through its Leisure*, ed. Sepp Linhart and Sabine Frühstück. Albany: SUNY Press, 1998. Pp. 139–161.

Bennett, John W. "Japanese Economic Growth." In *Aspects of Social Change in Modern Japan*, ed. R. P. Dore. Princeton: Princeton University Press, 1967. Pp. 411–453.

Bernett, Hajo. "Das Scheitern der Olympischen Spiele von 1940." *Stadion*, 6 (1980): 251–290.

Bickford, Lawrence. *Sumo and the Woodblock Print Masters*. Tokyo: Kodansha International, 1994.

*Bijutsu ni miru nihon no supōtsu*. Nagoya: Tokugawa Art Museum, 1994.

Bode, Rudolf. *Bewegung und Gestaltung*. Berlin: Weidekind, 1936.

Bolin, Anne. "Bodybuilding." In *Encyclopedia of World Sport*, ed. David Levinson and Karen Christensen, 3 vols. Santa Barbara: ABC-CLIO, 1996. 1:125–134.

Bolitho, Harold. "Frolicking Dragons: Mythic Terror and the Sumō Tradition." *ASSH Studies in Sports History*, 2 (1987): 2–22.

———. "Sumō and Popular Culture: The Tokugawa Period." In *The Japanese Trajectory: Modernization and Beyond*, ed. Gavan McCormack and Yoshio Sugimoto. Cambridge: Cambridge University Press, 1988. Pp. 17–32.

Bottenburg, Maarten van. *Verborgen Competitie: Over de Uiteenlopende Populariteit van Sporten*. Amsterdam: Bert Bakker, 1994.

Boudreau, Françoise, Ralph Folman, and Burt Konzak. "Psychological and Physical Changes in School-Age Karate Participants." *Journal of Asian Martial Arts*, 4:4 (1995): 50–69.

Bourdieu, Pierre. *La Distinction*. Paris: Editions de minuit, 1979.

Brousse, Michel. "Du Samouraî à l'athlète: l'essor du jûdô en France." *Sport/Histoire*, 3 (1989): 11–25

———. *Le Judo*. Geneva: Liber, 1996.

Brousse, Michel, and Jean-Paul Clément. "Le judo en France." In *Histoire des sports*, ed. Thierry Terret. Paris: L'Harmattan, 1996. Pp. 135–158.

Brousse, Michel, and David Matsumoto. *Judo*. Seoul: International Judo Federation, 1999.

Brown, Richard D. *Modernization*. New York: Hill & Wang, 1976.

Burks, Ardath W. *Japan*. Boulder: Westview, 1981.

Carr, Kevin Gray. "Judo." In *Encyclopedia of World Sport*, ed. David Levinson and Karen Christensen, 3 vols. Santa Barbara: ABC-Clio, 1996. 2:527–531.

————. "Making Way: War, Philosophy and Sport in Japanese *Jūdō*." *Journal of Sport History*, 20:2 (Summer 1993): 167–188.

Chogahara, Makoto, and Yasuo Yamaguchi. "Resocialization and Continuity of Involvement in Physical Activity among Elderly Japanese." *International Review of Sport Sociology*, 33:3 (September 1988): 277–289.

*Confessions of Lady Nijō*, trans. Karen Brazell. Stanford: Stanford University Press, 1976.

Connery, Donald S. "A Yank in Japan." *Sports Illustrated*, 16 (June 25, 1962): 60–73.

Cortazzi, Hugh. *Victorians in Japan*. London: Athlone Press, 1987.

Crawford, Andrew. "The Martian Yen: American Participation in the Aikido Tradition." *Journal of Asian Martial Arts*, 1:4 (1992): 28–43.

Crepeau, Richard C. "Pearl Harbor: A Failure of Baseball?" *Journal of Popular Culture*, 15:4 (Spring 1982): 67–74.

Cromartie, Warren, and Robert Whiting. *Slugging It Out in Japan*. New York: Kodansha, 1991.

Cuyler, Patricia. *Sumo: From Rite to Sport*. Tokyo: Weatherhill, 1980.

Daniels, Gordon. "Japanese Sport." In *Sport, Culture and Politics*, ed. J. C. Binfield and John Stevenson. Sheffield: Sheffield Academic Press, 1993. Pp. 168–187.

Davey, H. E. "The History and Legacy of Japan's Kokusai Budoin." *Journal of Asian Martial Arts*, 4:2 (1995): 54–63.

Dewanoumi Tomotaka, and Sakisaka Matsuhiko, *Ōzumō o miru tame no hon*. Tokyo: Dōbun shoin, 1985.

Diem, Carl. *Weltgeschichte des Sports*, 3rd ed. 2 vols. Frankfurt am Main: Cotta, 1971.

Donohue, John J. "Dancing in the Danger Zone." *Journal of Asian Martial Arts*, 1:1 (1992): 86–99.

————. *The Forge of the Spirit*. New York: Garland, 1991.

————. "Ideological Elasticity." *Journal of Asian Martial Arts*, 6:2 (1997): 10–25.

————. "The Ritual Dimension of *Karate-Do*." *Journal of Ritual Studies*, 7:1 (Winter 1993): 105–124.

Dore, R. P., ed. *Aspects of Social Change in Modern Japan*. Princeton: Princeton University Press, 1967.

Downer, Lesley. *The Brothers: The Saga of the Richest Family in Japan*. London: Chatto & Windus, 1994.

Draeger, Donn F. *The Martial Arts and Ways of Japan*. 3 vols. New York: Weatherhill, 1973–1974.

Draeger, Donn F., and Robert W. Smith. *Asian Fighting Arts*. Palo Alto: Kodansha International, 1969.

Duffy, Michael. "Mission Impossible." *Time*, January 20, 1992.

Dunning, Eric. "The Figurational Dynamics of Modern Sport." *Sportwissenschaft*, 9:4 (1979): 341–359.

————. *Sport Matters*. London: Routledge, 1999.

————. "The Structural-Functional Properties of Folk-Games and Modern Sports." *Sportwissenschaft*, 3:3 (1973): 215–232.

Dunning, Eric, and Kenneth Sheard. *Barbarians, Gentlemen and Players* Oxford: Martin Robertson, 1979.

Eguchi Hidehito. "Marine Sports and Leisure Are Growing Fast in Japan." *Business Japan,* 11 (November 1990): 129.

Eichberg, Henning. "Recording and Quantifying Is Not Natural.," *Stadion,* 3:2 (1977): 253–256.

Eisenstadt, S. N. *Japanese Civilization.* Chicago: University of Chicago Press, 1996.

Elias, Norbert, and Eric Dunning. *Quest for Excitement.* Oxford: Basil Blackwell, 1986.

———. *Sport im Zivilisationsprozeß.* Münster: LIT, 1983.

Esashi Shogō. *Josei supōtsu no shakaigaku.* Tokyo: Fumaidō, 1992.

Feather, N. T., and I. R. McKee. "Australian and Japanese Attitudes toward the Fall of High Achievers." *Australian Journal of Psychology,* 44:4 (1992): 87–93.

"55th Session of the International Olympic Committee, May 25–28, 1959." *Bulletin du C.I.O.* (August 15, 1959). Not paginated.

Frédéric, Louis. *Daily Life in Japan at the Time of the Samurai,* trans. Eileen M. Lowe. Tokyo: Charles E. Tuttle, 1973.

Friday, Karl F., with Seki Humitake. *Legacies of the Sword.* Honolulu: University of Hawaii Press, 1997.

Friedland, Jonathan. "Japan Shoots for Goal." *Far Eastern Economic Review.* 156 (June 17, 1993): 48–50.

Fujita Motoaki. "Supōtsu shūdan no un'ei keitai ni kan suru kenkyū." *Supōtsu shakaigaku kenkyū,* 3 (1995): 47–59.

Fujitake Akira. "Supōtsu shinbun." *Juristo zōkan sōgō tokushū,* 20 (1980): 214–219.

Fujiwara Kengo. "Physical Movement in the Aging Society of Japan." *International Review of Sport Sociology,* 22:2 (1987): 111–124.

Fujiyoshi Hisanori, and Tawara Takehiro. "Nanshiki tenisu." In *Saishin supōtsu daijiten,* ed. Kishino Yūzō. Tokyo: Taishūkan Shoten, 1987. Pp. 920–924.

Fukata Kyūya. "After Manaslu: Postwar Japanese Alpine Expeditions." *Japan Quarterly,* 12:3 (1965): 357–364.

Fukuoka T. "Research on Social Basis with Student Athletes at Upper Secondary School in Japan." *International Review of Sport Sociology,* 4 (1969): 53–58.

Fukusawa Hiroshi. "Kōreisha no yoka san'yo keisei yōin ni kan suru kenkyū." *Supōtsu shakaigaku kenkyū,* 4 (1996): 79–92.

Fukuzawa Yukichi. *Autobiography,* trans. Eiichi Kiyooka. New York: Schocken Books, 1972.

Funakoshi, Gichin. *Karate Dō: My Way of Life.* Tokyo: Kodansha, 1975.

Furuhashi, Hironoshin. "The Hosting of International Sports Events." *Japan 21st,* 39:6 (June 1994): 14–15.

Gabler, Hartmut. "Olympische Sieger und Siegerinnen." In *Olympischer Sport,* ed. Ommo Grupe. Schorndorf: Karl Hofmann, 1997. Pp. 181–209.

Galas, S. Matthew. "Kindred Spirits." *Journal of Asian Martial Arts,* 6:3 (1997): 20–47.

Gillmeister, Heiner. *Tennis.* Leicester: Leicester University Press, 1997.

Ginsberg, Laura. "The Hard Work of Working Out." *Journal of Sport and Social Issues,* 24:3 (August 2000): 260–281.

Goldstein, Carl. "Colours to the Mast." *Far Eastern Economic Review,* 151 (February 28, 1991): 66–67.

———. "The Corporate Pitch." *Far Eastern Economic Review,* 151 (February 28, 1991): 64–67.

———. "Japan's Spoilsports," *Far Eastern Economic Review,* 151 (February 28, 1991): 67–68.

Goldstein-Gidoni, Ofra. *Packaged Japaneseness.* Honolulu: University of Hawaii Press, 1997.

Goodger, B. C., and J. M. Goodger. "Judo in the Light of Theory and Sociological Research." *International Review of Sport Sociology,* 12:2 (1977): 5–34.

———. "Organizational and Cultural Change in Post-War British Judo." *International Review of Sport Sociology,* 15:1 (1980): 21–48.

Graburn, Nelson H. H. "Work and Play in the Japanese Countryside." In *The Culture of Japan as Seen through its Leisure,* ed. Sepp Linhart and Sabine Frühstück. Albany: SUNY Press, 1998. Pp. 195–212.

Grix, Arthur E. *Japan's Sport.* Berlin: Limpert, 1938.

Guttmann, Allen. *From Ritual to Record.* New York: Columbia University Press, 1978.

———. *Games and Empires.* New York: Columbia Unversity Press, 1996.

———. *The Games Must Go On: Avery Brundage and the Olympic Movement.* New York: Columbia University Press, 1984.

———. *The Olympics.* Urbana: University of Illinois Press, 1992.

———. *A Whole New Ball Game.* Chapel Hill: University of North Carolina Press, 1988.

———. *Women's Sports.* New York: Columbia University Press, 1991.

Hagiwara, Miyoko. "Japanese Women's Sports and Physical Education under the Influence of Their Traditional Costumes." In *Civilization in Sport History,* ed. Shigeo Shimizu. Kobe: Kobe University, 1987. Pp. 257–269.

Hakett, Roger F. "The Meiji Leaders and Modernization." In *Changing Japanese Attitudes toward Modernization,* ed. Marius B. Jansen. Princeton: Princeton University Press, 1965. Pp. 243–273.

Haley, Bruce. *The Healthy Body and Victorian Culture.* Cambridge, Mass.: Harvard University Press, 1978.

Hall, Francis. *Japan through American Eyes.* Princeton: Princeton University Press, 1992.

Hall, John Whitney. "Changing Conceptions of Modenization in Japan." In *Changing Japanese Attitudes toward Modernization,* ed. Marius B. Jansen. Princeton: Princeton University Press, 1965. Pp. 43–89.

———. *Japan: From Prehistory to Modern Times.* Tokyo: Charles E. Tuttle, 1971.

Hanson, Richard. "Letter from Korakuen." *Far Eastern Economic Review,* 138 (November 19, 1987): 116.

Hashimoto Kazuo. *Nihon supōtsu hōsōshi.* Tokyo: Taishūkan shoten, 1992.

Hata, Yoshie. "The Influence of Protestantism of [sic] Modern Physical Education in Japan." In *Civilization in Sport History*, ed. Shigeo Shimizu. Kobe: Kobe University, 1987. Pp. 77–86.

Hatano, Yoshiro, Ayako Ota, and Noriko Sudo. "Cross-Cultural Comparison of Public Image on Female Participation in Sport." In *Proceedings of FISU/CESU Conference*. Kobe: Kobe kokusai kōryū kaikan, 1985. Pp. 186–192.

Hayasaka Shōji. "Inuoumono." In *Saishin supōtsu daijiten*, ed. Kishino Yūzō. Tokyo: Taishūkan shoten, 1987. Pp. 81–82.

———. "Kasagake." In *Saishin supōtsu daijiten*, ed. Kishino Yūzō. Tokyo: Taishūkan shoten, 1987. Pp. 164–165.

———. "Yabusame." In *Saishin supōtsu daijiten*, ed. Kishino Yūzō. Tokyo: Taishūkan shoten, 1987. Pp. 1261–1263.

Hayase Keiichi. *Hirao Seiji hengen jizai ni*. Osaka: Mainichi shimbunsha, 1997.

Hayashi Ikuko and Yamamoto Tokuro. "*A Treatise on Gymnastics* (1828) no kenkyū." *Taiikushi kenkyū*, 7 (March 1990): 1–9.

Hazan, Baruch. *Olympic Sports and Propaganda Games*. New Brunswick: Transaction Books, 1982.

Hendry, Joy. *Understanding Japanese Society*. London: Croom, Helm, 1987.

Herrigel, Eugen. *Zen in der Kunst des Bogenschiessens*. Tübigen: Otto-Wilhelm Barth, 1975.

Hesselink, Reinier H. "The Warrior's Prayer: Tokugawa Yoshimune Revives the Yabusame Ceremony." *Journal of Asian Martial Arts*, 4:4 (1995): 40–49.

Higashi Michio. *1912 nen orimpikku, ano natsu no otokotachi*. Tokyo: Shinchō, 1996.

Higashimoto Haruo. "Supōtsu no shakai ni okeru 'iiwake.'" *Supōtsu shakaigaku kenkyū*, 2 (1994): 95–101.

Hirai Hajime. "'Supōtsu no chikyūka' o megutte." *Supōtsu shakaigaku kenkyū*, 2 (1994): 103–106.

Hirano Hideaki. "Shintai bunkaron no igi." *Supōtsu shakaigaku kenkyū*, 2 (1994): 23–33.

Hobsbawm, Eric, and Terence Ranger, eds. *The Invention of Tradition* Cambridge: Cambridge University Press, 1983.

Homma Shuku. "Archery as a Contest." In *Proceedings of the 1991 ISHPES Congress*, ed. Roland Renson, Teresa Gonzalez Aja, Gilbert Andrieu, Manfred Lämmer, and Roberta Park. Madrid: Instituto Nacional de Educación Fisica de Madrid, 1993. Pp. 106–113.

Horne, John D. "Aspects of Postmodernism and Body Culture." *Supōtsu shakaigaku kenkyū*, 2 (1994): 1–18.

———. "The Politics of Sport and Leisure in Japan." *International Review of Sport Sociology*, 33:2 (June 1998): 171–182.

———. "'Sakka' in Japan." *Media, Culture and Society*, 18:4 (October 1996): 527–547.

———. "Soccer in Japan: Is *Wa* All You Need?" *Culture, Sport, Society*, 2:3 (Autumn 1999): 212–229.

Hoshino, Harunaka. "Bladed Weapons." *Journal of Asian Martial Arts,* 2:1 (1993): 93–108.

Howell, Colin D. "On Metcalfe, Marx, and Materialism." *Sport History Review,* 29:1 (May 1998): 96–102.

Hulme, Derick L., Jr. *The Political Olympics.* New York: Praeger, 1990.

Hurst, G. Cameron III. *Armed Martial Arts of Japan: Swordsmanship and Archery.* New Haven: Yale University Press, 1998.

———. *Insei: Abdicated Sovereigns in the Politics of Late Heian Japan, 1086–1185.* New York: Columbia University Press, 1976.

Ikeda Masao. *Sumō no rekishi.* Tokyo: Heibonsha, 1977.

Imamura, Hiroyuki. "Philosophy and History of Japanese Martial Arts." *Journal of Asian Martial Arts,* 1:4 (1992): 51–62.

Imamura Yoshio. *Nihon taiiku shi.* Tokyo: Fumaidō, 1970.

Inagaki Masahiro. "Shizentaiiku no seiritsu katei ni tsuite." *Taiikushi kenkyū,* 1 (March 1984): 6–10.

———. *Supōtsu no kōkindai.* Tokyo: Sanseidō, 1995.

Inoue Shun. "Budō." In *The Culture of Japan as Seen through its Leisure,* ed. Sepp Linhart and Sabine Frühstück. Albany: SUNY Press, 1998. Pp. 83–93.

———. "The Invention of the Martial Arts." In *Mirror of Modernity: Invented Traditions of Modern Japan,* ed. Stephen Vlastos. Berkeley: University of California Press, 1998. Pp. 163–173.

Irie Katsumi. *Nihon fashizumu ka no taiikushiso.* Tokyo: Fumaidō, 1986.

———. *Nihon kindai taiiku no shisō kōzō.* Tokyo: Meiseki Shoten, 1988.

Ise Akifumi. *Hashiru!* Tokyo: Futabasha, 1996.

Ishii Masayuki. "Orimpizumu to tabunka shugi." *Taiiku no kagaku,* 46:8 (1996): 631–635.

Ishii Tsuneo, ed. *Puro yakyū no jiten,* Tokyo: Sanseidō, 1986.

Itai Keisuke. *Nakabon.* Tokyo: Shōgakkan, 2000.

Itō Akira. "Chikaraishi." In *Saishin supōtsu daijiten,* ed. Kishino Yūzō. Tokyo: Taishūkan shoten, 1987. Pp. 782–783.

———. "Tōkyō to Daitōku nai no chikaraishi no chōsa kenkyū." *Taiikushi kenkyū,* 4 (March 1987): 1–10.

———. "Tōkyōto Itabashiku nai no chikaraishi no chōsa kenkyū." *Taiikushi kenkyū,* 5 (March 1988): 34–40.

———. "Tōkyōto Suginamiku Ōmiya Ōmiya Hachimangū no chikaraishi no kenkyū." *Taiikushi kenkyū,* 2 (March 1985): 6–11.

Itō Kazuo. "Puro yakyū." In *Saishin supōtsu daijten,* ed. Kishino Yūzō. Tokyo: Taishūkan shoten, 1987. Pp. 1126–1135.

Itō Kimio. "The Invention of *Wa* and the Transformation of the Image of Prince Shōtoku in Modern Japan." In *Mirror of Modernity: Invented Traditions of Modern Japan,* ed. Stephen Vlastos. Berkeley: University of California Press, 1998. Pp. 37–47.

Ivy, Marilyn. *Discourses of the Vanishing.* Chicago: University of Chicago Press, 1995.

Iwaoka Hōmai. "Dakyū." In *Saishin supōtsu daijiten,* ed. Kishino Yūzō. Tokyo: Taishūkan shoten, 1987. Pp. 752–754.

Jansen, Marius B. *Japan and Its World.* Princeton: Princeton University Press, 1980.

Jansen, Marius B., ed. *Changing Japanese Attitudes toward Modernization.* Princeton: Princeton University Press, 1965.

Johnson, Elmer L. *The History of YMCA Physical Education.* Chicago: Follett, 1979.

Kalab, Kathleen A. "Playing Gateball: A Game of the Japanese Elderly." *Journal of Aging Studies,* 6:1 (1992): 23–40.

Kaneda, Eiko. "Trends in Traditional Women's Sumo in Japan." *International Journal of the History of Sport,* 16:3 (September 1999): 113–119.

Kaneyoshi Yasuyuki and Matsumoto Yoshiaki. *Gendai seikatsu no supōtsu bunka.* Tokyo: Taishūkan shoten, 1997.

Kano Jigoro. *Kodokan Judo.* Tokyo: Kodansha International, 1986.

Karaki, Kunihiko. "Die aufgegebenen Olympischen Spiele in Tokio 1940." *Hitotsubashi Journal of Arts and Sciences,* 23 (December 1982): 60–70.

Kashihara Masataka. "Puroresu wa naze supōtsu de wa nai no ka." *Supōtsu shakaigaku kenkyū,* 4 (1996): 51–62.

Kawahara Kazue. "'Fittonesu' genshō e no shiten." *Supōtsu shakaigaku kenkyū,* 3 (1995): 37–45.

Kawanari Yō. *Maboroshi no orimpikku.* Tokyo: Chikuma Shobō, 1992.

Kawanashi Masashi, Kitamura Takahiro, and Tomiyama Kōzō. "Chūkōnen supōtsu sankasha no seikatsu manzokudo—zenkoku supo-reku matsuri sankasha ni tsuite." *Supōtsu shakaigaku kenkyū,* 4 (1996): 93–105.

Keene, Donald. *The Japanese Discovery of Europe, 1720–1830.* Rev. ed. Stanford: Stanford Unversity Press, 1969.

———. "The Sino-Japanese War of 1894–95 and Its Cultural Effects in Japan." In *Tradition and Modernization in Japanese Culture,* ed. Donald H. Shively. Princeton: Princeton University Press, 1971. Pp. 121–175.

Kelly, William W. "An Anthropologist in the Bleachers: Cheering a Japanese Baseball Team." *Japan Quarterly,* 44:4 (October–December 1997): 66–79.

———. "Blood and Guts in Japanese Professional Baseball." In *The Culture of Japan as Seen through Its Leisure,* ed. Sepp Linhart and Sabine Frühstück. Albany: SUNY Press, 1998. Pp. 95–111.

———. "Learning to Swing: Oh Sadaharu and the Pedagogy and Practice of Japanese Baseball." In *Learning in Likely Places.* New York: Cambridge University Press, 1998. Pp. 265–285.

———. "'Men at Work': What Does Professional Baseball Demonstrate in Contemporary Japan?" (paper presented at a conference on "Sports and Body Culture in Modern Japan," Yale University, March 31–April 2, 2000).

Kemari hozonkai. *Kemari hozonkai kyūjūnenshi.* Kyoto: Kemari hozonkai, 1997.

Kenrick, Vivienne. *Horses in Japan.* London: J. A. Allen, 1964.

Kiku Kōichi. *"Kindai puro supōtsu" no rekishi shakaigaku.* Tokyo: Fumaidō, 1993.

King, Winston L. *Zen and the Way of the Sword*. New York: Oxford University Press, 1993.

Kinoshita Hideaki. *Supōtsu no kindai nihonshi*. Tokyo: Kyōrin shoin, 1970.

Kinser, Maggie. "Body Beautifuls [sic]." *Tokyo Journal*, 7:6 (September 1987): 36–39.

Kisanuki Hisayo, and Esashi Shōgo. "Sakkā no kansen dōki ni mirareru seisa no kentō." *Supōtsu shakaigaku kenkyū*, 4 (1996): 106–114.

Kishino Yūzō, ed. *Saishin supōtsu daijiten*. Tokyo: Taishūkan shoten, 1987.

Kiyota, Minoru. *Kendō*. London: Kegan Paul International, 1995.

Kiyokawa Masaji. *Supōtsu to seiji*. Tokyo: Baseball Magazine, 1987.

———. "'Swimming into History.'" *Citius Altius Fortius*, 5:3 (Fall 1997): 10–14.

Klaus, Franz. "Gedenken an Generalmajor Theodor von Lerch." *Zdarsky-Blätter*, 34–35 (December 1985–March 1986): 2–3, 5–13.

Knecht, Willi. *Der Boycott*. Cologne: Verlag Wissenschaft und Politik, 1980.

Könning, Willi. *Spitzensport in Japan*. Bonn: Dieter Born, 1990.

Komuku, Hiroshi. "Japanese Top-Athletes' Attitudes toward their Sports Careers." *International Review of Sport Sociology*, 17:2 (1982): 71–78.

Korube deitamu henshūshitsu, ed. *Orimpikku deita bukku*. Tokyo: Kolbe Publishing, 1984.

Koyama Takashige. "Nihon kyūdō gairon." In *Gendai kyūdō kōza*, ed. Uno Yōzaburō. Tokyo: Yūzankaku, 1980. Pp. 1–61.

Kozonoi Masaki. "Senzen no Kitakyūshū chihō ni okeru kigyōnai supōtsu no kenkyū." *Taiikushi kenkyū*, 9 (March 1992): 33–43.

Kōzu, Masaru. "The Development of Sports in Japanese Agricultural Districts." *Hitotsubashi Journal of Arts and Sciences*, 21:1 (1980): 40–51.

———. *Nihon kindai supōtsushi no teiryū*. Tokyo: Sōbun kikaku, 1994.

Krüger, Arnd, and Ito Akira. "On the Limitations of Eichberg's and Mandell's Theory of Sports and the Quantification in View of Chikaraishi." *Stadion*, 3:2 (1977): 244–252.

Kühnst, Peter. *Sports*. Dresden: Verlag der Kunst, 1996.

Kuhaulua, Jesse. *Takamiyama*. Tokyo: Kodansha, 1973.

Kusaka, Yuko. "The Development of Baseball Organizations in Japan." *International Review of Sport Sociology*, 22:4 (1987): 263–277.

———. "Nihon no shizenyū." *Supōtsu shakaigaku kenkyū*, 3 (1995): 27–36.

Lebra, Joyce. "Women in Sports." In *Women in Changing Japan*, ed Joyce Lebra, Joy Paulson, and Elizabeth Powers. Stanford: Stanford University Press, 1978. Pp. 255–262.

Lebra, Takie Sugiyama. *Japanese Women*. Honolulu: University of Hawaii Press, 1984.

Leonard, Wilbert M. II, and Hiroshi Komuku. "Japanese College Students' Attitudes toward Intercollegiate Athletics." *Journal of Sport Behavior*, 12:2 (June 1989): 59–76.

Lewis, Archibald. *Knights and Samurai.* London: Temple Smith, 1974.

Light, Richard. "A Centenary of Rugby and Masculinity in Japanese Schools and Universities." *Sporting Traditions,* 16:2 (May 2000): 87–104.

Linhart, Sepp, and Sabine Frühstück, eds. *The Culture of Japan as Seen through Its Leisure.* Albany: SUNY Press, 1998.

Long, Joe. "Jujutsu." *Journal of Asian Martial Arts,* 6:4 (1997): 62–75.

*Los Angeles Times.* August 10, 1928.

Loy, John W., James E. Curtis, and James M. Hillen. "Effects of Formal Structure on Mangerial Recruitment." *Sociology of Sport Journal,* 4:1 (March 1987): 1–16.

Lucas, John. *The Modern Olympic Games.* New York: A. S. Barnes, 1980.

McClain, James L. "Cultural Chauvinism and the Olympiads of East Asia." *International Journal of the History of Sport,* 7:3 (December 1990): 388–404.

McCormack, Gavan. "The Price of Affluence: The Political Economy of Japanese Leisure." *New Left Review,* 188 (1991): 121–134.

Machida Ryōichi. "Shinano ni okeru kemari no ryūkō." *Shinano,* 3:12 (1951): 42–50.

Maegerlein, Heinz. *Olympia 1960.* Frankfurt: Wilhlem Limpert, 1960.

Maezono Masakiyo. *Doriburu.* Tokyo: Baseball Magazine, 1996.

Magoun, Francis P. *History of Football.* Bochum-Langendreer: Kölner Anglistische Studien, 1966.

*Mainichi Shinbun.* January 21, 1900.

Mandell, Richard. "The Invention of the Sports Record." *Stadion,* 2:2 (1976): 250–264.

Mandell, Richard D. *The Nazi Olympics.* New York: Macmillan, 1971.

Manzenreiter, Wolfram. *Die soziale Konstruktion des japanischen Alpinismus.* Vienna: Institut für Ostasienwissenschaften, 2000.

Masujima Midori. *Samenai yume.* Tokyo: Za masada, 2000.

Masukawa Kōichi. "Supōtsu to kake." In *Saishin supōtsu daijiten,* ed. Koshina Yūzō. Tokyo: Taishūkan shoten, 1987. Pp. 624–627.

Matsumoto Junko. "Yamaguchiken Yoshikimura no ryōjō seinenkai 'undōbu' (1886–1937) ni kansuru shiteki kōsatsu." *Taiikushi kenkyū,* 10 (March 1993): 29–42.

Matsumura, Kazunori. "Sport and Social Change in the Japanese Rural Community." *International Review of Sport Sociology,* 28:2–3 (1993): 135–142.

May, William R. "Seishin" (unpublished paper, 1988).

———. "Sports." In *The Handbook of Japanese Popular Culture,* ed. Richard Gid Powers and Hidetoshi Kato. Westport: Greenwood Press, 1989. Pp. 167–195.

Mayeda, David Tokiharu. "From Model Minority to Economic Threat." *Journal of Sport and Social Issues,* 23:2 (May 99): 203–217.

Michihara Shinji. "Karatedō." In *Saishin supōtsu daijiten,* ed. Kishino Yūzō. Tokyo: Taishūkan shoten, 1987. Pp. 186–191.

Mishima, Yukio. *Acts of Worship,* trans. John Bester. Tokyo: Kodansha, 1989.

———. *Confessions of a Mask,* trans. Meredith Weatherby. New York: New Directions, 1958.

———. *Spring Snow,* trans. Michael Gallagher. Tokyo: Charles E. Tuttle, 1972.

———. *Sun and Steel,* trans. John Bester. New York: Grove, 1976.

Mitchell, Richard H. *Thought Control in Prewar Japan.* Ithaca: Cornell University Press, 1976.

Miyamoto Musashi. *The Book of Five Rings,* trans. Thomas Cleary. Boston: Shambhala, 1993.

Miyoshi, Masao. "Against the Native Grain." In *Postmodernism and Japan,* ed. Masao Miyoshi and H. D. Harootunian. Durham: Duke University Press, 1989. Pp. 143–168.

Miyoshi, Masao, and H. D. Harootunian, eds. *Postmodernism and Japan.* Durham: Duke University Press, 1989.

"Mizuno," *Olympic Magazine,* No. 11 (November 1996): 28–30.

Möller, Jörg. "Der deutsche Arzt Erwin von Bälz and die Entwicklung von Körperkultur und Sport in Japan." *Stadion,* 16:1 (1990): 129–141.

———. *Spiel und Sport am japanischen Kaiserhof.* Munich: Iudicium, 1993.

———. *Sumo-Kampf und Kult.* Sankt Augustin: Academia, 1990.

Mombushō kyōgi supōtsu kenkyūkai ed, *"Miru supōtsu" no shinkō.* Tokyo: Baseball Magazine, 1996.

Monday, Nyle C. "The Ryu-Ha System." *Journal of Asian Martial Arts,* 3:1 (1994): 72–81.

Moon, Okpyo. *From Paddy Field to Ski Slope.* Manchester: Manchester University Press, 1989.

Morikawa, Sadao. "Amateurism-Yesterday, Today and Tomorrow." *International Review of Sport Sociology,* 12:2 (1977): 61–72.

———. "Fundamental Problems of Studies in Amateur Sport." *International Review of Sport Sociology,* 19:1 (1979): 21–50.

Morikawa, Sadao, and John Rogers. "Sports Sociology in Japan." *International Review of Sport Sociology,* 22:1 (1987): 51–61.

Morley, Patricia. *The Mountain Is Moving: Japanese Women's Lives.* New York: New York University Press, 1999.

Morris, Kathleen. "How Japan Scored." *Financial World,* 164 (February 14, 1995): 82–85.

Morris-Suzuki, Tessa. "The Invention and Reinvention of 'Japanese Culture.'" *Journal of Asian Studies,* 54:3 (August 1995): 759–780.

Mosch, Norbert. "Die politsiche Funktion des Sports in Japan und Korea am Beispiel zweier Nationalsportarten: Judo und Taekwondo—Ein Vergleich" (Ph.D. dissertation; University of Vienna, 1987).

Mravic, Mark. "Scorecard: Say it Ain't Sumo!" *Sports Illustrated,* 92:7 (February 21, 2000): 24.

Müller, Günter R., and Dieter Kühnle. *Moskauer Spiele.* Gütersloh: Bertelsmann, 1980.

Müller, Norbert, and Joachim K. Rühl, eds. *Olympic Scientific Congress 1984 Official Report Sport History.* Niederhausern: Schors, 1985.

Muramatsu, Teijiro. *Westerners in the Modernization of Japan.* Tokyo: Hitachi, 1995.

Murasaki Shikibu. *Genji Monogatari,* trans. Edward Seidensticker. New York: Knopf, 1976.

Naismith, James. "Basketball." *American Physical Education Review,* 19:5 (May 1914): 339–351.

————. *Basketball.* New York: Association Press, 1941.

Najita Tetsuo, and Irwin Scheiner, eds. *Japanese Thought in the Tokugawa Period, 1600–1868.* Chicago: University of Chicago Press, 1978.

Nakamura Tamio. "Kindai budōshi kenkyūhō." *Taiikushi kenkyū,* 1 (March 1984): 21–25.

Nakamura Toshio. *Nihon teki supōtsu kankyō hihan.* Tokyo: Taishūkan shoten, 1995.

Nakamura Toshio, Izuhara Yoshiaki, and Todoriki Kenji. *Gendai supōtsuron: supōtsu no jidai o dō tsukuruka.* Tokyo: Taishūkan shoten, 1988.

Neide, Joan. "Martial Arts and Japanese Nationalism." *Journal of Asian Martial Arts,* 4:2 (1995): 34–41.

Newman, Bruce. "Japan—Coming on Strong." *Sports Illustrated,* 71:18 (August 21, 1989): 85.

Nihon sumō kyōkai hakubutsukan un'ei iin, ed. *Kinsei Nihon sumō shi.* 5 vols. Tokyo: Baseball Magazine, 1975–1981.

Nihon Supōtsu Shakaigakkai, ed. *Henyō suru gendai shakai to supōtsu.* Kyoto: Sekai shisōsha, 1998.

*Nihongi,* trans. W. G. Aston. 2 vols. Rutland: Charles E. Tuttle, 1972.

Nishimura Ayako. "Senzen kyōiku shingikai no shingi ni mirareru kōtō kyōiku kikan no taiiku mondai ni tsuite." *Taiikushi kenkyū,* 3 (March 1986): 8–15.

————. "Zenkoku kōtō jogakkōchō kaigi ni mirareru kōtō jogakkō no taiiku mondai." *Taiikushi kenkyū,* 5 (March 1988): 7–21.

Nishiyama Matsunosuke. *Edo Culture,* trans. Gerald Groemer. Honolulu: University of Hawaii Press, 1997.

Nishiyama Tetsuo. "Supōtsu no hon'yaku: dankyū seido to sono shūhen." *Supōtsu shakaigaku kenkyū,* 2 (1994): 35–51.

Nitobe, Inazo. *Bushido: The Soul of Japan.* Rutland: Charles E. Tuttle, 1969.

Nitta Ichirō. *Sumō no rekishi.* Tokyo: Yamakawa shuppansha, 1994.

Nogawa, Haruo, and Hiroka Maeda. "The Japanese Dream." In *Football Cultures and Identities,* ed. Gary Armstrong and Richard Giulianotti. Houndsmill: Macmillan, 1999. Pp. 223–233.

Nonomiya, Toru. "Lingianism and the Natural Method in Japan." In *Proceedings of the HISPA International Congress,* ed. J. A. Mangan. Glasgow: HISPA, 1985. Pp. 335–336.

Norflus, David. "Baseball: A Mirror of Japanese Society.," *Arena Newsletter,* 1:6 (October 1977): 9–12.

Nose Shūichi. "Shihan gakka torishirabe to taisō." *Taiikushi kenkyū*, 1 (March 1984): 11–15.

Obinata Katsumi. *Kodai kokka to nenjū gyōji*. Tokyo: Yoshikawa kōbunkan, 1993.

Obojski, Robert. *The Rise of Japanese Baseball Power*. Radnor: Chilton, 1975.

Oh, Sadaharu, and David Faulkner. *Sadaharu Oh*. New York: Times Books, 1984.

Ohara Toshihiko. *Hitome Kinue monogatari*. Tokyo: Asahi shinbunsha, 1990.

Oinuma Yoshihiro. "Ōzumō ni okeru heyaseido no rekishi." *Tōkai daigaku taiikugakubu kiyō*, 10 (1980): 11–16.

———. *Sumōshakai no kenkyū*. Tokyo: Fumaidō, 1994.

Oinuma, Yoshihiro, and Mitsuru Shimpo. "The Social System of the Sumo Training School." *International Review of Sport Sociology*, 18:1 (1983): 7–19.

*Ōkagami*, trans. Helen Craig McCullough. Princeton: Princeton University Press, 1980.

Ōkubō Hideaki. "Meiji 4–12 nen (1871–1879) no Kanazawa Igakukan ni okeru taisō kyōiku." *Taiikushi kenkyū*, 12 (March 1995): 1–10.

Olson, Harold James. "Japan at the Olympic Games, 1909–1938" (M.A. thesis; California State Polytechnic University, 1991).

Ōnaruto oyakata, moto. *Yaochō*. Tokyo: Rokusaisha, 1996.

Ono Akira. *Gendai supōtsu hihan*. Tokyo: Taishūkan shoten, 1996.

Ooms, Emily Groszos. *Women and Millenarian Protest in Japan*. Ithaca: Cornell University Press, 1993.

Ōtsuka Mieko. "Ono (Hatakeyama) Genzō ron." *Taiikushi kenkyū*, 8 (March 1991): 31–42.

———. "1920 nendai Hokkaidō taiiku ni tsuite: Mizuma Kazuto no taiiku riron o chūshin ni." *Taiikushi kenkyū*, 6 (March 1989): 38–48.

Peiser, Benny Josef. "Karate." In: *Encyclopedia of World Sport*, ed. David Levinson and Karen Christensen. 3 vols. Santa Barbara: ABC-CLIO, 1996. 2:541–545.

Pempel, T. J. "Contemporary Japanese Athletics." In *The Culture of Japan as Seen through its Leisure*, ed. Sepp Linhart and Sabine Frühstück. Albany: SUNY Press, 1998. Pp. 113–137.

Peng, Fred C., Tomoko Hongo, and Masako Nakawaki. "Nonverbal Expressions of Rituals in Japanese Sumo." *Semiotica*, 17:1 (1976): 1–12.

Perrin, Noel. *Giving Up the Gun*. Boston: Godine, 1979.

Plath, David W. "Land of the Rising Sunday." *Japan Quarterly*, 7:3 (1960): 357–361.

Polley, Martin. "Olympic Diplomacy: The British Government and the Projected 1940 Olympic Games." *International Journal of the History of Sport*, 9:2 (August 1992): 169–187.

Raita, Kyoko. "The Movement for the Promotion of Competitive Women's Sport in Japan, 1924–35." *International Journal of the History of Sport*, 16:3 (September 1999): 120–134.

———. "Nihon joshi orimpikku taikai to josei kyōgi supōtsu sanka sokushin undo." *Taiikushi kenkyū*, 13 (March 1996): 39–52.

Ratti, Oscar, and Adele Westbrook. *Secrets of the Samurai.* Rutland: Charles E. Tuttle, 1973.

Reader, Ian. "Studies of Japan, Area Studies, and the Challenge of Social Theory." *Monumenta Nipponica,* 53:2 (Summer 1998): 237–255.

———. "Sumo: The Recent History of an Ethical Model for Japanese Society." *International Journal of the History of Sport,* 6:3 (December 1989): 285–298.

Redmond, Gerald, ed. *Sport and Politics.* Champaign: Human Kinetics, 1986.

Reischauer, Edwin O. *The Japanese.* Cambridge, Mass.: Harvard University Press, 1977.

———. "A Union of Two Worlds." *Sports Illustrated,* 19 (December 23, 1963): 50–54.

Reischauer, Edwin O., and Albert M. Craig. *Japan.* Tokyo: Charles E. Tuttle, 1978.

Ren Hai. "China and the Olympic Movement." In *Sport and Physical Education in China,* ed. James Riordan and Robin Jones. London: E and FN Spon, 1999. Pp. 202–213.

Rimmer, Peter J. "Japanese Investment in Golf Course Development." *International Journal of Urban and Regional Research,* 18 (1994): 234–255.

Roden, Donald. "Baseball and the Quest for National Dignity in Meiji Japan." *American Historical Review,* 85:3 (June 1980): 511–534.

———. *Schooldays in Imperial Japan.* Berkeley: University of California Press, 1980.

Rogers, John M. "Arts of War in Time of Peace." *Monumenta Nipponica,* 45:4 (Fall 1990): 413–447.

Rosario, Louise do. "News-Stand Stars." *Far Eastern Economic Review,* 155 (December 24, 1992): 21.

Roscoe, N. K. "The Development of Sport in Japan." *Transactions and Proceedings of the Japan Society,* 30 (1933): 53–71.

Rosenberg, Daniel. "The Martial Arts and American Violence." *Journal of Asian Martial Arts,* 4:2 (1955): 11–33.

Rushin, Steve. "Planet Nagano." *Sports Illustrated,* 88:5 (February 9, 1998): 82–89.

Saeki, Toshio. "Sport in Japan." In *Sport in Asia and Africa,* ed. Eric A. Wagner. Westport: Greenwood Press, 1989. Pp. 51–82.

———. "The Conflict between Tradition and Modernity in a Sport Organization." *International Review of Sport Sociology,* 29:3 (1994): 301–313.

Sakai Tadamasa. *Nihon sumō shi.* 2 vols. Tokyo: Baseball Magazine, 1956–1964.

Sakaue, Yasuhiro. "Kendo." In *Encyclopedia of World Sport,* ed. David Levinson and Karen Christensen, 3 vols. Santa Barbara: ABC-CLIO, 1996. 2:547–550.

———. "Taishōki ni okeru Dainippon Butokukai . . . ." *Taiikushi kenkyū,* 7 (March 1990): 37–51.

Sanada Hisashi. "Kindai orimpikku sōsetsu no jidaiteki yōin." *Taiiku no kagaku,* 46:8 (1996): 626–630.

Sansom, George B. *A History of Japan.* 3 vols. Tokyo: Charles E. Tuttle, 1974.

————. *The Western World and Japan.* New York: Knopf, 1950.

Sasajima, Kohsuke. "History of Physical Education and Sport in Ancient Japan." *Canadian Journal of History of Sport,* 19:2 (December 1988): 57–61.

————. "History of Physical Education and Sport in Japan." In *Geschichte der Leibesübungen,* ed. Horst Ueberhorst, 6 vols. Berlin: Bartels & Wernitz, 1971–89. 4:190–214.

————. "Social Meaning of History of Sport and Its Social Role." *Zeitschrift für Kulturaustausch,* 27:4 (1977): 52–55.

Sasase Masashi. "Hokkaidō Teikoku Daigaku suki bu ni okeru tozan to kyōgi— 1912 nen-1926 nen no katsudō kiroku kara." *Taiikushi kenkyū,* 11 (March 1994): 41–54.

Sase Minoru. *Orimpikku: hirōtachi no nemuranai yoru.* Tokyo: Sekai bunkasha, 1996.

Sato, Hiroaki, ed. *The Sword and the Mind.* New York: Overlook Press, 1986.

Satō Jirō, ed. *Supōtsu mō hitotsu no fūkei.* Tokyo: Tokyo shimbun, 1995.

Satow, Ernest. *A Diplomat in Japan.* New York: ICG Muse, 2000.

Schaap, Dick. *An Illustrated History of the Olympics.* 3rd ed. New York: Knopf, 1976.

Seckler, Jonathan. "Swordsmanship and Neo-Confucianism." *Journal of Asian Martial Arts,* 1:2 (1992): 71–83.

Seidensticker, Edward. *Low City, High City.* New York: Knopf, 1983.

Sei Shōnagon. *Makura no sōshi,* ed. Ikeda Kikan, Kishigami Shinji, and Akiyama Ken. NKBT 19. Tokyo: Iwanami shoten, 1958.

Seiwa, Hiroko, and Chieko Onishi. "Women and Athletic Meetings in Japan"(unpublished paper, ISHPES Conference, Lyon, 1997).

Seki Harunami and Karaki Kunihiko. *Supōtsu wa dare no tame ni.* Tokyo: Taishūkan shoten, 1995.

Sharnoff, Lora. *Grand Sumo.* Rev, ed. New York: Weatherhill, 1993.

Shimizu Shigeo. "Amorosu 'Jimunasuchiku sho' (1839 nen) ni okeru supōtsu kyōgi no kannen." *Taiikushi kenkyū,* 8 (March 1991): 15–30.

————. "Orimpizumu wa naze yōsei sareta no ka." *Taiiku no kagaku,* 46:8 (1996): 614–620.

Shimizu, Shigeo, ed. *Civilization in Sport History.* Kobe: Kobe University, 1987.

Shine, Jerry. "*Honcho Bugei Shoden:* The Original Martial Arts Survey." *Journal of Asian Martial Arts,* 3:4 (1994): 104–107.

Sinclair, Robert J. "Baseball's Rising Sun." *Canadian Journal of History of Sport,* 16:2 (December 1985): 44–53.

Shishida Fumiaki. "Aikidō." In *Saishin supōtsu daijiten,* ed. Kishino Yūzō. Tokyo: Taishūkan shoten, 1987. Pp. 1–3.

Shively, Donald H. "The Japanization of the Middle Meij." In *Tradition and Modernization in Japanese Culture,* ed. Donald H. Shively. Princeton: Princeton University Press, 1971. Pp. 77–119.

————. "Nishimura Shigeki." In *Changing Japanese Attitudes toward Modernization,* ed. Marius B. Jansen. Princeton: Princeton University Press, 1965. Pp. 193–241.

Shively, Donald H., ed. *Tradition and Modernization in Japanese Culture.* Princeton: Princeton University Press, 1971.

Singleton, John, ed. *Learning in Likely Places.* Cambridge: Cambridge University Press, 1998.

Smith, Robert J. *Japanese Society.* Cambridge: Cambridge University Press, 1983

Sōgawa Tsuneo. "Gitchō." In *Saishin supōtsu daijiten,* ed. Kishino Yūzō. Tokyo: Taishūkan shoten, 1987. Pp. 201–203.

Sōgawa Tsuneo. *Kindai supōtsu no genzai.* Tokyo: Nihon tosho sentā, 1996. Sōgawa's name sometimes appears as "Samukawa" in American library catalogues.

Sollier, André, and Gyōburo Zsolt. *Japanese Archery: Zen in Action.* New York: Weatherhill, 1969.

Sonoda Sekiya. "Geitobōru." In *Saishin supōtsu daijiten,* ed. Kishino Yūzō. Tokyo: Taishūkan shoten, 1987. Pp. 275–276.

Soon Hee Whang."The Body as Culture: The Case of the Sumo Wrestler" (paper presented at a conference on "Sports and Body Culture in Modern Japan," Yale University, March 31–April 2, 2000).

———. "Bunka to shite no shintai: rikishi no ba'ai." *Supōtsu shakaigaku kenkyū,* 4 (1996): 23–33.

Soviak, Eugene. "On the Nature of Western Progress: The Journal of the Iwakura Embassy." In *Tradition and Modernization in Japanese Culture,* ed. Donald H. Shively. Princeton: Princeton University Press, 1971. Pp. 7–34.

Stearns, Peter N. "Modernization and Social History." *Journal of Social History,* 14:2 (Winter 1980): 189–210.

Stevens, John. *Abundant Peace.* Boston: Shambhala, 1987.

Stevens, John, and Rinjiro Shirata. *Aikido: The Way of Harmony.* Boston: Shambhala, 1984.

Stoddart, Brian. "Wide World of Golf." *Sociology of Sport Journal,* 7:4 (1990): 378–388.

Strutt, Joseph. *The Sports and Pastimes of the People of England.* 2nd ed. London: Thomas Tegg, 1838.

Sugawara, Ray. "The Study of Top Sportsmen in Japan." *International Review of Sport Sociology,* 7 (1972): 45–65.

Sugawara Rei. *Taiiku to supōtsu no shakaigaku.* Tokyo: Fumaidō, 1984.

Sugimoto Atsuo. *Supōtsu bunka no henyō.* Kyoto: Sekai shisōsha, 1995.

Suzuki Akisato. "Nara joshi kōtō shihan gakkō fuzoku shōgakkō jidai no Kawaguchi Hideaki no taiiku ni kansuru ichi kōsatsu." *Taiikushi kenkyū,* 9 (March 1992): 19–32.

Suzuki Akisato. "Taishō jiyū kyōiku ni okeru taiiku ni tsuite . . . ," *Taiikushi kenkyū,* 8 (March 1991): 43–54.

Suzuki Toshio. "Tokugawa bakufu shohōrei ni mirareru shomin no yūgi tōsei ni tsuite." *Nihon taiiku gakkai dai 30 kai taikai gō,* 1979. P. 80.

Tada Michitarō. *Asobi to nihonjin.* Tokyo: Chikuma Shobō, 1974.

Tahara, Junko. "Count Michimasa Soyeshima and the Cancellation of the XII Olympiad in Tokyo." *International Journal of the History of Sport,* 9:3 (December 1992): 467–472.

Takahashi, Hidesato. "Fan Clubs of Japanese Professional Baseball Teams" (paper presented at a conference on "Sports and Body Culture in Modern Japan," Yale University, March 31–April 2, 2000).

———. "Hiroshima shiminkyūjō ni okeru puroyakyū no shūgōteki ōen ni kansuru kenkyū." *Supōtsu shakaigaku kenkyū,* 2 (1994): 53–66.

Takahashi Yoshitaka. *Ōzumō no jiten.* Tokyo: Sanseidō, 1985.

Takenoshita, Kyuzo. "The Social Structure of the Sport Population in Japan." *International Review of Sport Sociology,* 2 (1967): 5–18.

*Tale of Flowering Fortunes (Eiga monogatari),* trans. William H. and Helen Craig McCullough. 2 vols. Stanford: Stanford University Press, 1980.

*Tale of the Heike,* trans. Kitagawa Hiroshi and Bruce Tsuchida. Tokyo: Tokyo University Press, 1975.

Tanada, Shinsuke. "Diffusion into the Orient: The Introduction of Western Sports in Kobe, Japan." *International Journal of the History of Sport,* 5:3 (December 1988): 372–376.

Tanaka Tokuhisa, and Yoshikawa Kumiko. *Supōtsu.* Tokyo: Kondō, 1990.

Tanaka Yoshihisa. *Gorufu to Nihonjin.* Tokyo: Iwanami shinsho, 1992.

Tanaka, Yoshiko. "The Role of the University in Women's Athletics in Japan." In *Proceedings of the FISU/CESU Conference.* Kobe: Kobe Kokusai Kōryū Kaikan, 1985. Pp. 338–345.

Tatano Hideo. *Supōtsu shakaigaku no riron to chōsa.* Tokyo: Fumaidō, 1998.

Thompson, Lee A. "The Invention of the *Yokozuna* and the Championship System, or, Futohaguro's Revenge." In *Mirror of Modernity: Invented Traditions of Modern Japan,* ed. Stephen Vlastos. Berkeley: University of California Press, 1998. Pp. 174–187.

———. "The Modernization of Sumo as a Sport" (Ph.D. dissertation, Osaka University, 1989).

———. "Professional Wrestling in Japan—Media and Message." *International Review of Sport Sociology,* 21:1 (1986): 65–80.

Tierney, Roderic Kenji. "Performing for the Nation: Sumō Becomes the 'National Sport'" (paper presented at a conference on "Sports and Body Culture in Modern Japan," Yale University, March 31–April 2, 2000).

Totten, George O. "Collective Bargaining and Works Councils as Innovations in Industrial Relations in Japan during the 1920s." In *Aspects of Social Change in Modern Japan,* ed. R. P. Dore. Princeton: Princeton University Press, 1967. Pp. 203–243.

Tsuganezawa Toshihiro. "Ōsaka Mainichi Shimbunsha no 'jigyō katsudō' to chiiki seikatsu bunka." In *Kindai Nihon no media ibento,* ed. Tsuganezawa Toshihiro. Tokyo: Dōbunkan, 1996. Pp. 217–248.

Tsunoda, Tadanobu. *The Japanese Brain: Uniqueness and Universality,* trans. Yoshinori Oiwa. Tokyo: Taishukan,1985 (1978).

Ueberhorst, Horst, ed. *Geschichte der Leibeübungen.* 6 vols. Berlin: Bartels & Wernitz, 1971–1989.

Ueshiba, Kisshōmaru. *Spirit of Aikidō,* trans. Taitetsu Unno. Tokyo: Kodansha International, 1984.

Uesugi Masayuki. "Shōhi shakai ni okeru supekuteitā supōtsu." *Supōtsu shakaigaku kenkyū,* 3 (1995): 1–11.

Uhlan, Edward, and Dana L. Thomas. *Shoriki.* New York: Exposition Press, 1957.

Uno Yōzaburō. *Gendai kyūdō kōza.* Tokyo: Yūzankaku, 1982.

Vamplew, Wray. *The Turf.* London: Allen Lane, 1976.

Varley, H. Paul. *Japanese Culture.* 3rd ed. Honolulu: University of Hawaii Press, 1984.

Vincenti, James J. "The Relationship between Female Status and Physical Strength in a Japanese University Athletic Club." *Journal of Sport and Social Issues,* 21:2 (May 1997): 189–210.

Vlastos, Stephen, ed. *Mirror of Modernity: Invented Traditions of Modern Japan.* Berkeley: University of California Press, 1998.

Wagg, Stephen, ed. *Giving the Game Away.* Leicester: University of Leicester Press, 1994.

Wakamori Tarō. *Sumō ima mukashi.* Tokyo: Kawade shobō shinsha, 1963.

Watanabe Tōru. "Daiichi kōtō (chū) gakkō no taisō kyōin ni tsuite." *Taiikushi kenkyū,* 3 (March 1986): 16–25.

——. "Kemari no tenkai ni tsuite no ichikōsatsu: Edo jidai no sōron wo chūshin to shite, kemari ni okeru iemoto seido ni tsuite." *Taiikugaku kiyō,* 3 (1966): 13–22.

——. "The Why of the Japanese Choice of Baseball." In *Civilization in Sport History,* ed. Shimizu Shigeo. Kobe: Kobe University, 1987. Pp. 113–128.

Watanabe Tōru, and Kuwayama Kōnen. *Kemari no kenkyū,* Tokyo: University of Tokyo Press, 1994.

Watson, Christopher. "Spiritual versus Martial Aikido." *Journal of Asian Martial Arts,* 5:1 (1996): 48–71.

Webb, Herschel. "The Development of an Orthodox Attitude toward the Imperial Institution in the Nineteenth Century." In *Changing Japanese Attitudes toward Modernization,* ed. Marius B. Jansen. Princeton: Princeton University Press, 1965. Pp. 167–191.

Weber, Max. *Wirtschaft und Gesellschaft.* 2 vols. 1920; Cologne: Kiepenheuer & Witsch, 1964.

Welky, David B. "Viking Girls, Mermaids, and Little Brown Men: U.S. Journalism and the 1932 Olympics." *Journal of Sport History,* 24:1 (Spring 1997): 24–49.

Wetherall, William. "Striking Sensitivities in Sumo's Inner Sactum." *Far Eastern Economic Review,* 126 (November 18, 1984): 50–51.

Whiting, Robert. *The Chrysanthemum and the Bat.* New York: Dodd, Mead, 1977.

———. *You Gotta Have Wa.* New York: Macmillan, 1989.

Wind, Herbert Warren. "Around the Mulberry Bush." *Sports Illustrated,* 8 (March 3, 1958): 56–64.

———. "The Bouncing Ball." *Sports Illustrated,* 8 (February 24, 1958): 52–62.

Wingate, Carrie. "Exploring Our Roots: Historical and Cultural Foundations of the Ideology of Karate-Do." *Journal of Asian Martial Arts,* 2:3 (1993): 11–35.

Wolfe, Robert E. II. "A Book of Five Rings." *Journal of Asian Martial Arts,* 1:2 (1992): 95–102.

Yamaguchi, Yasuo. "A Comparative Study of Adolescent Socialization into Sport: The Case of Japan and Canada." *International Review of Sport Sociology,* 19:1 (1984): 63–82.

———. "A Cross-National Study of Socialization into Physical Activity in Corporate Settings." *Sociology of Sport Journal,* 4:1 (March 1987): 61–77.

Yamaguchi Yasuo, Tohi Takashi, and Takami Akira. "Supōtsu yoka katsudō to kuoriti obu raifu." *Supōtsu shakaigaku kenkyū,* 4 (1996): 34–50.

Yamamoto Ikuei. *Musume to watashi.* Tokyo: Kiomizu shoin, 1996.

Yamamoto Norihito. "Daigakusei no raifusutairu to supōtsu no katsudō senkō." *Supōtsu shakaigaku kenkyū,* 3 (1995): 13–25.

Yamanaka Yū. "Noriyumi." In *Sekai dai hyakka jiten.* Tokyo: Heibonsha, 1988. 22: 265.

Yamashita Takayuki. "The Nagano Olympics: Inventing Japaneseness in a Global Imaginary" (paper presented at a conference on "Sports and Body Culture in Modern Japan," Yale University, March 31–April 2, 2000).

Yamashita Takayuki, and Kiku Koichi. "Yōroppa supōtsu shakaigaku no dōkō." *Supōtsu shakaigaku kenkyū,* 4 (1996): 1–12.

Yomiuri shimbun Ōsaka honsha undōbu, ed. *Za hīrō: sengo supōtsu no 40 nin.* Tokyo: Yomiuri shimbun, 1996.

Yorizumi Kazuaki. "Suēden taisō no waga kuni e no juyō katei ni kansuru ichikōsatsu." *Taiikushi kenkū,* 9 (March 1992): 1–18.

Yoshida Takeshi. "Supōtsuteki shakaikaron kara mita bān'auto kyōgi no henyō katei." *Supōtsu shakaigaku kenkyū,* 2 (1994): 67–79.

Yoshino, Kosaku. *Cultural Nationalism in Contemporary Japan.* London: Routledge, 1992.

# Index

**293**